# MANAGING GROUP AND INTERGROUP RELATIONS

*THE IRWIN-DORSEY SERIES IN BEHAVIORAL SCIENCE*

EDITOR JOHN F. MEE *Indiana University*

ARGYRIS *Interpersonal Competence and Organizational Effectiveness*

ARGYRIS *Organization and Innovation*

CARZO & YANOUZAS *Formal Organization: A Systems Approach*

CUMMINGS & SCOTT *Readings in Organizational Behavior and Human Performance*

DALTON & LAWRENCE (eds.) *Motivation and Control in Organizations*

DALTON & LAWRENCE (eds.) WITH GREINER *Organizational Change and Development*

DALTON & LAWRENCE (eds.) WITH LORSCH *Organizational Structure and Design*

GUEST *Organizational Change: The Effect of Successful Leadership*

KELLY *Organizational Behaviour*

KUHN *The Study of Society: A Unified Approach*

LAWRENCE & SEILER, WITH BAILEY, KATZ, ORTH, CLARK, BARNES, & TURNER *Organizational Behavior and Administration: Cases, Concepts, and Research Findings* rev. ed.

LORSCH & LAWRENCE (eds.) *Managing Group and Intergroup Relations*

LORSCH & LAWRENCE (eds.) *Studies in Organization Design*

LYNTON & PAREEK *Training for Development*

MASLOW *Eupsychian Management: A Journal*

MASSARIK & RATOOSH *Mathematical Explorations in Behavioral Science*

O'CONNELL *Managing Organizational Innovation*

ORTH, BAILEY, & WOLEK *Administering Research and Development: The Behavior of Scientists and Engineers in Organizations*

PORTER & LAWLER *Managerial Attitudes and Performance*

PRICE *Organizational Effectiveness: An Inventory of Propositions*

RUBENSTEIN & HABERSTROH (eds.) *Some Theories of Organization* rev. ed.

SCOTT *The Management of Conflict*

SCOTT & MITCHELL *Organization Theory: A Structural and Behavioral Analysis*

SEILER *Systems Analysis in Organizational Behavior*

WHYTE *Organizational Behavior: Theory and Application*

WHYTE & HAMILTON *Action Research for Management*

# MANAGING GROUP AND INTERGROUP RELATIONS

Edited by

**JAY W. LORSCH, S.M., D.B.A.**
Professor of Organizational Behavior

**PAUL R. LAWRENCE, M.B.A., D.C.S.**
Wallace Brett Donham Professor of Organizational Behavior

Both of the
Graduate School of Business Administration
Harvard University

1972

**RICHARD D. IRWIN, INC.**
**and**
**THE DORSEY PRESS**
HOMEWOOD, ILLINOIS 60430
IRWIN-DORSEY LIMITED, GEORGETOWN, ONTARIO

*First printing, June 1972*

Case material of the Harvard Graduate School of Business Administration is made possible by the cooperation of business firms who may wish to remain anonymous by having names, quantities, and other identifying details disguised while basic relationships are maintained. Cases are prepared as the basis for class discussion rather than to illustrate either effective or ineffective handling of administrative situations.

Library of Congress Catalog Card No. 73–190541

*Printed in the United States of America*

*To the Original Teachers of*
*Administrative Practices*

*Professors* Learned
Roethlisberger
Hower
Lombard
*and*
Glover

# Acknowledgments

WE WISH to express our gratitude to the following persons, who, as staff members of the Harvard Business School, played a role in preparing some of the cases in this book: Jeanne Deschamps, Richard Harmer, Russell Johnston, and Melvin Steckler. A similar debt is owed to Neil Millward, who, as visiting scholar at the Harvard Business School, wrote the Mayflower Company case.

Also, we are indebted to the following faculty colleagues, past and present, who directed the data gathering and writing of several of these cases: Larry Greiner, Robert Katz, and John A. Seiler.

We are equally grateful for the extremely important, if less direct, contributions made to the Human Behavior in Organizations course over the past few years by the following faculty colleagues: Stephen A. Allen III, Louis B. Barnes, J.B.M. Kassarjian, Harry Levinson, Eric Neilson, Alan Sheldon, and Richard E. Walton. Their contribution to this course is reflected in the nature of both the cases and readings included.

Thanks are also due to the publishers and authors who have given permission to use copyrighted material. The source of this material is noted with each piece. All cases, with the exception of Tubident, S.A., have been copyrighted individually by the President and Fellows of Harvard College. They are reprinted here by special permission and may not be reproduced in whole or in part without prior written consent. The same limitation also applies to the Tubident case, which was graciously provided for our use by INCAE (Instituto Centroamericano de Administracion de Empresas).

Finally we wish to acknowledge the invaluable help of Mrs. Susan Christiansen and Mrs. Ann Walter in the preparation of this manuscript.

Even though we recognize all these contributions of others, we also recognize our responsibility for any errors in this book.

Boston, Mass.
*June 1972*

J.W.L.
P.R.L.

# Contents

# Managing Intra- and Intergroup Relations

THE CASES and readings in this volume center on two classes of administrative issues which managers frequently encounter. First are the problems of managing relationships among members of a face-to-face work group and the relationship between the formally designated leaders of such groups and their subordinates. How does a manager achieve congruence between group goals and organizational purpose? How can group members and their superiors handle interpersonal hostility so it does not disrupt the group and/or does not impair group efficiency? What are the sources of power available to leaders of such groups and how can this power be effectively used? To what extent does the functioning of these groups lead to a resistance of changes in practices and procedures and how can the resistance be overcome when it occurs? As the cases which have been included illustrate, these problems of managing intragroup relations occur at all levels of an organization. They occur in top management groups (Textile Corporation of America), on the factory floor (Slade Company), and among professionals (The Times Herald). In fact, they seem also to evolve in organizations formed as an outlet for persons who seek escape from conventional work settings in utopian organizations such as communes (Bedrock).

Relations among groups within an organization is the second class of problems on which this volume focuses. Here the issue is how to achieve intergroup collaboration where it is required without reducing the differences in outlook which naturally evolve as various groups perform their respective tasks. Again, these problems occur among groups of managers (Tom Craig) near the factory floor (American Magnolite) and also can involve professionals (United Diesel).

To help students of administration to learn to deal with these problems, a variety of readings have been included. Dealing with the intragroup problem, there is one reading which provides a comprehensive framework for analyzing these issues—"The Individual in the Organization." For intergroup issues, two papers serve this purpose—"Diagnosing Interdepartmental Conflict" and "Understanding and Managing Intergroup Conflict." The other readings either report on specific research studies which illuminate these problems or deal with aspects of taking remedial action.

Even a quick perusal of these readings will lead to the conclusion that they do not suggest a simple solution to these human problems of administration. Rather, they provide ways of thinking from the behavioral sciences which can help the student diagnose the complex causes of the behavior described in the various cases and to think about action. It is then up to the student to use his diagnosis and his own judgment to decide what course of action is most likely to produce the results he desires with minimal side effects. To use a medical analogy, the readings are of value primarily to develop the skills of an internist in identifying the nature of the problem and the complex causes of ill health. However, no surgical tools or medicines are suggested as standard remedies. Rather, the student, like his managerial counterpart in the real world, must decide, based on his diagnosis and his appraisal of the options he has available, what action steps are likely to be most useful.

While the task of learning to handle the issues in these cases is a difficult one, it is also critical. For this reason, both the cases and the readings have been selected not only to deal with issues commonly faced by managers but also to increase the student's skill in dealing with administrative issues through his own behavior. The problems posed in these case situations generally do not require sweeping redesign of organizational and technological arrangements. Rather, they call for the responsible administrator to take action through interpersonal contacts with peers, superiors, and subordinates. It is our belief that this is the most frequent avenue open to administrators in coping with human problems. For, particularly in the early years of an administrator's career, but also throughout his working life, action through his own direct contact with others will be the most readily available tool in dealing with these issues.

# CASES ON GROUP ISSUES

## The Slade Company

Ralph Porter, production manager of the Slade Company, was concerned by reports of dishonesty among some employees in the plating department. From reliable sources, he had learned that a few men were punching the timecards of a number of their workmates who had left early. Porter had only recently joined the Slade organization. He judged from conversations with the previous production manager and other fellow managers that they were, in general, pleased with the overall performance of the plating department.

The Slade Company was a prosperous manufacturer of metal products designed for industrial application. Its manufacturing plant, located in central Michigan, employed nearly five hundred workers, who were engaged in producing a large variety of clamps, inserts, knobs, and similar items. Orders for these products were usually large and on a recurrent basis. The volume of orders fluctuated in response to business conditions in the primary industries which the company served. At the time of this case, sales volume had been high for over a year. The bases upon which the Slade Company secured orders, in rank of importance, were quality, delivery, and reasonable price.

The organization of manufacturing operations at the Slade plant is shown in Exhibit 1. The departments listed there are, from left to right, approximately in the order in which material flowed through the plant. The diemaking and setup operations required the greatest degree of skill, supplied by highly paid, long-service craftsmen. The finishing departments, divided operationally and geographically between plating and painting, attracted less highly trained but relatively skilled workers, some of whom had been employed by the company for many years. The remaining operations were largely unskilled in nature and were characterized by relatively low pay and high rate of turnover of personnel.

The plating room was the sole occupant of the top floor of the plant. Exhibit 2 shows the floor plan, the disposition of workers, and the flow of work throughout the department. Thirty-eight men and women worked in the department, plating or oxidizing the metal parts or preparing parts for the application of paint at another location in the plant. The department's work occurred in response to orders communicated by production schedules, which were revised daily. Schedule revisions, caused by last-minute order increases or rush requests from customers, resulted in short-term volume fluctuations, particularly in the plating, painting, and shipping departments. Exhibit 3 outlines the activities of the various jobs, their interrelationships, and the type of work in which each specialized. Exhibit 4 rates the various types of jobs in terms of the technical skill, physical effort, discomfort, and training time associated with their performance.

**EXHIBIT 1**

Manufacturing Organization

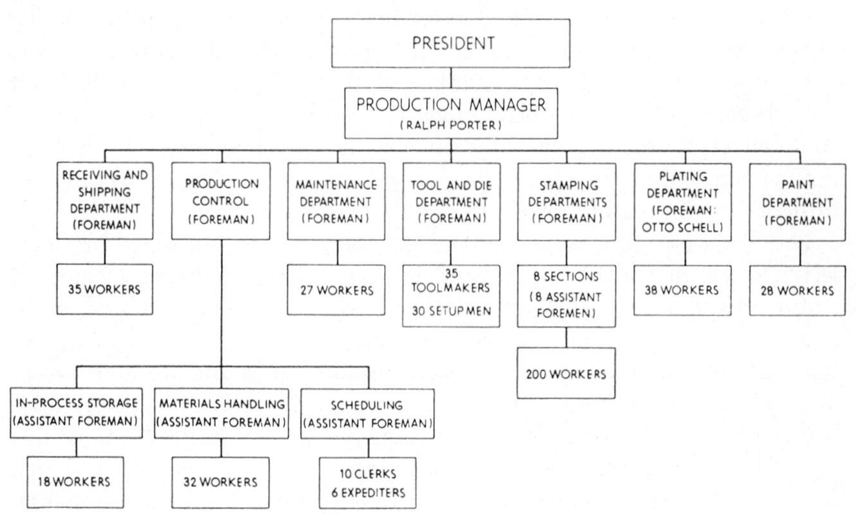


The activities which took place in the plating room were of three main types:

1. Acid dipping, in which parts were etched by being placed in baskets which were manually immersed and agitated in an acid solution.
2. Barrel tumbling, in which parts were roughened or smoothed by being loaded into machine-powered revolving drums containing abrasive, caustic, or corrosive solutions.
3. Plating—either manual, in which parts were loaded on racks and were immersed by hand through the plating sequence; or automatic, in which racks or baskets were manually loaded with parts which were then carried by a conveyor system through the plating sequence.

Within these main divisions, there were a number of variables, such as cycle times, chemical formulas, abrasive mixtures, and so forth, which distinguished particular jobs as they have been categorized in Exhibit 3.

**EXHIBIT 2**

Plating Room Layout

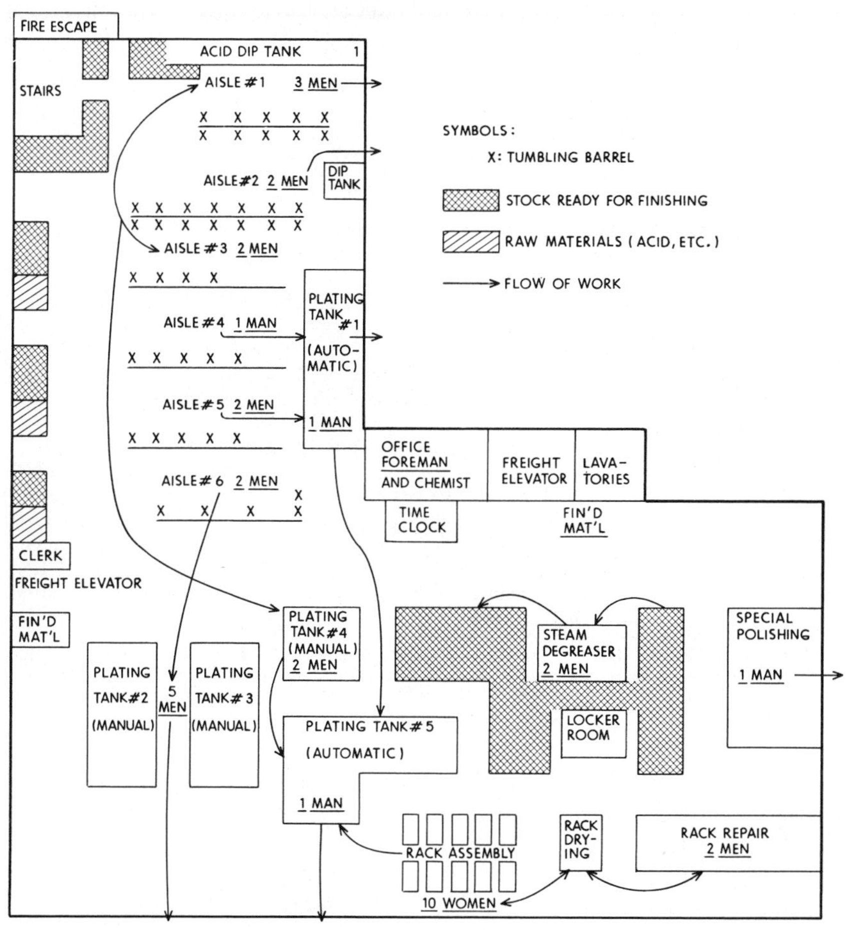


The work of the plating room was received in batch lots whose size averaged a thousand pieces. The clerk moved each batch, which was accompanied by a routing slip, to its first operation. This routing slip indicated the operations to be performed and when each major operation on the batch was scheduled to be completed, so that the finished product could be shipped on time. From the accumulation of orders before him, each man was to organize his own work schedule so as to make optimal

**EXHIBIT 3**

Outline of Work Flow, Plating Room

| | |
|---|---|
| AISLE 1: | Worked closely with Aisle 3 in preparation of parts by barrel tumbling and acid dipping for high-quality* plating in Tanks 4 and 5. Also did a considerable quantity of highly specialized, high-quality acid-etching work not requiring further processing. |
| AISLE 2: | Tumbled items of regular quality and design in preparation for painting. Less frequently, did oxidation dipping work of regular quality, but sometimes of special design, not requiring further processing. |
| AISLE 3: | Worked closely with Aisle 1 on high-quality tumbling work for Tanks 4 and 5. |
| AISLES 4 AND 5: | Produced regular tumbling work for Tank 1. |
| AISLE 6: | Did high-quality tumbling work for special products plated in Tanks 2 and 3. |
| TANK 1: | Worked on standard, automated plating of regular quality not further processed in plating room, and regular work further processed in Tank 5. |
| TANKS 2 AND 3: | Produced special, high-quality plating work not requiring further processing. |
| TANK 4: | Did special, high-quality plating work further plated in Tank 5. |
| TANK 5: | Automated production of high- and regular-quality, special- and regular-design plated parts sent directly to shipping. |
| RACK ASSEMBLY: | Placed parts to be plated in Tank 5 on racks. |
| RACK REPAIR: | Performed routine replacement and repair of racks used in Tank 5. |
| POLISHING: | Processed, by manual or semimanual methods, odd-lot special orders which were sent directly to shipping. Also, sorted and reclaimed parts rejected by inspectors in the shipping department. |
| DEGREASING: | Took incoming raw stock, processed it through caustic solution, and placed clean stock in storage ready for processing elsewhere in the plating room. |

* Definition of terms: *High or regular quality:* The quality of finishes could broadly be distinguished by the thickness of plate and/or care in preparation. *Regular or special work:* The complexity of work depended on the routine or special character of design and finish specifications.

use of equipment, materials, and time. Upon completion of an order, each man moved the lot to its next work position or to the finished material location near the freight elevator.

The plating room was under the direct supervision of the foreman, Otto Schell, who worked a regular 8:00-to-5:00 day, five days a week. The foreman spent a good deal of his working time attending to maintenance and repair of equipment, procuring supplies, handling late schedule changes, and seeing that his people were at their proper work locations.

Working conditions in the plating room varied considerably. That part of the department containing the tumbling barrels and the plating machines was constantly awash, alternately with cold water, steaming acid, or caustic soda. Men working in this part of the room wore knee boots, long rubber aprons, and high-gauntlet rubber gloves. This uniform,

**EXHIBIT 4**

Skill Indices by Job Group*

| *Jobs* | *Technical Skill Required* | *Physical Effort Required* | *Degree of Discomfort Involved* | *Degree of Training Required*† |
|---|---|---|---|---|
| Aisle 1 | 1 | 1 | 1 | 1 |
| Tanks 2–4 | 3 | 2 | 1 | 2 |
| Aisles 2–6 | 5 | 1 | 1 | 5 |
| Tank 5 | 1 | 5 | 7 | 2 |
| Tank 1 | 8 | 5 | 5 | 7 |
| Degreasing | 9 | 3 | 7 | 10 |
| Polishing | 6 | 9 | 9 | 7 |
| Rack assembly and repair | 10 | 10 | 10 | 10 |

* Rated on scales of 1 (the greatest) to 10 (the least) in each category.
† The amount of experience required to assume complete responsibility for the job.

consistent with the general atmosphere of the "wet" part of the room, was hot in summer, cold in winter. In contrast, the remainder of the room was dry, was relatively odor-free, and provided reasonably stable temperature and humidity conditions for those who worked there.

The men and women employed in the plating room are listed in Exhibit 5. This exhibit provides certain personal data on each department member, including a productivity-skill rating (based on subjective and objective appraisals of potential performance), as reported by the members of the department.

The pay scale implied by Exhibit 5 was low for the central Michigan area. The average starting wage for factory work in the community was about $1.25. However, working hours for the plating room were long (from 60 hours to a possible and frequently available 76 hours per week). The first 60 hours (the normal five-day week) were paid for on straight-time rates. Saturday work was paid for at time and one half; Sunday pay was calculated on a double-time basis.

As Exhibit 5 indicates, Philip Kirk, a worker in Aisle 2, provided the data for this case. After he had been a member of the department for several months, Kirk noted that certain members of the department tended to seek each other out during free time on and off the job. He then observed that these informal associations were enduring, built upon common activities and shared ideas about what was and what was not legitimate behavior in the department. His estimate of the pattern of these associations is diagrammed in Exhibit 6.

The Sarto group, so named because Tony Sarto was its most respected member and the one who acted as arbiter between the other members, was the largest in the department. The group, except for Louis Patrici, Al Bartolo, and Frank Bonzani (who spelled each other during break

## EXHIBIT 5

Plating Room Personnel

| *Location* | *Name* | *Age* | *Marital Status* | *Company Seniority* | *Department Seniority* | *Pay* | *Education* | *Familial Relationships* | *Productivity-Skill Rating** |
|---|---|---|---|---|---|---|---|---|---|
| Aisle 1 | Tony Sarto | 30 | M | 13 yrs. | 13 yrs. | $1.50 | High school | Louis Patrici, uncle; Pete Facelli, cousin | 1 |
| | Pete Facelli | 26 | M | 8 yrs. | 8 yrs. | 1.30 | High school | Louis Patrici, uncle; Tony Sarto, cousin | 2 |
| | Joe Iambi | 31 | M | 5 yrs. | 5 yrs. | 1.20 | 2 yrs. high school | | 2 |
| Aisle 2 | Herman Schell | 48 | S | 26 yrs. | 26 yrs. | 1.45 | Grade school | Otto Schell, brother | 8 |
| | Philip Kirk | 23 | M | 1 yr. | 1 yr. | 0.90 | College | | ..† |
| Aisle 3 | Dom Pantaleoni | 31 | M | 10 yrs. | 10 yrs. | 1.30 | 1 yr. high school | | 2 |
| | Sal Maletta | 32 | M | 12 yrs. | 12 yrs. | 1.30 | 3 yrs. high school | | 3 |
| Aisle 4 | Bob Pearson | 22 | S | 4 yrs. | 4 yrs. | 1.15 | High school | Father in tool and die dept. | 1 |
| Aisle 5 | Charlie Malone | 44 | M | 22 yrs. | 8 yrs. | 1.25 | Grade school | | 7 |
| | John Lacey | 41 | S | 9 yrs. | 5 yrs. | 1.20 | 1 yr. high school | Brother in paint dept. | 7 |
| Aisle 6 | Jim Martin | 30 | S | 7 yrs. | 7 yrs. | 1.25 | High school | | 4 |
| | Bill Mensch | 41 | M | 6 yrs. | 2 yrs. | 1.10 | Grade school | | 4 |

* On a potential scale of 1 (top) to 10 (bottom), as evaluated by the men in the department.

† Kirk was the source of data for this case and, as such, was in a biased position to report accurately perceptions about himself.

EXHIBIT 5–Continued

| Location | Name | Age | Marital Status | Company Seniority | Department Seniority | Pay | Education | Familial Relationships | Productivity-Skill Rating* |
|---|---|---|---|---|---|---|---|---|---|
| Tank 1 | Henry La Forte | 38 | M | 14 yrs. | 6 yrs. | $1.25 | High school | | 6 |
| Tanks 2–3 | Ralph Parker | 25 | S | 7 yrs. | 7 yrs. | 1.20 | High school | | 4 |
| | Ed Harding | 27 | S | 8 yrs. | 8 yrs. | 1.20 | High school | | 4 |
| | George Flood | 22 | S | 5 yrs. | 5 yrs. | 1.15 | High school | | 5 |
| | Harry Clark | 29 | M | 8 yrs. | 8 yrs. | 1.20 | High school | | 3 |
| | Tom Bond | 25 | S | 6 yrs. | 6 yrs. | 1.20 | High school | | 4 |
| Tank 4 | Frank Bonzani | 27 | M | 9 yrs. | 9 yrs. | 1.25 | High school | | 2 |
| | Al Bartolo | 24 | M | 6 yrs. | 6 yrs. | 1.25 | High school | | 3 |
| Tank 5 | Louis Patrici | 47 | S | 14 yrs. | 14 yrs. | 1.45 | 2 yrs. college | Tony Sarto, nephew Pete Facelli, nephew | 1 |
| Rack Assembly | 10 women | 30–40 | 9M, 1S | 10 yrs. (av.) | 10 yrs. (av.) | 1.05 | Grade school (av.) | 6 with husbands in company | 4 (av.) |
| Rack Maintenance | Will Partridge | 57 | M | 14 yrs. | 2 yrs. | 1.20 | Grade school | | 7 |
| | Lloyd Swan | 62 | M | 3 yrs. | 3 yrs. | 1.10 | Grade school | | 7 |
| Degreasing | Dave Susi | 45 | S | 1 yr. | 1 yr. | 1.05 | High school | | 5 |
| | Mike Maher | 41 | M | 4 yrs. | 4 yrs. | 1.05 | Grade school | | 6 |
| Polishing | Russ Perkins | 49 | M | 12 yrs. | 2 yrs. | 1.20 | High school | | 4 |
| Foreman | Otto Schell | 56 | M | 35 yrs. | 35 yrs. | (Not available) | High school | Herman Schell, brother | 3 |
| Clerk | Bill Pierce | 32 | M | 10 yrs. | 4 yrs. | 1.15 | High school | | 4 |
| Chemist | Frank Rutlage | 24 | S | 2 yrs. | 2 yrs. | (Not available) | 2 yrs. college | | 6 |

**EXHIBIT 6**

Informal Groupings in the Plating Room

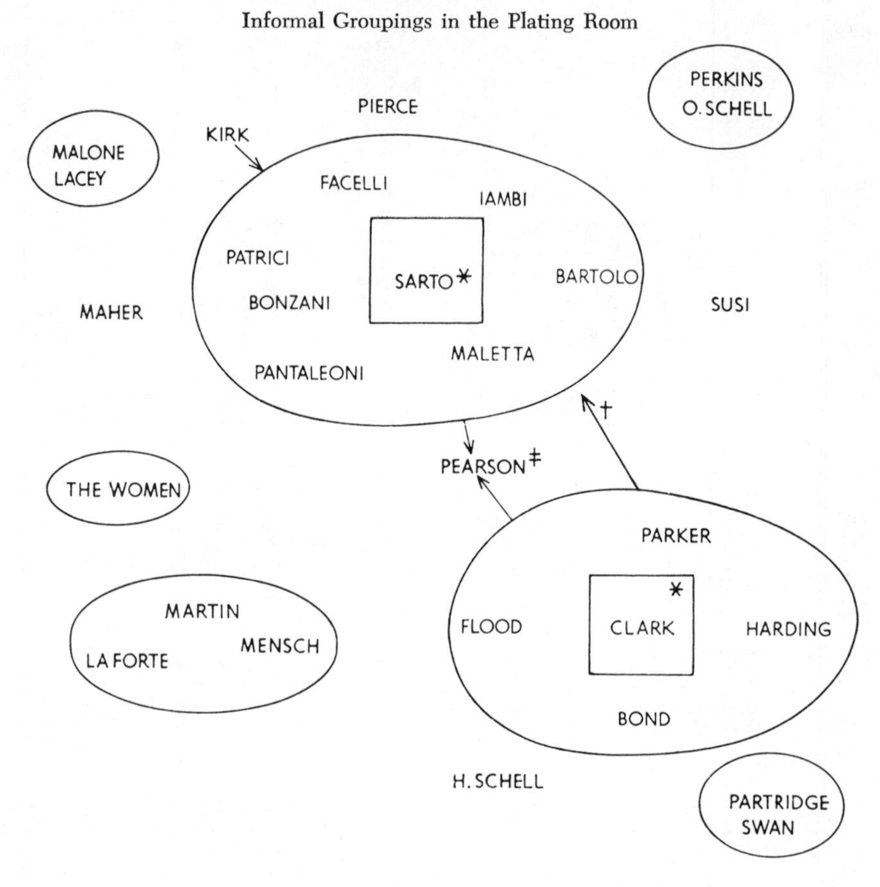


* The boxes indicate those men who clearly demonstrated leadership behavior (most closely personified the values shared by their groups, were most often sought for help and arbitration, and so forth).

† While the two- and three-man groupings had little informal contact outside their own boundaries, the five-man group did seek to join the largest group in extraplant social affairs. These were relatively infrequent.

‡ Though not an active member of any group, Bob Pearson was regarded with affection by the two large groups.

periods), invariably ate lunch together on the fire escape near Aisle 1. On those Saturdays and Sundays when overtime work was required, the Sarto group operated as a team, regardless of weekday work assignments, to get overtime work completed as quickly as possible. (Few department members not affiliated with either the Sarto or the Clark groups worked on weekends.) Off the job, Sarto group members often joined in parties or weekend trips. Sarto's summer camp was a frequent rendezvous.

Sarto's group was also the most cohesive one in the department in terms of its organized punch-in and punch-out system. Since the men were regularly scheduled to work from 7:00 A.M. to 7:00 P.M. weekdays, and since all supervision was removed at 5:00 P.M., it was possible almost every day to finish a "day's work" by 5:30 and leave the plant. What is more, if one man were to stay until 7:00 P.M., he could punch the time cards of a number of men and help them gain free time without pay loss. (This system operated on weekends, also, at which times members of supervision were present, if at all, only for short periods.) In Sarto's group the duty of staying late rotated, so that no man did so more than once a week. In addition, the group members would punch a man in in the morning if he were unavoidably delayed. However, such a practice never occurred without prior notice from the man who expected to be late and never if the tardiness was expected to last beyond 8:00 A.M., the start of the day for the foreman.

Sarto explained the logic behind the system to Kirk:

> You know that our hourly pay rate is quite low, compared to other companies. What makes this the best place to work is the feeling of security you get. No one ever gets laid off in this department. With all the hours in the week, all the company ever has to do is shorten the work week when orders fall off. We have to tighten our belts, but we can all get along. When things are going well, as they are now, the company is only interested in getting out the work. It doesn't help to get it out faster than it's really needed—so we go home a little early whenever we can. Of course, some guys abuse this sort of thing—like Herman—but others work even harder, and it averages out.
>
> Whenever an extra order has to be pushed through, naturally I work until 7:00. So do a lot of the others. I believe that if I stay until my work is caught up and my equipment is in good shape, that's all the company wants of me. They leave us alone and expect us to produce—and we do.

When Kirk asked Sarto if he would not rather work shorter hours at higher pay in a union shop (Slade employees were not organized), he just laughed and said: "It wouldn't come close to an even trade."

The members of Sarto's group were explicit about what constituted a fair day's work. Customarily, they cited Herman Schell, Kirk's work partner and the foreman's brother, as a man who consistently produced below that level. Kirk received an informal orientation from Herman during his first days on the job. As Herman put it:

> I've worked at this job for a good many years, and I expect to stay here a good many more. You're just starting out, and you don't know which end is up yet. We spend a lot of time in here; and no matter how hard we work, the pile of work never goes down. There's always more to take its place. And I think you've found out by now that this isn't light work. You can wear yourself out fast if you're not smart. Look at Pearson up in Aisle 4. There's a kid who's just

going to burn himself out. He won't last long. If he thinks he's going to get somewhere working like that, he's nuts. They'll give him all the work he can take. He makes it tough on everybody else and on himself, too.

Kirk reported further on his observations of the department:

As nearly as I could tell, two things seemed to determine whether or not Sarto's group or any others came in for weekend work on Saturday or Sunday. It seemed usually to be caused by rush orders that were received late in the week, although I suspect it was sometimes caused by the men having spent insufficient time on the job during the previous week.

Tony and his group couldn't understand Herman. While Herman arrived late, Tony was always half an hour early. If there was a push to get out an extra amount of work, almost everyone but Herman would work that much harder. Herman never worked overtime on weekends, while Tony's group and the men on the manual tanks almost always did. When the first, exploratory time study of the department was made, no one in the aisles slowed down, except Herman, with the possible exception, to a lesser degree, of Charlie Malone. I did hear that the men in the dry end of the room slowed down so much you could hardly see them move; but we had little to do with them, anyway. While the men I knew best seemed to find a rather full life in their work, Herman never really got involved. No wonder they couldn't understand each other.

There was quite a different feeling about Bobby Pearson. Without the slightest doubt, Bob worked harder than anyone else in the room. Because of the tremendous variety of work produced, it was hard to make output comparisons, but I'm sure I wouldn't be far wrong in saying that Bob put out twice as much as Herman and 50 percent more than almost anyone else in the aisles. No one but Herman and a few old-timers at the dry end ever criticized Bobby for his efforts. Tony and his group seemed to feel a distant affection for Bob, but the only contact they or anyone else had with him consisted of brief greetings.

To the men in Tony's group the most severe penalty that could be inflicted on a man was exclusion. This they did to both Pearson and Herman. Pearson, however, was tolerated; Herman was not. Evidently, Herman felt his exclusion keenly, though he answered it with derision and aggression. Herman kept up a steady stream of stories concerning his attempts to gain acceptance outside the company. He wrote popular music which was always rejected by publishers. He attempted to join several social and athletic clubs, mostly without success. His favorite pastime was fishing. He told me that fishermen were friendly, and he enjoyed meeting new people whenever he went fishing. But he was particularly quick to explain that he preferred to keep his distance from the men in the department.

Tony's group emphasized more than just quantity in judging a man's work. Among them had grown a confidence that they could master and even improve upon any known finishing technique. Tony himself symbolized this skill. Before him, Tony's father had operated Aisle 1 and had trained Tony to take his place. Tony in his turn was training his cousin Pete. When a new finishing problem arose from a change in customer specifications, the foreman, the department chemist, or any of the men directly involved would come to Tony for help, and

Tony would give it willingly. For example, when a part with a special plastic embossing was designed, Tony was the only one who could discover how to treat the metal without damaging the plastic. To a lesser degree, the other members of the group were also inventive about the problems which arose in their own sections.

Herman, for his part, talked incessantly, about his feats in design and finish creations. As far as I could tell during the year I worked in the department, the objects of these stories were obsolete or of minor importance. What's more, I never saw any department member seek Herman's help.

Willingness to be of help was a trait Sarto's group prized. The most valued help of all was of a personal kind, though work help was also important. The members of Sarto's group were constantly lending and borrowing money, cars, clothing, and tools among themselves and, less frequently, with other members of the department. Their daily lunch bag procedure typified the "common property" feeling among them. Everyone's lunch was opened and added to a common pile, from which each member of the group chose his meal.

On the other hand, Herman refused to help others in any way. He never left his aisle to aid those near him who were in the midst of a rush of work or a machine failure, though this was customary throughout most of the department. I can distinctly recall the picture of Herman leaning on the hot and cold water faucets which were located directly above each tumbling barrel. He would stand gazing into the tumbling pieces for hours. To the passing, casual visitor, he looked busy; and as he told me, that's just what he wanted. He, of course, expected me to act this same way, and it was this enforced boredom that I found virtually intolerable.

More than this, Herman took no responsibility for breaking in his assigned helpers as they first entered the department, or thereafter. He had had four helpers in the space of little more than a year. Each had asked for a transfer to another department, publicly citing the work as cause, privately blaming Herman. Tony was the one who taught me the ropes when I first entered the department.

The men who congregated around Harry Clark tended to talk like and copy the behavior of the Sarto group, though they never approached the degree of inventive skill or the amount of helping activities that Tony's group did. They sought outside social contact with the Sarto group; and several times a year, the two groups went "on the town" together. Clark's group did maintain a high level of performance in the volume of work they turned out.

The remainder of the people in the department stayed pretty much to themselves or associated in pairs or triplets. None of these people were as inventive, as helpful, or as productive as Sarto's or Clark's groups, but most of them gave verbal support to the same values as those groups held.

The distinction between the two organized groups and the rest of the department was clearest in the punching-out routine. The women could not work past 3:00 P.M., so they were not involved. Malone and Lacey, Partridge and Swan, and Martin, La Forte, and Mensch arranged within their small groups for punch-outs, or they remained beyond 5:00 and slept or read when they finished their work. Perkins and Pierce went home when the foreman did. Herman Schell, Susi, and Maher had no punch-out organization to rely upon. Susi and

Maher invariably stayed in the department until 7:00 P.M. Herman was reported to have established an arrangement with Partridge whereby the latter punched Herman out for a fee. Such a practice was unthinkable from the point of view of Sarto's group. It evidently did not occur often because Herman usually went to sleep behind piles of work when his brother left or, particularly during the fishing season, punched himself out early. He constantly railed against the dishonesty of other men in the department, yet urged me to punch him out on several "emergency occasions."

Just before I left the Slade Company to return to school after fourteen months on the job, I had a casual conversation with Mr. Porter, the production manager, in which he asked me how I had enjoyed my experience with the organization. During the conversation, I learned that he knew of the punch-out system in the plating department. What's more, he told me, he was wondering if he ought to "blow the lid off the whole mess."

# Work Group Ownership of an Improved Tool*

The Whirlwind Aircraft Corporation was a leader in its field and especially noted for its development of the modern supercharger. Work in connection with the latter mechanism called for special skill and ability. Every detail of the supercharger had to be perfect to satisfy the exacting requirements of the aircraft industry.

In 1941 (before Pearl Harbor), Lathe Department 15–D was turning out three types of impeller, each contoured to within 0.002 inch and machined to a mirrorlike finish. The impellers were made from an aluminum alloy and finished on a cam-back lathe.

The work was carried on in four shifts, two men on each. The personnel in the finishing section were as follows:

1. *First Shift*—7 A.M. to 3 P.M. Sunday and Monday off.
   a) Jean Latour, master mechanic, French Canadian, forty-five years of age. Latour had set up the job and trained the men who worked with him on the first shift.
   b) Pierre DuFresne, master mechanic, French Canadian, thirty-six years of age. Both these men had trained the workers needed for the other shifts.
2. *Second Shift*—3 P.M. to 11 P.M. Friday and Saturday off.
   a) Albert Durand, master mechanic, French Canadian, thirty-two years of age; trained by Latour and using his lathe.
   b) Robert Benet, master mechanic, French Canadian, thirty-one years of age; trained by DuFresne and using his lathe.
3. *Third Shift*—11 P.M. to 7 A.M. Tuesday and Wednesday off.
   a) Philippe Doret, master mechanic, French Canadian, thirty-one years of age; trained by Latour and using his lathe.
   b) Henri Barbet, master mechanic, French Canadian, thirty years of age; trained by DuFresne and using his lathe.
4. *Stagger Shift*—Monday, 7 A.M. to 3 P.M.; Tuesday, 11 P.M. to 7 A.M.; Wednesday, 11 P.M. to 7 A.M.; Thursday, off; Friday, 3 P.M. to 11 P.M.; Saturday, 3 P.M. to 11 P.M.; Sunday, off.
   a) George MacNair, master mechanic, Scotch, thirty-two years of age; trained by Latour and using his lathe.
   b) William Reader, master mechanic, English, thirty years of age; trained by DuFresne and using his lathe.

* The following case was reprinted with permission from *Personnel Administration: A Point of View and a Method,* by Paul Pigors and Charles A. Myers (New York: McGraw-Hill Book Co., Inc., 1956).

Owing to various factors (such as the small number of workers involved, the preponderance of one nationality, and the fact that Latour and DuFresne had trained the other workers), these eight men considered themselves as members of one work group. Such a feeling of solidarity is unusual among workers on different shifts, despite the fact that they use the same machines.

The men received a base rate of $1.03 an hour and worked on incentive. Each man usually turned out 22 units a shift, thus earning an average of $1.19 an hour. Management supplied Rex 95 High-Speed Tool-Bits, which workers ground to suit themselves. Two tools were used: one square bit with a slight radius for recess cutting, the other bit with a 45-degree angle for chamfering and smooth finish. When used, both tools were set close together, the worker adjusting the lathe from one operation to the other. The difficulty with this setup was that during the rotation of the lathe, the aluminum waste would melt and fuse between the two toolbits. Periodically the lathe had to be stopped so that the toolbits could be freed from the welded aluminum and reground.

At the request of the supervisor of Lathe Department 15–D, the methods department had been working on his tool problem. Up to the time of this case, no solution had been found. To make a firsthand study of the difficulty, the methods department had recently assigned one of their staff, Mr. MacBride, to investigate the problem in the lathe department itself. Mr. MacBride's working hours covered parts of both the first and second shifts. MacBride was a young man, twenty-six years of age, and a newcomer to the methods department. For the three months prior to this assignment, he had held the post of "suggestion man," a position which enabled newcomers to the methods department to familiarize themselves with the plant setup. The job consisted in collecting, from boxes in departments throughout the plant, suggestions submitted by employees and making a preliminary evaluation of these ideas. The current assignment of studying the tool situation in Lathe Department 15–D, with a view to cutting costs, was his first special task. He devoted himself to this problem with great zeal but did not succeed in winning the confidence of the workers. In pursuance of their usual philosophy: "Keep your mouth shut if you see anyone with a suit on," they volunteered no information and took the stand that, since the methods man had been given this assignment, it was up to him to carry it out.

While MacBride was working on this problem, Pierre DuFresne hit upon a solution. One day he successfully contrived a tool which combined the two bits into one. This eliminated the space between the two toolbits which in the past had caught the molten aluminum waste and allowed it to become welded to the cutting edges. The new toolbit had two advantages: it eliminated the frequent machine stoppage for cleaning and regrinding the old-type tools; and it enabled the operator to run the lathe at a higher speed. These advantages made it possible for the operator to increase his efficiency 50%.

DuFresne tried to make copies of the new tool, but was unable to do so. Apparently the new development had been a "lucky accident" during grinding which he could not duplicate. After several unsuccessful attempts, he took the new tool to his former teacher, Jean Latour. The latter succeeded in making a drawing and turning out duplicate toolbits on a small grinding wheel in the shop. At first the two men decided to keep the new tool to themselves. Later, however, they shared the improvement with their fellow workers on the second shift. Similarly it was passed on to the other shifts. But all these men kept the new development a closely guarded secret as far as "outsiders" were concerned. At the end of the shift, each locked the improved toolbit securely in his toolchest.

Both DuFresne, the originator of the new tool, and Latour, its draftsman and designer, decided not to submit the idea as a suggestion but to keep it as the property of their group. Why was this decision made? The answer lies partly in the suggestion system and partly in the attitude of Latour and DuFresne toward other features of company work life and toward their group.

According to an informational bulletin issued by the company, the purpose of the suggestion system was to "provide an orderly method of submitting and considering ideas and recommendations of employees to management; to provide a means for recognizing and rewarding individual ingenuity; and to promote cooperation." Awards for accepted suggestions were made in the following manner: "After checking the savings and expense involved in an adopted suggestion [the suggestion committee] determined the amount of the award to be paid, based upon the savings predicted upon a year's use of the suggestion." "It is the intention of the committee . . . to be liberal in the awards, which are expected to adequately compensate for the interest shown in presenting suggestions." In pursuance of this policy, it was customary to grant the suggestor an award equivalent to the savings of an entire month.

As a monetary return, both DuFresne and Latour considered an award based on one month's saving as inadequate. They also argued that such awards were really taken out of the worker's pockets. Their reasoning was as follows: All awards for adopted suggestions were paid out of undistributed profits. Since the company also had a profit-sharing plan, the money was taken from a fund that would be given to the workers anyway, which merely meant robbing Peter to pay Paul. In any case, the payment was not likely to be large and probably would be less than they could accumulate if increased incentive payments could be maintained over an extended period without discovery. Thus there was little in favor of submitting the new tool as a suggestion.

Latour and DuFresne also felt that there were definite hazards to the group if their secret were disclosed. They feared that once the tool became company property, its efficiency might lead to layoff of some members in their group, or at least make work less tolerable by leading to an increased quota at a lower price per unit. They also feared that there might be a change in scheduled work assignments. For instance, the lathe department worked on three different types of impeller. One type was a routine job and aside from the difficulty caused by the old-type tool, presented no problem. For certain technical reasons, the other two types were more difficult to make. Even Latour, an exceptionally skilled craftsman, had sometimes found it hard to make the expected quota before the new tool was developed. Unless the work load was carefully balanced by scheduling easier and more difficult types, some of the operators were unable to make standard time.

The decision to keep the tool for their own group was in keeping with Latour's work philosophy. He had a strong feeling of loyalty to his own group and had demonstrated this in the past by offering for their use several improvements of his own. For example, he made available to all workers in his group a set of special gauge blocks which were used in aligning work on lathes. To protect himself in case mistakes were traced to these gauges, he wrote on them: "Personnel (*sic*) Property—Do not use. Jean Latour."

Through informal agreement with their fellow workers, Latour and DuFresne "pegged production" at an efficiency rate that in their opinion would not arouse management's suspicion or lead to a restudy of the job, with possible cutting of the rate. This enabled them to earn an extra 10% incentive earnings. The other 40% in additional efficiency was used as follows: The operators established a reputation for a high degree of accuracy and finish. They set a record for no spoilage and were able to apply the time gained on the easier type of impeller to work on the other types which required greater care and more expert workmanship.

The foreman of the lathe department learned about the new tool soon after it was put into use but was satisfied to let the men handle the situation in their own way. He reasoned that at little expense he was able to get out production of high quality. There was no defective work, and the men were contented.

Mr. MacBride was left in a very unsatisfactory position. He had not succeeded in working out a solution of his own. Like the foreman, he got wind of the fact that the men had devised a new tool. He urged them to submit a drawing of it through the suggestion system, but this advice was not taken, and the men made it plain that they did not care to discuss with him the reasons for this position.

Having no success in his direct contact with the workers, Mr. MacBride appealed to the foreman, asking him to secure a copy of the new tool. The foreman replied that the men would certainly decline to give him a copy and would resent as an injustice any effort on his part to force them to submit a drawing. Instead he suggested that MacBride should persuade DuFresne to show him the tool. This MacBride attempted to do, but met with no success in his efforts to ingratiate himself with DuFresne. When he persisted in his attempts, DuFresne decided to throw him off the track. He left in his lathe a toolbit which was an unsuccessful copy of the original discovery. At shift change, MacBride was delighted to find what he supposed to be the improved tool. He hastily copied it and submitted a drawing to the tool department. When a tool was made up according to these specifications it naturally failed to do what was expected of it. The workers, when they heard of this through the "grapevine," were delighted. DuFresne did not hesitate to crow over MacBride, pointing out that his underhanded methods had met with their just reward.

The foreman did not take any official notice of the conflict between DuFresne and MacBride. Then MacBride complained to the foreman that DuFresne was openly boasting of his trick and ridiculing him before other workers. Thereupon, the foreman talked to DuFresne, but the latter insisted that his ruse had been justified as a means of self-protection.

When he was rebuffed by DuFresne, the foreman felt that he had lost control of the situation. He could no longer conceal from himself that he was confronted by a more complex situation than what initially he had defined as a "tool problem." His attention was drawn to the fact that the state of affairs in his department was a tangle of several interrelated problems. Each problem urgently called for decision that involved understanding and practical judgment. But having for so long failed to see the situation as a whole, he now found himself in a dilemma.

He wished to keep the goodwill of the work group, but he could not countenance the continued friction between DuFresne and MacBride. Certainly, he could not openly abet his operators in obstructing the work of a methods man. His superintendent would now certainly hear of it and would be displeased to learn that a foreman had failed to tell him of such an important technical improvement. Furthermore he knew that the aircraft industry was expanding at this time and that the demand for impellers had increased to such an extent that management was planning to set up an entire new plant unit devoted to this product.

# Claremont Instrument Company

One of the problems facing the supervisory staff of the Claremont Instrument Company in the summer of 1948 was that of "horseplay" among employees in the glass department. For some time this question had troubled the management of the company. Efforts had been made to discourage employees from throwing water-soaked waste at each other and from engaging in water fights with buckets or fire hoses. Efforts to tighten up shop discipline had also resulted in orders to cut down on "visiting" with other employees. These efforts were made on the grounds that whatever took an employee away from his regular job would interfere with production or might cause injury to the employees or the plant machinery.

Production was a matter of some concern to the officials of the company, particularly since the war. In spite of a large backlog of unfilled orders, there were indications that domestic and foreign competition in the relatively near future might begin to cut into the company's business. Anything which could help to increase the salable output of the company was welcomed by the officers; at the same time, anything which might cut down overhead operating expenses, or improve the quality of the product, or cut down on manufacturing wastage was equally encouraged.

The Claremont Instrument Company had been located for many years in a community in western Massachusetts with a population of approximately 18,000. The company employed approximately 500 people. None of these people were organized in a union for collective bargaining purposes. The company produced a varied line of laboratory equipment and supplies. Many of its products were fabricated principally from glass, and over the years the company had built up a reputation for producing products of the highest quality. To a considerable extent this reputation for quality rested upon the company's ability to produce very delicate glass components to exacting quality standard. These glass components were produced from molten glass in the glass department. Exhibit 1 presents a partial organization chart of the company.

The entire glass department was located in one wing of the company's main factory. In this department the glass components such as tubes, bottles, decanters, and glass-measuring devices were made from molten glass. Some of these glass parts were produced by hand-blowing operations,

**EXHIBIT 1**

Partial Organization Chart

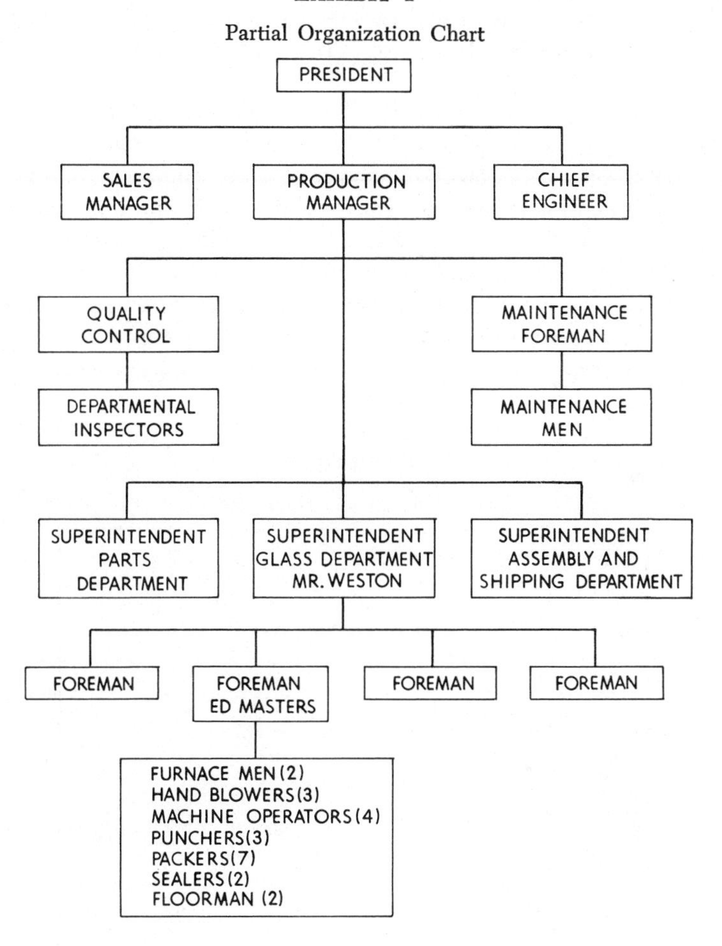


but most of them were produced on bottle-making machinery which in effect blew the molten glass into a mold. This operation of blowing the glass by hand or by machine was the most critical operation in the department and required a high degree of skill. Immediately following the blowing operation some of the parts were "punched." The "puncher" was a mechanical apparatus into which the glass components were placed; as the machine revolved, a small gas flame melted the glass in a small area and blew a hole in the glass component. Next the parts were placed on a mechanical conveyor where they were annealed by an air-cooling process. Then the parts were picked off the conveyor by women known as packers, whose duty was to inspect them for defects of many kinds and to give them temporary packaging in cardboard cartons for transit to other parts of the factory. The final operation in the department was performed by sealers, whose job it was to seal these cardboard cartons and place them in stacks for temporary storage. Exhibit 2 is a floor plan of the glass department.

The glass department was operated on a continuous, twenty-four-hour, seven-day-a-week basis, because of the necessity of keeping the tanks of molten glass hot and operating all the time. Four complete shifts worked in the department. The different shifts rotated as to the hours of the day they worked. Roughly each shift spent two weeks at a time on the day shift, on the evening shift, and on the night shift. Each shift worked on the average five days a week, but their days off came at varying times throughout the week. The glass department was located in a separate wing of the plant and the employees of the department used a special entrance and a special time clock.

**EXHIBIT 2**

Floor Plan of Glass Department

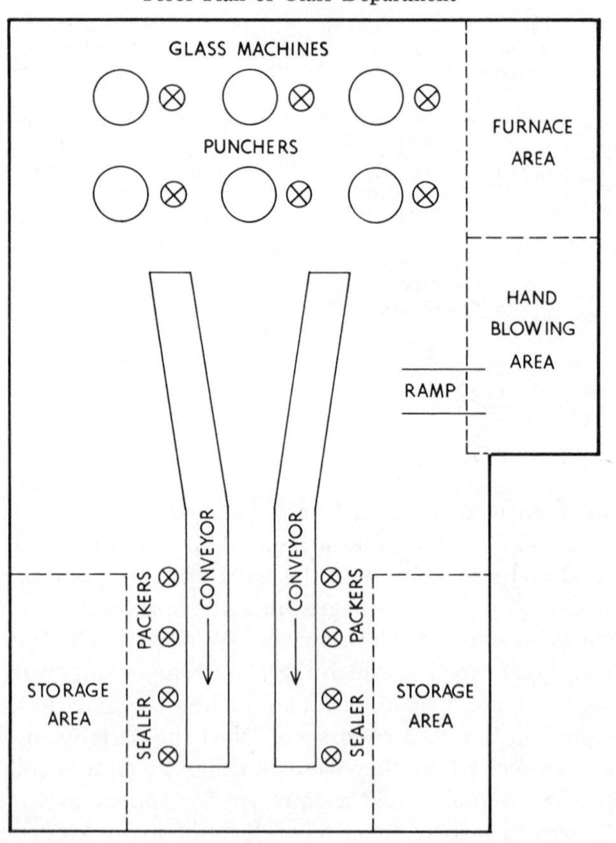

Each of the four shifts employed about twenty-three people. Each shift had its own foreman and assistant foreman and hourly workers as indicated in Exhibit 1. All these workers were men, with the exception of the packers. The foreman was a full-time supervisor, but the assistant foreman usually operated a glass machine and only substituted for the foreman in his absence. The furnace men prepared the molten glass for the glass blowers while the floormen cleaned up broken glass and other waste and filled in on odd jobs.

An inspector from the quality-control department and a maintenance man from the maintenance department were assigned on a full-time basis to each of the four shifts. The inspector worked with the packers and was responsible for the quality of all glass components. The maintenance man was responsible for the maintenance and satisfactory operation of all machinery in the department.

Several physical conditions made work in the glass department unique in the plant. The fact that the glass furnaces were located in this department meant that the department was always unusually hot. The glass-blowing machines were run principally by compressed air, and each movement of a machine part was accompanied by the hiss of escaping air. This noise combined with the occasional sound of breaking glass made it impossible for the members of the department to converse in a normal tone. An oil vapor was used to coat the inside of the molds on the glass machines, and when the hot glass poured into the mold, a smoke was given off that circulated throughout the department.

In the summer of 1948, Ralph Boynton, a student at the Harvard Business School, took a summer job as one of the floormen on one of the shifts working in the glass department. While on this job, he made the above observations about the Claremont Instrument Company in general and the glass department in particular. In the course of the summer, Ralph became particularly interested in the practice of engaging in horseplay, and the description that follows was based on his observations.

The foreman of Boynton's shift, Ed Masters, had worked a number of years in the glass department and had been promoted to foreman from the position of operator of one of the glass machines. In Ralph's opinion the foreman was generally liked by the shift employees. One of them commented to Ralph, "If everything is going okay, you don't see Ed around. If anything goes wrong, he's right there to try and fix it up." Another one of them commented, "He pitches right in—gives us a hand—but he never says much." Frequently when a glass machine was producing glass components of unacceptable quality, Ralph noticed the foreman and the maintenance man working with a machine operator to get the machine in proper adjustment. On one occasion Ralph was assigned the job of substituting for one of the sealers. Shortly after Ralph had started his work

Ed Masters came around and asked how he was doing. Ralph replied that he was doing fine and that it was quite a trick to toss the cartons into the proper positions on the stack. Ed replied, "You keep at it, and it won't be long before you get the hang of it. You'll be tired for a while, but you'll get used to it. I found I could do it and I am a 'ninety-seven-pound weakling.' "

Ralph also picked up a variety of comments from the employees about one another. The shift maintenance man, Bert, referred to the men on the shift as "a good bunch of guys." One of the packers referred with pride to one of the machine operators, "that guy can get out more good bottles than anybody else." On one occasion, when the glass components were coming off the end of the conveyor at a very slow rate, one of the packers went around to the glass machines to find out what the trouble was. When she came back she reported to the rest of the packers, "Ollie is having trouble with his machine. It's out of adjustment but he will get it fixed in a few minutes." Ralph noticed that a record was kept of the total daily output of each shift of packers. These women seemed anxious to reach a certain minimum output on each shift. When the components were coming through slowly, he heard such comments as, "This is a bad night." If the work had been coming slowly, the packers regularly started "robbing the conveyor" toward the end of the shift. This was the practice of reaching up along the conveyor and picking off components for packaging before they reached the packer's usual work position.

A short time after Ralph started to work, the company employed another new floorman for the shift. This new man quickly picked up the nickname of "Windy." The following were some of Windy's typical comments: "My objective is the paycheck and quitting time." "I love work so much I could lay down and go to sleep right beside it." "These guys are all dopes. If we had a union in here, we would get more money." "I hate this night work. I am quitting as soon as I get another job." Most of the other employees paid little attention to Windy. One of the sealers commented about him, "If bull were snow, Windy would be a blizzard." One night Windy commented to three of the men, "This is a lousy place. They wouldn't get away with this stuff if we had a union. Why don't the four of us start one right here?" None of the group replied to this comment.

Ralph had a number of opportunities to witness the horseplay that concerned the management. At least one horseplay episode seemed to occur on every eight-hour shift. For example, one night while Ralph stood watching Ollie, one of the machine operators, at his work, Ollie called Ralph's attention to the fact that Sam, the operator of the adjacent machine, was about to get soaked.

"Watch him now," Ollie said with a grin, "last night he got Bert and now Bert is laying for him. You watch now." Ralph caught sight of Bert warily circling behind the machines with an oil can in his hand. Sam had been sitting and quietly watching the bottles come off his machine. Suddenly Bert sprang out and fired six or seven shots of water at Sam. When the water hit him, Sam immediately jumped up and fired a ball of wet waste which he had concealed for this occasion. He threw it at Bert and hit him in the chest with it. It left a large wet patch on his shirt. Bert stood his ground squirting his can until Sam started to chase him. Then he ran off. Sam wiped his face and sat down again. Then he got up and came over to Ollie and Ralph. Sam shouted, "By Jesus, I am going to give him a good soaking." Ollie and Ralph nodded in agreement. Later Ollie commented to Ralph, "It may take as long as three hours for Sam to work up a good plan to get even, but Bert is going to get it good."

Sam was ready to get back at Bert as soon as he could be lured close enough to the machine. Sam pretended to watch his machine but kept his eye out for Bert. In a little while Bert walked jauntily by Sam's machine. They grinned at each other and shouted insults and challenges. Bert went over to a bench to fix something and Sam slipped around behind his machine, pulled down the fire hose and let Bert have a full blast chasing him up along the conveyor as Bert retreated. Sam then turned off the hose, reeled it back up and went back to his machine.

All the other employees on the scene had stopped to watch this episode and seemed to enjoy it. They commented that it was a good soaking. Bert came back to the machines after a while, grinning, and hurling insults while he stood by Sam's machine to dry off from the heat of the machine. The other operators kidded him some, and then everyone went back to work seriously.

A little later the foreman came through the department and noticed the large puddle of water on the floor. He instructed Bert to put some sawdust on the puddle to soak up the water. Ralph was told later that Ed Masters had told Bert, "I want more work and less of this horsing around." A few minutes later Ed Masters and Bert were discussing a small repair job that had to be done that evening.

On another occasion Ralph asked Ollie what he thought of the horseplay. Ollie commented, "It's something each guy has to make up his own mind about. Personally, I don't go in for it. I have got all the raises and merit increases that have come along, and I know Bert hasn't had a raise in over a year. Whenever something starts, I always look back at my machine so that I can be sure that nothing goes wrong while I am looking away. Personally, I just don't care—you have to have some fun, but personally, I don't go in for it."

Just at this point Al, one of the punchers, came down from the men's lavatory ready to take his turn on one of the punch machines. He was a moment or two early and stood talking to Sam. Ollie got up from where he had been talking to Ralph and started to holler, "Hey, Al—hey, Al." The other operators took up the chant, and all of them picked up pieces of wood or pipe and started drumming on the waste barrels near their machines. Al took up a long piece of pipe and joined in. After a minute or two, one of the operators stopped, and the drumming ended quickly. Al lit a cigarette and stepped up to take the machine for his turn.

Ralph later had an opportunity to ask Bert what he thought of the horseplay. Bert said, "You have to have some horseplay or you get rusty. You have to keep your hand in." Ralph noted that Bert's work kept him busy less than anyone else, since his duties were primarily to act as an emergency repairman and maintenance man. Ralph asked, "Why doesn't Ollie get into the horseplay?" Bert replied, "Ollie can't take it. He likes to get other people, but he can't take it when he gets it. You have got to be fair about this. If you get some guy, you are surer than hell you will get it back yourself. Now you take Sam and me. We've been playing like that for a long time. He don't lose his temper, and I don't lose mine. I knew I was going to get that hose the other night; that was why I was baiting him with a squirt gun." Ralph asked, "Does Ed Masters mind it very much?" Bert answered, "Hell, he's just like the rest of us. He knows you've got to have some of that stuff, only he gets bawled out by the superintendent if they see anything going on like that. That's why we don't play around much on the day shift. But on the night shift, that's when we have fun. The only reason we don't squirt the foreman is because he's the foreman. As far as we're concerned, he is no different from us. Besides he ain't my boss anyway. I'm maintenance. I don't care what he says."

About the middle of the summer, the superintendent of the glass department returned from his vacation and immediately thereafter an effort was made by him through the foremen to "tighten up" on shop discipline. The men on the machines and the punchers were forbidden to walk up to the other end of the conveyor to talk to the packers and sealers and vice versa. The foreman starting making occasional comments like "keep moving" when he saw a small group together in conversation. On one occasion a small group stood watching some activity outside the plant. Ed came by and quite curtly said, "Break it up." Everyone seemed quite shocked at how abrupt he was.

About this same time, the word was passed around among the employees that a big push was on to step up the output of a certain product in order to make a tight delivery schedule. Everyone seemed to be putting a little extra effort into getting this job done. Ralph thought he noticed that the foreman was getting more and more "jumpy" at this time. On one occasion Ed commented to some of the employees, "I am bitter today." One of the machine operators asked him what the trouble was, and Ed made some comment about a foremen's meeting where the superintendent was telling them that the playing around and visiting would have to stop.

One night a short time later, Ralph saw that preparations were being made for an unusually elaborate trap for soaking Jim, one of the sealers who had recently begun to take part in the water fights. A full bucket of water was tied to the ceiling with a trip rope at the bottom in such a way that the entire contents would be emptied on Jim when he least suspected it. Many of the employees made a point of being on hand when the trap was sprung. It worked perfectly, and Jim was given a complete soaking. Ralph thought Jim took it in good spirit since he turned quickly to counter-attack the people who had soaked him. Shortly after all the crew had gone back to work, Ruth, one of the packers, was coming down the ramp from the area where the hand-blowing operations were performed. She was carrying some of the glass components. Ruth slipped on some of the water that had been spilled during the recent fight and fell down. She was slightly burned by some of the hot glass she was carrying. Those who saw this happen rushed to her help. The burn, while not serious, required first-aid attention and the assistant foreman went with Ruth to the company dispensary for treatment. Ralph thought that the employees all felt rather sheepish about the accident. Ruth was one of the more popular girls in the department. The word went around among the employees that a report on the nature and cause of the accident would have to be made out and sent to higher management. Everyone was wondering what would happen.

# Tubident, S.A.*

## PART I

"YES, WE HAVE a serious organizational problem around here. My supervisors don't know how to supervise, and I just can't control production the way we must in this business. Until about a year ago, I used male foremen to supervise the female workers on our production lines, but we had a lot of playing around that hurt both morale and production. I think I have that problem solved. But I still have discipline problems, and high quality and volume standards are always in danger. My supervisors just aren't aggressive enough."

Sr. Lopez, a founding stockholder and the general manager of Tubident, S.A. was explaining his supervision problem to a casewriter from the Harvard Business School who visited the plant in the summer of 1966. "I can't explain this problem sitting in this office. Let's go out to the plant floor so I can show you how the production lines operate. Then I can explain what's wrong with my supervisors."

### COMPANY BACKGROUND

The Tubident plant was located near a poor residential area in the outskirts of the capital city of Cozuela. Cozuela was a member of a recently established protected trade area composed of a number of neighboring nations in Latin America. The company was founded in 1962 by Sr. Lopez and two investors well known in the country with the hope of obtaining the contract to supply metal tubes for the recently established local plant of a large international toothpaste manufacturer. Although importing tubes from abroad, the management of the company had refused to encourage the initiation of Tubident, despite the promise of substantial cost savings. Packaging was considered to be of primary sales importance and the firm maintained rigorous quality standards which it doubted that Tubident could meet. Reliable delivery was also considered essential and it was noted that local firms with limited mechanical experience and an untrained workforce sometimes suffered unexpected delays. Although discouraged by their failure to achieve a supplier contract and by the resulting uncertainty of their market prospects, Tubident organizers decided to initiate the enterprise anyway, and success had gradually followed. After four years, the firm had become the exclusive metal tube supplier to its initial customer and to a number of other toothpaste, cosmetic, and detergent firms in the area, increasing many times both its volume and the types of tubes it produced. Recently, a line of plastic extruding machines had been added and a second expansion of plant facilities was contemplated.

Investors gave much credit for the success of the enterprise to Sr. Lopez. Trained in a technical institute in Europe, he had several years of production experience with local firms, frequently working in process design and equipment installation. At Tubident, Sr. Lopez had designed and set up the plant, and served as sales executive, purchasing agent, and financial officer, as well as general manager. (See Exhibit 1 for Tubident's organization chart.)

**EXHIBIT 1**

Organization Chart, 1966

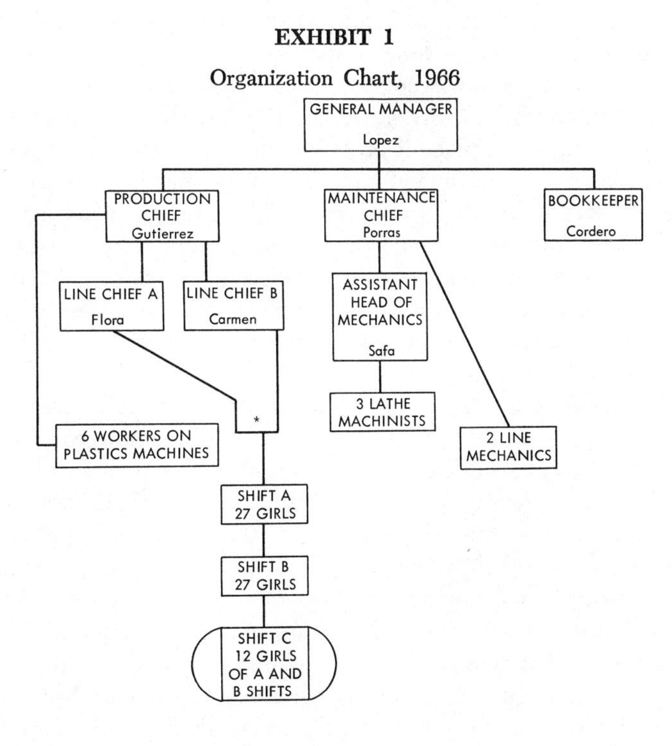


* The dual responsibility of the two line chiefs represents the fact that each chief supervised each of the two shifts for different parts of each day.

## PRODUCTION

All production facilities were located in the central factory area. A small volume of plastic bottles and other extruded plastic containers was produced in this area, but the principal product was toothpaste tubes of a variety of types and sizes. Crude types were produced from small aluminum washers on the company's extrusion machine, which was equipped with a synchronized screw machine to thread the neck and carve the collar design. Crude tubes were stored in large wire baskets until they were needed for finished processing on the two tube production lines. At the first four stations on the production lines, tubes were passed on a conveyer through an oven for heat treating to create the proper degree of flexibility —soft enough to be squeezed easily yet hard enough to withstand further processing. Then tubes were given their exterior color base on the lacquering machine, which contained three revolving cylinders on which the tubes were rolled through a lacquer base. An overhead conveyor then passed the tubes through a drying oven and to the printing machine station. The mechanical operation of the printing machine was similar to that of the lacquerer, except that the tubes were rolled against a mat which applied a design and written message. The work of the unloaders at the lacquering and printing machines required manual speed, dexterity, and good vision. The machines were preset to discharge roughly a tube per second. The unloader had to remove the tube by the neck, inspect it for various kinds of defects, place it precisely on a hook on the conveyor, and wipe excess lacquer from the cylinder before the machine moved through its next cycle. Next, the tubes were conveyed through a second drying oven to the packing table where packers removed them from the hooks, inspected them, screwed on plastic caps, removed excess ink from the interiors, and boxed them for shipment. Above every machine was a sign indicating the cost to the plant of each hour of downtime. Exhibit 2 is a floor plan of the factory area.

The tube production lines were operated on a two-shift basis, six days a week. Two complete shifts, composed entirely of women, worked on the line. Because of a government regulation requiring a half-hour lunch break for straight eight-hour shifts, the two shifts' crews worked alternate four-hour periods, 6 to 10 A.M.–2 to 6 P.M. and 10 A.M. to 2 P.M.–6 to 10 P.M. Work crews exchanged shifts every week. Approximately eight months out of the year, a third shift was added. It operated one of the two production lines between 10 P.M. and 6 A.M. Permission to work women after 10 P.M. had to be renewed periodically by the Ministry of Labor and sometimes required weeks of negotiation, during which period the late shift had to be discontinued. To man the night operations, workers were selected from the two permanent day crews and were replaced on the day shifts by permanently employed extras who otherwise performed service jobs in the plant. Night workers were paid one and one half times the day rate.

Each day shift employed approximately 27 women. Women at the oven and the lacquering and printing machines worked in teams of two, while four to five women worked at each packing table. Exhibit 2 also shows the distribution of workers across the floor. The forelady and her mechanic worked straight eight-hour shifts and thus supervised each of the two shift crews for four hours a day. When a night shift was operated, each forelady and mechanic team worked 12 consecutive hours a day. The

**EXHIBIT 2**

Factory Floor Plan, 1966

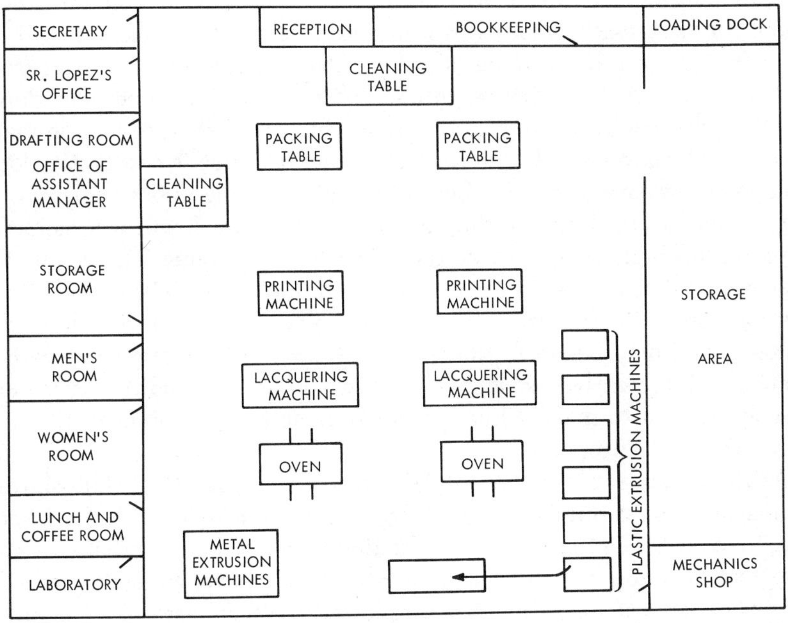

SECRETARY
RECEPTION
BOOKKEEPING
LOADING DOCK
SR. LOPEZ'S OFFICE
CLEANING TABLE
DRAFTING ROOM
PACKING TABLE
PACKING TABLE
OFFICE OF ASSISTANT MANAGER
CLEANING TABLE
STORAGE ROOM
PRINTING MACHINE
PRINTING MACHINE
STORAGE AREA
MEN'S ROOM
LACQUERING MACHINE
LACQUERING MACHINE
PLASTIC EXTRUSION MACHINES
WOMEN'S ROOM
OVEN
OVEN
LUNCH AND COFFEE ROOM
METAL EXTRUSION MACHINES
LABORATORY
MECHANICS SHOP

forelady was officially responsible for assigning girls their duties, maintaining discipline, and doing odd jobs such as filling the ink buckets and making simple adjustments to the machinery. The mechanic was responsible for all maintenance, setups, and satisfactory operations of all machinery on the lines. Although one of the girls at the packing table was designated as the inspector and held responsible for quality control, Sr. Lopez said, "I hold every girl responsible for quality production." A production manager was responsible for the overall operation.

Several physical conditions affected the work in the plant. Heat from the ovens made the area unusually hot, especially at midday. The lacquering machines gave off a pungent odor, which was nauseous to some of the women. Noise from the machines, particularly from the extruders, made normal conversation difficult. The factory floor was surrounded by offices and supplementary rooms, all opening onto it. People constantly walked back and forth across the floor, inventories were piled in free spots, and women worked at two or three cleaning tables, giving the impression of crowding and great activity.

## INCIDENT ON THE PLANT FLOOR

As he guided the casewriter past the machines during his explanation of the operation, Sr. Lopez indicated a lacquering machine which had been brought to a halt, its two operators standing idly beside it. "That is exactly the problem I was telling you about in the office. That machine is down. The chain is slack. In another two minutes the printing machine will be idled for lack of tubes coming out of the drying oven. Five minutes from now, the packers will have no tubes. The minute a machine goes down like that, the mechanic ought to be on it. Gutierrez (the production manager) should never let this kind of thing happen, but it constantly does. Will you excuse me a minute? I've got to get this thing under control."

Sr. Lopez walked over to the girls and spoke with them for a moment. Then he left and went towards the laboratory, emerging a few minutes later with a mustached man in a white shirt and slacks. They spoke for a few minutes with the girls and then bent over the machine, which the white-shirted man began to tinker with. A man in levis appeared with a wrench and screwdriver, spoke with the two other men, and then also bent over and began to make adjustments. After about five minutes, the machine was back in operation.

As Sr. Lopez was returning to the casewriter with the white-shirted man, a secretary ran up saying that Sr. Lopez had a phone call. Sr. Lopez said, "This is Sr. Gutierrez, our production manager here. Perhaps he can help you clear up any technical questions you have while I take this call." He again excused himself and followed the secretary off the floor.

Sr. Gutierrez began to talk about the technical problems of the machinery and the job of keeping the lines running. The casewriter, however, had noticed a number of things about which he had questions and began by asking Gutierrez why he had seen a few girls sitting alone on packing boxes cleaning tubes while others worked in groups.

GUTIERREZ: It disturbs Sr. Lopez to see the girls talking too much. On the lines, it's hard enough keeping the talking down so that they can check the printing and lacquering on each tube. When they get into groups to clean defectives, sometimes one of them really begins to act up, and the rest of the girls become silly and really loud. This distracts the girls in the group and also others working on the line. So we sometimes have to put the troublemakers to work by themselves.

CASEWRITER: Why do the girls have to be quiet on the lines?

GUTIERREZ: It's not that they really have to be quiet. It's just that they have to concentrate to spot defectives caused by their machine and by previous operations. Each of the machines can produce its own type of defective. For example, the extrusion machine could produce defects in shape or design; improper oven temperature or conveyer speed can make the tube too hard or too soft. Lacquer might be too thick and smudge or crack. And the most difficult one, of course, is the printing machine, which might produce a few flawed letters of tiny type. Because of the speed of the machines, the checking we require is tough and requires great concentration.

The casewriter asked Sr. Gutierrez what his biggest problem was in supervising the girls on the line. He said: "Sometimes the girls get the mechanics to fuss with the machines when it isn't necessary, or they stop them every half hour for cleaning. Now, you can't say anything about this because it's hard to judge whether the tubes are right. Sr. Lopez is a real stickler for quality, and if you've told the girls to get the machine going and he comes in and spots a tube he doesn't like, you're not doing your job."

CASEWRITER: What does Sr. Lopez have to do with supervising the plant operation?

GUTIERREZ: Unfortunately, (smiling broadly) everything. When he gets to the plant in the morning, the first thing he does after hanging up his coat is to come out here. He looks at the quality of the printing and the lacquering, the tube shape and its feel, the oven temperatures and the conveyer speeds, or a machine we're repairing, and he always has suggestions. He picks a tube off the line (Sr. Gutierrez picked up an imaginary tube, raised it to within a couple of inches from his face, and scrutinized it with his head cocked and one eye closed) and says to me, "Gutierrez, don't you believe this tube could use a little more ink?" It's a very good question.

CASEWRITER: Does this bother you?

GUTIERREZ: No, not really. I've been with this plant since the beginning. And by now, I'm used to it. Besides, if there's a mistake out here, it is my responsibility. Sr. Lopez knows this machinery and he knows the quality that our customers want better than any of us. So he's helping, not hurting me, when he points out errors . . . (Sr. Gutierrez thought a moment). No, I'm very appreciative of Sr. Lopez's help. But Porras, who was production manager before me and who is now chief mechanic, used to blow up whenever Cordero, the bookkeeper, came out here. Cordero doesn't know anything about machines, yet he'd come running out here all the time, waving his papers about wastage or defectives or production rates. And he didn't care who he talked to. I guess he's learned better, though, because he doesn't do it now except when Sr. Lopez is out of the country. Since he owns a few shares of stock, I guess he feels responsible for filling in for Sr. Lopez.

## THE PROBLEM OF SUPERVISION

At this point, Sr. Lopez returned and accompanied the writer to the office saying, "You've seen the operation and understand how it works. Let's have some coffee and I'll explain my supervisor problem. Let me start from the beginning. When we began to produce here, we decided to use women for a variety of reasons. Most important, female labor is less expensive than male labor, and the work on the line requires no special knowledge or technical skill and is not heavy. We took only young women, and, as is natural, women who weren't ugly, in order to give the plant a more attractive appearance. We thought that young women wouldn't have children and thus would be able to work more freely in a factory. We also felt they would be more energetic and thus able to boost production. We used male line chiefs, who supervised the girls and also served as mechanics.

"But having males supervise all-women crews led to nothing but trouble. Almost immediately, some of the girls began to complain that the line chiefs were showing preference towards certain other girls. The girls said that the sweethearts were given the best jobs so that they could make the best pay and were treated far more leniently than the others. You can imagine the kind of thing: a favorite says she feels badly or wants to be excused for the day, so naturally the man has a soft heart and gives her time off or sends her to rest in the coffee room. Naturally, the less attractive girls must have resented being denied these privileges. I suppose that sometimes the line chief lost interest in an old favorite and to make the point, he perhaps treated her a little harder than the others. Maybe the discarded girl felt resentful and wanted to get even with him.

"Two things worried me about this: one, I want good morale, and, two, I could imagine what was going on at night. None of the administrators are here at night and the shift chief would really have a chance to fool around. Fooling around, he would lose everyone's respect and be unable to maintain discipline. And if he were fooling around, he would have to give a chance to the mechanics too. You can imagine the kind of problem that I could have on my hands.

"Of course, had I had proof of any of this, someone would have gotten fired on the spot, but everytime I brought it up, it was staunchly denied.

"What was I to do? I liked the idea of outright replacing the young girls with older, uglier women who would be more responsible, less chatty, and less attractive to line chiefs. But that would have meant loss of the training time I'd already invested and possible labor problems which might have jeopardized the night shift. Furthermore, all that severance pay would have been expensive. And anyway, I don't believe in treating workers that way.

"My other idea was to replace the male shift foremen with women. We heard that women were working when they didn't feel well because they were embarrassed to tell their supervisors. Also, women are emotional and get easily upset when men are gruff, which often happened because the foremen were in a hurry or angry at something. With a forelady, the workers would feel more comfortable and would be able to communicate better. But I didn't want to do this because I didn't want to lose my men, who were by this time good mechanics, and I also feared that the foreladies would be unable to maintain discipline, especially at night when there were no administrators around. I just couldn't picture a woman obeying another woman. I also wondered if a woman would be able to get the mechanics to cooperate.

"There was my original problem. What would you have done?"

CASEWRITER: It sounds very complicated. How did you handle it?

LOPEZ: It proved easier than I had thought, and I made both moves. I replaced the young girls gradually as they left the plant of their own accord. We still have a lot of the earlier workers with us, but you can see the older ones scattered through the lines, and they are much more satisfactory. As for the shift chiefs, I got rid of those who had been causing the trouble. We picked our two best women and assigned them as foreladies. We got rid of all the men who had been causing the trouble. The good men, who liked learning about machines, were made mechanics of the new plastics line which we were opening. At the same time, I created a separate mechanics staff with Porras, our old production chief and best mechanic, as head. Then I assigned a mechanic from that staff to work with each of the foreladies. Gutierrez, one of our old line foremen, was made production manager.

CASEWRITER: And what were the results?

LOPEZ: Well, I have no more complaints of favoritism, and my production jumped considerably. But the basic problems of quality and volume are always with us, and I have to be constantly on top of them, or they will get out of hand.

CASEWRITER: Could you explain these problems?

LOPEZ: I guess the simplest way is to explain a little more about the people I've got. The girls don't always pay attention and aren't the most intelligent of workers. For example, lots of times they miss the defectives as they pass through. That's why I try to get everyone to watch for defectives. And girls aren't mechanical and I don't want them fooling around with the machines. Lots of times they aren't even able to judge whether something is really wrong. That's why the mechanics must jump right in whenever the girls think there is a problem, and often when they don't see anything, too. The trouble with mechanics is that they are often more interested in exploring interesting technical problems than they are in getting a machine fixed and the line back in operation. That's why the production manager must always be on top of them. But you saw out there what happens all the time. People don't move when problems occur.

Basically the biggest problem facing most businesses in this country is that no one knows what supervision means—we just don't have well-qualified supervisors. Most chiefs are accustomed to working with the government. There, they have no pressure to produce, nor do they learn to put pressure on others. When there is no pressure, people get sloppy. It's not just that my supervisors don't know how to do their job, they get frustrated with it and want to quit. One of my foreladies now wants to go back to the lines. And the one before her smashed her thumb and had to be given other work. That's why I have to be on top of things all the time.

CASEWRITER: Could you explain how you do keep on top of things.

LOPEZ: The biggest thing is to be on the floor as much as possible. Whenever I find a defective or see a machine down, I point it out to the workers and supervisors. It's been a tremendous educational job explaining to everyone what a quality tube is and persuading the foremen and mechanics to move when something goes wrong. I used to hold weekly assemblies with the whole crew at which I'd explain problems I'd discovered and the need to improve. I just don't have time for that anymore, but I think that the large signs you saw above each machine helped the personnel to understand the importance of keeping the machines running.

CASEWRITER: What kind of production records do you keep?

LOPEZ: I only really have daily and weekly totals and they aren't that helpful. I had thought that the girls might take an interest in these and perhaps the groups would work to see who could produce more. But the production of the two groups always seems to be about equal and the inspector who keeps the records tells me that nobody ever looks at them.

One interesting thing, though, that puzzles all of us is that when we run our night shift, we sometimes get on one line three quarters of what we produce on two lines in the daytime. Even taking into account the fact that we do most of our setups in the daytime, we still get proportionately more production at night. We can't understand this because the forelady and mechanic are there alone and don't have any backup from the administration.

CASEWRITER: Is there any explanation?

LOPEZ: I don't know. One reason might be that the machines are all prepared in the daytime, so that they run throughout the night without breaking down. But this doesn't seem valid because our worst time for breakdowns is the four hours around midday, and the machines generally run pretty well in the later afternoon and early evening, when they should be wearing down from their morning tuneups. The most satisfactory explanation I can think of is that the cool temperature at night is a factor. When it is very hot, as it is around noontime, the ink flow is uneven and the machines require constant minor adjustments. The nights are much fresher, and perhaps the ink flow is smoother. To be truthful, I can't figure out the answer but it's got me curious.

The casewriter expressed an interest in spending a few days in the plant in order to gain an insight into the problems of supervision. He also hoped to learn more about the night shift.

LOPEZ: Yes, that's a good idea, though I think the night thing's a fluke caused by the more favorable temperature. I doubt whether there is anything in the night conditions which could be reproduced in the daytime, though I'd be mighty interested to know if there were.

The casewriter visited the plant for a number of days, observing the operations and conversing with the workers to learn more about supervision and the night shift at Tubident. One day, he encountered one of the foreladies, Flora, appearing very upset. (Flora had been supervising the line for about two months, having previously worked on the lacquering machine. Sr. Gutierrez had told the casewriter that he had selected Flora as supervisor because "she is one of our most serious workers. She always stays alone and never gets into trouble.") The casewriter asked her what was the matter. "The girls are rude and spoiled. Whenever you reprimand one for a mistake, she talks back to you. I get in trouble when the girls talk too much. I used to get along with them when I was their work partner but now they won't respect me or do what I tell them. The trouble is that Sr. Gutierrez didn't send around a note authorizing me as chief and explaining how the girls would have to treat me. I get very upset when things aren't done well. The girls say I'm bad-tempered. It isn't that; it's just that Sr. Lopez told me very strictly how I was supposed to do this job, and I'm trying to do it. Sr. Lopez hates to see defectives on the floor. This morning the girls have been throwing them all over the place. I said very pleasantly, 'Couldn't you pick those up and keep your places clean?' They just gave me dirty looks and didn't do anything about the mess. I know I must be doing something wrong, and I told Sr. Lopez I didn't want the job any more. He just told me to reprimand the girls sternly or suspend them for a few days. I can't suspend them because they are as poor as I am. Now I'm going to go tell Sr. Gutierrez to ask the girls himself to pick up the things instead of telling me to do it. I'm also going to ask him to write me a note authorizing me to be chief."

A short time later, the casewriter spoke with some of the girls about Flora. One of them said, "She bawled me out yesterday for not having asked permission to go to the restroom. I'd like to say something to her but I guess I'd better not. She forgets that when she was a worker, she did the same thing when none of the bosses was around."

Later in the day, the casewriter encountered Flora leaving the floor. She said tearfully, "I don't know what to do. I can't go to Sr. Gutierrez everytime something happens. I just asked them nicely not to talk too loudly. They said, 'Why can't we talk? We're working with our hands, not with our mouths.'" She excused herself and hurried away.

Later that day the casewriter was discussing the work of the foreladies with Sr. Gutierrez. Mariela, the former forelady, had seriously injured her hand and had been assigned to work in the warehouse. The casewriter asked Gutierrez how the injury had occurred.

GUTIERREZ: Well, I'm not really sure. She wasn't very clear about it. She said that she was cleaning the printing machine and stepped on the start lever. (Pause) But I can't see how she could have done that. (Pause) Maybe one of the girls did it.

CASEWRITER: Do you mean intentionally?

SR. GUTIERREZ: No, of course not.

CASEWRITER: Then, why wouldn't she have mentioned it?

SR. GUTIERREZ: (pause): Maybe she didn't want to get anyone else involved. She probably would have wanted to keep it quiet if it had happened that way.

The casewriter tried to observe the relationships among the workers and to discover their feelings about each other and their jobs. He noticed that some of the younger looking girls, who comprised about two thirds of the line workers and manned the faster operations, often came into the plant laughing in small groups and gathered to converse in the coffee room or around the machines before taking their places on the lines. Older women and a few of the younger girls came and left by themselves. The girls made a number of comments about one another to the writer. Josefina, a sweet-looking girl, appeared to be very popular. She said, "We are all good friends around here. We tease each other a lot and talk about our boyfriends." Another girl said, "This was my first job. I'd heard stories of how badly some of my friends were treated where they worked, but everyone here is very nice. Even the bosses are friendly." Many of the women were the sole support of their children, and those without children usually gave money to their parents. While some of the younger ones said they enjoyed working where there were friends instead of staying at home where there was just housework, other young ones seemed to share the attitude of the older women, that work meant only earning money for their families.

The casewriter noticed one very pretty girl named Sara, who always entered and left the plant alone and barely talked to anybody. She always came dressed up and appeared bored and sullen. When the casewriter asked Sr. Gutierrez about her, he said that she had been part of a group of the original workers. They had learned their jobs fairly well but had become more and more talkative, noisy, and playful and had distracted the other workers and upset everyone. Gutierrez said he had finally felt obliged to talk to Sara about her boisterousness and had urged her to become independent of the "troublemakers." She had accepted his scolding and now worked alone, bothering no one. He now considered her one of his best workers.

The casewriter asked her how she felt about her work and the other workers. "I used to have many friends; Maria, Roxana, Teresa, Josefina, Julieta, and I were the first workers and used to have a lot of fun. Most of them are still here, but they gossip and start rumors and it's better not to get mixed up with them. Now I work my four hours thinking about what I'll do when I leave, and I don't have to pay so much attention when the girls feel like working and keep pushing me to hurry. I used to go to the inspector's table to see how much we had produced when the machines were good and we felt like working. Our shift used to be better than A. But I don't know who's better now, because I don't bother to look."

One day, when the machines were stopped and Gutierrez and the mechanics were conferring on what was to be done, the casewriter struck up a conversation with Maria, one of the popular workers, about supervision on the day shift. She said, "Do you know how many chiefs we have around here?—everyone from the manager to that mechanic over there. They all give us orders. One tells you the tubes are O.K. Another says they aren't and wants to adjust the machine. It's good, though. They do our work for us." The writer turned to Julieta. She told him, "The job is boring. We like to talk and sing, but it's hard to know when they [the management] will get mad at us for talking, so we always try to talk just loudly enough to hear one another over the noise of the machines."

Another girl, discussing the desire of the workers to talk and sing, mentioned that they had previously had a radio. "We used to have music on the radio, but the bosses liked formal music. Finally they decided we weren't paying enough attention to our work. We weren't sorry because we didn't like that kind of music anyway."

Carmen, the other shift chief, was a short, slim woman, striking in her dignified demeanor. One afternoon, she and Neddy, her mechanic, had just come on duty with the two o'clock shift (composed of the women who had already worked from 6 to 10 A.M.). None of the bosses was in the plant that afternoon. The changeover was effected with much joviality. Before the girls took their places at the machines, Carmen ran around cleaning up defectives and joking with everyone. One worker commented to the casewriter that this was "going to be a good afternoon." Soon the lines were going full steam. Carmen began to run around the machines, filling ink wells at one, picking up stray defectives at another, with a pleasant word to each of the girls as she passed.

Occasionally, someone would shut a machine down, clean the roller for about 30 seconds, and get it going again. Suddenly, Josefina, at one of the lacquering machines, said to the loader at the machine, "Tell Carmen to get over here quickly. I'm running out of ink." The word was passed down the line to Carmen, who was helping the packers because they'd fallen behind. Carmen grabbed an ink bucket, filled it from a barrel, and ran over to fill Sara's well. Immediately after that, as Neddy strolled in from the mechanics room, the two girls at the printer on the other line shouted, "Carmen, Carmen!" A chorus of laughing voices rose, "Carmen, Carmen! Neddy, Neddy!" Carmen and Neddy started towards the printing machine, then looked around and laughed with the others. Everyone kept working. As Carmen passed the casewriter, she said, "We're way ahead today." At one point, Julieta's machine was stopped. Carmen immediately ran over. One of the extras, who was sweeping the floor, dropped her broom and ran to look for Neddy in the machine shop. Soon Neddy, Carmen, and Julieta were working on the machine and got it started rapidly.

As the afternoon wore on, various girls quickly asked extras to take their places and went out for coffee. The casewriter asked Carmen why she wasn't insisting that they ask for permission. "Whenever the bosses aren't around I don't insist. But when it gets out of hand, I go up to one of them and say (she frowns sternly and wags her finger), 'You know you're supposed to ask permission.' " The casewriter said, "You mean when the bosses are around?" She just laughed and ran over to help the packers again. Watching her work at the packing table, the casewriter remembered what Carmen had told him about her job: "My job is to help the girls do their work. My other job is to please everybody. For example, when the bosses are around, I tell the girls to keep the talking down, and if there are defectives lying on the floor, I clean them up fast."

A little later, the casewriter saw Julieta in the coffee room and asked her why things were going so well today. "Today we all just feel good and want to see how much we can turn out. We had a terrible time this morning because Flora was mad at us for talking and Sr. Lopez kept coming around. It's really fun when Carmen and Neddy are here alone. I want to learn about mechanics, and Carmen and Neddy let me help. You know, the chiefs don't like us to work on the machines, and we can't do it when they're around. Also, Carmen helps us, and she never bosses us around unless there's a reason."

The production of that day was unusually high. On the following day, it was very hot in the plant. No one seemed animated, and a few girls commented that they didn't feel much like working. At almost any moment, at least one machine could be seen stopped with its operator spending a long time cleaning it. Carmen commented to the casewriter, "It's too hot in here, and the girls are tired and don't feel like working fast. You can't blame them, and you can't keep them from stopping the machines because one of the bosses usually agrees that the machine needs adjustment."

Gutierrez, shaking his head over the slow progress of the work, said, "One problem today is that a part on one of the printing machines is causing trouble because it's worn out. The mechanics are building me a new part and once we get it in, the machine will stay in adjustment much longer. They've been working on the part since eight this morning. Come into the machine shop and I'll show it to you." In the machine shop, they saw the mechanics gathered in a group in one corner. On the bench lay the new printing part apparently untouched. Sr. Gutierrez looked at the part, then at the mechanics, cursed to himself, and walked out.

Though there was no night shift during the casewriter's visit at Tubident, he tried to discover why night production was higher by questioning the workers. Carmen's reply was:

> I like working the night shift best. I need the extra income for my child and I'm grateful to be able to earn time and a half for the extra work. The work at night is much simpler, because you don't have to worry about anything except the machines and the girls. We only run one line, and the mechanic and I can easily attend to this. The girls take care of their machines and keep them running. When they call you over at night, you know they really need your help.

There's a good spirit at night. I think the girls realize that all the management is interested in the next morning is the number of boxes of tubes we produced the night before. We say to them, "Let's really turn it on so they can see how much we've done." We want them to see we've been working hard and not sleeping or playing games. If we have a breakdown, need more mechanics, or don't produce enough tubes, it might not be worth the management's while to keep the night shift going. And all of us want the extra money.

The casewriter asked other girls how they felt about night work and following are some of the answers:

Sure we get tired. Lots of times one of the girls will get so tired she almost goes to sleep at the machine. But we do everything we can to keep her awake; we turn on the radio real loud, or we'll sing special songs, or her companion will tell jokes and laugh or tell her everything she can think of about her boyfriend. Pretty soon she gets over it and feels fine again.

. . . . . . . . . . . . . . . . . . .

We have a good time. Even Flora gets along.

. . . . . . . . . . . . . . . . . . .

The reason we produce more is that we're a well-selected group. Some girls get sick or fall asleep at night. They aren't selected for the shift. It's kind of an honor to be chosen for night work.

. . . . . . . . . . . . . . . . . . .

At night, you are really responsible for your machine. You have to decide whether it is running properly and whether the tubes are properly soft and have the right amount of lacquer on them. You only stop the machine if something is seriously wrong. If you see one tiny bad line or speck on the print, you know it's not important and keep going. When you *do* stop the machine, you get to fix it. You may talk things over with the chief, but you really feel responsible to keep things under control yourself, because nobody's going to do it for you.

We get all greasy but change everything around with the pliers until the ink is coming out just right. Of course, we've got to hurry, because we want to produce a lot for the morning. I can fix and adjust the machine in lots of little ways. You're not supposed to do that in the daytime.

. . . . . . . . . . . . . . . . . . .

One day the casewriter noticed that Flora was back on the line and that Carmen was working as forelady for both day shifts. When he asked what had happened, Sr. Gutierrez replied, "She finally just refused to be chief anymore. She'd been getting more and more moody lately. When the girls called her for help, she'd get upset that they weren't doing their work. She thought the girls were just trying to bother her. She came to me finally complaining about a group of girls who were ignoring her orders, she said, and insulting her, too. She asked me to do something. I felt it was my obligation to call the three girls together to ask for their cooperation. I explained to them what Sra. Flora had said and that she was new and didn't know any better. They said they hadn't done anything and that Sra. Flora must be making it up.

"Sra. Flora had gone to see Sr. Lopez, wanting to switch back to the line and after my meeting with the girls, Sr. Lopez decided that it was important enough to call another meeting of the three girls, him, and me, this time inviting Sra. Flora. Flora explained what disturbed her but the girls couldn't understand it. They denied it all. We decided that it wasn't right for her to be upset and that it would be better to get another line chief. Carmen's working 16 hours temporarily until we choose a replacement."

## POSTSCRIPT

When the casewriter had completed his observations, he returned with a rough draft of the case to check with Sr. Lopez on the accuracy of statements attributed to him, and to obtain approval for clearance use of the case. When he arrived, Sr. Lopez welcomed him with a smile. "Here's the man who really understands what I'm up against. Now you can tell me how I can train these supervisors of mine better."

Sipping coffee, the casewriter learned that Sr. Lopez was considering replacing Flora with Mariela, depending upon the latter's recovering the use of her thumb, "since she's one of our most experienced girls. She really knows what I want and it will be easier to work with her than breaking in a new girl. I know what we need out there, and it's very hard breaking a new person in. I don't have the time for it I used to have. Well enough of that. Let's see what you've got."

Sr. Lopez took the case and began reading. When he reached the section early in the case commenting on his success in achieving high quality standards, he stopped, looked in his desk, and handed the casewriter a recent letter from a principal customer, congratulating Lopez on the consistent good quality of the Tubident products and commending Sr. Lopez personally for his achievement.

For the next hour Sr. Lopez continued to read, making occasional corrections or comments and frequently chuckling. As he finished, he looked up at the casewriter, smiled, and said: "Well, I think you've got it all down here. We've had a real job on our hands and still do. It will make an interesting case for your students. Now if you'll wait a minute while I make my rounds, I'll drive you into town for lunch."

The casewriter followed Sr. Lopez into the plant, watched him remove the tubes from the line to check them carefully, occasionally stopping to point out a problem to the girls. Once Sr. Lopez looked over at the casewriter, grinning, and said, "Just like in your case, eh?" Then he took the casewriter's arm and they left for lunch.

# American Radiatronics Corporation

THE AMERICAN Radiatronics Corporation was one of the leading producers and an early pioneer in the nuclear electronics industry. The company manufactured a line of nuclear instrumentation specialties and other electronic devices for nuclear applications. This case reports the results of a study of the nuclear tube assembly room, one of the production rooms of the Baltimore, Maryland, plant of the company. In this room the company's regular line of electronic tubes was assembled, tested, and prepared for shipment.

The casewriter's attention was initially called to the nuclear tube assembly room in a conversation he had with Ralph Langley, general foreman of the process department. In expressing his views about the various problems and plans he had in connection with each segment of the several production units in this department, Langley described the tube room group as the most successful and, from certain standpoints, the most interesting.

The casewriter followed up this lead by securing some additional background facts on the tube room. He found that, prior to Langley's assuming leadership of the department, some 24 months earlier, the girls in the room had acquired the reputation of being agitators, hotheads, and persistent troublemakers. Production was down, costs had gotten out of hand, and deliveries had become very unpredictable. Some thought had been given to eliminating the entire operation.

Some data on labor efficiency during the subsequent 24 months are presented in Exhibit 1. During the most recent three-month period the tube room's direct and allocated[1] monthly costs had averaged $12,350, while the actual sales value of the room's monthly production for the same three months averaged $35,800.

A recent special management report presented some additional figures of interest. Between January of the previous year and March of the current year, the group had shown a 53 percent improvement in the dollar output of product per man-hour of work, direct labor efficiency had increased approximately 23 to 25 percent, and there had been about 11 to

[1] Indirect costs were allocated to the department at the rate of 425 percent of direct labor dollars.

12 percent improvement in the raw material utilization on tubes produced. During this same period, they operated at 81 percent of their expense budget. In other words, they had used some $4,000 less on miscellaneous expenses than had been budgeted for such items. During this time period the hourly wages of the girls working in the room had risen from an average of $1.45 per hour to $1.75 per hour.

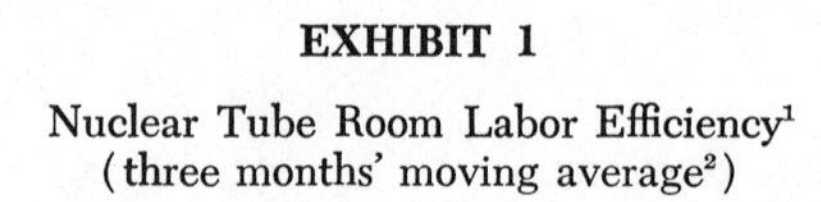

**EXHIBIT 1**

Nuclear Tube Room Labor Efficiency[1]
(three months' moving average[2])

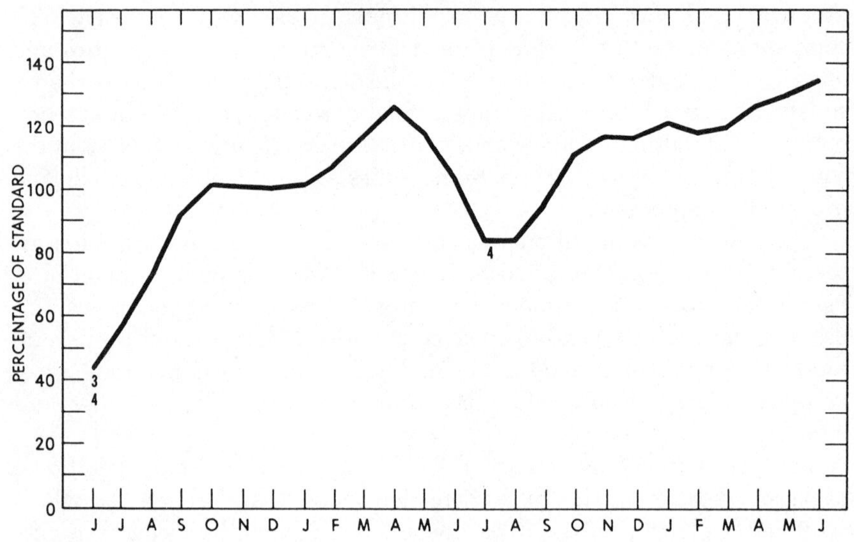


[1] Standard hours produced divided by hours on rated jobs (approximately 90 percent of time is spent on rated jobs).

[2] All percentages are calculated on new standards.

[3] Prior to this period, labor efficiency figures are not available; however, the best estimates attainable indicate that efficiencies were averaging between 40 and 50 percent of standard.

[4] Somewhat lower labor efficiencies are expected during the hot summer months than during the remainder of the year.

In summary, the profit position for tube manufacturing operations as a whole was now one of the best in the company, where previously the activity had been operating at a loss. This record of progress had been widely recognized throughout the company.

In commenting about the group, Langley said:

The more or less unique or different aspect of this performance was that it was accomplished by the group itself—not so much by any tangible thing that I or management had done. These people, who had previously been considered a problem group, are now performing in an efficient and profitable way; and they have a very active interest in seeing not only the group in which they were engaged, but the company as a whole, progress and make profits. It seems to me that this is quite an impressive thing for them to have accomplished by their own efforts.

As a result of this conversation with Langley and the other information he had obtained, the casewriter decided he would like to learn more about the tube room and how it operated. He arranged, therefore, on his next visit to the plant, to ask the company president, Frank Halbert, for permission to study the department.

In approving the study, Halbert said, in part: "I hope you find what you are looking for. It would be tremendously important for the whole economy to bust through this 'least work for the most pay' idea workers in this country have." Later, he said: "Do you really think there is any substitute for fear as a motivator? I doubt it. All of these fringe benefits and things won't do it; we've certainly learned that."

About Langley and operations in the tube room, Halbert commented approximately as follows:

I don't want to downgrade Ralph Langley or anything like that—I think he has been extremely successful in what he is doing—but it should be kept in mind that the tube room is not such a tough place to handle. We have some real trouble spots in other parts of the company. The tube room, after all, because of the kind of work done there, lends itself to the girls' seeing the connection between what they do and the final product. The work has challenge; it's interesting. There are opportunities there for satisfaction in the work itself that you couldn't begin to find in these other places.

### Background Facts about the Company and Its Products

In the course of his investigation, the casewriter learned a number of background facts about American Radiatronics Corporation and the conditions under which its tube manufacturing activities were conducted. The history of the company epitomized the pattern of development followed by many young companies that had taken part in the postwar nuclear electronics boom. Starting in a small garage workshop on a back street in Baltimore, the company had been founded approximately ten years earlier by two young scientists convinced of the coming industrial applications for nuclear processes and instrumentation. After an early period of rapid growth and a later series of mergers, the company prospered and finally stabilized at a level of sales in the range of $14 million annually. It remained at this volume for several years. In most recent years the company had been experiencing increasingly tightening competition from other young companies that had also grown to formidable strength of size and resources, and from older electronics firms that had more recently decided to enter the burgeoning nuclear field. The later history of the company was marked also by a number of shifts in the top management structure; the present management team had been installed approximately two years earlier.

The Baltimore plant contained the main factory and home office headquarters for the company. Located in an industrial park area on Baltimore's outskirts, the plant employed approximately six hundred people, most of whom commuted to work from Baltimore and its outlying suburbs. Well over half the company's sales volume was derived from the Baltimore plant's operations.

### The Nuclear Tube Assembly Room

The nuclear tube assembly room was one of several production units in the plant's process department. Under Langley's direction the department produced a variety of equipment parts, some of which went into larger equipment units manufactured by the company, while others were sold directly to customers. Exhibit 2 shows a partial organization chart of the company down to the level of this department's organization. Besides the nuclear tube assembly room, there were three other production units in the department, each housed in an adjacent separate room. The products and manufacturing processes for each of the production units were such that the work of one group was not linked to that of the others.

**EXHIBIT 2**

**Partial Organization Chart**

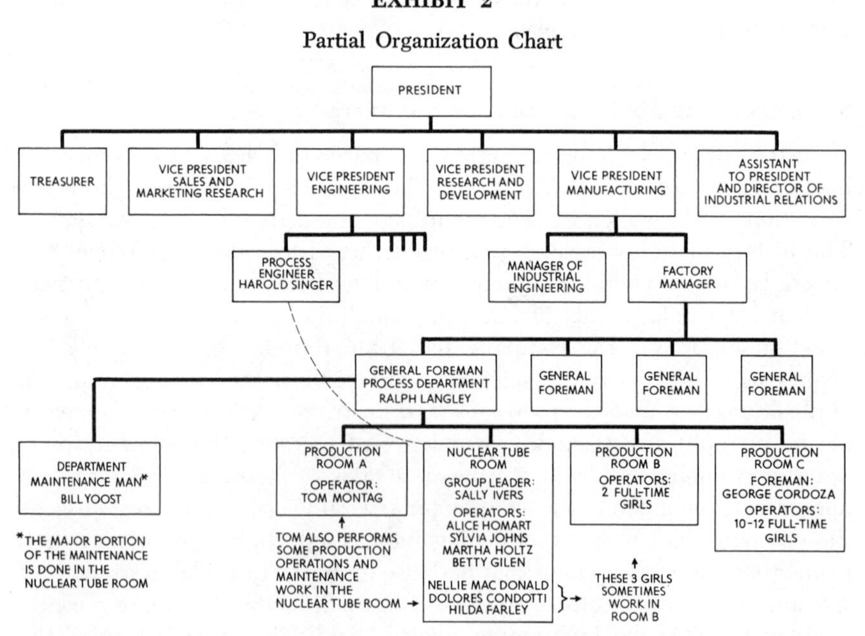

The nuclear tube assembly room produced all of the company's regular line of electronic tubes. These products varied considerably in size, shape, design, and materials. In appearance, they ranged from delicate glass vials three or four inches in length to massive steel chambers with bolted covers. Some were all-glass construction; still others consisted of all-metal assemblies, with numerous variations in the thickness and kind of metals employed. In all, approximately twenty-five different types of tubes were manufactured on a regular production basis, although not all styles were in production at the same time. A normal production month would call for eight to ten separate tube styles to be produced in quantities varying between three and five hundred per style. A number of miscellaneous small jobs consisting of repair, modifications, or experimental "mockup" of regular and/or experimental tubes were also assigned to the room each month. Out of the total number of tube types produced, four major tube styles accounted for approximately 80 to 84 percent of the dollar value of the room's output.

### The Production Process

The production process varied with each style of tube, depending upon the materials employed, the mechanical design of the tube, and the particular electronic properties called for by its function. The precise relationship between a given tube's design and its performance was not always clearly known. Certain tube designs were developed over the years by trial-and-error methods until a workable tube design was achieved, while others were developed from known formulations and in accordance with standard design procedures. For this reason, there was always an element of change in the air concerning details of the maufacturing process. For each tube a set of written standard operating procedures was developed by the company engineers to describe each assembly operation required; but from the viewpoint of production personnel, the history of modification and innovation that surrounded the evolution of many tube designs and production methods tended to imply that the process of developing ultimate designs was not yet at an end.

Most of the operations performed in the assembly process were of a handwork nature, in which a variety of jigs, small implements, heating torches, and special-purpose machines were employed. Customarily, the work was performed on a batch of parts at a time until a sufficient inventory of parts was accumulated to allow a number of tubes to be assembled in one operation.

The work of the tube room was roughly divided into (1) glasswork, which consisted of making tube shells and internal glass parts; (2) metalwork, wherein internal metal springs, wires, grids, leads, etc., were made and prepared for use; (3) tube assembly, at which time the entire tube was put together; (4) vacuum testing and exhausting, where tubes were leak-tested, exhausted, and filled with special gases; and (5) electronic testing, where the tube was tested as a functioning unit. After final testing, tubes were labeled, recorded according to individual serial numbers, and packaged for shipment or inventory storage. At all stages of assembly, tubes were given visual and electrical tests to minimize defective parts or subassemblies finding their way to final assembly. All testing and quality control measures were performed by the production workers themselves, including the final test before packaging.

### The Production Workers

The major part of the production work in the tube room was performed by eight women, one of whom served as group leader for the others. Each worker performed several kinds of operations, although each had, at the same time, one or more operations which she regarded as her particular specialty. These special jobs, which were part of the regular production process, had emerged over time as the most suitable work for a girl to do in view of her skills, her preferences, and the needs of the department. They were the most frequently recurring operations performed, accounting for roughly 50 percent or more of her time, and were the chief identifying characteristic of each girl's job. In all, an almost infinite variety of combinations of worker and job were practiced in the room. It was not uncommon for several girls, each at different times, and occasionally at the same time, to perform the same operations. Not even the special jobs were necessarily exclusive, as usually at least two girls had the special skills required to do a given job; and in case of absences or emergencies, one would take over for the other.

The tube room production staff was augmented by two men, one of whom served as maintenance man for the whole department, while the other worked in the tube room part time assisting in various production operations. He did this when not busy in Room A, his normal work assignment, a single-man operation which did not keep him busy full time.

Some additional personal and job information about these people and the department general foreman, Langley, are given in Exhibit 3.

### Pay Rates and Employee Evaluation

As shown in Exhibit 3, the employees of the tube room were paid on an hourly basis. Pay grades were established for each job classification by the industrial relations department according to an evaluation of the amount of skill and knowledge required of a worker in the job. Within each pay grade, there was an established range through which the hourly wage rate could progress. An employee's progression within range was

**EXHIBIT 3**

Job and Personal Information—Tube Room Personnel

| *Name* | *Job Classification* | *Pay* | *Age* | *Seniority with Company* | *Seniority in Tube Room* | *Education* | *Ethnicity* | *Marital Status* |
|---|---|---|---|---|---|---|---|---|
| Ralph Langley | Department general foreman | Not available | 41 | 3 yrs. | 2 yrs. | MS in physics | Yankee | M |
| Bill Yoost | Maintenance mechanic | $2.20/hr. | 39 | 3 yrs. | 2 yrs. | High school and trade school | Yankee | M |
| Sally Ivers | Group leader, production worker AA | $2.17/hr. | 43 | 12 yrs. | 12 yrs. | High school | Yankee | S |
| Alice Homart | Production worker AA | $2.05/hr. | 53 | 3 yrs. | 3 yrs. | High school | Yankee | Widow |
| Nellie MacDonald | Production worker A | $1.85/hr. | 46 | 5 yrs. | 5 yrs. | College, 1 yr. | Yankee | M |
| Hilda Farley | Production worker A | $1.81/hr. | 46 | 11 yrs. | 1 yr. | Grammar school | Irish | S |
| Martha Holtz | Production worker A | $1.76/hr. | 56 | 6 yrs. | 4 yrs. | 9 yrs. in Germany | German | M |
| Betty Gilen | Production worker A | $1.74/hr. | 42 | 4 yrs. | 4 yrs. | High school and art school (3 yrs.) | Yankee | W |
| Sylvia Johns | Production worker A | $1.71/hr. | 42 | 1 yr. | 1 yr. | Junior high school | Belgian | W |
| Tom Montag | Production worker B | $1.63/hr. | 26 | ½ yr. | ½ yr. | High school | French | M |
| Dolores Condotti | Production worker B | $1.61/hr. | 31 | 3 yrs. | 3 yrs. | Junior high school | Lithuanian | M |

determined by periodic merit reviews. At intervals of four months, each employee was rated by his department general foreman on evaluation forms designed to reveal his strengths and weaknesses. These evaluation forms were forwarded to the industrial relations department, where eligibility for pay increases was determined. The tube room workers were not unionized, although certain other manufacturing groups in the company had been organized some years previously by a large international trade union.

### Work Standards and Output Records

Approximately 95 percent of the tube assembly operations performed by the girls had been figured into standard hours by the company's industrial engineers. These standard hours were used in costing out direct labor costs for tube manufacturing operations by the accounting department, and they served as a standard of efficiency against which the room's actual performance was measured. Tube production for the total group was determined weekly when a physical inventory was taken of all finished and in-process tubes. Thus, labor invested in defective or destroyed tube parts or assemblies was "lost" to the group in figuring its net labor efficiencies. Monthly summaries of weekly efficiency figures were submitted to higher management for examination and review. Exhibit 1 presents these monthly efficiency figures for the previous twenty-four months.

All the labor efficiency figures in Exhibit 1 were based on revised standards put into effect three months prior to the study. The former standards, which had been set against the group's historical performance some years previously, had become inadequate in relation to the level of output then being achieved by the group. Consequently, Langley had initiated a review of all standards, "tube by tube, operation by operation," revising the allowed hours downward between 23 and 59 percent on individual tubes to an average 34 percent decrease on major tube types.

When Langley first took over supervision of the tube room group, the work force consisted of fourteen production workers. In the ensuing six months, improvements in the group's performance created a surplus of labor which, because of a relatively stable volume of operations, required a series of layoffs to be made. It was during this period that the original force was reduced to the present eight. The layoffs were made in two steps, with the girls selected for layoff primarily on the basis of seniority, with some secondary attention to the variety of work the girls could do, and the quantity and quality of their work. Langley commented:

> Those that stayed seemed to take it all right, even though none of them knew for sure whether she would be staying or not. They understood. One girl in the group I fired outright because of her attitude. She just couldn't and wouldn't fit in with the others. We had a long history of trouble with her.

During the twenty-four months since Langley took over the department, there were no major changes in the production facilities, manufacturing methods, or basic tube types in production. Much of the equipment in use was considered to be of antiquated and inefficient design. The improvements in group performance which were noted during this period were attributed primarily to improvements in labor efficiency and to informal production method innovations. Some minor alterations in tube design were made by the company's scientific personnel, and a number of such changes were initiated by members of the work group themselves; but as these changes were made, their laborsaving effects were largely incorporated into revised work standards.

### How the Tube Room Group Operated

The most immediate and apparent feature of the room was its physical layout and the location of various work positions within it. The room itself was a large, gray, concrete-floored enclosure approximately 60 feet long by 50 feet across. Closely assembled rows of tables, workbenches, production machines, and test stands filled its central portions, while an ordered clutter of miscellaneous cabinets, shelves, benches, and additional production equipment banked its wall areas. A row of windows looked into Production Room C, immediately adjacent. A single door provided access and egress for the room.

Exhibit 4 shows some details of the room's layout and the locations at which various people worked during a one-week observation period. Movement throughout the room was frequent and widespread, and the occasions were very seldom in which at least one or two people were not in motion. The changing of settled work positions was likely to occur at any time during a day. Bantering, horseplay, and visiting were frequent occurrences; and at times, even periods of total inactivity, such as when a girl appeared to be daydreaming or silently contemplating her work were observed. The pattern of activity did not appear to vary with the comings and goings of Sally Ivers, Langley, or any of the other supervisory personnel.

### Work Assignments and Supervisory Practices

In performing their work, the girls customarily obtained their working instructions from Sally. This usually occurred first thing in the morning, when there was a short flurry of milling around, donning of work smocks, setting up and adjustment of production equipment, and arrangement of parts, supplies, etc., preparatory to going to work. Throughout this, Sally would move from girl to girl, checking, answering questions, and discussing the day's work schedule. At times, this instruction giving would occur during the workday as a girl finished the batch of work she had

**EXHIBIT 4**

Tube Room Layout and Observed Work Positions during One-Week Period

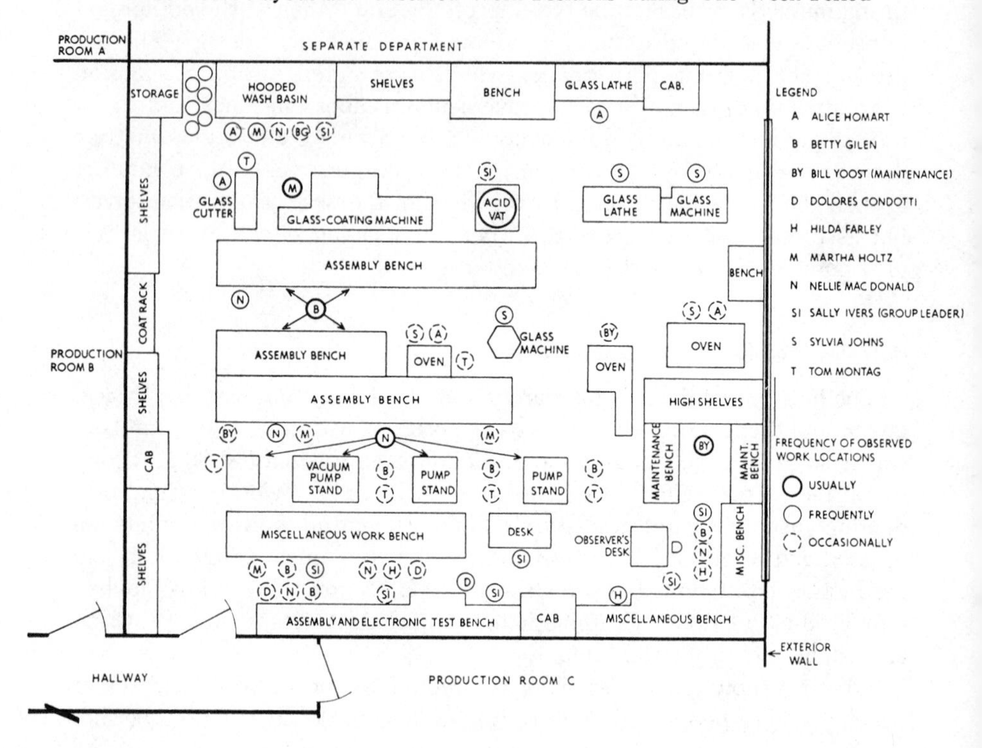


been on. Often, the exchange would be phrased as: "O.K. if I go to so and so now?" and "Sure." Or if more detailed instructions were required, Sally and the other girl would go over to the appropriate work station and discuss the details together. On a number of occasions, changes in work position or kind of work being performed took place without any apparent prior consultation with Sally.

One of the most concrete features of work scheduling practices in the tube room was a monthly production schedule delivered to the group by the company's production planning department just before the first of each month. Sally spoke about this in the following manner:

SALLY IVERS: We get this production schedule sheet here on my desk the first of every month from production planning, showing the kinds and numbers of tubes we will have to produce for the month. Ralph Langley and I then look it over, and we make our plans for how we want to schedule the different jobs that need doing. We usually start with the toughest orders first—that is, the longest, or those we think we will have some trouble with—so that by the end of the month we will have just the smaller jobs to do.

CASEWRITER: How do you use the standard times shown on the sheet?

SALLY: We don't pay too much attention to them. They tell us what the standard time is for each of the tubes to be produced. If we make the standard time, that is good, and we usually do. In fact, very often we beat the standard time. You know, we have been doing a very good job here.

CASEWRITER: What if you don't make your schedule? That is, what if you don't make production for a month? Suppose you were near the end of a month and you saw that you were not going to make it, what would you do?

SALLY: We usually make it. If we don't, we don't get too upset because we can always make it up some other time; and besides, usually if we don't make it, there is a good reason for it.

Langley also commented about this same production sheet and how he and Sally used it in scheduling work.

RALPH LANGLEY: When the production sheet comes in to us, Sally and I look it over. Sometimes, we figure that they're asking for too many parts of one kind or not enough of another, so we change it. We look at the numbers on the sheet, then we check the stock, and then we sort of think about whether or not the figures look right.

CASEWRITER: What do you mean by "whether the figures look right?"

LANGLEY: Well, I mean sometimes the production planning people can make a mistake like anyone else. Sometimes, the company has so many tubes of one kind in stock that I just know they couldn't have wanted that many, so I will second-guess them. I keep an eye on the main company inventory, you know; it's in the room right over there down the hall. All I have to do is walk in and look around, and I can see how many of what kind of tubes are in stock there; and often, I happen to know how the sales are running on particular tubes.

You know, sometimes people from the sales department come down and ask questions about things—questions about tubes, how much they cost, whether we are having any particular difficulty with them. In fact, I have often spoken directly with customers. Of course, I am not supposed to do that, that is not right, but they will often refer a customer to me to talk about a particular tube; and in this way, I have a feeling of how the sales of different kinds of tubes are going.

With this information about sales, inventory, stock situation, and the general work load we are operating under here, I am able to make some pretty fair guesses about the figures that production planning has set up—that is, whether we should follow their figures or adjust them slightly. Sometimes, we miss, but not very often. Usually, it has worked out in the past that our estimates of what the best schedule should be are good. In fact, it has happened more than once that the people from production planning would come to me and ask for my opinion on how many tubes I think they should put on the production planning sheet.

One of the production girls, Betty Gilen, spoke about the production schedule in the following manner:

BETTY GILEN: The day you'll see satisfaction written all over everyone's face is the last working day of the production month when we've met schedule. The last days before the end of the month, you'll see the girls walking to the production record over there, checking that, then checking the production schedule again on Sally's desk; and when they've made it, they really feel good. I know I do, and you'll see what I mean when you see the others acting that way, too.

Now, this is provided they haven't been pushed. This is important, because we meet our own schedule. No one says anything to us, no one is breathing down our backs. We do it ourselves. It's really amazing the change that begins to come over people when they move into the last part of the month and see we're going to have to step it up in order to make our quota. Everyone works a little harder, everyone tries to get her part of the work out of the way a little faster and on to the next girl. We really start to work hard, hand in hand with one another. It's a wonderful thing to watch. This is what makes this department work together so well. It's the cement that binds us as a team, you might say. Everyone, and I would say there's not a single exception to this, is willing to cooperate; and we all feel the same way about meeting the schedule—as I said, as long as no one is pushing us, as long as we're doing it ourselves.

### Attitudes toward the Work

In the course of his investigation, the casewriter held a number of conversations with other girls also about their work and how they felt about it. Here is the way several of them spoke during these conversations:

MARTHA HOLTZ: One of the things I do is make the anodes for these tubes. We used to make them out of stainless steel, but now we always make them out of platinum. You know, that was funny. One day, about six months ago, while we were still making them out of stainless steel, I made a mistake and made them out of platinum instead, and I made up a whole batch of them that way before I realized it. When I finished, I told Sally Ivers about it and said: "I made a mistake. I made these anodes out of platinum instead of stainless steel." She said: "That's all right, Martha; let's test them out this way and see how they are." They tested out perfectly, so she told Ralph Langley about it; and the next time I made anodes for that tube, Sally told me to make them out of platinum again because they had tested out so well. Always before, we had trouble testing out a whole batch of them without having some bad ones; and you know, since we've been making them out of platinum, we have had hardly any bad ones at all. And to think, just because I'd made a mistake!

. . . . . . . . . . . . . . . . . . . . . . . . . . . .

ALICE HOMART (*referring to some tube stem assemblies she is reworking from a batch made a few days earlier*): We've been having a lot of trouble with leaking stems lately, and we're trying to figure out where the trouble is by studying these stems from rejected tubes. I'm spending quite a bit of time right now trying to find the trouble.

CASEWRITER: How do you feel about spending your time examining these defective stems when it takes you away from regular production?

ALICE: I'm concerned about it. This is a headache, all the trouble we're having. That's why I'm spending so much of my time now trying to figure out what went wrong, so that we can get the production rate back up again. That makes sense, doesn't it? If I just ignored this trouble we're having and kept making stems, and if they were bad, we wouldn't really be getting any production out at all, would we?

CASEWRITER: I guess that's right. Does anyone ever say anything to you when you get behind on production?

ALICE: You bet they do. We hear about it, all right; and believe me, we hear about these leaky tubes, too. Nellie MacDonald shoots them right back at us when they don't make her leak test. That's what we're here for. No one stands over our shoulder counting what we do, but we know how many finished tubes we make and how many the production schedule calls for. Besides, it's always nicer when things are going along without any trouble. You know, we're not supposed to do this (*indicating the defective stem she is examining*); this is not our job.

CASEWRITER: Whose job is it?

ALICE: Well, no one's really, but we're not engineers. We're just production girls. We're not supposed to know the technical parts of this kind of work. The only thing is—there's no one else at the plant here who knows much more about this kind of work than we do. There's just us here in the room, so I guess it's up to Sylvia Johns and myself to figure out what goes wrong when we have trouble. Ralph Langley can help us sometimes, but he can't do everything. Besides, we're closer to the work.

. . . . . . . . . . . . . . . . .

SYLVIA JOHNS: I'm a glass blower. I learned the business from my husband in Philadelphia, where we operated a neon sign glass company for 25 years before he died. I had to go back to work after he died, and that's why I'm here. I like my work here. It's a good job, but it wasn't easy for me to find the kind of work I like to do after my husband died. Actually, glass blowing is all I do here, and it's what I prefer doing, too. I never work much on tube assembly, although I guess I would if I had to. Glasswork is really my line. After all, 25 years—I know it. My husband taught me well before he died.

. . . . . . . . . . . . . . . . .

CASEWRITER (*addressing Dolores Condotti at a work station where he has not seen her before*): What are you doing here?

DOLORES CONDOTTI: Making springs.

CASEWRITER: What are "springs"? [They appeared to be small-diameter coil springs with long wire tails protruding from them at right angles.]

DOLORES (*after several attempts to describe the function of a spring in a tube*): Oh, here, let me show you. (*Leading the casewriter over to a nearby cabinet, she opens it, removes a tube from a box, smashes the thin mica window in one end of it with a loud bang, and shows him the location of the spring.*)

CASEWRITER (*after they have returned to Dolores' work station*): What was that tube you just smashed?

DOLORES: Oh, that was just an extra one. There's something wrong with it. That's why it was in that box in the cabinet. The other tubes in there were good ones for inventory. I make springs about twice a month. They say I'm the best spring maker here. I don't know if they really mean it or not, or if they're just trying to make me feel willing to make springs so no one else will have to do it.

. . . . . . . . . . . . . . . .

CASEWRITER (*standing beside Betty Gilen at her customary workbench*): Could you tell me the name of this place here where you seem to be working most often?

BETTY: You could call this the heavy metal tube station. You see, I make all of the heavy tubes in here, and I guess I'm a sort of a specialist in it. But we're not making very many at the rate we're going now. I can only make tubes that the parts fit in, and these parts don't fit. You see this cover here? You see this container here? Well, these two parts are supposed to go together, and they don't. Somebody goofed. These covers are made in the machine shop, and the containers are made by a vendor, and you can see that the cover doesn't position right on the container, and that won't pass inspection. It holds on all right, but it's got to look real pretty. They're fussy about appearance, you know.

CASEWRITER: Does this delay affect you personally?

BETTY: Personally is right. It's driving me crazy. This is a big order, and we're way behind on it. We won't get them done—can't work on them at all. This means I haven't got anything to do. It means I've got to hunt jobs. It means the day is sixteen hours long for me these days. I fiddle here; I fiddle there; I don't really get anything done. I like to keep busy. It's really much better if you can just stay in one spot, have your work lined up, and go ahead and do it. You know, it's a lot harder to find work than it is to do the work itself.

CASEWRITER: Where else do you sometimes work?

BETTY: Oh, you'll find me over at the glass machine; you'll find me at the wash basin, and you've probably seen me quite a bit over at the pump stand there. You see, I do all the glass-welding. That is, I do all the glasswork in connecting tubes to the vacuum outlets. It's not that it takes any kind of particular genius to do it. It's not a matter of intelligence, but I'm kind of familiar with that type of work. As I say, I do all kinds of things. If you want to see where I'm working, you'd better look fast because I won't be there long.

## Employee Attitudes toward Each Other

Here is how several of the girls talked and behaved with respect to their relations with one another:

ALICE (*in response to a question about why there were two separate coffee groups*): Why, I never thought about that until you mentioned it now. It's always been that way; I've never paid any attention to it. We've always had the two groups, but it doesn't mean anything. We're all friendly with one another.

CASEWRITER: How do you decide when to start and stop?

ALICE: Well, the company says we can have a break at 10:00 and 3:00, and we're supposed to have ten minutes; but Ralph Langley says it's up to us how long we take, just so we get our work out. So we don't go by the company rule. We just have our coffee, and then break up when we're through and go back to work.

CASEWRITER: How do you come to break up?

ALICE: I really don't know; we just stop. Sometimes, we take twenty minutes or so; sometimes quite a bit less. At the end of the month, if we're rushed, we'll cut it pretty short; but no one ever says anything to us. Ralph has told us it's up to us girls, so we just gauge it by how busy we are.

### Work Incidents

Following are two examples of work interactions witnessed by the casewriter which were fairly typical of the general patterns of work behavior he observed.

***Incident No. 1.*** Nellie MacDonald needed a new valve installed on her vacuum pump machine, a maintenance service often performed by Montag when he was working in the tube room.

NELLIE MACDONALD: Hey, Tom, I need a valve put on.

TOM MONTAG: Yah, yah. [Tom was at the other end of the room, moving a heavy tank cylinder toward the pump stand.]

NELLIE: Well, come on, I'm in a hurry. If you'd stay in here where you belong instead of hiding away in Room A, you'd get these things done (*all this said in a lighthearted, jocular tone of voice*).

MONTAG (*approaching pump stand and Nellie with the heavy metal bottle*): Watch out; get out of the way, or you'll get this bottle on your toes!

NELLIE: You do that, and I'll lay you out flat.

MONTAG (*winking to other girls nearby*): She can do it, too.

. . . . . . . . . . . . . . . . . . . .

***Incident No. 2.*** One day, as the casewriter was working at his observation desk, he heard a loud pop and the sound of breaking glass. Looking up, he saw Betty standing at the finished tubes inventory cabinet, with the door open, and a tray of finished tubes in her hand. At her feet were the remains of a broken tube (retail value, about $45). Sally was standing about eight feet away, working at a bench, with her back to Betty. Nellie was at her pump stand about the same distance away. Sally did not look up, but continued steadily with her work. The noise was very audible and quite out of the ordinary of normal sounds in the room. Its point of origin, that is, from the direction of the finished tube cabinet, was also quite clear. Nellie, from her pump stand, looked over to Betty, shook her head slowly from side to side, and said, "Tsk, tsk, tsk," and then made a comment having something to do with what had caused the tube to fall out of the cabinet. Betty's elbow and tray were resting close to the shelf from which the broken tube had obviously fallen. Betty corrected her position and at the same time looked forlornly at the smashed tube. Nellie walked over to the other side of the room, obtained a broom and dustpan, and began to sweep up the mess, disposing of it in a trash can. Betty proceeded to the electronic test stand with the tray of tubes she had been carrying. It would have been very easy for Betty to put the tray down and clean up the broken glass herself. Throughout the incident, neither Betty nor Nellie glanced in Sally's direction, nor did Sally ever change the pace of her work or look up.

### Ralph Langley's Behavior

The casewriter's own observations of Langley's behavior were that he had apparently developed relationships with the group in a way which allowed him to retain a high degree of involvement in the affairs of the room without extensive personal presence on his part. The casewriter had noticed over a two-week period of time the following general pattern of behavior on Langley's part: He would make a tour of the room each morning near the beginning of the workday, speaking briefly with nearly everyone in the room when doing so (although usually in different order from day to day); and he would take part in various technical discussions that accompanied the start of a day's work. From then on, he would reappear at fairly regular intervals, two or three times during the day, or when some kind of unusual work event occurred.

During his periods of absence from the room, he visited the other rooms of his department, attended conferences and other scheduled meetings, paid informal visits to members of other departments in the company, or, as was more customary for extended periods of time, retired to his desk in one corner of Room B, next door to the tube room.

It was to this desk that members of the tube room group would come when they had a question or a problem. Any one of the girls or two men from the tube room were equally likely to visit Langley at his desk; and unless the situations prompting the visit were unusually complicated or pressing, he would respond with a few words of explanation, approval, or a promise to "do something about it." During a two-day period in which Langley once happened to spend nearly all his time at his desk, these visits averaged about six or seven per day. His characteristic demeanor during interactions with subordinates was grave and intently serious, although his face would often break into fleeting, eye-twinkling smiles. Seldom effusive, he nevertheless usually managed to convey by his bearing and verbal behavior an impression of friendliness and personal interest toward those with whom he happened to be dealing at any one time and an impression of calm, unhurried confidence in addressing the problems of his office.

### Comments of the Girls about Langley

The occasions were very seldom during the conversations with members of the tube room work group that reference was not made at one time or another to Langley, the department general foreman. The comments made were almost universally approving.

SALLY: If anything does go wrong around here, we first of all try to find out what the trouble is ourselves; and if that doesn't work, we go to get Ralph. Ralph always helps us out. Ralph always knows the answers.

. . . . . . . . . . . . . . . . . .

BETTY: Ralph is fair, and he knows what he is doing.

. . . . . . . . . . . . . . . . . .

MARTHA (*in connection with a rumor that Ralph Langley was being considered for promotion to a bigger job*): Ralph, he's the best. I don't know what we would do without him. He is always so fair, treats us all alike. We're very proud of Ralph. We would miss him terribly if he left.

. . . . . . . . . . . . . . . . . .

NELLIE (*in response to a question concerning whether she could recall a recent event which had made her feel particularly good or bad*): Well, I'm not sure what it is you are after with that question; but if you would like to know how I feel about Ralph's maybe being promoted, for one thing, I'll tell you. I would be very pleased for Ralph, very proud of him. We all would be. He deserves a promotion, and it's time he went on to bigger things. But as for me, it would mean I'd lost my purpose for working. It would never be the same again. I can't tell you exactly how I would feel; but when I first heard he might be leaving us, I was stunned. That guy made our work something it had never been before. I would never be able to feel the same way about George. [George Cordoza was also rumored to be Ralph's replacement.] George is all right. He's pleasant, and he's a nice guy, but I have a respect for Ralph I'd never be able to develop for George. And it's not only respect I feel for Ralph, but I have a very close relationship with him. Not outside of work at all; I mean here on the job. Ralph is my friend.

I always enjoy coming to work. I look forward to it every morning. We're a zany bunch in there—real screwballs—you couldn't find a bunch of people anywhere with more different personalities than we have. You've seen the way we horse around, the stunts we pull, and we don't feel the least bit embarrassed about it. We can get away with anything; but when it comes to our work, there's no one better than we are, either. My pump stand here, for instance, means everything in the world to me. There's a lot about it I don't understand, but I think about it all the time. I guess you'd say it's the biggest and most important thing in my life to me right now. I used to have a much bigger job in another company than the one I have right now. Believe it or not, I was once a floorlady during the war in a department that had 350 people in it, and many of them were men. That was a big job. Now, this is just a small department here, and I'm not over anyone, but I feel important. I feel there's a purpose in my life. I'm responsible for the pump stand, and it's a critical part of the operation in there. I can't describe to you really how I feel about it. It's a part of me, and I'm a part of it. I worry about how it's going. I'm checking it over all the time, and I'm turning out a lot of work on it.

But you see, it's not only the pump stand. It's how Ralph and people like him can make you feel about it. You know, Ralph is a very intelligent man. He has a great deal of technical knowledge, and he knows how to use it. But there are a lot of bright people around American Radiatronics and other companies like this one. There are only a few of them, though, that can use their knowledge to make a dumb person like me feel important. I know I'm not very bright, and it doesn't take much for anyone to make me feel really stupid, but Ralph has never done that. He's always made me feel that I am smart rather than dumb, that I've got ideas that are useful. Now, my knowledge about the pump stand is very limited, and I lean a great deal on Ralph to help me out of scrapes; but you know, every time I talk over a problem with him, I feel as though I'm learning something. And I *am* learning! It seems as though Ralph has a way of using his superior knowledge to help a person build up his own knowledge. He gives it to you—he doesn't use it on you. That's how I feel about Ralph as a friend, as the best boss I've ever had.

Then again, there's something else. Right now, we've run into a problem on the pump stand. There's something wrong in the exhaust manifold system. We're not getting the tubes clean enough. Sally and I have gone over and over the system, and we don't know what it is. We will wait for Ralph until he has time, and we know eventually he will help us out. Sure, we've got an engineer assigned to the department, that is, someone who is supposed to take care of these problems for us. We're not supposed to; we're just production girls, not supposed to know anything. And, brother, is he convinced of that! I'd walk out of the plant before I'd turn to him for help on my pump. In the first place, he doesn't really know much about them; and in the second place, with what little he does know, he can make you feel so darned stupid in such a short time that you could scream. We don't need him in here and don't want him. So you see, without Ralph, we would have no one. If he left us, we'd have really lost something, and we would know it.

## Ralph Langley

The casewriter talked to Langley on a number of occasions about his perceptions of his job and his concepts of himself as an administrator. Following are excerpts from some of these conversations.

***Conversation No. 1.*** How Langley talked about his relations with the tube room production girls.

LANGLEY (*speaking about what had been responsible for the marked improvement in the group's performance over the past two years*): I would say it was mostly a matter of treating the girls in there the way they wanted to be treated, the way they needed to be treated in order that they might feel as though they were part of American Radiatronics. When I first took over the department, one of the first things I told my girls was that as far as I was concerned, all I wanted them to do was to do the best job they could, to forget about standards, to forget about any kind of pressure or expectation other than just doing as well as they knew how.

I told them I felt they were working for American Radiatronics and not for me, that my job was to help them and not tell them what to do, that they were strictly on their own as far as getting out production was concerned, as far as scheduling their work was concerned, pacing themselves, watching their own waste, and so on. I stressed over and over again that they were to forget about standards, figuratively to throw the standards out, pretend they didn't even exist —if they didn't make standard, to forget about it, not worry about it—just to do the best job they knew how. If they got into trouble, they could ask me for help, and I would give it to them.

Above all, I told them, we were going to be interested in making a better tube and learning how to do our job better at all times. They didn't believe me at first, and some of them gave me a really rough time. But gradually, they learned I meant what I said, and things began to improve. Some of the girls who gave me the most trouble are now the most productive and helpful ones.

I have no supervisor in the room, as you know. I have Sally, who is group leader for the others. But each girl in the room is responsible for her own operation. If she gets into trouble, or if she has a question, she's free to come to me directly. I then work out her problems with her personally. I go in to them every now and then, just now and then, to keep an eye on things and to stay in touch. I check the production record to see how things are going, and I always speak to the girls. I try to be careful, whenever I come into the room, to see that I always talk to a different girl first each time. This way, each girl feels she is getting her fair share of attention. Now, these girls are not all the same. Some of them are pretty tough customers. Nellie MacDonald, in particular, has given me quite a lot of trouble in the past. So I'm extra careful in working with her.

I keep no secrets from the girls. They know as much about this operation, about what is going on in the top offices, as I do. I'm completely honest with them, and I ask that they be honest with me. And this has paid off, too, because none of my girls are afraid to admit their mistakes and they're always anxious to learn how to do something better. Of course, I may be exaggerating this a little bit. I have noticed lately that there is almost a tinge of neuroticism in the way several of the group have become so concerned about production and quality. It causes a little stir now and then. But anyway, most of the girls in there can perform any operation in the place, and they trade off. They know that as far as I'm concerned, it's up to them to decide how they want to distribute or organize their work.

Quite often, the department gets some extra work to do from one of the other departments, work that is not a part of the regular job in there. When we do get that, I just turn it over to one of the girls. She'll do it. The girls don't worry much about doing these extra jobs because they know that as far as I'm concerned, as long as they're doing their jobs the best they can, that's all I care about.

People have to be motivated. All people do. These girls are just the same as you and I. We like to feel we're important. We like to feel we're doing something worthwhile and that we're learning. We like to have a direction to be going in and know whether we are getting any place or standing still. I try to act this way with the girls. I'm always careful and insistent they're given full credit for everything they do. As far as I'm concerned, whatever is done in that room is their responsibility and their accomplishment. I keep out of their hair. When I talk with them, I talk with them about whatever is of interest to them. If it's about their families, fine; if it's about the work, fine.

Sometimes, when I see that things are not going so well—and they don't always go just right—I'm careful to avoid any distressing or threatening discussion. For instance, sometimes the production orders I bring in are downright staggering in the demands they represent for the girls. When I know I have a particularly tough one coming along, I'm careful to wait until the right time to tell the girls about it.

You know, I have a budget, but I don't use my budget to control my people. Rather, I use it as something which they themselves can get satisfaction out of. For instance, we have cut our operating expenses way down since I took over; but I didn't do it, my people did it. Our department maintenance man, Bill Yoost, administers our supplies expense budget himself. He does all his own ordering, and he does it in accordance with the amount of money he has available in his budget. These are supplies that are used not only by himself but by the girls in the department as well. Since they all know that it's up to them to control their expenses, they do it. If someone from another department comes and tries to borrow something which they know has been charged against their budget, they simply won't allow it. They'll say: "No, you'll run our expense budget over. You'll have to get it somewhere else."

I go over the budget with Bill once a month, whenever it comes out. We talk about it. From then on, it's up to him. I keep an eye on it every now and then just to see that he isn't running too far out on a limb; and if I see something wrong, I'll ask him about it. But if he tells me that he's making out all right, I let him go.

***Conversation No. 2.*** How Langley talked about the use of work standards.

LANGLEY: I believe in work standards as a broken yardstick of measurement that has no inherent validity but does have a practical value. To me, the function of the standards is to serve as a guidepost on the side of the road to tell us where we are today in relation to where we were yesterday and where we think we can go tomorrow. They provide management a means of determining in advance what they can sell their products for while being competitive and profitable.

I've indoctrinated my people not to take standards as having any intrinsic value in themselves, but rather to use them just as a guide. It isn't the standard that should determine how they work or pace themselves; instead, the energy, drive, and interest they put in their work should be determined by how they *feel* about their work. I tell my people: "Try to do the best you can comfortably and independent of what the standard says you should do. In other words, you should be taking your incentive from yourselves." But I also emphasize that it is of vital interest to the company, and therefore to themselves, that they make the operation as profitable as possible, because in a sense they are the company. Management is not the company; the stockholders are not the company; it's a combination. They, the workers, are just as meaningfully the company as management or the stockholders are, and in many ways even more so. I drive into them that they, as individuals and as a group, have a big stake in the company's profitability because one of the important satisfactions available to them is being engaged in a successful profitable activity. "After all," I tell them, "work is a way of life, and we've got to be getting something out of it as people. One of these things that can be important is the knowledge that we are connected with a successful operation that we helped make that way."

***Conversation No. 3.*** How Langley talked about the production schedule and other required features of his department's operation.

LANGLEY: Now, take the production schedule; that's sacred! That is a must. Under all circumstances, we must produce the schedule.

CASEWRITER: Is this because your superiors have imposed the schedule on you that same way, too?

LANGLEY: No, it's because I want it that way. This is what we're in business for. We want to get goods out the door. The way we go about doing that will, of course, make a difference in how successfully we accomplish the things not directly connected with production that are also real and important. But we want to keep the record straight. There is no wavering or compromise on the schedule. That will not be tolerated, and everyone knows it.

There are three things I am very firm on in the department. One of them is the production schedule. Another is the employee evaluation sheets. These sheets are absolutely required by management, and I can't get around them. I don't like them; I think they can do more harm than good at times; but they are there, and I have to go along with them.

The third thing is that I expect my people in this department to get along with one another. I say to the girls: "You must adjust to and with the group—become a part of it. At least, you must have a willingness to try to do this." I think they all know this; I've told them so directly, and I've talked about and around it repeatedly on every occasion I could. This doesn't mean I forbid people to have personal differences. That would be stupid. But I do require that they overcome whatever personal differences they might have to the extent of being able to function cooperatively with one another.

CASEWRITER: What would you do if someone did not live up to this requirement?

LANGLEY: Out she would go.

CASEWRITER: You mean you would fire her? Have you ever done so?

LANGLEY: I have. Two years ago, I had to get rid of one girl who just had to fight with everyone she worked with. I tried my best to help her, but it did no good. So I fired her; and everyone knew why, too.

### How an Outsider in the Company Saw the Nuclear Tube Room

One day the casewriter had an opportunity to visit briefly with someone from outside Langley's department who was at the same time familiar with the tube room activity and its customary mode of operation. The man was Harold Singer, a process engineer from the company's central engineering department. Singer was one of a group of men who served as technical specialists for various operating departments in the company and who also spent a considerable portion of their time on product development and long-range planning activities. A portion of Singer's remarks are reproduced below in the approximate form in which they were made:

HAROLD SINGER: I really can't understand how this operation makes money. The products are primitive in design, no changes have been made in years, and there's no engineering control of any kind. Everything is run on a casual, hit-or-miss basis. It shouldn't make money, but somehow it does. . . .

Dollarwise, they're doing a pretty good job in here, as far as it goes; but they've got one overriding weakness in the way they are presently set up. Do you realize the girls do all their own testing in here? The same girls that make the tubes test them. It just isn't logical. It's against human nature. You can't trust the same people who make something to test it also. It's not healthy. They'll always try to protect themselves. This group of test equipment over here should be operated by a distinctly separate group of people completely removed from the production and under different supervision. That's the only basis under which you can get reliable testing and guard against infiltration of loyalties back and forth between manufacture and testing. . . .

We've got plans in the works for taking on this place and really making it over. And when we do, we'll see to it that the testing operations are carried on in a separate department. We'll really whip this operation into shape. . . .

There's a tremendous potential in this kind of activity, but it's never been exploited. We've got designs on the board right now that would revolutionize the way of doing things around here if we could get them going. I'd like to make this a model showplace for the company. Right now, it's the worst in the company. Look at all this dirt around and the disorganization. . . .

This place has never been under engineering control. That's the trouble with it. The products and processes here now are what they've traditionally been almost from the start. Most of the product design changes that have been made have been developed and put into practice by the production people themselves. That's not good. Too much can creep into an organization that way that isn't good for it. They design their own products, they alter and maintain their own production equipment and processes, and they are free to go off in all different directions at once.

The first thing we would do if we could get hold of this room would be to put every operation under close engineering surveillance. The whole setup needs to be revamped and overhauled from one end to the other. We'll do it, too. You won't recognize it two years from now. Some of the new products we have in mind will call for a level of sophistication in production methods, equipment design, and cleanliness that'll make this look sick. You've seen pictures of how some of these production departments look in other companies—cleanliness precautions that make them look like operating rooms, temperature and humidity controls, all white-painted walls and equipment. That's what we'll have here. Personnel is right now looking into available sources of production girls for us; and when we start getting them in here and training them properly, and install modern production methods with a true mass production setup, then you'll see what this department can do. . . .

I'd like to think time zero for this department's operations in this company's history will start three months from now. We've got all the preliminary design work and process system concepts worked out already; and in about three months, we'll begin to pick up some real speed. Two years from now, you won't know the place. In contrast, everything that will have gone on before will be nothing. Take a good look around at what you see in here right now; you'll never see it again. Before long, it will be like looking back at the covered wagon era.

# Bedrock[1]

ABOUT TO LEAVE after a short visit at Bedrock, a communal farm in central Oregon, the casewriter asked Alex Winston, the commune's founder, what the most difficult problem was that he was facing at the moment. Alex answered:

The thing that has caused me the most worry lately has been the question of how to hold the group together.

Let me explain. . . .

A lot of people have left Bedrock in the last few weeks. There were some I was glad to see go. But there were others that left that I wish hadn't. I don't try to persuade anyone to stay when he says he's leaving, because each person has to work out his own trip. And I don't have any goal of keeping everyone here that wants to try it out. There are a lot who are not ready for this kind of life; the demands of the work usually weeds them out. But there have been some others who seemed ready to commit themselves to something like Bedrock as a permanent trip. They were willing to do the work; they seemed to be doing okay otherwise. But then, after some minor argument, they'd split.

Alex related the case of Roger Crawford as an example of someone who had appeared ready for communal life, but had left:

Roger had been here several months. He had something going with the land. He felt he could get very close to it . . . said he had some of his best highs out in the field plowing. Roger was also very good at getting close to the other people here at Bedrock. Everyone liked him a lot. He was easygoing and friendly. I relied on him a lot to smooth feelings when people got in arguments. He was good at easing tensions.

Well, a couple Saturday nights ago some people came to visit a member of the commune who has since left. It was late at night, everyone was high on pot, and a loud argument had broken out. Apparently it was between Carl (Carl Harris was a co-founder of the commune and seemed to the casewriter to be the number two man in the commune's informal hierarchy) and these visitors—I can't remember for sure. I was asleep and it woke me up. So I came downstairs and told the visitors to leave. (When there's a hassle, you can't solve anything when there are a lot of outsiders around.) There was some argument, and I knocked a glass out of a guy's hand and then threw them out of the house. I guess I really blew up.

---

[1] All names have been disguised.

Well, the next morning at breakfast, Roger announced that he'd decided this wasn't his kind of trip. And he got up from the table and left. Nothing more was said. Some members left with him. Some more left the next couple of days. By the end of the week, half the commune had left.

Roger's leaving was a real loss to the commune. Some other good people left, too.

Alex said there were still others at Bedrock who may be about to leave:

Right now, Sandy is thinking about leaving and going back to school. Her going wouldn't be that bad; she doesn't contribute that much.

But Mark can make a big contribution to the group; and last night I overheard him telling Brent that he may not stay around, either. He was saying something about his not liking the way Carl is pushing people around.

I'm not afraid the group is going to fall completely apart. But it does concern me that we're losing some good people. I'm not sure what I can do about it.

## THE BACKGROUND OF ALEXANDER WINSTON AND THE FOUNDING OF BEDROCK

Bedrock was founded by Alex Winston and seven others in early December 1969. All of the eight founders had had some experience in communes before and were trying again to put together a commune that could last. From their experience, they had learned that the right fit between the needs of the individual and the needs of the group was difficult to achieve. They had each migrated from commune to commune looking for a group where the fit felt good. Bedrock was another attempt at forming such a group.

Alex put up the money for Bedrock. He was the oldest son of a wealthy Californian, who himself had inherited his money from his father. Alex described his parents to the casewriter:

My father was a playboy during his twenties. Then, as he started into his thirties, he starting developing a paunch and got scared, I guess. He met a salesgirl and married her after six weeks.

That was my mother. She was a total zero. She was dumb. She made no contribution to society at all. She simply consumed and consumed and consumed. And I think it was marrying her that ruined him. He could have pulled out of his playboy days and made something of himself. But she swallowed him up into her warm body. And he never got out.

Now, in the despair of her old age, she's turned to religion; and he has turned to historical novels, reading about the kind of man he wanted to be. His ideal was Abraham Lincoln.

My father had a strong sense of ethics, but he was too weak to live up to them. Where he could have made a mark in the world like his father, he essentially lived off the inheritance. I really feel sorry for him. The one thing I did get from my father is his sense of ethics and integrity—but I'm working at living by it; he couldn't.

Alex's share of the inheritance was in a trust account and was turned over to him on his twenty-first birthday.

Alex withdrew from straight society gradually. He majored in architecture through one year of graduate school; but gave up his studies because, he explained, "I discovered that the practice of architecture is 90 percent salesmanship and 10 percent design. I'm not a salesman."

Alex then tried painting in San Francisco. There he married his first wife. But he found the community of artists there, in his terms, "desperate, shallow, and artificial"; so he bought a house and some land in Monroe, Oregon, as a place to live and paint. He and his wife furnished Thanbrun (a name the house already had) with antiques; and Alex was on his way to becoming a pillar of the community.

However, in Monroe, Alex became interested in radical politics, and found his way into several anarchist groups in the Eugene area. He found that they were more talk than action, however, and he left them and his wife to join a commune in the Monroe area. However, that commune began disintegrating, as Alex reported it, when the FBI came in and arrested a draft dodger among them and threatened to charge the others with harboring a criminal.

At that time Alex left for the East Coast with another woman in the commune, who was separated from her husband. They stopped in Idaho and each got divorced and then moved on to New York, where they were married and lived together for a year.

From there, Alex went to Union Farm in Maine, a communal group that had been operating for about five years. Union Farm had, however, evolved from a commune into a more conventional agrarian community with only a communal school. Dissatisfied with the changes, Alex left Union Farm after four months to return to Monroe.

Back in Monroe he found a single person had held on at the original commune. With him and some others, Alex began a new commune in the house his first wife had vacated. Then, Alex told the casewriter, "Soon the FBI came again looking for draft dodgers. This time I threw them off the land, because they had no search warrant. Early the next morning the agents reappeared with ten state troopers. They slapped handcuffs on me and hauled me off to jail. I spent one night in jail. It cost me $1,000 before I was acquitted of the charges against me."

By that time the new commune had begun to dissolve. Alex returned to the East Coast with Ruth, a member of the commune, and journeyed there from commune to commune, until on Halloween night, 1969, Alex visited Hoch, an economically successful commune in New Hampshire, founded by some Ph.D. dropouts from Massachusetts. There he met Carl and persuaded Carl and Iris to come back with him and Ruth to Oregon and start up a new commune.

They returned, purchased the land and house adjoining the original property, and founded Bedrock in early December.

. . . . . . . . . . . . . . . . . . .

Alex described the evolution of the commune to its present state:

> The average age of the founders was around 26–27. Most had been in other communes. We lived in both Thanbrun and the new house, which are about ¼ mile apart. A result of this was that we got divided into two groups.
>
> One group left with their leader last February over a disagreement. We then decided to all live together here at the new house. In the meantime, Carl had recruited about seven or eight young boys from Portland. That lowered the average age to around 22–23. Most of them were not ready for this kind of commitment and they left gradually over the next two months. Rick is the only one left of that group. Now older couples are coming or planning to come. I've received letters from two couples in the Southwest. I expect they will be more stable and more committed to the way of life we're trying to build here. You have to be ready for this kind of trip before you're willing to work as hard as we work here.

## THE PHYSICAL SURROUNDINGS AT BEDROCK

Bedrock farm covers about 350 acres of primarily hardwood forest, four miles west of Monroe, Oregon. Already in a remote area, the commune's house stood at the end of a one-mile private road that itself crossed a large ravine. Therefore, the house was not visible from the road; nor could any part of the Monroe community be seen from the house.

Bedrock's new, two-story communal house stood in the center of a large clearing. In front of the house were several acres of cultivated land, most of it planted. Attached to the left side of the house was a board and polyethylene greenhouse. To the left-rear, 50 yards from the house, near the far edge of the clearing, stood an animal shed. To the right of the house were three small shelters of asbestos sheeting bent into bowed A-frame structures, the open ends draped with polyethylene sheeting.

The inside of the house was not furnished like the average American home. There were no curtains, no stuffed furniture, and no carpets. The walls were only half-painted. No Rembrandt reproductions nor mountain scenes hung on them. A bare light bulb dangled from the ceiling.

In the living room were a bed frame and another bed of five stacked mattresses, a short bookcase filled with books, a record player and a pair of headphones, an upright piano, and an old sewing machine. Hanging in the uncurtained window were several fly strips that, by the size of their catch, appeared to have outlived their usefulness.

The living room extended into a dining room filled by a large 4′ x 12′ table made of two 4′ x 8′ sheets of unfinished plywood overlapped and fastened together on heavy legs salvaged from an earlier table. In the center of the table stood a centerpiece of three glasses of semiwilted daisies and wildflowers.

Several posters were hanging on the wall of the dining room. One of them was a map of the firewood-logging roads. Another said, "If you're going to be anything today, BE NICE." Another was a poster warning of the evils of marijuana. Still another was a list of daily household chores for the women:

1. wipe table
2. sweep floor
3. clean oven
4. laundry
5. wash dishes
6. wash windows
7. make bread
8. make beds

The open side of the dining room extended into the kitchen and, further, to a laundry room. They claimed the standard modern appliances: two ovens and a range, color coordinated to the reddish-brown brick wall they were built into, a large matching refrigerator-freezer, and an automatic washer.

## THE MEMBERS OF BEDROCK

At the time of the casewriter's visit, Bedrock's membership consisted of ten adults and four children. (See Exhibit 1 for data on the adults.) The casewriter talked with most of the adults about their own backgrounds, their reasons for dropping out, and why they chose to be at Bedrock. It appeared to the casewriter that they knew relatively little about each other's backgrounds. The reason they gave for not inquiring into each other's histories was that what matters is what you are and do after you come to Bedrock, not what you were before. "We accept a person for what he is, not what he was."

None of the members of Bedrock were dressed like the showcase hippies of Harvard Square. There were no suede vests, no flowered shirts, no beaded headbands, no peace medallions on leather straps. The men had beards of varying fullness. Some had long hair that was smoothly combed; others' looked, to the casewriter, like it could defeat any comb that dared to challenge it. Their apparel ranged from overalls and work boots to jeans and a khaki jacket and work boots. As a group, the men looked like they had stepped out of the 19th century. The women wore slacks and jeans and sweatshirts.

## EXHIBIT 1

Members of Bedrock

| *Name* | *Partners* | *Time at Bedrock* | *Age* | *Education Background* | *Previous Communal Experience* | *Activity before Communal Experiences* | *Children* | |
|---|---|---|---|---|---|---|---|---|
| | | | | | | | *Name* | *Age* |
| Alex | ┐ | 7 months | 33 | 1 yr. grad school | 4 communes | Painter | | |
| Ruth | ┘ | 7 months | 27 | High school | 2 communes | Store clerk | Noah | 3 weeks |
| Carl | | 7 months | 32 | High school | 2 communes | Greenwich Village | | |
| Iris | ┐ | 7 months | 24 | 1 yr. college | 1 commune | Greenwich Village | Baboo | 10 months |
| Rick | ┘ | 6 months | 19 | High school grad | none | Portland Center | | |
| Brent | ┐ | 2 months | 27 | College grad | none | Welfare group in San Francisco | | |
| Janet | ┘ | 2 months | 25 | College grad | none | | Misha | 2 years |
| Sandy | | 6 weeks | 19 | 1 yr. college | none | College | | |
| Ellen | | 3 weeks | 26 | (unknown) | none | Store clerk | Matthew | 4 years |
| Mark | | 4 days (3 weeks in Dec.) | 21 | 1 yr. college | none | Underground university | | |

## Alex

Alex had slightly graying brown hair and a full beard that surrounded his freckled, small-featured face. He wore a cotton shirt, bib overalls, and heavy work boots.

Alex explained his own motivation in turning to communal living:

All the institutions in the system—schools, churches, business, government—are cold machines that process you like a piece of metal, twisting, bending, warping you into a new part of the ever-expanding machine network. They're not interested in you; they're interested only in your body as a producer and consumer. You have no identity of your own. You're defined in terms of your job, what size house you have, where you live. No one is interested in you as a person. So you're brainwashed to do work you don't like, to be able to buy things you "need" to have people think well of you. You're taught to compete. The system pits people against people. But you're really not working for yourself; you're working for the machine. You're taught to consume, only because your consumption will keep the machine going.

Somewhere along the way, you finally realize you're working for the wrong things. The rewards the system gives you don't really satisfy your needs. You discover its all irrelevant, barren, empty, hollow. When you discover that, you're no longer motivated to play the game. Like, I worked hard all the way through high school trying to get good grades, to be a class officer, to get a letter in sports—when, what I really wanted was to get laid. And I never did get laid.

What is important is that people learn to grow together with other people. People need to learn to cooperate, not to compete. I struggled for a long time with the question of "how do you get people together?" When I was involved in the anarchist groups in Eugene, I came to the conclusion that, in the setting of a farm, the obvious economic facts of life would force people to learn to cooperate.

If we succeed and show others it can be done, maybe we can change the system. Maybe just that much (holds thumb and forefinger half inch apart before face). But even if we can make it change one small budge, for us, I'll feel successful.

Living and working on the land does appeal to me. But I could have simply bought a farm and operated it myself. I didn't. I started the commune, instead, because of my firm conviction that people need to learn to cooperate, and they can do it here. This hasn't been easy, but I think this is the right thing to do, and I won't back off. I don't want to.

Even though I've put up the money, I'm not really risking any more here than anyone else is. They're all investing their lives in it.

## Ruth

Ruth, the only black at Bedrock, grew up in a ghetto family of ten children. She had first decided to try communal living when she lived in Oakland. Her work as a store clerk was providing her little satisfaction. She tried experimenting part-time with hippie-artistic life. Some friends who were in Alex's commune at Thanbrun were visiting in Oakland and invited her to join them; so she quit her job and went to Oregon. It was there that she met Alex.

When that commune disbanded, Ruth left with Alex on his trek through communes in the East and returned with him to Oregon to start up Bedrock.

Ruth said she saw no reason to go back into regular society:

They're working for the wrong things there. Here we're working for each other. We've got a group. We've got land and trees and animals. The air and water are clean. Why should I go back to the city? What can it offer me that I haven't got here?

### Brent and Janet

Brent and Janet were the only married couple at Bedrock in the legal sense. Brent had smoothly combed brown hair that reached down to cover the back of his neck and a full, bushy beard on a young and friendly face that denied its twenty-seven years. He wore a G.I. fatigue shirt, a remnant of his stint in Germany with the U.S. Army. From Washington state, Brent had been reclassified and joined up after graduating from college in English literature. Janet joined him a year later in Germany after finishing college, and taught kindergarten there until his release. Returning to the United States, they lived in San Francisco for a year. They then started looking for a commune, heard about Bedrock, and moved to Oregon. They had been at the commune with their two-year-old daughter, Misha, for about two months. Janet wore a light blue sweatshirt, her hair pulled back in a pony tail.

Brent explained why he came to Bedrock:

Straight America is not a happy place to live in. The country is ridden with guilt over the thousands of young Americans' lives wasted on a war they now suspect was immoral from the start. Yet, at the same time, they're desperate, trying to save face and not admit, even to themselves, the senselessness of Vietnam. The majority of the country is racist, and, with the encouragement of the Nixon administration, is going to stay that way. The country is gagging on its own pollution. And as long as Madison Avenue keeps Joe America on the individualistic, stuff-your-own-gut consumer treadmill, there'll be no money to take care of pollution. Cities are falling into decay, turning into battlegrounds between blacks, students, and the police.

There's nothing there to hold me. Once I thought I could change things. But it's all too large—the Establishment, the institutions. Some guys may want to fight the dinosaurs; but that's not my trip.

For a while we just dropped out. We went to San Francisco and stayed with a group there. We lived off welfare checks. But that was leeching off a system you didn't want to be a part of. We decided to find a group that was paying its own way. That's how we ended up at Bedrock.

I think we're a lot like the original Americans up here. They left a system they thought was too far gone to try to bring it back. They started over as we are doing. We're trying to make ourselves self-reliant here. We're not cutting ourselves completely off. We pay our taxes; we buy services from the outside, like utilities and medicine. But we're also working out our lives on our terms. We've got a lot more control over our lives because we're functioning in a group that is small enough that each of us feels a responsibility for the others. We know each other and can trust and rely on each other. We're all in this together.

It's not like on the outside, where a man leads two lives—one at work and one at home. Here everything I do relates to the one group. My life is a lot more integrated; it isn't fragmented into work and family sectors. I can see the results of my work; I can see my impact on other people's lives. I get to cooperate with people rather than compete against them.

But, probably the most important factor is the land. The land is really the key to Bedrock. Here we learn to work together with nature, not fight against it. To plant and cultivate and harvest is the ultimate trip. You get a feeling for your place in the whole scheme of things. And it feels good. I'm ready to make this my life's trip.

Janet added:

Life in straight America had very little to offer me. You work to buy things that are made to wear out so you have to buy them again. A woman spends her life imprisoned alone in a house in suburbia. Here I've got the company of the other women during the day. Here I'm also contributing to the welfare of a group I know. I can see the results of my efforts.

In addition, our kids have a better chance of growing up without our hangups here because we all act as parents for the kids once they're finished nursing. With a bunch of parents to identify with, the kids won't get warped in one direction. I think it's a lot better way.

### Iris

Iris was physically small, had long, red, frizzy hair and a childlike, wide-eyed look that contradicted her otherwise worn appearance. Deserted by her mother as a child, she grew up with relatives. A high school honors student in Connecticut, Iris lived in Greenwich Village for a year, where she met Carl. They were in a group that was arrested for drug use. Everyone received a suspended sentence except Carl, who had to serve six months in jail. Iris signed a statement that she was his common-law wife so she could visit him for that period. Upon his release, they went to New Hampshire and joined Hoch. Later Carl left for Boston to form his own commune and Iris left to work and attend art school part time in

New York. Upon discovering she was pregnant, she returned to Hoch. Iris explained:

> There's something about the family as far as the commune is concerned. It's like a healthier place. Hoch seemed like it could satisfy more of my needs at the time, so I could get involved in a healthier way than doing what I was doing.

Carl also returned later, after his attempt at starting a new commune ended in failure. Iris said she left Hoch to help found Bedrock out of a sense of adventure and a desire to see the communal experience develop from the beginning. Iris found she preferred communal living:

> One thing, your work is directly involved with your living, and like it's not separated, you know. Like you don't *go* to work. Like it's involved. There's more satisfaction as far as that goes . . . and as the way you learn to deal with people as far as, not someone you're working with, but someone you're involved with, or like on all kinds of levels. There's a definite financial advantage—as far as what we're able to achieve and to share that none of us would be able to do alone. We're able to share, and we therefore have more in a way; even though none of us really has anything.

Iris added that communal living made extra emotional demands of the members:

> There seems to be more pressure involved. It's like running an engine, a big powerful engine. You have to let off steam, whatever. There's a lot of power at work—the changes we're going through.

#### Rick

Rick's only apparel was a pair of bib overalls and, pulled down over his long unruly hair, a brown, battered, wide-brimmed felt hat with an orange embroidered headband. Rick talked about his decision to live at Bedrock:

> For my last two years in high school, I worked at living the straight scene. I was really disgusted at the state of things—the war, police violence, discrimination. That didn't equal the freedom I'd been told our country stood for. I didn't want to be any part of it. I had friends who were dropping out; and I felt like dropping out—I could see no future in it. But my high school counselor persuaded me to really give the system a try. So for two years I worked at being straight. I finally couldn't take it; so I dropped out. I went back to dropping acid and taking dope.
>
> Ever since I was a kid, I wanted to be a farmer. When I was little, my father and I used to talk about how we'd have a farm together. Well, it turned out it really didn't mean that much to him. He's a factory worker; and we're in completely different worlds. Well, after I graduated, I went to work for my uncle up in Washington . . . wrapping hoagie sandwiches. That wasn't my idea of

doing something meaningful. So, one day I was thinking about splitting and he jumped all over me. I wanted to take a walk to think things out and he ordered me to get to work. "You know what happens when you don't do what I tell you," he threatened me. So I split. I rolled up my clothes into a bag and went to Portland.

I wanted to do some good somewhere. I'd heard of the Portland Center, where they counsel kids with drug problems and runaways, and that kind of stuff. So I went there. They gave me a place to sleep, and I'd help with the telephones. Sometime, when a guy didn't show up, I'd take his place. Other than that I was one of those freaks who walks around all day without a job.

Carl had come to Portland Center looking for guys to join the commune. I'd thought about living in a commune before, but the kind where you lie around and screw and get stoned. Anyway, I decided to give it a try. One day after Christmas, Carl brought a bunch of us—I think there were seven of us guys, between seventeen and nineteen—down to Bedrock. It was December 27. I've been here ever since—that is, except for three times I went back to Portland.

But I'm not going back anymore. I finally learned it's a bad scene. Portland was like my graduation into life. But it took going back several times to realize how screwed up it was. I'd get fed up with it here. Carl and Alex were always making the decisions. It was like a dictatorship. I thought I'd be freer in the city. So I'd go back to Portland and it reminded me what the city was—so I'd come back to Bedrock. The third time I went I was only gone a day. I left because I didn't feel like I was really a part of things here. I called back and talked to Iris and found out they did miss me, that they did think I did important work. So I came back.

I learned I wasn't mature, or aware, enough to try to understand people. Now when I get uptight about something, I force myself to stay, to talk it out, to try to understand.

Well, I guess one of the advantages of Bedrock is that it isn't as easy as other places. It's part of character development, part of my education. It's not only hard work; a lot of it is emotional, dealing with people. Getting to know different types. Learning to live with them while I change them as I go or allow them to change me.

My parents have been up to see me. My father is in a completely different world from me. So he doesn't get involved in mine; and I don't in his. With my mother, it's a different thing. She's always said, "Do what you want, as long as you're happy." She really meant it, too. And I've always been able to be open with her. I even told her about my drugs in high school. When they were here, she said if I was happy here, it was okay with her. The only thing she said before she came was that if someone was going around naked while she was here, she'd split. So everyone kept his clothes on out of respect for her.

### Mark

Mark was from Calgary. He had come to Bedrock in December with some other fellows who were joining the commune and then left with one of them several weeks later, because it was Christmas time and he wanted to see his family. In Calgary, he tried several different jobs, but, in his words, "I quit because I didn't like the 9-to-5 obligation. And I didn't like the idea of working for someone else's profit." Out hitchhiking, he got a lift in the direction of Oregon, and ended up at Bedrock.

I attended Guelph College in Ontario and took some classes in psychology, philosophy, sociology, and history. After talking to some of my philosophy professors, I came to the conclusion that they were as screwed up as anyone else, that they didn't know what life was about, nor did they know how to create a satisfying life for themselves. They were in a spiritual limbo; they had no real sense of purpose in their lives. And I felt like a stranger in society, myself, personally impotent and aimless. So I decided to leave school and go out and do some research on my own.

I tried several jobs, but found that the work I could get gave me no personal satisfaction. What kind of fulfillment can you get from turning a screw, or filling a gas tank, or selling a hairbrush? I was looking for some kind of work that would be inherently satisfying in itself. I couldn't find it.

For a while I worked for an underground university set up in a Calgary dormitory. It mocked the system well enough. I sold Bachelor's degrees for $15, Master's for $20, and Ph.D.'s for $25. You had to pass an exam of three questions for each degree, too. Questions like "Who discovered America?" and "What does life mean?" But the whole scene was mostly drugs and group sex classes. There wasn't much substance to it. So I split and came back here. . . .

The view is good here.

I think that here I can maybe learn what really is and what isn't. Like the work . . . I like to do it. I don't do it for the bread or to impress anybody. I do it because it feels good. You plant, you weed, you harvest . . . It's a whole thing. You're not just some cog in a wheel. Working on the land puts you in tune with reality. It's a real harmony.

Besides that, it's a case of finding out what you can do. Here you are given responsibility and you accept whatever responsibility you can take. And you work on that, which is always a good thing. You realize your responsibilities. Like a certain amount of things are handed to you on a platter, but you realize that you have to make up for them, too, at the same time. Not everything's free.

I thought my parents would be quite pleased that I was working on the land. They were farmers in their youth, working with the same kind of equipment we use. Instead they're quite put out. They don't like the idea of my working eight to ten hours a day and not getting paid for it.

### Sandy

Sandy had short dark hair and a distant, faraway look when she talked. Sandy had become discouraged with college her freshman year and had dropped out. She wandered around for a while and ended up at Bedrock. It now looked as if she would be returning to school.

### Ellen

Ellen had talked to friends about the idea of starting a commune before and had come to Bedrock after her apartment in San Francisco had been burned out. She told the casewriter:

I'm not going to stay here forever because I'm alone with my kid and most of the ones who have been here a while are in couples. Everything is quite structured. There's no chance to do your own thing—for example, crafts and something like that. It's not as easy to get personally involved here as if everyone had put in as much as the next person. Alex is the authority figure because it's his thing.

### Carl

Carl had been associated with various communes for the last five years. Before that he had been in the Marines, and had lived in New York, where he had met Iris. He had been in and out of Hoch several times and had tried starting his own commune once. All he'd say about it was that it broke up after about six months because of differences of opinion. Of all the commune members, Carl was the most reluctant to talk about his background.

Carl explained why he had gone the commune route:

Because the world on the outside is so screwed up. Morally, economically, politically, sexually. Their idea of the good life is a bunch of crap. It's too far gone out there. The world's beyond reforming. We're an outpost, a testing ground. We're getting ready for when the whole system outside blows up. The Village, Haight, welfare . . . they're part of the system—leeches on it. They'll go when it goes.

He told the casewriter what he had learned from his experiences with communal living. He said there were three important things:

First, for a commune to hold together, everyone has to have a lot of tolerance for each other. For example, there are a lot of dumb things people here at Bedrock do that I just have to overlook.

The second thing is that jealousy breaks up a commune. Jealousy cannot be tolerated in commune members. If anyone shows any jealousy, he should not be shown any sympathy. On the contrary, he should be ridiculed.

The third, and most important, thing I've learned is that drugs help a lot. When people get stoned on drugs, they'll do antisocial things that they wouldn't do otherwise. When they find these things not only condoned, but encouraged, by the others, that tends to pull them more solidly together as a group.

Carl said the commune could maintain itself economically. He said that Hoch had for six years, that it was worth $160,000 now, and that, if Bedrock were larger and well organized, they could not help but make big profits with all the free labor.

### THE WORK

The casewriter heard it restated several different times and ways that the fundamental rule of Bedrock was that no one could stay who did not work. What work one did on a particular day was determined, first, by what needed to be done, and second, by what one's own capabilities and preferences were. As Alex pointed out, "We can't afford the luxury of everyone doing his own thing."

Alex also felt that, as a rule, if there were problems between people, more could be accomplished by hard work on the land than by taking work time to talk them out. He explained, "Some people are a lot better at that kind of session than others." Alex seldom allowed time off from work for discussion of personal problems.

The work of the commune could be divided into five main categories:

1. firewood logging
2. organic gardening
3. livestock and work animals
4. construction
5. housework

***Firewood Logging.*** This was done during the winter and early spring months when gardening was not possible. They sold the firewood to a local dealer.

***Organic Gardening.*** This required selecting the crops, planning the planting time, procuring sufficient manure for fertilization, planting, caring for the crops, harvesting, and selling what would not be consumed by the commune. Six acres had been cleared and planted. The crops were:

green beans
baby green beans
shell beans
wax beans
summer squash
butternut squash
Hubbard squash
zucchini squash
Boston lettuce
buttercup lettuce
romaine lettuce
cherry top lettuce
Simson lettuce
tomatoes
cherry tomatoes
radishes
white radishes
peas
onions
scallions
beets
carrots
cabbage
turnips
chard
cauliflower
hot peppers
kale
endive
cucumbers
sweet corn
eggplant
watermelon

They planned to sell some of their surplus crops through their own roadside stand and some to a wholesaler in Portland.

***Livestock and Work Animals.*** The livestock was grown for consumption by the commune. It included three cows (one's name was Yum-yum because she was future meat for the commune), and three calves, six pigs, nine sheep, a goat, a shed full of chicks, and a few ducks and geese. There were four horses and a colt for pulling wagons and plows. Bedrock had no mechanized farm equipment outside of the truck. "What's better, covering a field with horses' shit or a tractor's exhaust?" Brent rhetorically asked.

***Construction.*** As yet, only minor construction had been done by the commune members. However, plans had been made for a new barn and additional living quarters that would be built before winter.

***Housework.*** As a rule, the women did the housework—cleaning house, laundry, tending children, preparing and cleaning up after meals. However, it was not unusual for a woman to engage in the lighter work the men were doing. On Sundays, the men did the dishes.

An attempt was made to include everyone in on the childrearing—the idea being that a child was less likely to pick up any one person's personal biases if he identified with a large number of parents.

No matter what work one did, everyone followed the same time schedule:

| | |
|---|---|
| 5:30 | up |
| 5:30– 6:00 | coffee, discussion of day's work assignments |
| 6:00– 7:00 | work and chores |
| 7:00– 7:30 | breakfast |
| 7:30–12:00 | work |
| 12:00– 1:00 | lunch |
| 1:00– 4:00 | work |
| 4:00– 5:00 | chores |
| 5:00– 6:00 | dinner |
| 6:00– on | free |

Alex said he had no trouble personally in enforcing the work rule. "Unless everyone works, we have no chance of succeeding," he said. "It doesn't bother me at all to go out and yell at a guy who won't get up in the morning or chew a guy out who's screwing around instead of working. He's wrecking it for the rest of the group—and he has no right to."

## ORGANIZATION

Alex and Carl were the only members of the "Board of Directors," an informal designation for the group that counseled with each other to make major decisions. Admission to the board was by Alex's consent, on the bases of time spent at the commune, maturity, and personal commitment to the commune.

Alex delegated responsibility to others on the basis of their skill and experience. On that basis, Carl, who had once worked as a landscape architect's assistant, had major responsibility for the fields, which claimed the majority of the work hours. Although Alex could overrule any of his decisions, by virtue of his experience, Carl made most of the decisions concerning planting.

Alex was gradually turning responsibility for the horses and the livestock over to Rick, as he perceived Rick becoming more "mature." Brent had assumed the job of keeping the commune's financial books. None of the women had been delegated specific responsibilities.

Everyday each member was required to turn in a work slip stating how many hours he (or she) had worked, and at which jobs. These data were posted to time accounts for each job at the commune. There was an account for each crop, each category of animal, for building projects, housework, and the firewood project. There were also accounts to record sales and expenses in each category. At intervals during the year, the hours in each account would be translated into $ figures on the basis of the average living expenses for a commune member (the current average was around $85 a month). These $ equivalents to the hours worked would be added as an expense to each category. In that way, each category could be treated similar to a profit center, with the intent to determine whether a category was paying for itself or not, and which categories were the most profitable.

Brent had started the use of work slips only two weeks previous. There had been initial resistance to turning in work slips on the part of some of the commune members. They complained that the work slips were restrictive—that that was one of the things everyone at Bedrock was trying to get away from. Rick once turned his hours in carved on a 2 x 4 block. Another time he wrote three short plays on subjects that symbolically related to the work he had done that day. Ruth once turned her hours in on a banana peel. But Alex explained that the records were necessary in order to be fair with the government, when it came to taxes, while at the same time not being unfair to themselves. Carl continued ridiculing the use of the work slips.

No one was paid for his work. Meals, clothes, and medical care were paid for from the commune's fund.

A new member was not required to make any financial investment in the commune upon entering. In fact, Alex encouraged new members to keep a bank account, property, or other assets as a "side bet," so that no one would stay at Bedrock simply because he couldn't afford to leave. However, no one was allowed to use his outside assets for personal purchases while a member of the commune. If the new member had an automobile, he had the option of locking it up, leaving it unused for the duration of his membership, or retaining ownership, but turning its use over to the commune.

Defectors from the commune were not reimbursed for any of their labor upon leaving. Alex had, however, paid for bus fare to their homes for some people who had left Bedrock.

## TWO NIGHTS AND A DAY AT BEDROCK

Following are excerpts from the casewriter's log, recorded during a visit he and his wife, Dorothy, made at Bedrock. The casewriter came to Bedrock interested in observing behavior that would provide clues to the following questions:

1. How are roles defined in the group? Who gets what role and why?
2. How do the members deal with each other interpersonally? How do they handle conflict?
3. What factors (environmental, task, organizational, personal, and social) tend to act for and against drawing the group together?
4. What "hangups" do I have that will get in the way of understanding the commune members from their point of view?

***Sunday at 7:00*** **P.M.** When we arrived, most of the members of Bedrock were seated around the dining room table on long, backless benches, smoking self-rolled cigarettes and drinking Kool-aid and "tree frog," a weak spirit they made from potatoes. After short introductions, we joined them at the table. Carl, Ellen, and Sandy were absent.

Although we felt self-conscious, no one else seemed too changed by our presence. Iris and Ruth were engrossed in breast-feeding their babies. Rick tried engaging Alex in a "psychoanalysis" of the meaning behind a drawing of a turtle that he had done. Janet offered Dorothy some wild strawberries from a bowlful they'd picked that afternoon, and Brent poured us both some of the home brew.

***7:30*** **P.M.** Just as we were looking for some way to get out of finishing our home brew unnoticed, Sandy walked in. She and Ellen had spent the weekend at Smithson, a progressive undergraduate school in northern Oregon. Soon after they got there, Ellen had disappeared with Little Billy, a former Bedrock member; so Sandy came home alone. Rick made some crack at Matthew about the benefits of being an orphan. Ruth wondered aloud whether Ellen would be back in time for work Monday morning.

At the same time, Alex and Brent were talking about a construction project planned for the near future. A barn would be built adjacent to the house on the north side to provide easy access to the animals during the winter months. Additional permanent living quarters extending from the greenhouse end of the house were also planned.

While this was going on, Misha and Matthew were pounding on the piano and singing their own tunes. So when I asked Alex about the construction plans, he remarked that one of the top priorities was a special room for the kids, so there could be some quiet for the adults.

***8:05*** **P.M.** Rick asked if he could play his rock record. Looking at his watch, Alex said no, that it was after 8:00 P.M. Rick pleaded jokingly for a weakening of the rule, promising he would break the record if he could play it once now. I asked Alex about the record rule. He rolled himself a cigarette from a can of Bugler tobacco, leaned back in the rattan chair at the head of the table, and explained to me:

> We've tried to stay away from rules and restrictions because that's what we were trying to get away from. But for a long time there was a lot of tension about rock records. I don't like them, and some of the others don't. But anybody could put one on and play it as loud as he wanted. The result was that we never had any quiet around here. Finally, someone turned the cup over and we held a meeting on it.[1] It turned out that, because those of us who couldn't take it any longer had done so much griping about it, by the time we had a vote on it, we had gotten on the others' nerves so much that everyone was happy to restrict it to 6:30 to 8:00 in the evening.

I asked Alex if any other things had caused a lot of tension. He answered:

> At first there were a lot of tensions because there were so many of us. Fortunately, some of the guys had been in the Army and were able to help get things organized.
>
> Then for quite a while, we had a lot of trouble with people being too sick to work—that is, they made themselves too sick. There was a lot of tension over that. It was hard to talk about it, about what you thought they were doing. Then someone who had been in the Army came up with a name for it. He called it the G.I. Shuffle. Now if someone says they're sick, you can simply ask if he has the G.I. Shuffle—and we do ask. We've found the problem comes up much less frequently since we've named it. Another thing people have trouble with is this thing of trying to do a job by yourself when more than one person can do it better. That is in direct opposition to what we're trying to do. It comes from the prevailing Western attitude toward individualism and the ridiculous individual attitudes and stances it engenders, which we recognize as sick. The point is that the job is much too big for any one person—in fact, that any life-project is too big for any one man. That's a simple idea; but it has a lot of meaning for us. At the same time, it's very difficult to explain and talk about it when someone's actions go against that idea. So we end up expressing it as a joke, chiding the person with "I'll do it all myself" in a friendly, kidding way. That seems to convey the message pretty well.

I asked them about the issue of monogamy versus polygamy in the commune. They told me that there was no set policy. Sexual choices were left to the individual. They said that, as a rule, pairs tend to form, as much

---

[1] On the wall of the dining room was a small stand holding an orange melmac cup in an upright position. When someone wanted to discuss a problem and perhaps get it resolved by a decision of the group, he would turn the cup upside down on its stand. Subsequently, a meeting would be called for that evening. The person who had overturned the cup would start the meeting, holding the cup before him on the table. After he finished, the cup was passed to each person around the table. A person could speak only when the cup was before him on the table. That way one couldn't interrupt another and everyone got his chance to speak. When the cup had gone all the way around the table without anyone saying anything, the meeting was over.

in order to have a particular someone to talk personal problems out with as for sexual reasons. The pairings resulted in a pseudo monogamy that was as ignored as it was recognized.

*8:20* P.M. It was getting dark, so we excused ourselves to set up our tent for the night and headed out the back door. Alex offered us one of the shelters, but we declined in favor of our own provision—a tent.

*8:30* P.M. As we were pitching the tent, a person robed in white emerged from a trail out of the woods behind us, followed by a middle-age couple in civilian dress carrying green boughs. As they approached, we saw that what appeared to be white robes were actually two sheets, one draped over the shoulders, the other wrapped around the loins in diaper fashion. The wearer, Carl, was large and muscular, with long disheveled blonde hair. The two disciples were from San Francisco and had heard about Bedrock driving through Oregon and came by to take a look. Both talked effusively and enthusiastically about Bedrock and were in a rush to get back to California because it was getting dark.

*8:50* P.M. By the time the tent was set up and we had returned to the house, the Californians had left. All the group but Alex and Ruth were sitting around the table. Alex and Ruth had gone to Ruth's room.

*9:30* P.M. Someone asked us what we did in Boston. We told them that Dorothy was a music school student and I was a casewriter. I was explaining what a case was when Carl broke in, challenging the idea that anything worthwhile could be drawn from formal education. Carl said a number of Ph.D. friends of his had renounced academia for communal life and had been very successful in their decision.

Just then, Alex walked in wearing only a T-shirt and work boots and suggested that it was late and time to go to bed if we planned on getting up on time in the morning. One of the women said it was a lot easier to get up when Roger was here. Rick and the other women agreed. They explained to us that Roger used to get up at 5:00 A.M. and came around calling out "one bell." That would wake everyone up; but they could go back to sleep for a few more winks. Then he'd call out "two bells" at 5:15. At 5:30 was "three bells," and everyone got up. Roger would then read poetry to the group or sing.

Alex turned the conversation to Monday's work. The talk centered on how much mulch they needed and where they could get it and whether new sides should be put on the truck to haul it. The discussion seemed open; that is, it appeared that all the men participated in it and freely disagreed with each other. Brent, Mark, and Rick made suggestions to Carl and Alex, and then voiced to Carl and Alex agreement or disagreement with judgments they made. There was little interchange among Brent, Mark, or Rick; each of their remarks was directed primarily at Carl or Alex or both. Carl and Alex made the decisions; and Alex appeared to have the final say.

It was decided to put off fixing the sides of the truck and getting mulch until Tuesday and devote Monday to planting. We then all turned in for the night.

***Monday, 5:30*** **A.M.** Alex's alarm rang at 5:30. He got up and woke Brent, whose job it now was to wake up everyone else. We joined each other around the table for a cup of coffee before the men would do the chores and the women fix breakfast. I mentioned that I was not accustomed to getting up so early; and we were told again about Roger and the morning ritual, as if nothing had been said about him the night before. Several of the women said that they really missed Roger.

***6:00*** **A.M.** Brent invited me to help with the chores; so while Dorothy helped fix breakfast I joined him and Rick, Mark, and Matthew out in the animal shed.

***7:00*** **A.M.** Breakfast was poached eggs, apple turnovers, and wheat mush. We stood in line and served ourselves from containers on the kitchen counter. Carl ate quickly, got up, hanging the buckets of curdled milk in cheese cloths for cottage cheese, and then went from the kitchen out the back door. (It seemed strange to me that Carl would be the one making the cottage cheese.) He reappeared outside in the greenhouse with a watering can, caring for some large tomato plants on a top shelf.

Ruth said something about plants that big not belonging in the greenhouse, to which Rick said, "That's his trip. He's a plant freak." "He's a freak, period," replied Ruth. Everyone laughed. Ruth then turned to us and said that Carl talks about people behind their backs, that he drags down the people he doesn't like, and that, if he didn't like us, he'd criticize us after we left. No one voiced disagreement with her.

***7:30*** **A.M.** After Carl returned to the table, the conversation among the men centered on what size of rubber hose to attach to a tank they had to make a "liquid shit" spreader. Carl, Brent, and Alex were the most active in the conversation.

Then the discussion turned to the tasks that would be worked on that day. Rick said he planned to work on the mare's hooves and train Rudolph, the colt. Mark and Brent wanted to build the new sides for the Dodge truck. But Alex rejected that; since the commune was short of hands, the essential things should be done first. And planting the crops was most essential; so we'd do that.

***7:45*** **A.M.** Carl then started making the assignments. He drew a small map of the fields in front of the house and marked on it where Brent and Rick were to dump loads of hay to be spread over the day's planting. Mark, Dorothy, and I got the job of raking the field, planting, and spreading the hay. Iris had already started the laundry, so the other women were left to decide who would fix lunch.

***8:00*** **A.M.** Dorothy, Mark, and I started raking the field lengthwise. Then I suggested raking across the width, to avoid the large accumulations of rocks that would result from longer raking paths. We switched. Then Carl walked over and told us to rake from the middle of the width out to both edges. We did that.

In a few minutes, Brent and Rick pulled the team of horses up beside us with a load of hay and Matthew on top. Brent told Matthew to stand in front of the horses and hold their reins so they would not move while he and Rick unloaded the hay. Matthew looked a little frightened. Rick told him not to be scared, just to stand there and let the horses eat him.

Brent told us we were raking wrong. He said to rake the stones all to one edge, not from the middle out. Mark told him Carl had said to do it this way. He said, "Okay."

Mark loosened up the ground and dug small holes with a hoe. Dorothy and I transplanted cabbage from flats Carl had cultivated. When Mark got too far ahead of us, he'd help with the planting.

After dumping another load of hay, Brent came over with some sugar cubes for us. Mark said they'd give us a fast pick up, and popped a couple in his mouth. We paused, looked at each other, hesitant, then each took one and sucked on it.

I asked Mark to characterize Alex's influence at Bedrock. He said it was a "benevolent dictatorship." I also asked him the cause of the blowup that resulted in the departure of Roger and the other commune members. He said he didn't know what happened; he had come back four days after the blowup and no one had talked about it.

While we were planting, Carl came by twice to make sure we were doing it correctly. He also called me aside twice—once to show me how to plant the lettuce once we had finished with the cabbage, and once to show me which additional cabbage flats and lettuce flats to use. It seemed strange to me that Carl would give me the instructions instead of Mark; I was only a visitor to the commune.

***12:00 noon.*** Lunch: a rice and pork concoction, green salad, home baked bread, coffee, fresh milk and Kool-aid. Once again, Carl ate quickly and left.

I asked Alex about Bedrock's relations with the outside world. He said their relations with the townspeople were pretty good, that he had seen few people as willing as the Oregonians were to let others do their own thing. Alex pointed out that he's on friendly personal terms with the sheriff and has been elected town auditor two years in a row. He continued: "Our only really bad experience as a commune with the Establishment is the harrassment we've gotten from the FBI over draft dodgers and the threat of drug raids."

Here he digressed:

> The only dope we keep around is marijuana. We have two categories of marijuana—medicinal and recreational. I've found marijuana works very well

for reducing pain; I've applied it successfully that way a number of times here. Then sometimes we have some extra for recreational purposes—on weekends, I, myself, think it's much more safe than alcohol. People are more docile under marijuana.

I keep both the medicinal and recreational marijuana locked up. And only I can dispense it. That's a firm rule. By the way, we haven't had any for quite a while. It's become very difficult to get.

Alex went on to point out that Bedrock is not plugged into the nation's media and advertising network. Bedrock has no television. The commune subscribes to no newspaper or magazine.

He also said that, on the average, a member rarely leaves the commune, except on weekends—and then they usually go in groups of three or four. And few outsiders from the neighborhood visit Bedrock. One reason may be its geographical isolation. Other reasons the commune members gave for not having many visitors, was the outsiders' aversion to their unorthodox appearance (the long hair and beards on the men) and their practice of wearing no clothes whenever the weather permitted.

After our conversation, Alex joined Carl out at the animal shed to pick out a sheep to sell to a local farmer coming by later in the afternoon. After he had gone, I asked about the blowup the previous weekend. Everyone seemed hesitant to talk about it. All that was said was that there was an argument late at night, and the next day Roger and some of the others left. Sandy said she hoped Roger would come back. Iris and Rick agreed; they hoped he would too.

I also asked who made the work assignments when both Carl and Roger were around. Brent objected to my question. He said that each person chose himself what he did, and that if you didn't like your assignment, you could object and they'll talk it over.

***12:45* P.M.** After lunch, Mark and I returned to the planting. Dorothy decided to stay in the house and help prepare dinner. Brent and Rick decided to spend the afternoon shoeing the horses.

Carl checked by twice that afternoon to see how we were doing with the lettuce. The second time, around 2:30 P.M., he brought with him two flats of chrysanthemums and called me aside to show me how he wanted them planted. After Carl left, I asked Mark why Carl got the role of supervisor. He answered that leadership goes to the guy with experience and expertise, and Carl had once worked as a landscape architect's assistant. Mark also said that he himself had had a little farming experience before coming to Bedrock; and it was his opinion that Carl's judgment, when it comes to crops, is often not very good.

I also remarked that it surprised me that Carl was giving me the instructions rather than him. Mark answered that he and Carl did not get along very well. They hadn't when Mark was at Bedrock before in December, and they didn't now. In December, Mark explained, he challenged Carl quite often on how to do things, and Carl didn't like that. He said Carl didn't seem too pleased when he came back to Bedrock.

As our conversation continued, Mark appeared increasingly worked up. He said he was ticked off that Carl had us planting chrysanthemums. He recalled Alex's statement that morning that, because we were short of people, only the essential things should be done first. Planting flowers was not essential. He then said he was going to hold off and wait a while and see what was going on—that he was ready to take off if he didn't like it.

***3:15* P.M.** I went looking for Carl to ask him a question about the chrysanthemum planting. Not finding him outside, I asked about him in the house and was told he was in his room on the second floor.

The second floor was unfinished in the sense that the plasterboard walls and wood frame were unpainted, there were no ceilings in the rooms, and there were no doors, except on Carl and Alex's rooms. Tie-dyed curtains hung in the doorways. Where I could see into the rooms, there were stacks of mattresses on the floors. I called out for Carl and heard him answer from behind his door. Not opening it, he asked what I wanted. I asked my question. He answered it, and I left.

***4:00* P.M.** We knocked off. Ellen had returned. Ellen looked out of place at Bedrock. She was the only woman who wore make up, and she wore a lot, including thick false eyelashes. She wore black sandals, brown silk slacks, and a multihued red silk tunic. Ellen was also overweight.

Ellen had spent the weekend with Little Billy high on LSD and hash. She was telling the others how great it was; Brent and Rick chided her for being selfish and not bringing any back.

Carl and Alex were outside. Rick told us that around 2 o'clock he had caught Carl napping on the stack of mattresses in the living room. He had jokingly scolded him and told him "Go to your own room to sleep; you're setting a bad example."

***4:15* P.M.** Everyone went outside or upstairs and Dorothy and I were alone on the main floor. She told me about her afternoon. After 1:00 P.M., when the men had gone back to their work, Iris cleared the table and started doing the dishes. The rest of the women found something else to do than work. Janet said she wasn't feeling well, and went upstairs. Ruth went to her room to check on Noah. Sandy wandered outside.

By 2:00 P.M., Ruth, Janet, and Sandy were on the living room floor. Ruth was nursing Noah and Janet was playing with Misha. Sandy talked with them. She made a face as she said she didn't like sleeping with Mark out in the shelter. Ruth told Sandy she was fickle. Iris added, "You can't be picky."

Carl came in and made some small talk with the two women in what Dorothy characterized as a patronizing tone. He then stretched out on the stack of mattresses and appeared to be beginning a nap when Rick "caught" him. Later Carl, unprompted, tried to justify himself to Alex, saying he had worked during most of the lunch hour.

Dorothy had learned that the whole commune as a group had gone on an "outing" only once. That was when they bought pizza to celebrate Carl's leaving after an argument. He returned the next day, however.

To Dorothy it appeared that the women in general were not as committed to the idea of the commune as the men. They had a good deal of free time, yet they were not completing the household tasks on the list posted on the wall. She thought that "the women are staying with their men, while the men play out their fantasies." The most committed of the women seemed to be Iris; the least, Sandy and Ellen.

***4:20* P.M.** Brought up to date, I was on my way out to the tent when Carl came in and joined Dorothy in the kitchen. He poured himself a cup of milk and took two fistfuls of cookies (about one third of them) from the counter. I backtracked, sat down across the table from him, and asked him questions to keep him occupied.

***4:30* P.M.** Rick and Iris came in and asked Carl if they could go to the auction with him. When he said he wanted to go alone this time, they began pleading and begging, half jokingly. It was to no avail. After he had finished a third handful of cookies and two more cups of milk, Carl left alone in the panel truck for the auction, accompanied only by a single sheep for sale.

***4:50* P.M.** When Iris went upstairs to see to Baboo, her son, Rick remained behind to tell me about the work he had done with the horses. Unsolicited, he drew me diagrams of how to shoe a horse, explained how he made his own bridles, and brought me up to date on the techniques he was using to train Rudolph, the colt. Rick hoped to enter Rudolph in the pulling competition at the local fair. His enthusiasm for working with the horses was obvious.

***6:00* P.M.** Dinner consisted of pork spareribs, dandelion salad, leftover rice, milk, and Kool-aid. The few cookies Carl had left behind were for dessert.

***6:45* P.M.** Dorothy and I excused ourselves to go lie down in the tent. An hour later we returned to the house.

***7:45* P.M.** In the living room and the dining room were Brent, Mark, Rick, Janet, and Ellen. Alex and Ruth were spending the evening in Ruth's room. Sandy and Matthew were missing. Misha was upstairs asleep. Mark was playing his guitar and singing; Brent was trying to read a book; Janet was setting up the handloom; and Rick and Ellen were talking. Rick and Iris had gotten permission from Alex to bathe in the house (the standard place was the beaver pond) and had finished bathing. Rick was wearing nothing but his hat with the orange embroidered headband.

Brent and Mark joined in the conversation when it turned to drugs. Brent told them how cheap pot was in Amsterdam. Rick and Brent teased Ellen again about not bringing anything back from Smithson.

***10:00* P.M.** We turned in.

***Tuesday, 5:30* A.M.** This time Carl came down naked, with his overalls and T-shirt draped over his arm. He dressed in front of us at the breakfast table. I wondered how Dorothy was reacting to all this.

We found out that Sandy and Matthew had hitchhiked to the auction and had come home with Carl around 10:30 P.M. Carl left before the sheep had been auctioned, so he did not know how much they'd gotten for it.

***6:00* A.M.** Before breakfast, while Brent and Rick did the chores, Mark and I worked at nailing extra planks on the side posts of the Dodge truck.

***7:00* A.M.** When we had just gone in for breakfast, Carl followed us in and asked Mark where the hammer was he had been using. Mark said he'd left it in the truck, because he wasn't finished. Carl chewed him out in front of the others, telling him to *always* put the tools away when he wasn't using them—that too many things were misplaced already and other people needed the tools, too. Brent turned and mimicked Carl, as Carl was walking out. Apparently, Alex heard Carl's reviling from upstairs, because when he came down for breakfast, he lightly scolded Carl before the group for not returning the seed catalog to its proper place. He pointed out that the catalog was a tool, too.

The conversation over breakfast was a more elaborated version of the previous night's drug discussion. People talked about times they had gotten various drugs at bargain prices and what their favorite drugs and combinations of drugs were.

***8:30* A.M.** After breakfast, Dorothy helped Iris clean up the table and washed dishes while I packed our equipment and talked with Alex. I asked him if he expected Bedrock to succeed:

> I wouldn't have started it if I didn't think it could work. We've made a lot of mistakes this first year; but that's to be expected. Economically, I'm sure we can make it, if everyone works. And no one stays who doesn't put in a full day's work; that's our fundamental rule. We just have to get our timing with the crops and our marketing in good shape and we'll make it pay for itself.
>
> We know the strong economic base is necessary; but it is not sufficient. Unless we succeed through cooperation, the whole thing will have been a failure.
>
> The commune has to go through developmental stages before it has reached the point where we really want it. Like, right now it needs a strong leader. I've seen too many groups fall apart because they didn't have a strong leader when they got started. There are too many big decisions that need to be made in a consistent way. A democracy just doesn't work then. On the other hand, the leader can't be arbitrary, because then the members will leave. I give reasons for decisions. I delegate authority for different responsibilities. But until this thing gets on its feet, I must have the final say. Some of the people that helped

found the commune left, I'm sure, partially because they didn't like the way Carl and I were running things. But you can't have chaos.

Once the group is organized well enough that it's supporting itself economically, then I think the leader can step back and give up some of his power. I plan to do that when we've gotten that far. Until then, I supply the money and I make the big decisions.

When the commune does get itself on a sound economic footing, it will be made a legal body, like a corporation or a trust, and all my personal outlays will be converted into a long-term loan to that body, payable only in money earned by the commune. Then, as long as the commune functions well enough to meet its payments, I will have no more control over decisions than any other member.

It was then that he raised the problem of holding the group together and keeping good members. He said he thought part of the problem might be Carl:

Some of the commune members have objected to rough treatment they've gotten from Carl. He is sometimes hostile and aggressive. However, during the first months of the commune, when people had to be expelled from the other house when we returned from the East, and when my right to decide the directions the commune would go were being challenged by others, and when we had to get rid of freeloaders who weren't going to work, Carl's roughness and aggressiveness were resources I was glad I could draw on.

But lately, his way of handling problems hasn't been needed. Now the objectives of the commune have become fairly firmly established. Dissenters usually simply leave rather than challenge my leadership. I've learned from Carl how to get fired up when it's really necessary.

However, Carl hasn't changed his style much; he's still pretty rough and aggressive. But now he's directing it toward properly functioning members of the group.

I think Carl's behavior may be a factor in some of the members' leaving. That may have been part of the reason why Roger left. In a sense, Roger and Carl were rivals for leadership in the commune. Carl was in charge of the fields because of his experience. So he was overseeing most of the work and making a lot of the decisions about when things would be done and what people would do. On the other hand, Roger was better liked by most of the commune members, especially the younger ones. He showed more interest in them as people, and just had a more easygoing personality. So, in a sense, he was a leader, too. People would go to him with their problems. He also had this weird thing about singing songs and reading poetry in the morning that some of the people liked. Carl and Roger didn't particularly like each other, it seemed.

But that's getting away from the point, which is that Carl is bugging some good people who are here now. It may be it's just because he's always telling them what to do. And they don't like that and get touchy. I don't know. What I do know is that we're not as together as we should be.

Several members of the group have dropped hints here and there that I ought to expel Carl from Bedrock. I have mixed feelings about that. Carl was a lot of help to me in organizing the commune and stood by me as the commune went through some difficult times. He has also provided most of the knowledge we needed for planting the crops. I don't even know everything we've got planted out there. That's been his area of responsibility.

Carl, on the other hand, thinks the problem stems from another source—that we're not using drugs as we could to get the group together. I'm very hesitant about the group drug trip.

Right now it's every man for himself as long as he doesn't let it get in the way of the work. And since we work eight to ten hours a day and everyone has to get up at 5:30, that essentially means no drugs except on weekends. Then a guy can freak out or do whatever he wants. It's his own thing then. But not when the group has to rely on him for work.

Some of the other people in the commune would like to go the group drug route, too, I think. But I'm hesitant about it myself. I think people should deal with each other as they are really, not as they are under the influence of drugs—or alcohol, for that matter. I won't try to talk seriously with a guy on dope. He's just not there. He's not responsible; he's not rational.

So I don't like the idea of group drugs and the things that go along with it. However, I still haven't completely dropped that option.

I want to do something to better the situation; at the same time, I won't compromise my integrity.

# The Times-Herald[1]

THE TIMES-HERALD, one of the major daily newspapers in a large middle-western city, published afternoon and evening editions, six days a week as well as a single Sunday edition. The paper was founded in the late nineteenth century by Samuel B. Fischer and was managed by his descendants in 1962. Its stated publishing policy was to remain impartial in political disputes and to report news in an objective manner avoiding sensational issues.

As Exhibit 1 indicates, the editorial department of *The Times-Herald* was under the direct supervision of Bob Smith,[2] managing editor. While assistant managing editors and the associate editor supervised the news reporters, feature reporters, and columnists, the rewriting and editing functions were the direct responsibility of the city editor and the news editor. Joe O'Malley, the city editor, managed the city desk which directed the daily reporting of local news and the writing of stories. Thus, while the assistant managing editor assigned reporters to major events or "beats" for coverage, the city editor directed the daily gathering of news. Stories were either written by reporters or telephoned by them to rewrite men who converted the news items into finished stories. National and foreign news was gathered predominantly by one of the several wire services which *The Times-Herald* subscribed to, although *The Times-Herald* occasionally sent senior reporters to cover world events of particular interest to readers. The wire-service copy and the local stories from the city desk were all routed through the news desk, which was supervised by Fred Dugan, news editor.[3] Fred and the copy editors on the news desk (desk men) edited the copy and decided which stories would be included in the paper. Exhibits 2 and 3 provide a floor plan of the city room and the news desk, respectively.

After the news had been processed by the men on the news desk, the copy which was to be included in the paper was dropped through a chute

[1] All names have been disguised.

[2] All editorial department personnel, including the managing editor, were referred to by their first names.

[3] While this case deals with the day news desk there was also a smaller desk ("the lobster desk") of four men who worked from midnight to 8:00 A.M. preparing news for the early editions. This group was also the responsibility of Fred Dugan.

(see Exhibits 2 and 3) to the composing room two floors below. Here the make-up editor, Gene Little (a member of the news desk, who spent most of his time in the composing room), laid out the front page. Gene

**EXHIBIT 1**

Organization of Editorial Department*

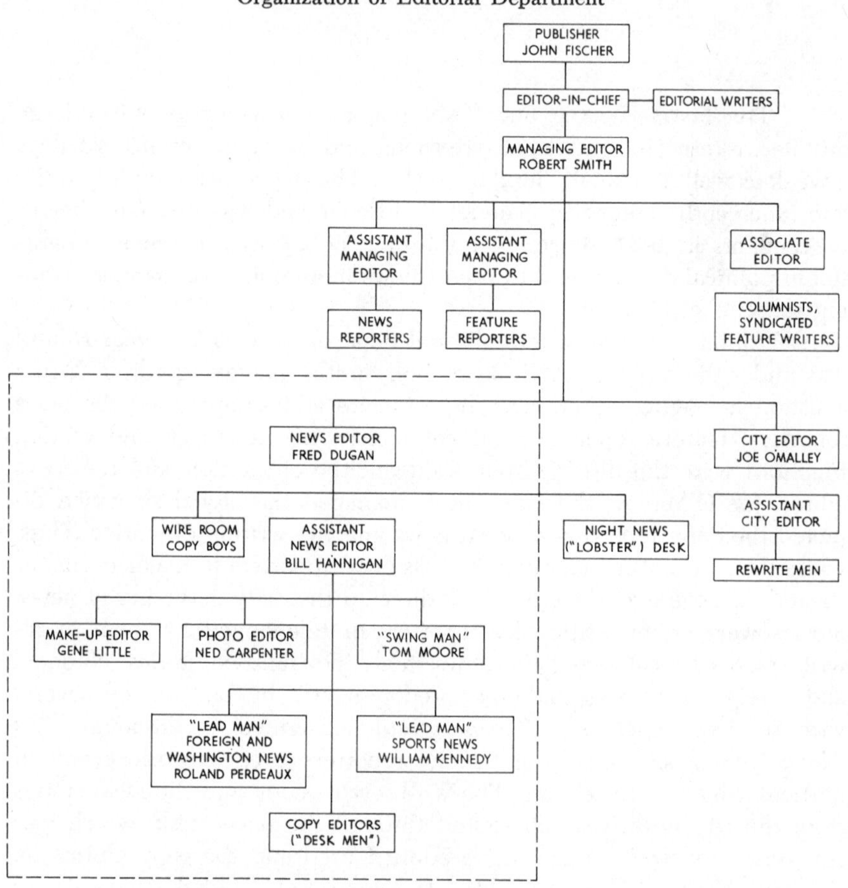


* This is the casewriter's conception of the organization since no formal chart existed. Dotted line encloses news desk positions.

also helped composing room personnel solve any layout problems as they fitted news into spaces not occupied by previously laid out advertising copy on the inside pages. After the layout had been completed, the edition was ready for printing.

In addition to the news editor and the make-up editor there were several other supervisory positions on the news desk. The assistant news editor, William Hannigan, referred to in newspaper parlance as the "slot man," assigned the stories to the various desk men and reviewed the edited results before sending them to the composing room. As Exhibit 3 indicates, the news desk was divided into three sections, one for local and national (other than Washington, D.C.) news, one for foreign and Washington news, and one for sports. The slot man made

**EXHIBIT 2**

The City Room of *The Times-Herald**

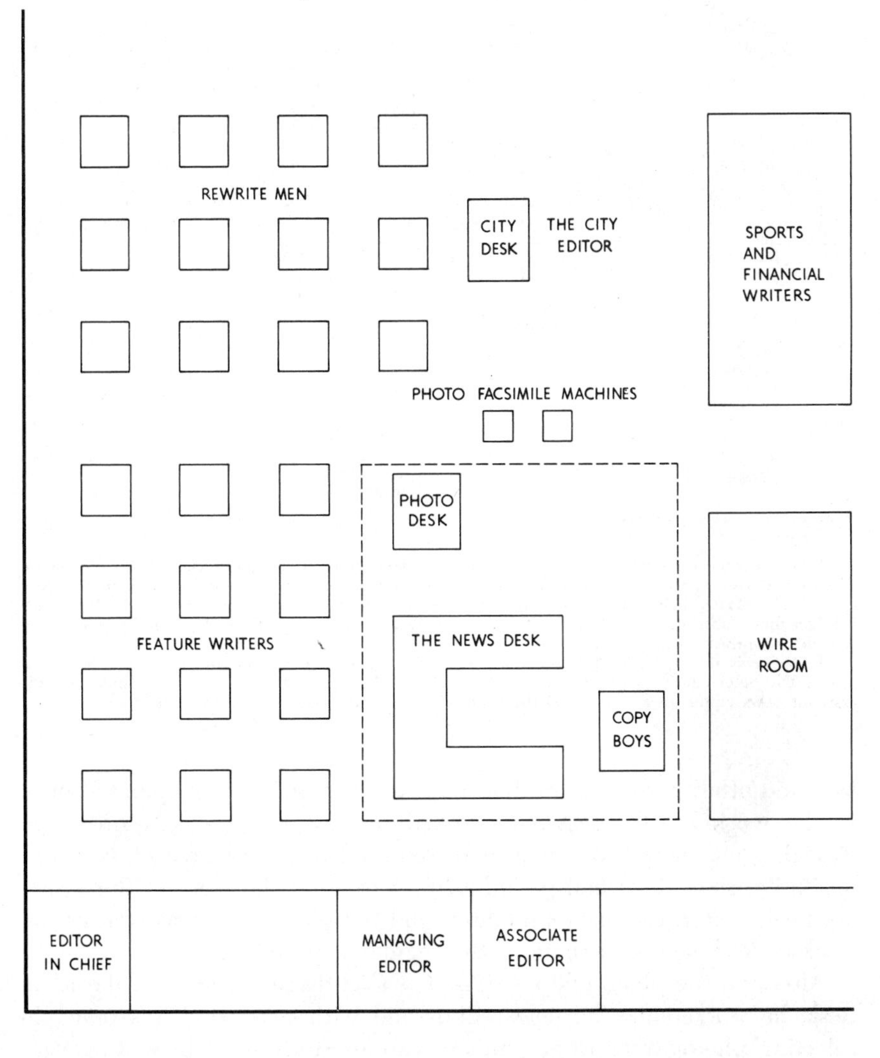


* Dotted line encloses all news desk positions except for make-up editor who worked in composing room.

assignments directly to the desk men working on local news, but for other news worked through "lead men," Rolly Perdeaux for Washington and foreign news and Will Kennedy for sports news. These lead men supervised one or two desk men in editing their particular category of copy. Another supervisory position on the desk was the "swing man," Thomas Moore, who, as his title implies, substituted for supervi-

**EXHIBIT 3**

*The Times-Herald* News Desk*

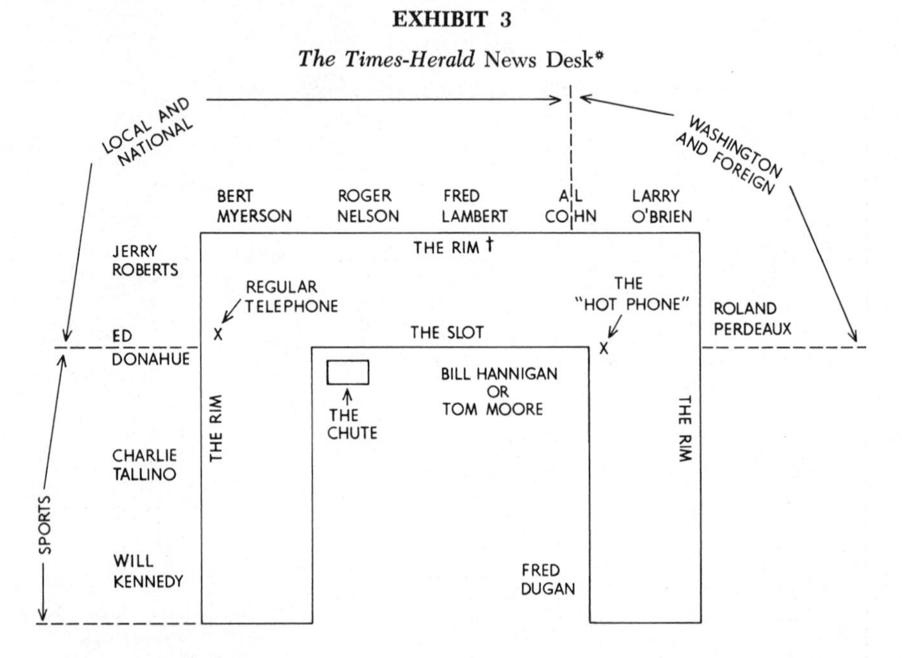


* Two members of the news desk staff are not shown on this diagram. Gene Little (make-up editor) and Ned Carpenter (photo editor) held jobs requiring them to work away from the desk (see Exhibit 2). Although the desk men rotated seats, this figure represents a typical seating chart. Ed Donahue substituted for Charlie Tallino and Will Kennedy on their days off and Al Cohn sometimes worked on local news.

† The news desk of *The Times-Herald,* as at most newspapers, was arranged in a horseshoe shape. The outer edge was referred to as "the rim" and the inner edge as "the slot." Thus since the assistant news editor always occupied the center he was traditionally called the "slot man."

sory and other personnel on their days off. The news desk operated on a six-day week, but the desk men worked only five of the six. According to Fred Dugan, the job of swing man required a high degree of skill and flexibility, since Tom had periodically to perform the work of the assistant news editor, the make-up editor, and the photo editor, as well as the work of lead men and some of the regular copy editors.

Although the photo editor's desk was slightly removed from the news desk, he worked for the news editor and with other desk personnel in selecting photographs to accompany various stories and in writing captions for them.

### The Men on the Desk

As Exhibit 4 indicates, most of the copy editors had long journalistic careers behind them. By tradition, the desk at *The Times-Herald,* as at most newspapers, had been staffed with senior men who, because of age or family responsibility, no longer desired to work the long and irregular hours required of reporters, and who displayed a skill at, and an interest in, copy editing. Recently, however, Fred Dugan had become concerned that there were not enough younger men on the desk to provide a balanced appraisal of news copy and to provide continuity as the older men retired. He also believed that younger men were needed to provide long-range replacements for the executive positions on the desk. He therefore arranged to have several younger men assigned to the desk. While they had less experience than their seniors, these newcomers came to the copy desk after several years of experience in various phases of reporting and editorial work, either with *The Times-Herald,* or with other papers. In order to make room for these younger men, Bob Smith had transferred copy editors who indicated suitable interest and competence to the position of chief editor of a feature department or to senior writer's jobs in these departments. In the spring of 1962, Fred Dugan was attempting to evaluate the effects of this change in the complexion of the copy editor's position on the operation of the desk.

Fred spoke about the use of younger men on the desk:

> There is a feeling among many newspapermen that the copy desk is the end of the line. The feeling in the trade is that older people end up on the desk, but you can't put out a successful paper on that basis. At the present time in the newspaper business obtaining good copy editors is the most pressing employment problem. If you were to look at smaller papers, the old age of the desk men might be a striking feature, but on a big paper such as ours things are too fast moving to operate this way. We have to continue to try to bring younger men in as copy editors.

When a man came to work for the desk from outside *The Times-Herald,* he sometimes worked as a part-timer before being given a permanent desk position. For example, this was the way Bert Myerson, one of the newer desk men, was originally brought to *The Times-Herald* from another local paper. As Fred Dugan explained, "We wanted him on a part-time basis to see if we liked him and he liked us. He worked out well, so we put him on full time. He is one of our promising younger men now."

Many of the desk men had initially become interested in a journalistic career while working on school newspapers, beginning work at *The Times-Herald* as copy boys in the evening or during the summer while they were going to college. Roger Nelson was one of these. "Rog" went

## EXHIBIT 4

Desk Personnel

| Name | Position | Age* | Service at The Times-Herald | Service on News Desk† | Prior Journalistic Experience |
|---|---|---|---|---|---|
| Fred Dugan | News editor | 48 | 32 | 28 | Copy boy, copy editor on *The Times-Herald* |
| Bill Hannigan | Asst. news editor (slot man) | 52 | 33 | 22 | Copy boy, reporter, copy editor on *The Times-Herald* |
| Tom Moore | Swing man | 42 | 20 | 16* | Copy boy, reporter, copy editor on *The Times-Herald* |
| Gene Little | Make-up editor | 48 | 27 | 16 | Copy boy, reporter, copy editor on *The Times-Herald* |
| Ned Carpenter | Photo editor | 55 | 20 | 20 | Several positions on small-town newspapers |
| Roland Perdeaux | Lead man, foreign and Washington | 58 | 33 | 33 | Reporter on a small-town newspaper; copy editor on *The Times-Herald* |
| Will Kennedy | Lead man—sports | 40 | 22 | 10 | Copy boy, sports writer, copy editor on *The Times-Herald* |
| Fred Lambert | Desk man—local | 56 | 13 | 13 | Reporter, copy editor on another metropolitan newspaper |
| Roger Nelson | Desk man—local | 55 | 28 | 28 | Reporter on small-town newspaper |
| Al Cohn | Desk man—local or foreign | 62 | 34 | 34* | Reporter on another metropolitan newspaper |
| Ed Donahue | Desk man—local or sports | 36 | 6 | 6 | Copy boy and reporter on another metropolitan newspaper |
| Jerry Roberts | Desk man—local | 72 | 20 | 20 | District manager for wire-service, wire-service reporter |
| Bert Myerson | Desk man—local | 32 | 2 | 2 | Reporter on another metropolitan daily |
| Larry O'Brien | Desk man—foreign | 50 | 4 | 4 | Reporter and copy editor on metropolitan daily |
| Charlie Tallino | Desk man—sports and local | 38 | 2 | 2* | Several positions on a neighborhood weekly newspaper |

* *The Times-Herald* had no regular retirement age. Personnel worked until they felt they wanted to retire.

† Asterisk indicates service on lobster desk as well as day desk. Al Cohn and Tom Moore had been on day desk about one year while Charlie Tallino had been on day desk six months.

to work for a small-city newspaper during a summer vacation from the University of Chicago, where he was majoring in fine arts. After graduation he returned to this paper and a few years later joined *The Times-Herald* as a copy editor. A few men like Will Kennedy, whose father had been a well-known sports cartoonist, had become interested in working for *The Times-Herald* because of family connections.

Bert Myerson spoke of his attitudes about work on the desk:

The desk used to be a dead end. Now it appears that this may not be so. The progression used to be reporter, rewrite, desk. Now that some of the other fellows [former copy writers] have moved on as feature and editorial writers, I'm hopeful it means you can move from the desk to other things. On the desk you are learning newspaper technology, but you don't have an opportunity to learn about any one area in depth. Yet the work on the desk is interesting, because we see such a variety of stuff.

"Rolly" Perdeaux, who was the lead man on foreign and Washington news, exemplified the attitude of the senior desk men:

My wife says I'm like a fireman. I can't wait to get to work. I think the thing that makes us like this business so much is the opportunity for creativity. Everybody feels that they have a part in putting out the paper. If you ask the reporters, pressmen, or the mailmen, they'll also say, just like we do, that without them the paper wouldn't go out.

But working on the desk is particularly interesting, because it is the nerve center of the paper. We are extremely important as a last outpost between the public and the news sources.

The desk men were concerned about maintaining journalistic standards in editing the news. Comments such as these were typical:

A speech by Khrushchev is a tough one to handle. You don't want to make it too big, yet it is news. If you let them get too much propaganda out of it by giving them a big headline, you can panic the public. You are doing a disservice to the public and your country.

. . . . . . . . . . . . . . . . . . . . . .

We have a responsibility to the public. I'm proud to work for *The Times-Herald,* because we make an effort not to be jingoistic, or warmongers. We take time to make a "head" accurate and not misleading, but still to make it appealing to the public.

We want the story to be fair, and we don't want it to be offensive. When we know one of the competitors is going to break a story, we want to get it in and beat him to it.

. . . . . . . . . . . . . . . . . . . . . .

When the [wire-service] describes the color of somebody's beard or what he was wearing, it is O.K., but when it is what somebody says, they are usually wrong, so I don't like to use their stuff.

. . . . . . . . . . . . . . . . . . . . . . . . . . . . . .

The casewriter observed that these standards were not only valued by the desk men, but were also reflected in comments by employees in other parts of *The Times-Herald* and in the paper's editorial policy. Bill Hannigan, the slot man, explained:

It may be difficult to recognize our rules, because they are not written down, but we do have them. By the time a man gets to the news desk he has learned *The Times-Herald* way of doing things. We don't go for sensationalism. We are straight down the line politically and we try to be fair to all sides. Since everybody knows these things, they get done quietly and unobtrusively. By the time something get past the rewrite men, the city editor, past the men over there [pointing to the desk men on the rim] and past me, it should agree with *The Times-Herald* policies. I check things over to make sure they are right. However, the boys in the composing room will often catch something and call me to see if it got by us, and it often did. They don't have any technical responsibility for this down there, but they help us.

Assignments of men to the various positions on the desk were based on three criteria: availability of openings, ability of the men, and, particularly, their interest. Will Kennedy and Charlie Tallino, who edited sports copy, discussed the assignment process:

WILL: Take for example Perdeaux. Washington and foreign news is his job. He's a good man for it—lecturer and world traveler. He teaches at [a local university]. He used to lecture a lot about foreign affairs. He has traveled to the Holy Land and Rome in the last few years.

CHARLIE: Right, you get into an area because you have an interest in it and like it.

WILL: It wouldn't do to have someone on our job who knows nothing about sports.

Will Kennedy also explained how Tom Moore had been assigned the job of swing man.

Tom came over from the lobster desk and was jumped over some of the others. Lam and Roger didn't want to run around that much, so Fred gave it to the younger man. It depends somewhat on what people want. None of the other guys would want to be on sports.

While permanent assignments were made on this basis, the fact that the desk operated on a six-day week made it necessary for several of the men in addition to the swing man to rotate between various positions. It was usually the newer men on the desk who moved from one position to another, while the senior men generally remained at a regular position.

One exception to this was Al Cohn, who rotated between working on foreign and Washington news and local news whenever he wanted. Fred Dugan explained Al's almost daily shifts in assignments:

> I don't really care where Al lands, as long as all the seats are occupied. He is one of our senior citizens, and we let him work wherever he feels like sitting down when he comes in each morning.

Supervisory personnel on the desk were usually selected from among desk personnel or from persons working in other parts of the paper with prior experience on the desk. Comments such as this one by Will Kennedy were typical of the sentiments the men expressed about the supervisors.

> Fred [Dugan] is really creative. He is not satisfied to let the front page remain the same through many editions. He really works to make it the best possible.[4]

Al Cohn, who had recently transferred from the lobster desk, expressed a similar view:

> On the lobster desk I was brass, here I am just one of the boys. I transferred over though because my wife had been ill and also because I saw it as a chance to work with Fred, who is really a bright guy. I've watched him ever since he started as a copy boy. As far as we are concerned, he's a case of the right man on the right job.

### A Day on the News Desk

The city room was in full operation from 6:30 A.M. to 5:00 P.M. each day. The period between midnight and 8:00 was referred to as the "lobster shift" and was manned by a skeleton crew which stood by in case of a sudden important news development and also processed routine incoming news for use in the early, "bulldog," edition. The men on the day news desk began to arrive at 6:00 A.M. The first to arrive was usually Larry O'Brien, the "early man." He sorted copy from the lobster shift and began making rough selections about what copy was suitable for inclusion in the first edition. At about 7:00 Fred Dugan and Bill Hannigan arrived and familiarized themselves with the important stories by talking with Larry O'Brien. The following exchange might be typical:

---

[4] The day news desk was responsible for putting out six editions which went to press at the following times: 9:20 A.M., 11:50 A.M., 1:00 P.M., 3:10 P.M., 3:50 P.M. Copy for each edition had to be sent to the composing room at least forty-five minutes before these press times. How much variation there was between editions was a function of the news developments on a particular day. Generally, however, there would be some changes between each edition, so that the final edition would have little resemblance to the early edition. It was not uncommon to have the entire front page remade in the course of one or two editions.

LARRY: Well, we've got a revolution going in Burma this morning. The new man's name is Lee Win. That should fit any headline.

BILL (*laughs*): "Lee Win—Wins," huh? Well, I guess we'll want to use that unless something better breaks. What else have you got . . . ?

By 7:30 most of the other desk men had arrived and begun work. As each man came in, he stopped by the locker room and removed his street wear and suit coat, since everyone including the editor-in-chief worked in his shirt sleeves. At the desk, each man brushed off the area in front of his chair and made certain that the copy boys had filled the paste pots and supplied him with paper pads. If there was no work immediately available, the men began to thumb through the last edition from the evening before.

If there were any late arrivals, they might be greeted like Rolly Perdeaux welcomed Al Cohn when the latter arrived ten minutes late one morning:

AL: 'Morning, boys.

ROLLY: Well, are you the early man for tomorrow?

AL: You're confused. I'm not the early man, I'm the late man.

Fred Dugan was informed each morning by the business office how much space he would have available for news copy in that day's editions. The amount of news space was determined by the amount of advertising sold and the size newspaper which could be sold profitably with this amount of advertising. Thus, it was necessary when heavy news days coincided with light advertising to eliminate news copy which would ordinarily warrant inclusion in the paper. The casewriter noticed that the copy editors were all concerned when such a "tight paper" occurred and frequently complained about not being able to include important stories. Fred Dugan was responsible for allocating news space within the paper to local and national, Washington and foreign, and sports news. When news space was limited, Fred usually first cut the size of the sports page before eliminating important stories from the regular news pages.

Once the size of the paper was determined and the work at the desk gained momentum, Bill Hannigan reviewed stories as they came in from the city desk and the wire services. Sports and Washington and foreign news was passed on to the respective lead man, but Bill himself made the decision as to what local and national news items were to be included in the edition. If he wanted it to go in, the copy was given to one of the desk men on the rim who edited it for accuracy, grammatical correctness, style, and length, and then wrote the headline. Basically, the same procedure was followed by Will Kennedy and Rolly Perdeaux in their sections, although they also worked directly on some of the copy themselves, usually the major stories. The length of the story and the size of type for the headline were specified by Bill Hannigan, for local and national news as well as major foreign and Washington stories, although Will Kennedy made his own decisions about the sports page, since he was also responsible for its layout.

When a copy editor had finished a particular story he pasted the parts of the story to a sheet of paper on which he had written the headline, the page the story was to run on (although this was only specified for the major stories), and the edition it should run in, and handed all this back to Bill Hannigan or his lead man. After a check to see if the story had come out the way he had expected, the supervisor dropped it into the chute leading to the composing room.

Tom Moore explained the philosophy of the supervisors at the desk with regard to reviewing stories.

> We believe in a little checking up, but generally the people are mature enough to take care of their own jobs. We usually just give the story a quick once over because the men know how to handle them. With a new man or a major story we might take more time.

Al Cohn and Lam Lambert discussed the way most of the men felt about having their work reviewed:

> AL: You'll never find another desk like this. Nobody's afraid of anyone else, including the boss. If someone makes a mistake we let him know about it. We expect some mistakes. We recognize, because of the time pressures, that people will make mistakes.
>
> LAM: If somebody makes a mistake we explain what's wrong so it won't happen again, instead of firing him like they do on some other papers.
>
> AL: Yes, *The Times-Herald* has a much calmer, better work atmosphere than the other papers in town.

The casewriter observed that while most of the desk men showed no concern about supervisory review of completed stories, Charlie Tallino was an exception. On several occasions the casewriter noticed Charlie watching nervously as Bill Hannigan looked over his work on local news stories. When Bill dropped the story into the chute without comment, Charlie gave an audible sigh of relief. On a particular morning Charlie was working on an important story on the death of prize fighter Bennie Paret which was to appear on the front page. Charlie gave the story to Tom Moore, who was working in the slot that day, and watched carefully as Tom read it. Fred Dugan stopped and looked over Tom's shoulder at the story and then picked it up and brought it back to Charlie saying, "I don't like the head too well. Can't we do better than this?" Charlie replied, "I'll get it," and again worked on the headline for several minutes, after which Fred returned and they discussed it further. Fred finally suggested a word which Charlie said, "was just the one I was looking for," and the story was dropped to the composing room. Charlie told the casewriter, after this incident, "Fred really has a gift for finding the right 'head' for a story. He makes it seem easy."

The front page was the particular domain of Fred Dugan himself. He determined the major part of its content and sometimes wrote the lead headline and edited the lead story, although these tasks were often assigned to Bert Myerson, Roger Nelson, Al Cohn, or Fred Lambert who performed them with little supervision. Bill Hannigan, Rolly Perdeaux, and Will Kennedy kept Fred informed of major stories which might deserve front page attention. In Fred's absence, Bill Hannigan made decisions on front page content, as well as performing Fred's other duties.

The desk men continued working on stories as long as there was copy available. When there was a slack period, which might occur several times during the day, they spent most of their time either reading earlier editions of *The Times-Herald,* looking for "typos" (typographical errors) or reading competitive newspapers to see how they were handling stories that *The Times-Herald* had run in earlier editions. The desk man who found a "typo" would cut the article out, paste it to a sheet of paper and mark it with the appropriate proofreader's symbols. He would then drop it down the chute. The casewriter observed on several occasions that the more experienced desk men would be assigned stories which kept them at work for long periods, while at the same time, Ed, Charlie, and Bert were reading newspapers or chatting.

While the men worked they discussed current stories, political and world events, or family and personal problems. Frequently they asked each other for help on a particular story or headline. For example, Rog Nelson asked Al Cohn and Larry O'Brien for help in the phrasing of a headline on the nuclear test-ban negotiations:

ROG: Should we use "No-Give on Part of Russians" in the headline?

AL: I don't think you've got the right meaning there.

LARRY: You are inventing the word and really using a verb as a noun. It sounds awkward to me. Why don't you try "Russians Won't Give."

ROG: Let me see how that works.

There was also a great deal of joking between the men on the desk. For example, one day early in March as Ed Donahue was ordering coffee from the cafeteria, he asked Al Cohn if he would like anything, and the following exchange occurred:

AL: What's the special for today?

ED: I'm not sure, but they are going to have Kelly green matzoh balls for St. Patrick's Day.

AL: Is that so? Passover isn't for a couple of weeks yet, but get me a green bagel with my coffee.

ED: You want sour cream with it?

AL: No, that's high on cholesterol.

On another occasion Ed Donahue and Will Kennedy spent most of a morning joking with Charlie Tallino about the latter's having crashed a St. Patrick's Day open house by wearing a green tie.

One morning Al Cohn was sitting alongside Bert Myerson carrying on a one-sided conversation with him, while Bert was working. Ed Donahue removed a small piece of cotton from his desk drawer and took it to Bert with the whispered suggestion that he stuff it in his ear, "to stop Al from banging on it." Bert smiled and winked in response. This was done so quietly that neither Al nor the other desk men were aware of the incident. After Al had left for lunch, Ed recounted the incident to several of the other desk men who appeared to find it amusing and exchanged several jokes about Al's tendency to "bang on your ear." This conversation ended abruptly when Bill Hannigan looked up from a story he was reading and said, "Come on, Ed."

Humorous exchanges were not confined to the perimeter of the news desk. For example, a former desk man, now a financial writer, often engaged in humorous banter with the desk men as he dropped stories into the chute. One morning he approached the chute with a story which he stuck under Will Kennedy's nose:

WILL: I wondered what you guys had been doing in that cubbyhole of yours all these years.

FINANCIAL WRITER: This is the treasury balance. You guys may not know it but you can't put out the paper without the treasury balance. (*Laughter from the desk men.*)

WILL: As far as I can tell you are just like the feature writers—you don't know what live news is any more. . . .

During the period the casewriter was at *The Times-Herald* the desk men joined with the reporters and rewrite men in joking about a new glass-enclosed booth for the telephone operators which was being constructed near the city desk. The booth was designated as "the communal shower bath," "the sidewalk toilet," and by Al Cohn as "an isolation booth for noisy desk men."

The desk men sometimes found themselves the target of jokes. Charlie Tallino was checking a list of returning servicemen which had been prepared by a rewrite man when he found on the list the name of "Herschel Harshbarger," a pseudonym used on hotel registers by one of the star *Times-Herald* reporters. After Charlie disclosed his discovery to the other copy editors they all watched with amusement as he went over to "straighten out" the rewrite man.

The desk men also spent time discussing how *The Times-Herald* news coverage compared to that of competitive papers. For example, one morning Will Kennedy noted that a story carried by other local papers was not appearing in *The Times-Herald.* After a flurry of activity as several men tried to determine why this had happened, Bill Hannigan discovered that, "the story came in late yesterday and the lobster shift should have handled it." This precipitated a general discussion of how the lobster desk failed to pass on stories, with everyone stopping work to join in the criticism of the lobster desk. The casewriter noticed that although several of the desk men had at one time or another worked the lobster desk, they all frequently criticized it as the cause of mistakes which occurred during the day. This often happened even when it appeared to the casewriter that one of the day desk men might have been expected to catch the error. On another occasion the casewriter observed one of the feature writers come to the desk and ask to borrow a typewriter. Ed Donahue nodded his assent. Several hours later Will Kennedy wanted to use the typewriter and asked where it was. Ed and Charlie Tallino informed him that, "The damn features boys stole it again." Ed and Charlie then went off, cursing, to find the machine, and bring it back "where it belongs!"

Fred Dugan did not usually take an active part in the joking and conversation, but he often joined in the laughter and occasionally made a contribution. While Bill Hannigan was a frequent participant in all the exchanges around the desk, the casewriter noticed that Tom Moore did not contribute to the conversations and often showed no reaction to the joking.

Exhibit 5 provides a summary of all these contacts. It is based on approximately eighteen hours of observation over a six-day period.

This pattern of working and socializing continued throughout the morning with only occasional interruptions. The first of these came between 9:30 and 10:00 each morning when Bill Hannigan or Jerry Roberts would suggest that it was time for coffee. Usually without being asked, Charlie Tallino would make up the coffee list, asking each man what he wanted, even though this usually involved hunting for Fred Dugan and Ned Carpenter, the photo editor, who often were in some far corner of the city room. The only member of the desk who did not order coffee with them was Gene Little, make-up editor, who was working in the composing room. The list would then be given to a copy boy who would bring the order back from the cafeteria. While Charlie prepared the list most of the time, there were occasions when Ed Donahue and Bert Myerson would perform this task. One morning Bert Myerson suggested humorously to Al Cohn that he make up the coffee list. Al ignored his entreaties until Lam Lambert said, "Come on, Al, are you buying?" Al then made up the list.

Another interruption in the work routine occurred at 10:30 when Gene Little, who spent 90 percent of his time in the composing room, brought up copies of the first edition to the desk men. This was the signal, if the work load permitted, for everybody to take a few minutes

**EXHIBIT 5**

Nonrequired Interactions

| RECIPIENTS \ INITIATORS | SPORTS: KENNEDY | SPORTS: DONAHUE | SPORTS: TALLINO | LOCAL: LAMBERT | LOCAL: ROBERTS | LOCAL: MYERSON | LOCAL: NELSON | LOCAL: COHN | FOREIGN: O'BRIEN | FOREIGN: PERDEAUX | EXECUTIVES: LITTLE | EXECUTIVES: CARPENTER | EXECUTIVES: MOORE | EXECUTIVES: HANNIGAN | EXECUTIVES: DUGAN | OUTSIDE PERSONNEL† | TOTAL RECEIVED |
|---|---|---|---|---|---|---|---|---|---|---|---|---|---|---|---|---|---|
| SPORTS: KENNEDY | X | 6 | 10 | | | | | | | 1 | | | | 3 | 2 | 8 | 30 |
| SPORTS: DONAHUE | 5 | X | | | 1 | | 1 | | | | | | 1 | 2 | 1 | 1 | 12 |
| SPORTS: TALLINO | 2 | 1 | X | | 1 | | | | | | | | | 1 | | | 5 |
| LOCAL: LAMBERT | 3 | 3 | 1 | X | 3 | 1 | | 2 | 1 | | | | | | 1 | 7 | 22 |
| LOCAL: ROBERTS | 1 | 3 | 1 | | X | | | 1 | | | | | | 2 | | | 8 |
| LOCAL: MYERSON | 1 | 3 | | 2 | 3 | X | 1 | 2 | | | | | | 2 | 1 | | 15 |
| LOCAL: NELSON | 1 | | | 2 | 1 | 2 | X | 1 | | | | | | 2 | 1 | | 10 |
| LOCAL: COHN | | 2 | 1 | 4 | 2 | 1 | | X | 3 | | 1 | 1 | | 1 | 1 | | 17 |
| FOREIGN: O'BRIEN | | | | 1 | | | | 2 | X | 2 | | | | | | | 5 |
| FOREIGN: PERDEAUX | 1 | 1 | | 1 | | | | 1 | 4 | X | | | 2 | 3 | 5 | 3 | 21 |
| EXECUTIVES: LITTLE | | 1 | 1 | 1 | | | | | | | X | | | | 2 | | 5 |
| EXECUTIVES: CARPENTER | | | 4 | | | | | | | | 1 | X | | 1 | 1 | | 7 |
| EXECUTIVES: MOORE | | 1 | 1 | | | | | | | | | | X | | 3 | 1 | 6 |
| EXECUTIVES: HANNIGAN | 4 | 3 | 1 | | 1 | | 1 | 1 | 1 | 5 | 1 | | 3 | X | 2 | 3 | 26 |
| EXECUTIVES: DUGAN | | | | | | | | | | 2 | 4 | 5 | 4 | 2 | X | 6 | 23 |
| TOTAL INITIATED | 18 | 24 | 20 | 11 | 12 | 4 | 3 | 10 | 9 | 10 | 7 | 6 | 10 | 19 | 20 | 29 | 212 |
| SURPLUS OF RECEIPTS (DEFICIT OF RECEIPTS)* | 12 | (12) | (15) | 11 | (4) | 11 | 7 | 7 | (4) | 11 | (2) | 1 | (4) | 7 | 3 | X | |
| WORKED ON MAJOR STORIES OR SUPERVISOR | YES | NO | NO | YES | NO | YES | YES | YES | NO | YES | YES | YES | YES | YES | YES | | |

* This represents the difference in interactions received and initiated. A surplus indicates more receipts than initiations and a deficit the opposite condition.

† Outsider refers to interactions received from personnel other than news desk personnel.

and scan the paper. A few minutes later a copy boy would appear with copies of the same edition for all city room personnel, including the men at the news desk.

Gene Little described this early edition as "our first and our worst. We get better as the day goes along, but we don't have time to catch everything on this early one." While Gene was in the composing room most of the day, he was in constant contact with Bill Hannigan and Fred Dugan over "the hot phone" which provided a direct link between the news desk and the composing room. The casewriter observed that while the hot phone was in easy reach of most of the men on "the rim," only the slot man or news editor answered it. If the persons occupying these positions were away from the desk, Rolly Perdeaux would answer the telephone after it had rung several times. There was another telephone near the sports men which was used for routine calls. This was usually answered by Charlie Tallino.

Another interruption in work activity might occur when the publisher's secretary arrived to take up a collection for a retirement or engagement gift, or to set the time for an office party celebrating such events. On one such occasion she came to tell the copy editors that a retirement party was set for 3:00 that afternoon. When Charlie Tallino heard this he became quite upset, because he had not made a contribution when the collection was made a few days earlier on his day off. He offered to contribute to the gift, but the secretary said she had already purchased it, and invited Charlie to the party anyway. Charlie continued to insist that he wanted to give something, until Jerry Roberts said, "That's O.K., Charlie, we've got the money we need. We all miss giving once in a while."

About 11:30 the desk men began to leave for lunch. Because of the necessity of continually staffing the desk, only two or three men could be absent simultaneously. Each man obtained permission from the slot man before going to eat. For the most part the men ate in the company cafeteria. Whom they ate with seemed to the casewriter to depend upon when they and others were free to leave the desk. When two desk men left together, they would usually sit together in the cafeteria, joining friends from other parts of the paper. If a desk man went to lunch alone, he would either join other desk men who were already in the cafeteria, or friends from other parts of the paper, depending upon where seats were vacant.

Fred Dugan, Tom Moore, and Bill Hannigan always went to lunch at different times. Fred usually ate with the assistant managing editor or with other senior personnel. Bill Hannigan usually brought his lunch and ate in a lounge adjoining the cafeteria, reading a competitive newspaper as he ate. Tom Moore also brought his lunch and ate alone in the sports room, which was vacant at that time of day. As he ate, Tom read the *New York Times*.

Activities in the afternoon continued in a fashion similar to those of the morning, although the desk men might seek other diversions if there were a light work load. Will Kennedy and Ed Donahue often worked crossword puzzles. Al Cohn sometimes occupied himself by writing poems, which he then gave Lam Lambert to read. Lam and Al might then spend several minutes discussing possible rhymes and meters.

The general conversation around the desk often shifted to other subjects. On one day it might be Jerry Roberts recounting the retirement party for the 90-year-old church editor who had retired the week before. According to Jerry, "She had been prevailed upon to retire because she had been getting a bit cantankerous in her dealing with the ministers." Another day the conversation might focus on a "think piece" Rolly Perdeaux had written for the Sunday edition on the Algerian problem.[5] Rolly would be the center of attention as he answered questions about the situation and received compliments about the article.

At several points during the day, telephone calls from the general public were received over the regular telephone asking for information about baseball scores or how long it had taken Colonel Glenn to complete one orbit around the earth. The copy editors individually and as a group went to great lengths to attempt to find answers to these questions. Charlie Tallino delighted in telling stories about how he and Will Kennedy had settled barroom brawls over the telephone by providing answers to various queries about sports statistics.

When news was light, a group of former desk men would often congregate around the chute after they had dropped in a feature article or other copy discussing current issues or gossiping about mutual acquaintances with the men on the desk. These sessions were usually characterized by the same humorous banter that prevailed among the copy editors.

Frequently, often as much as once an hour, Joe O'Malley, the city editor, would bring an important breaking story to the news desk himself, usually with a shout explaining the story to everyone within earshot, "There's been a murder in the west end. . . ." "A school bus accident out in [a suburb]. Nobody's seriously hurt, as far as we know. We've got a man on the way out there." Joe would often stop alongside the news desk and chat with the desk men about the local political situation or an important local trial. From time to time he would register a complaint with Fred Dugan, Bill Hannigan, or other desk personnel about the manner in which one of the local stories had been handled. Typical of these complaints was one Joe brought to Ned Carpenter, photo editor:

JOE: Hey, Ned, the caption on the picture of that building that burnt down on the south side isn't right. My man out there said the building was worth $150,000, not $100,000, like you said in the caption. The trouble is the photographer took the picture of the short side of the building. It runs for a block on the other side.

Before Ned could reply, Bill Hannigan, who was seated at the news desk several yards from Ned and Joe, interrupted.

BILL: Joe, what do you guys think they made in that shack, ten dollar bills?

---

[5] The managing editor occasionally asked qualified desk men to write an article of this nature. They were given extra compensation for this work.

Joe laughed at Bill's rebuttal and began talking to him about a political scandal which was being covered in that day's paper. No other mention was made of the caption.

Each of these trips by Joe to the news desk made the casewriter especially aware of the contrast between the two sides of the city room. The men at the news desk spent almost the entire day at their positions, working and talking in quiet conversational tones, even when they were joking with each other. Stories were brought to them by copy boys, rewrite men, and O'Malley. The only other interruptions were the occasional visits of feature writers and other personnel who dropped stories in the chute and chatted quietly. Around the news desk a calm, businesslike atmosphere prevailed. In contrast, the city desk always seemed to be at a high level of motion and noise. Joe O'Malley would be shouting instructions to rewrite men and to reporters across the room; telephones would be ringing interminably; reporters would be standing in a group laughing and talking loudly—all of which contributed to the general din.

On heavy news days the pressure of deadlines became more apparent to the casewriter and he noticed that casual conversation around the news desk became less prevalent. For example, on the day that Colonel John Glenn was welcomed by a huge crowd in New York City, there was also a major airplane disaster. This made it necessary to revise the front page in a matter of less than an hour to give major prominence to the airline accident. Activity around the desk became intense, and unnecessary conversation subsided. The men worked together calmly without outward signs of tension. When the changes had finally been made, Joe O'Malley passed by the desk and remarked, "Well, we took the heat off Glenn by having an airplane crash." This was greeted by laughter as Will Kennedy said, "You've got to be kind of cold-blooded to be a city editor."

The desk men were conscious of working under pressure. Al Cohn recalled his experiences during the Army-McCarthy hearings:

> I had to condense thirty columns of copy into sixteen columns each night for thirty nights. The tension got so terrific I had a skin eruption and had to be out for a month. You can't keep going night after night from midnight to 8 A.M. without let up. Someone else would have had a coronary.

Bill Hannigan indicated that the copy editors worked under more pressure than men on other parts of the paper:

> Different parts of the paper are different. In the business office they have more of a routine. Here and over there (*pointing to the city desk*) we have to worry about the clock, six deadlines a day. With us it is a little more difficult than with them [the city desk] since we make the final decision on whether a story goes in or not. After all this time we get used to the pressure and it doesn't bother us much.

Several men explained that cooperation among desk men was important. Rolly put it this way:

> There is a real spirit of cooperation to get the best results. Everyone knows that three heads are better than one. Teamwork is very important to deal with the semantic problems we work on. If someone's ideas are better than the ones you have, you are glad to accept them. Of course, we all are human and sometimes you are unhappy at a change. I got mad once [30 years ago] when they changed my headline. I'd only been here a few years then.

Larry O'Brien expressed a similar view:

> I've noticed that there seems to be more teamwork on a news desk or city desk than with a comparable business operation. There seems to be an *ésprit de corps*. You may not like some of the people you work with, but I have noticed that here and on other papers we work together.

The casewriter seldom saw persons around the news desk show anger openly. However, on one occasion, one of the feature editors stormed around the news desk, asking why a certain story had not been included in an early edition. The desk men continued their work and seemed not to notice the outburst. After the feature editor had left, Lam Lambert explained, "We just ignore people who do that." Several weeks later Jerry Roberts and Al Cohn became involved in a discussion about working conditions on other newspapers and an argument resulted. As the two began to argue heatedly, Ed Donahue broke in:

> ED: You two want to put on the gloves?
>
> LAM: They argue like a bunch of Unitarians. Being the only Unitarian here, I can speak with authority.
>
> ED: And the only damn Republican.
>
> LAM: Keep your evaluations to yourself.

Ed and Lam exchanged winks, as Jerry and Al changed the topic of conversation and began to reminisce about mutual friends who had retired from *The Times-Herald.*

The desk men frequently discussed the performance of former desk men who had left the desk for various reasons. While these appraisals were usually favorable, a journalism instructor at a local college who had worked on the desk temporarily one summer often came in for critical comment. According to the men on the desk, "He might have been able to teach the stuff, but he sure couldn't do it. . . ." "He was always banging on your ears about his house or about some such thing. He made so much noise sometimes we couldn't get the work out. We thought he would drive us crazy."

In addition to regular news activities, one of the copy editors was assigned each month to maintain the "rack." This was a backlog file of short news items with no time limitations which could be inserted in the paper as filler whenever they were needed. Fred Dugan made this assignment without keeping any formal record of who had performed it in past months. During the period the casewriter was at *The Times-Herald,* Bert Myerson had spent slightly more than a month working on the rack. One afternoon Fred Dugan noticed him working on a stack of material from the rack and said, "Well, I guess I'll have to spring you pretty soon. How long have you been on it? It's been over a month hasn't it?" Bert replied, "Just about."

Two days later, on Bert's day off, Bill Hannigan asked Larry O'Brien to work on the rack for the day. Larry communicated with facial expressions that he was not pleased at the assignment and finally said, "Can't you get someone else, Bill?" Bill nodded his assent and assigned Larry to work on foreign news instead. Several minutes later, when Ed Donahue arrived, he was assigned to the rack for that day. A few days later Fred assigned Lam Lambert to take over the rack from Bert. Shortly after this change was made, the following conversation occurred between Gene Little and Bill Hannigan. Gene had been looking over the rack material stored in the composing room.

GENE: Lam can ease up on the rack. We have loads of material down there.

BILL: O.K., I'll tell him. (*He turned to Lam.*) I think you can lay off that stuff for awhile. Gene thinks we have plenty.

Fred Dugan explained the men's attitude toward the rack:

They consider the rack job onerous, because the rack stuff isn't breaking and exciting, like other news on the desk. They seem to feel the same way about it a reader does when he sees it in the paper. It is filler which can be skipped.

During the course of the day the desk men often made suggestions about handling various stories. The casewriter noticed that when the suggestions were made by Rolly, Lam, Roger, Al, Larry, Jerry, or Will, Fred Dugan and Bill Hannigan listened carefully and often adopted the suggestions. When the suggestions were made by Bert or Ed, Fred and Bill always listened attentively, but never seemed to act on them. Charlie Tallino was not observed making any suggestions, but carried out his work according to original instructions.

At about 3:00 the desk men began to wind up their work, and the men who had arrived earliest put their pencils and equipment into drawers and leisurely got ready to leave. They often stopped to chat with reporters or rewrite men or stayed at the desk reading the paper. By 4:00 the desk men all had gone for the day.

### Other Social Activities

In addition to regular contacts at work, the desk men saw each other outside on several social occasions. They and former copy editors had formed a social club known as the GADS (Gourmets' and Drinkers' Society). Each member contributed fifty cents a month; the proceeds were used to finance two social gatherings for members and their wives, one in the spring and one in the fall. Although responsibility for the planning of these functions was rotated among members, there was one officer, the president-treasurer, Lam Lambert.

The men who worked on the desk also joined other *Times-Herald* editorial department employees for occasional parties. A recent party was organized by several reporters in honor of "Herschel Harshbarger," the mythical character mentioned earlier. Jerry Roberts explained why these parties were held. "We had such a good time at retirement and engagement parties that we decided to get together more often." Since desk personnel lived in different parts of the metropolitan area, they did not see each other frequently except for these organized social events.

### Executives' Evaluation of the Desk's Performance

Both Bob Smith, managing editor, and Fred Dugan told the casewriter that the performance of the desk was satisfactory to them both in terms of the quality of stories and headlines and in terms of the desk's ability to meet deadlines. Fred Dugan explained it this way:

> I think we have a good organization now. Many of the men have been well trained in several positions, so their ability isn't limited and they are able to adjust to any situation which may arise. Beside a knowledge of his position, a desk man must be well rounded, must be able to work quickly, and must have the poise to work under stress. Our men have these qualities; they couldn't be on the desk unless they did.
>
> While reporting and writing may decide the quality of a newspaper, it is the appearance and presentation of these things which attracts the reader. A paper without all of these things is missing 50 percent of its opportunity. Our goal on the desk is to try to make our 50 percent of the task [presentation and appearance] as effective as possible. I believe we now do a good job at these things, but we are always striving to improve.
>
> In the past and on other newspapers the desk is an old man's job, but we can't operate that way on this paper, because the news is moving too quickly for the older men to handle. We have gotten some younger men on the desk, and it is beginning to work well. But finding qualified young men is a problem. There are men around the paper who have worked on the desk during vacations and have done a good job, but they aren't temperamentally suited to desk work. They find the work too confining for them, and therefore I know having them on the desk wouldn't be mutually satisfactory. These men have the ability but not the desire. They would rather be moving, traveling, writing, and seeing their names on by-lines instead of accepting the more confining anonymous life of the copy editor. Of course the copy editor has the advantage of regular hours and no out-of-town assignments as well as a good group of fellows to work with.

## APPENDIX A

## TECHNICAL NOTE ON THE ROLE OF COPY EDITORS

Below are excerpts from *Headlines and Deadlines, A Manual for Copy Editors* by Robert E. Garst and Theodore M. Bernstein, both assistant managing editors of the *New York Times,* which help to explain the position of a copy editor (desk man) in the technology of the newspaper and in the journalism profession, as well as the skills required for this position.[1]

. . . . . . . . . . . . . . . . . . .

### From the Preface

Copy editing is one field in which the demand for workers usually exceeds the supply. This is likely to be permanently so because in an ideal sense there will never be a copy editor who knows enough to fill the requirements of his job thoroughly. The ideal copy editor would not only have a complete mastery over the technical phases of his work, such as the editing of copy and the writing of headlines, but would possess sound and swift judgment, would be an expert rhetorician and grammarian and would be thoroughly versed in government, politics, astrophysics, home gardening, shoes, ships, sealing wax and all subjects that find or are likely to find a place in the kaleidoscopic enterprise that is the modern newspaper.

. . . . . . . . . . . . . . . . . . .

### From Chapter 1, "Newspaper Organization"

The emphasis in newspaper work has long—too long, perhaps—been put upon the reporter. While there is no wish to take from him credit for his many superb contributions to the excellence of the modern newspaper, it ought to be realized that there is a man who stands between him and his critical public—the copy editor. The sparkling, swift, entertaining story, signed by John Jones of *The Daily Star,* draws comment and approbation, but it is not often recognized by even his fellows that the copy editor's share in the creation of the gem may be as great if not greater than that of John Jones, Reporter.

It is not seldom that the wit, ingenuity and craftsmanship of the copy editor rescue from the limbo of unread newspaper stories the uninspired work of John Jones. It is the editorial pencil as much as the reportorial typewriter that puts before the public daily the readable information of the world's happenings. It is the copy editor who is essentially the guardian of what gets into the newspaper and how it looks when it gets there. He detects the errors, corrects the English, cuts out the dead wood of verbiage, tones the story up to its proper pitch or down to the level required by good taste or the libel laws.

The appeal of the reporter's work is great; the activity, the contact with the world, with its great men and with its ideas, make the stimulation of the job unparalleled in any profession. But the copy editor is closer to the heart of the newspaper's power; he is indeed its heart. Under his pencil flow the accounts

---

[1] Robert E. Garst and Theodore M. Bernstein, *Headlines and Deadlines, A Manual for Copy Editors* (New York: Columbia University Press, 1961).

of all important happenings anywhere. This sense of closeness to vital things, plus the capacity to shape information about them so that their importance will be shown in true perspective make the copy desk job second to none.

FROM CHAPTER 2, "THE COPY EDITOR"

Errors creep into newspaper copy from many sources. News passes through many hands; it is garbled in transmission; it is written and rewritten by men of varied ages, education and temperament; it is read and edited under similar conditions. Wrong perspective or partisanship, too much enthusiasm or too little, may handicap a story. The very speed with which newspapers must be printed permits mistakes to slip by the many persons who handle news in its course through the news machine. The continuous struggle of the newspaper is to eliminate errors. Many checks have been set up against them and the chief of these is the copy editor.

The copy editor is virtually the last man between his newspaper and the public. The copy may have been read several times before it reaches him, but its ultimate form, phraseology and spirit rest in his hands. Mistakes or poor writing that pass him are almost certain to reach the reader in print. They may be detected in the office in time to be corrected, but many such blunders are never discovered except by the newspaper reader.

The greatest weapon of the copy editor in his efforts to eliminate errors is an alertness that challenges every fact, every name, virtually every word. Every fact should be checked. Those that appear incorrect and cannot be verified must be eliminated. Statements that are absurd or dangerous are deleted without question. Likewise the facts should be weighed against one another to insure consistency.

The function of the copy editor is critical, not creative. In no circumstances should he rewrite a story completely. If it cannot be saved except by being rewritten, that work should be done by a rewrite man or by the reporter who wrote the original story. The desk man must cope with the material that is given him and make the most of it by recasting, striking out superfluous words, substituting active or colorful words for dead ones, expressing a phrase in a word and by other similar means.

. . . . . . . . . . . . . . . . . . 

With a unanimity that is somewhat disconcerting to the copy editor, reporters profess to regard him as a mutilator of good copy and there is some ground for this opinion. There are some desk men temperamentally unfitted to make the most of another man's writing; their conception of what a story should be is so strong that virtual rewriting is the only course they can follow. Such men must be restrained and if they remain copy editors, trained to the viewpoint of the editorial pencil rather than to that of the reportorial typewriter. The general aim of the copy desk is to preserve as far as possible the words of the reporter, if they express what he desires to convey, and to retain the spirit imparted by him, if it is proper. As the final link in a long and expensive process, the copy editor can destroy the honest work of many reporters.

The business of writing and editing news is a cooperative undertaking, demanding the best of many brains. There is no place for pride of authorship. The desk man should recognize and retain the merits of the story given to him to edit, the reporter should recognize that the copy editor often saves him from grave mistakes and generally improves his work.

. . . . . . . . . . . . . . . . . . . . . .

The education, experience and knowledge of the copy editor cannot be too broad. The more he has learned, seen or knows, the greater his value to the newspaper. He should have a wide knowledge of names, places and events; he must be well-informed in the arts, sciences and social trends; he should know history and literature and be familiar with the machinery of government and laws.

It is imperative that he be acquainted with his own city, if he is an editor of local copy. He must know its geography, its people, its government, its officials, its buildings. If he is an editor of national copy he must have a wide knowledge of national politics, movements, figures and events. Copy editors dealing with legislation in the national or in state capitals should have detailed information about the machinery of legislatures. If the editor is dealing with foreign copy he must know much about the politics, economics and government of the countries concerned and of their recent history at the least. Finally, the copy editor must have common sense. The logic he uses to test the reasonableness of assertions in news stories is the same logic he applies in everyday affairs.

# Stuart Aircraft

"I'VE BECOME quite concerned about the losses in the managerial ranks at our newly acquired CANCOVER [Canadian Coverings Limited] operations," Jim McGregor told the casewriter. McGregor was vice president for manufacturing of Stuart Aircraft, a large West Coast producer of commercial and business jets.

First we lost several Americans that we transferred up there after the acquisition. Now we're losing Fred Colby, sales and purchasing manager at CANCOVER and the top Canadian that we retained, and I'm afraid that after he goes, others will follow. Fred has accepted an offer to head Canadian operations for one of our subcontractors, Banks Tool, at a sizable salary increase. I sure hate to lose him and I'm going to try to talk him out of leaving. I guess Fred really didn't get much salary advance after taxes in the takeover when you consider that the old CANCOVER management paid his country club membership and made arrangements for gas and an automobile. I can remedy that some when I talk to him. But I have a hunch that the only thing that would have interested Fred when we took over was the job at the top, and I was afraid to take that kind of risk with a man I didn't know. Seat covers and interior trim for aircraft may not seem like a big item, and as a percentage of production costs, it's not; but there are a lot of combinations of materials and colors. There are rapid changes in requirements and short lead times. And a couple of commercial jets setting on the apron waiting for interior trim is a very disconcerting sight to a production man. I'm also mad about our profit performance in the six months since we took over and I'm pushing them on that. We're still in the red and when we shut down our Boise plant and bought CANCOVER, we expected a $500,000 annual profit using the Boise cost as a transfer price.

## THE ACQUISITION

In July, 1968, Stuart Aircraft sold their Airfit division located in Boise, Idaho, to Consul Products, a conglomerate. About 20 percent of Airfit's sales were aircraft parts, and about half of this amount was parts for interior trim (seat covers, curtains, partitions, rugs, etc.). Because the workers in the aircraft segment of the business were paid higher wages, Consul had no desire to retain the aircraft operations (which amounted to about $8 million in annual sales). Stuart Aircraft therefore had to find another source of supply for these items.

The alternatives considered initially were:

1. Relocate in Boise, Idaho. This had advantages in terms of work force retention but would result in high labor costs.
2. Move to a site in Salem, Oregon. This would result in lower labor costs but it would take some time to build a plant and an effective organization.
3. Consolidate all interior trim production in Omaha, Nebraska, where 35 percent of Stuart's requirements were produced at the time. However, the Omaha facility was already crowded.
4. Buy the necessary trim from Canadian Covering Limited (CANCOVER), an existing and independent supplier.

In the early fall of 1968, Stuart management discovered the possibility of purchasing the CANCOVER operations in Banff, Alberta. The owners of CANCOVER were all over 60 and anxious to end their responsibilities at CANCOVER; if they sold the company, Canadian tax treatment of capital gains would permit them to retain a large portion of the sale price. To Stuart management this new alternative presented certain advantages: low labor costs in an established organization, tight control over operations, and increased Canadian-produced content of Stuart's jets (a strong tax factor in export sales to Canada). These advantages more than compensated for the additional day of delivery time for parts coming from CANCOVER to the United States due to customs procedures.

After CANCOVER negotiated a three-year union contract with the Canadian local (reaching $3 per hour in the third year), Stuart was able to arrange for a favorable purchase price. The sale was announced on January 5, 1969. One of the former owners immediately flew to Trinidad and bought a beach club, and the other two owners retired to their homes near Banff.

## CANCOVER

### Before Acquisition

Prior to the acquisition by Stuart Aircraft, Canadian Coverings Limited was a small, privately owned firm located in Banff, Alberta. Of the three owners, two had been inactive and the third, Mel Bruce, had become somewhat restless. Fred Colby, sales and purchasing manager, reported directly to Bruce, but in recent years he had acquired considerable latitude in running CANCOVER operations. These operations were characterized by informal organization, control systems, and decision-making procedures. CANCOVER had a reputation as a dependable, high-quality producer of seat covers and other interior trim.

At the time of the purchase by Stuart Aircraft, CANCOVER was producing about 15 percent of Stuart's requirements for trim. These sales represented about 80 percent of CANCOVER's current business; the remaining sales included seats for snowmobiles, interior trim for a small producer of private aircraft, and a subcontract for interior trim for military "spotter" aircraft. Once the news of the sales of the Airfit division broke, management of the Canadian firm moved quickly to seek additional business from Stuart. CANCOVER had been experiencing declining sales for several years. All other major aircraft producers had acquired a captive source of supply for trim. Zarren Aircraft's move to a captive source several years previously had meant the loss of a substantial portion of CANCOVER's business. Employment had fallen from 200 to 65. During the period after the loss of the Zarren contract, management had made a desperate effort to find new sales opportunities but results had been meager and the prospects looked grim.

### Post-Acquisition Developments

The original post-acquisition plan called for continued production of all trim for the Stuart 800 at present locations (15 percent at CANCOVER, 50 percent at Boise in a facility retained by Stuart, 35 percent at Omaha). Upon phase-out of production on the 800 in May, 1969, the Boise facility would be closed, and during a one-month lull before production began on the Stuart 1107 all necessary equipment, material, and staff would be moved to CANCOVER. Prior to that key personnel would travel to Banff occasionally to help CANCOVER "gear up" for their new role. The long-range plan called for building a new plant in Banff to consolidate all of Stuart's trim production at one location.

The first hitch in the plans occurred when Stuart employees at Boise began to leave for other jobs sooner than expected. The final terms of the Airfit sale had included arrangements for 150 hourly workers and 20 supervisors to be retained by Stuart to complete production on the 800 trim prior to closing down in Boise. Charles Bartlett, who had been assistant plant manager in charge of production for Airfit, was retained by Stuart and placed in charge of the Boise trim operations. Bartlett was directed to inform the Stuart personnel in Boise of all alternatives for trim sources, except the negotiations for purchase of CANCOVER. They were also told by Jim McGregor, vice president of manufacturing for Stuart Aircraft, "Stuart will have a job for you," regardless of the outcome of the location decision. The first news of the negotiations for CANCOVER reached some union members at Boise through the international union offices.

Shortly after official announcement of the CANCOVER purchase, Consul Products began a drastic reduction in work force at the former Airfit plant. The hourly payroll was reduced from 3,500 to 1,200, and 300 salaried employees were terminated. Stuart employees in Boise, seeing the possibility of a return to the Airfit operations eliminated, became concerned about their future. Bartlett, who was to become production manager at CANCOVER, relayed the employees' concern to McGregor. He was told that Stuart would pay most relocation costs for all staff members and that the company management particularly wanted five or six key Boise employees to transfer to Banff. Despite these assurances, personnel losses accelerated, forcing a shift of some trim work for the 800 from Boise to Banff.

Stuart was unsuccessful in gaining employee commitments for the move to Canada. Eight or nine key people had been sent to Canada to appraise the prospects but all found the wages, fringe benefits, tax situation, cost of living, and the idea of moving to Canada unappealing. As Tom Anderson, quality control manager at Boise, told the casewriter, "Banff is a beautiful, active town of 25,000 in the summer, but the Americans were seeing it with over 4 feet of snow. I've never seen a place that looked so dead. I thought, 'Maybe spring doesn't even come here.' " Jim McGregor, Charles Bartlett, and Bert Parsons, who was selected as new plant manager for CANCOVER, met on April 30 individually with those key men who were left in Boise. Some of the offers originally made to these men were improved, involving salary increases, even though doing this meant salary inequity problems with some employees of the prior CANCOVER organization. Several American managers received offers of $300–400 per month more than Canadians were receiving at the same level. Still there were no decisions to transfer to Canada, even though continuing personnel losses caused further transfer of 800 trim work to Banff. The work transfer forced some staff members to spend 2–3 days per week in Banff even though they would not move permanently. Stuart managers reassured people that they would be given a job within the company, and interviews at other plants were arranged. However, no Boise personnel accepted offers at other plants. Stuart then offered "extra benefits" to people who would remain at Boise until final closedown. Production at Boise dwindled. Prior to closing, four men, including Charles Bartlett, agreed to transfer to Banff. (See Exhibit 1.)

Meanwhile, back at Banff the Canadians were having some problems. The shift of work from Boise meant not only an increase in volume but an increase in the combinations of colors and styles, making production more complex. This shift placed a strain on a limited production control system already stretched by the changeover to Stuart's mode of operation. Much of the CANCOVER equipment and inventory was outdated and was therefore removed to make room for equipment brought in from Boise. A new production layout had to be developed in an antiquated four-story building with inadequate space and numerous materials handling problems. New products and methods had to be taught simultaneously with a buildup in work force (from 65 hourly employees to over 200 in less than eight months). The push to expand production forced considerable interaction and joint decision making among department managers to resolve

## EXHIBIT 1

### Canadian Covering Ltd., June 10, 1969

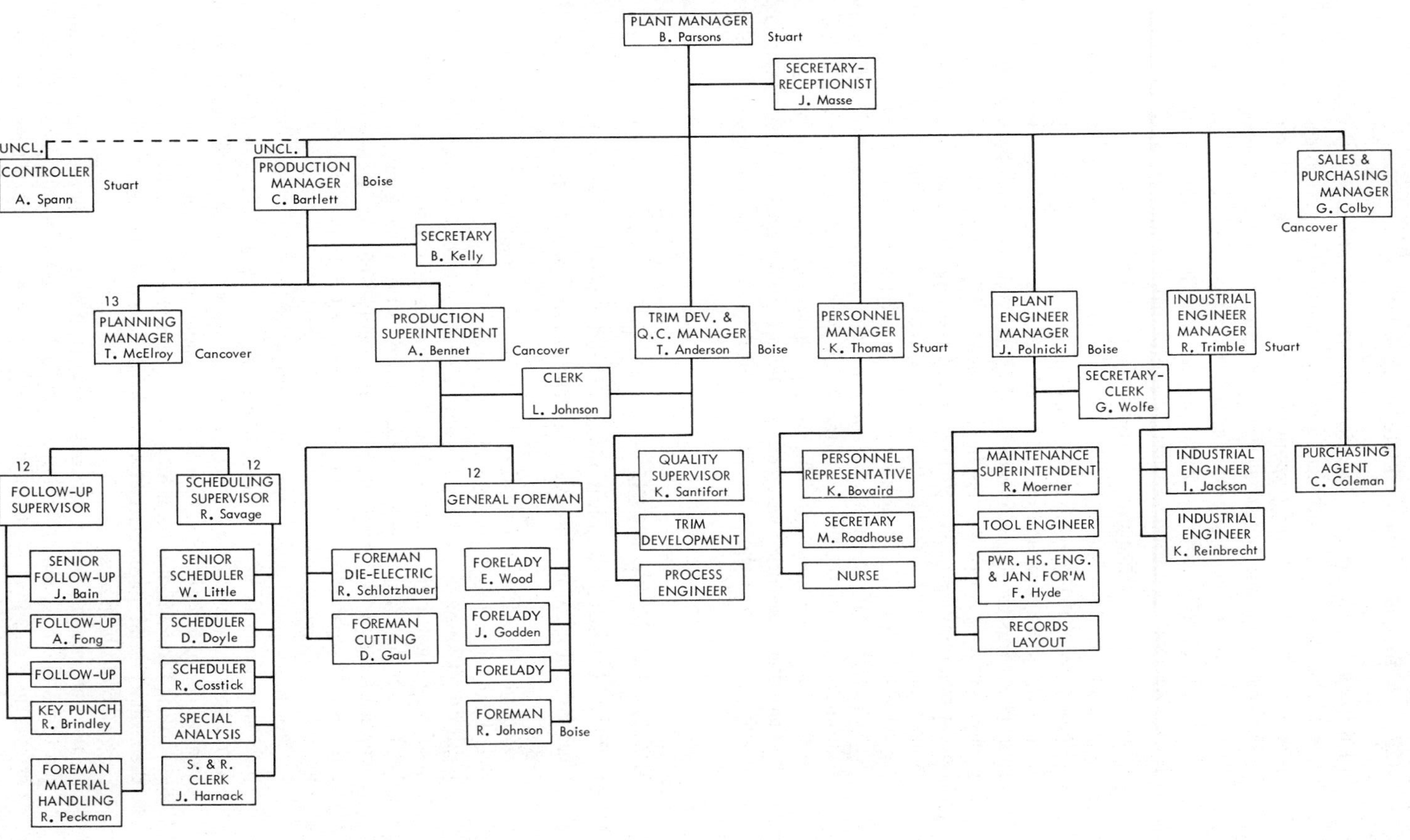

problems such as space allocation, quality of materials, delivery schedules, re-scheduling of production in response to changed requirements from the home office, shifting personnel, and so on. These problems were further complicated by the fact that the managers' offices were spread over three floors of the building. Some antipathy arose between members of the old CANCOVER management and the Americans, particularly those from Boise. As Bob Trimble, industrial engineering manager and an American who had been with Stuart in the United States, put it:

The CANCOVER people are good people. They know their jobs but they have a different approach and different intensity about things. I guess it comes from the diversity of background and ideas. We need to tell them what is expected, but as it is I think they have a feeling of being pushed. We have a pretty headstrong crew here. The people from Boise tend to be argumentative—maybe you got things done there by shouting and really raising sand, but the Canadians are sensitive about it. There's a tendency for the Boise managers to say that the CANCOVER equipment is junk and their methods are backward and the Boise equipment and methods are better. I just find the Boise people tougher and pushier than the Canadians. They're aggressive and tend to grab the show while the Canadians are more reserved. Frankly, I prefer dealing with CANCOVER people. But I think they're a little bit afraid—afraid to talk up—to buck Stuart people.

## THE CANCOVER VIEWPOINT

Tim McElroy, planning manager, a Scot who had been with CANCOVER prior to the takeover, described some of the problems he faced:

Our people have been kind of scared at what might happen—kind of defensive. I talked to Jim McGregor in January and I was pretty well reassured, but I still didn't know what my job would be for a while—I was apprehensive. Economically I got a good deal out of it. Professionally I'm not any worse off and I'm learning to enjoy it. For a while I wasn't sure it was going to go. It's taking some submerging of personalities. I had a pretty free rein all over the production area. Now I've had to learn to keep my nose out of some parts of it and get used to taking orders again.

The Boise plant was a trim facility and a very good one. They had built their own methods and organizations. We operated on a shoestring here and didn't spend money unless we had to since it was a proprietor's place—not like a corporation. We got used to making decisions on the spot and pretty informally—we didn't have to inform a home office and wait around for them to make up their mind. And paperwork—boy!—I wish I could recover half of the cost of paper around here now.

We had enough vanity to think we were doing things the right way and so did they. There's been a tendency to try to overshout people. There's been a lot of overtime and hustle and bustle, and people have gotten tired. You see the switchover to 1107 production started in April and we didn't get the one-month shutdown to get ready because of the extra work from Boise. About that time the flow of information from other plants and the home office was way worse than perfect. It created a lot of problems. Some of those people didn't even know where we were—somewhere north of Seattle.

The one big plus we've had here is that the union is desperate for this to go. It was a case of business coming into Canada from the United States and it's been going the other way a lot in the last few years. People took it as a challenge and their pride was on the line. Stuart was putting their bets on a Canadian outfit and people wanted to make it work. Remember too that our business had really declined—we had gone from 200 down to 65 people in the last several years. So Stuart coming in here was like a shot of adrenalin. We're already back to 200 and will add even more. The pay for women is good—probably the best in the area—and we're probably in the top quarter on men's pay. So the hourly people are behind us. Developing trust is the key to the thing and developing some friendships—getting almost to a family sort of arrangement.

Fred Colby, sales and purchasing manager, had been with CANCOVER for over thirty years prior to the Stuart takeover. He was leaving to become manager of an aircraft parts supplier in a nearby town:

I've never worked for anyone else since I was a kid. Before the takeover I worked for a family company directly for the owner. I want to see if I can take over and do the whole job as boss . . . and of course there's money involved too. It's a desire on my part to see just what my capabilities are. Even before Stuart I was interested but I just couldn't leave them. I had a pretty free rein before and a lot of responsibility, but now with Bert (the plant manager) and Charles (Bartlett) here I've gotten frustrated, I guess. I guess I just feel like they don't need me. Really deep down that's it. This other company has been after me for a while and finally I talked to them. The job is managing director of Canadian operations and the salary is far more than my needs. Well, after a couple of visits and some sleepless nights I said "O.K."

You know, Charles (Bartlett) ran the show at Boise and he has the same problems as I have. I was into everything and all of a sudden you don't have the authority. The American personnel naturally did things differently but I must say we did a few things right here. I've told Charles Bartlett and his men, "Just because you did it that way in Boise doesn't make it right."

It's kind of hard to wait on decisions from a home office after so many years of making them all on the spot. It must be rough on Tim (McElroy) because his job of production planning is one of the roughest jobs in Stuart. A mistake there can stop the entire delivery schedule. He's had a lot of information problems . . . who to contact for this or that. I notice he goes ahead and does something and then—boom "What have I done?"

## THE VIEWPOINT OF STUART MANAGERS

Charles Bartlett, the new production manager at CANCOVER, had lunch with the casewriter, during which he talked with pride about the educational accomplishments of his children, who were in graduate school in the United States. He talked also about his and his wife's activities in scouts, church, and other community activities with "the kids." They had not formed many new relationships since coming to Banff. Bartlett was described by other Stuart managers as hard driving, powerful, and very loyal to his Boise people. He talked at length about the problems these men had faced during the phase-out and how he regretted that most of them had left Stuart. Bartlett's regret suggested a feeling of responsibility for their rights:

I wish I could have done more for them. I tried to help them as much as possible. I still get calls from companies asking about them. I thought all the people who came here were treated well on economics but they are all leaving. Tom Anderson's (development and quality control manager) wife just wouldn't make the move. He came up hoping she would relent. He gave it a try but she had a job making about $5,000 a year working a couple of days a week as a tool designer. Another fellow, a young foreman named Johnson, had some problems with his love life and left. This is kind of an isolated place for a bachelor.

Just recently John Polnicki (plant engineering manager from Boise) accepted an offer from another company in the States. He had just bought a house here the week before but the offer was too good to turn down. So now I'm the only one from Boise who'll be left when Tom and John leave this month. I came because the other interesting jobs required relocation and also to maintain service with the company. I've been with them about 30 years. I lost money on the transfer after taxes, which are a lot higher here, but I was hoping for a bit slower pace on the job. It's been hectic traveling back and forth between plants and kind of hard to adapt to the new organization. We've had to be careful not to say, "This is the way we did it in Boise." I'm not completely relaxed in my job now and it's very disappointing to me to see Tom and John leave. I'll be all alone then and I feel trapped and caged in. I'll miss having someone I can talk to. Usually when a manager goes to a new place he takes along someone he can depend on—someone who talks the same language. It helps a lot. Those things are choking me, but maybe I'll get over it. I can't help but wonder if I've made the right decisions, but I feel morally committed to the company.

The plant controller, Art Spann, was a Canadian who had been with Stuart since receiving his Master's degree in management from MIT in the early 1960s. Spann reported directly to the corporate controller rather than to the plant manager. He strongly felt his responsibility for installing adequate control and reporting systems at Banff. He talked about the problems he had experienced at CANCOVER:

Records were in bad shape, Even the payroll was sloppy. Fringes were a mess. Hall (the bookkeeper) had been here for 40–45 years and it was hard to get him to change because of his age . . . and he's a little stubborn. It's not easy for him to change and understand the new systems.

They never had a standard cost system, so we started trying to get some labor distributions from the floor and it has been a real hassle. There's still resistance . . . they look on it as a waste of time. The main resistance is that they don't know the reasons for it and the second is the pressure for production. The girl foremen are worse than the men because the men are from other companies where they got used to it. Basically production comes first and finance is a poor second but we're going to make it work. There's no choice about it.

## MANAGERIAL CONFRONTATION

A meeting of the managers in Plant Manager Bert Parson's office produced several heated exchanges between Art Spann and Charles Bartlett over foreman training and reporting procedures, and between Bartlett and Fred Colby over vendor and material quality problems. Bartlett appeared to win both arguments by forcefully burying both opponents under a long recitation of the problems which they were causing him in his efforts to increase production.

Bert Parsons, plant manager, discussed his views of the situation after the meeting:

I'm happy about the apparent attitude of the hourly worker. They have been very cooperative and have worked hard to get this thing going. This pleases me no end. I just hope we don't ruin it. But this management thing . . . I've never worked with such a hard-headed group. We'd do a better job if these guys didn't fight all the time. Art Spann is very, very critical of poor bookkeeping in the time sheets and so on. He's got reason to be concerned. But I'm concerned about the problem and we're doing our best and we're working on this thing. But this fighting business is tough and I'm fed up. And I've gotten tough with Art a couple of times. I've had the most trouble with the Boise people. I've often said, "What are we fighting about? We're just discussing this thing." But Charles is a great one for the sky is falling stuff. He has a tendency to grab the show. At Boise the way to get things done was to shout and make things sound as rough as possible. That may sound strange but that's the way the atmosphere was there. It's been rough enough here as it is. There's been a lot of pressure on people to get production up to our planned levels and now we're losing key people. Fred Colby is going to the home office next week to talk to Jim McGregor and I'm still hopeful that we can change his mind. I've tried using him as an unofficial trouble shooter but he has been frustrated by a loss of responsibility. Fred is also pretty involved in local society and we've got a mismatch in titles with the other companies here. For example, I'm just a plant manager, whereas most of the other plants around are run by VP's. This can be a big thing in small-town social circles.

# Textile Corporation of America

IN 1963 the Textile Corporation of America (TEXCORP) was formed from three family-owned companies: (1) Smith-Abbott Mills, centered in Fitchburg, Massachusetts, and directed by William Abbott; (2) North Carolina Mills, owned by the Ford family and headed by Robert Ford; (3) Carolina Cotton Company, a single large mill located in South Carolina and owned by John Rand. The three family companies had not been direct competitors. Smith-Abbott Mills produced high-grade spun rayon and wool blended fabric, North Carolina Mills specialized in fine cotton fabrics and staple synthetic fabrics, and the Carolina Cotton Company made high-quality print cloth. By combining their firms' resources, Abbott, Ford, and Rand became owners of a major firm in the fine textiles industry, with sales in 1963 of 45 million.

Due to family loyalties and the strength of long-standing reporting relationships, TEXCORP existed as a single company in name only. Few functions were integrated, although accounting for all three firms was done at the corporate office in New York City. Because his North Carolina Mills represented the largest portion of the TEXCORP (1963 sales of 25 million), Robert Ford and his management team were able to dominate the company through 1966. William Abbott, the wealthy owner of Smith-Abbott Mills, avoided direct participation in TEXCORP management. He kept an office in the New York headquarters, attended board meetings, and watched the Fitchburg operations, but much of his time was spent vacationing in Europe or playing golf. In 1967, Mr. Abbott decided to spend more time in New York City.

By 1967 it was clear that the fine cotton fabric market was declining in importance in the United States. In June of 1967, representatives of the National Chemical Company were approached by TEXCORP management at the suggestion of William Abbott. National Chemical was a multinational corporation with 1967 sales of over $2 billion. They had recently begun to diversify into nonchemical markets, and several TEXCORP executives were personal friends of National executives. These informal relationships led to official discussions, and National Chemical purchased TEXCORP in early 1968.

In the exchange of TEXCORP stock for National Chemical stock, all of the directors of TEXCORP became wealthy men. TEXCORP's directors controlled 68 percent of the voting stock of the company when it was purchased by National Chemical. William Abbott became one of the largest individual shareholders of National Chemical common stock. Robert Ford, then 65 years old, agreed to step down as President of TEXCORP and William Abbott became the chief executive. Mr. Ford, although not entirely happy with the management arrangements, had considerable financial security in that his family's trust fund now owned over $10 million of National Chemical stock. Richard Hicks, the National Chemical vice president responsible for TEXCORP, felt that Mr. Abbott would make a better chief executive than Ford, and encouraged the management transition. Abbott made several organizational changes himself at this time. Andrew Thompson, who had been the star salesman for Smith-Abbott Mills, was promoted to vice president of sales for Smith-Abbott Mills. Walter Hogan, a former plant manager for Smith-Abbott Mills, became vice president of manufacturing.

TEXCORP's sales in 1967 had risen to $65 million. Profits had grown from 1963 through 1966, but had dipped somewhat in 1967 to $2 million. Exhibit 1 outlines the TEXCORP organization in February of 1968, and Exhibit 2 presents the background of key personnel.

### John Mitchell, MBA

John Mitchell, 27, was married and had one child. He grew up in Darien, Connecticut, and graduated from Harvard College in 1963. Mitchell had chosen Harvard because it was supposed to be a very liberal school. For the first two years he remained conservative, but during his junior and senior years he committed himself as a political liberal. He took courses in religion and psychology and briefly considered being a minister. After graduation he thought about entering law school or medical school, but his father wanted him to go to HBS. After receiving his MBA in 1965, he joined a Peace Corp project in the Far East, where he taught industrial psychology.

John Mitchell liked to think of himself as good at the "gamesmanship" of life. His interest in psychology led to a certain degree of introspection and he prided himself on his ability to describe the games people played. In high school, for example, Mitchell was often called an "apple polisher" because his school work seemed to follow the particular concerns of his various teachers. He was a straight-A student. In college, he hardly ever cut classes, and was a Dean's List student for four years. He was active in athletics, and was a starting fullback for the Harvard team. John Mitchell even considered football a "psychological game." Commenting on his football experiences, he said:

> If the coach was in a mean mood, you growl and hit somebody . . . if not, you joke and try and have fun. Hell, the guys that were on the field to make the

**EXHIBIT 1**

February 1968: TEXCORP Organization

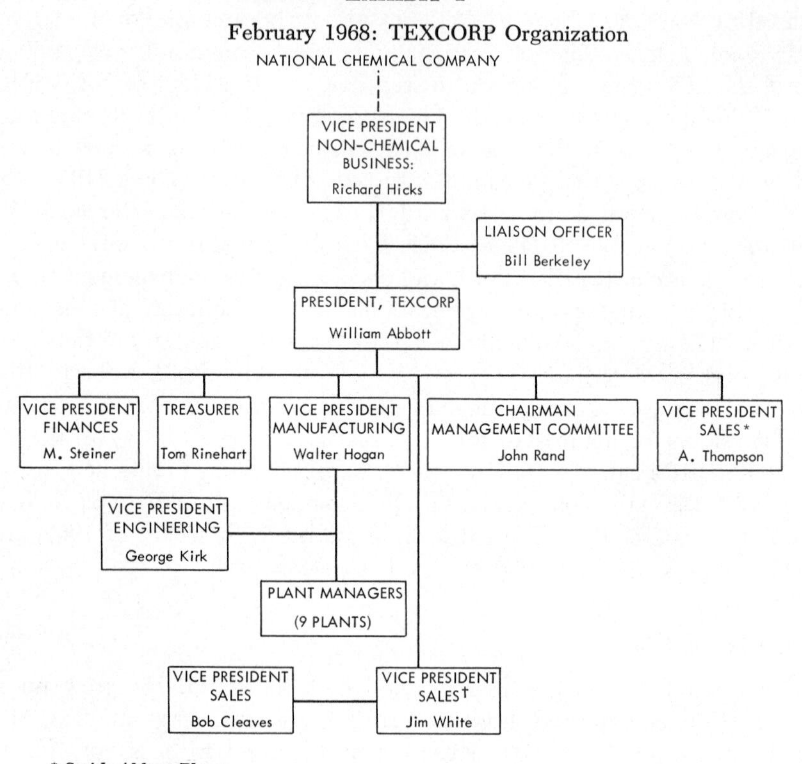


* Smith-Abbott Plant
† North Carolina Mills

big plays not only *did* the right thing in practice, but *thought* and *said* the right thing too. . . . It's all a fantastically complicated game.

Mitchell earned a varsity letter each year in college.

Mitchell's experiences overseas strengthened his political "liberalism" (labeled "radicalism" by his mother). While at the Business School, he had participated in many lengthy discussions about the businessman's social responsibilities. John Mitchell was sometimes shocked by what he considered to be the narrow-mindedness of some of his classmates, and he often wondered if the business world could offer him the satisfactions he believed he needed in life.

His interest in psychology eventually led Mitchell to a one-year research project while at the Harvard Business School, and the co-authorship of a book on psychological aspects of motivation.

In 1968 Mitchell decided to return to the United States. He did not think he had the patience to be an effective teacher, although he had been very successful as a teacher in the Peace Corps. The business world

**EXHIBIT 2**

Personal Background of TEXCORP Personnel

| *Name* | *Age* | *Background* |
|---|---|---|
| William Abbott* | 55 | Former president of Smith-Abbot Mills, ex All-American football player from Princeton, independently wealthy. |
| Andrew Thompson | 41 | Former salesman for Smith-Abbott Mills, former professional golfer, long-time friend of William Abbott. |
| Walter Hogan* | 62 | Former plant manager of Smith-Abbott Mills, former football coach, long-time friend of William Abbott and Mr. Abbott's father. (Founder of Smith-Abbott Mills.) |
| John Rand* | 66 | Former president of Carolina Cotton, Harvard College '25, independently wealthy. |
| Martin Steiner | 42 | Former chief financial officer for North Carolina Mills. |
| George Kirk | 45 | Hired in 1964, chief engineer for four TEXCORP engineers, offices located in North Carolina. |
| Sam Jarvis* | 54 | Plant manager of Carolina Cotton Plant, brother-in-law of John Rand. |
| Bob Hogan | 36 | Plant manager of Smith-Abbott Mills, son of Walter Hogan. |
| Jim White | 55 | Former sales manager of North Carolina Mills. |
| Bob Cleaves* | 42 | Former president of a small textile company bought out by TEXCORP in 1964, independently wealthy, a bachelor. |
| Tom Rinehart* | 63 | Treasurer of TEXCORP, former treasurer of North Carolina Mills. |
| Bill Davis | 50 | Plant manager of largest North Carolina Mills plant, appointed in 1965, son-in-law of John Rand. |
| Bill Berkeley | 29 | MBA from Berkeley, hired by National Chemical in 1967, worked for Hicks since December, 1967. |
| Richard Hicks | 50 | Vice president of National Chemical, HBS class of '49, known as a "real professional" to other National Chemical executives. |

* Indicates that an employment contract was in effect. (These contracts lasted through 1971 and guaranteed the men salaries ranging from $40,000–$70,000 per year.)

in the United States in 1968 further challenged him because of the new emphasis being placed on social responsibility. Mitchell hoped he could find a job that offered an outlet for his growing social conscience. Also, he was anxious to test himself in a real business organization:

> I wanted to see if I could compete with my classmates from HBS. But at the same time I love travel, love other cultures. But I kept wondering, if I were back in the States, would I be such a hot shot?

### National Chemical Company

Richard Hicks, the vice president of National Chemical and responsible for TEXCORP, heard about Mitchell through family friends. Hicks was in charge of National's nonchemical operations, and he wrote Mitchell and asked him to come to National Chemical's offices in New York to talk about the company's operations overseas. When they met, Mitchell told Hicks that the chemical industry didn't really interest him, because it was dominated by large corporations; however, after many meetings and several offers, Mitchell agreed to go to work as assistant to the president of TEXCORP, William Abbott. Mitchell would be trained for a year in the textile business and then go to a textile mill that National was planning to buy overseas. The job sounded ideal to Mitchell. He could test himself in the world of big business and also indulge his interest in travel and living abroad. The Mitchells rented a small house in Darien.

In July of 1968, Mitchell went to work at TEXCORP, which was located in an office building about ten blocks from the National Chemical headquarters in New York. William Abbott had been told very little about his new assistant, except that he was to train him for a year. Since Mitchell knew nothing about the textile business, he asked to spend two months in the mills—part of this time as a loom operator, which he did, even though this was theoretically against union regulations.

Mitchell's initial impressions about TEXCORP and TEXCORP management were very favorable. Andrew Thompson, the VP in charge of textile products and the number two man at TEXCORP, was a very outgoing and personable man, and Mr. Abbott told Mitchell to see Thompson if there were any "problem" with his training. John Mitchell spent most of his time at the large Smith-Abbott Mill in Fitchburg. Although the workers believed him to be a "spy from the chemical company" at first, they soon relaxed and Mitchell developed several strong friendships. Since he was living in a motel in Fitchburg without his family, he spent 12 to 14 hours a day at the mill and got to know the personnel on both the day and the night shifts.

When he returned to New York in September, Mitchell found that there was nothing planned for him to do. Although Abbott spoke to him every day in his office for about 20 minutes in order to find out how he was getting along, Mitchell felt that no one was really interested in what he did. Consequently, he willingly accepted responsibility for helping to collect and organize the financial figures for the first TEXCORP five-year plan. (Systematic planning was one of the most well developed management techniques at National Chemical.)

Mitchell was beginning to learn more about headquarters personnel at TEXCORP. He observed that four offices, which he called "Executive Row," were large, spacious, and thickly carpeted, while the rest of the TEXCORP offices were relatively modest. The four offices were occupied by William Abbott, Walter Hogan, John Rand, and Tom Rinehart. Mitchell was surprised to discover that Rand and Rinehart were rarely involved in the regular management meetings, and Hogan was not highly respected by many of the headquarters personnel.

Although he got along well with all the TEXCORP executives, Mitchell found that he had too little in common with them to spend much time socializing:

> I was too young and unimportant. Also, I didn't play golf and I didn't drink. I had tomato juice at lunch while they were boozing it up.

Bill Berkeley, who was the "liaison man" assigned to TEXCORP by Richard Hicks, became Mitchell's closest friend, since they were the same age approximately, and the only men at TEXCORP under 40. Also, both Mitchell and Berkeley reported to Hicks:

> Bill Berkeley and I got along very well. . . . Berkeley spent half of every day over at TEXCORP talking to Abbott or one of the financial VP's about liaison work. You know, fill this form in, the appropriations meeting is next month, etc.

Mitchell was distressed at the unsophisticated level of management he found at TEXCORP, and he developed the habit of having long, one-sided conversations with his wife when he arrived home each evening:

> What a day! Discovered that I was the only—get this!—the only guy who could use a slide rule in TEXCORP, except for Kirk . . . But he's an engineer . . . I don't know. It sure seems like some of those men waste a lot of time and stuff trying to butter-up Bill Abbott, and there's so little real *analysis*. Hell, no!! I'm not "buttering him up" with my slide rule! You ever tried doing 20 discounted cash flows without one!?!

As October wore on, John Mitchell began to feel frustrated and bored. One day he went around the TEXCORP office asking executives if they had any jobs or projects he might help them with. He spent a day filing expense reports, and three days drawing graphs and charts showing loom utilization for the first half of 1968. He later told his wife:

It's kind of dull right now. I didn't think it would be like this. What? Sure, I've talked to Andy. He doesn't know what to do with me. Let's face it . . . none of them really know what to do with me. First I was a "spy," you know. Now I'm a "bright kid with a lot of potential." I don't want to be underfoot all the time. You can only ask a guy for work so many times, then you just have to try and make work. What a drag.

And, in early November:

Well, I finally talked to Andy today. Told him I was really going out of my mind. And I talked to Bob Cleaves. Anyway, they both told me I should lay it on the line to Abbott. "Talk to him at Oscar's," they said. (Oscar's was a large bar and restaurant often frequented by TEXCORP executives.) I'm going to ask him for more responsibility. Hell, I've got absolutely zero now. He must know how I feel . . . but he's so damn silent. No one ever knows what's on his mind. . . . Except Andy, of course. Those two are like father and son.

Because William Abbott seemed constantly preoccupied and was often out of the office, Mitchell was reluctant to speak to him about his job. ("If I catch him wrong, he'll just see me as a complainer, or, worse, an overly ambitious 'whiz kid,'" he explained to his wife.) Abbott ran TEXCORP with the help of the two executives who had come with him from Smith-Abbott Mills in Fitchburg, Andrew Thompson and Walter Hogan. Thompson and Abbott were particularly close, and virtually all company decisions were made by these two men. Abbott had also continued to direct Smith-Abbott Mills personally, and he and Thompson spent five to eight days a month in Fitchburg. Finally, in mid-December, Mitchell followed Thompson's advice and asked William Abbott if he could speak to him at Oscar's after work.

Mitchell discovered that his boss was much easier to talk to at Oscar's. Abbott liked to drink, and Mitchell found it relatively easy to ask his boss for a line position with specific responsibilities. Abbott replied that he would like to have a boy like Mitchell on his "team" and would give him a position if he would pledge to stay "with him" for three years. As the evening progressed, Mitchell observed that Abbott spoke more and more about "loyalty" and the value of a man who would "stick it out." Mitchell was reluctant to commit himself to any time period, and at 10:30, when the two left Oscar's, he remarked that he would "certainly stick it out if things went well."

During the second week of November, Mitchell had spoken to Richard Hicks. It was their first meeting since July, and Mitchell had requested it because he had heard that the National Chemical Company's plans to purchase an overseas textile firm had "fallen through." Richard Hicks' dynamic personality had been a large part of Mitchell's decision to work at TEXCORP and he enjoyed the 30-minute meeting with the National Chemical vice president. However, he learned that plans for expansion into overseas textiles had been delayed indefinitely. That night he warned his wife:

> Don't pack those bags for Europe, Baby; probably will never need them. Yeah, the deal fell through . . . looks like it's TEXCORP or nothing. . . . Anyway, the glamour has worn off a little; how about you? Good, if things go well, maybe we can rent a little bigger house next year.

This change in Mitchell's original career goals forced him to examine his present situation at TEXCORP even more closely.

## TEXCORP PERFORMANCE

For the next month, Mitchell continued to make work for himself. In order to keep completely busy, he fulfilled a long-time desire and signed on as a volunteer consultant for the New York Urban Coalition. Beginning in December, Mitchell spent at least two nights a week working late in New York City. He found the excitement and satisfaction of volunteer work made his late arrival home almost worthwhile. (Mitchell often skipped dinner and arrived home at midnight.) But in December, the November financial statements were released and the usual good humor in the TEXCORP offices became strained. Sales had dropped sharply, and most of the plants were losing money:

> They're all waiting for some kind of axe to fall from Hicks. Man, were the figures rotten. One of our plants was showing a 22 percent loss before taxes! I don't know what National is going to do, but I hope they do it fast. What do you mean, *I* should do something?! Who am I? Anyway, I think there is a project I could do.

The disappointing financial statements brought no immediate response from the Chemical company. TEXCORP managers, however, began to express their concern to Mitchell. Andrew Thompson and Walter Hogan pointed to the relatively stable performance of the Smith-Abbott plants, and at management meetings they emphasized the need to upgrade the plant efficiency at Carolina Cotton. Sam Jarvis, Carolina's plant manager, complained openly to Mitchell and other TEXCORP executives that his product mix was unprofitable because several North Carolina Mills plants were now producing what he used to produce and he was never given the money he needed to buy needed new equipment, Bill Berkeley spent two or three days each week at the TEXCORP executive offices. Berkeley and Mitchell often spoke about TEXCORP organizational problems and the need for reform. Berkeley was often asked what, if anything, the Chemical company was going to do about TEXCORP in light of the poor operating statistics, and his usual reply was one of assurance. "Calm down, fellas," Mitchell heard him say. "Just get out there and sell a little, and we'll do all right." Privately Berkeley admitted to Mitchell that he knew Hicks was concerned about the poor performance, but he didn't know if major policy changes were planned.

By the end of December, it was obvious that the year-end financial statements would also show sharp declines in sales and profitability. Although Andrew Thompson was beginning a two-week vacation in California and William Abbott was on a week's vacation in Florida, John Mitchell decided to put together a marketing research study of TEXCORP'S two biggest plants. Rather than "clear" this study with the two absent executives, he approached the two plant managers involved and they responded enthusiastically to his proposed studies. For the next several weeks, Mitchell spent most of his time in Fitchburg and South Carolina (the location of the two plants he decided to study).

The poor performance reflected in the late 1968 financial reports prompted a minor TEXCORP reorganization in December. Mr. Hicks moved to create operating divisions and attempted to formally alter the old family reporting and communications channels. After close consultation with William Abbott, he announced the formation of temporary committees to run three operating divisions. Each committee would have a chairman, and the chairmanship would rotate every quarter. It was understood that this was a short-term and temporary arrangement, and that permanent division managers would be appointed as soon as possible. Andrew Thompson was made chairman of the Consumer Products Division (primarily high-grade spun rayon and wool blends), Jim White (former VP of sales for the South Carolina Mills) was made chairman of the Industrial Products Division (fine cottons and synthetic fabrics), and the chairmanship of the Specialty Products Division was left vacant. Exhibit 3 illustrates the new organization. This chart was drawn up by Bill Berkeley, but was never identified as "official." The presence of the "unofficial reorganization chart," however, was known and accepted by TEXCORP executives.

Mitchell completed his first marketing study in mid-January. The study included an analysis of profitability by product line and by major customer, and was enthusiastically accepted by the plant manager. Mitchell sent a copy of his study to William Abbott but Mr. Abbott did not comment on it.

### A Request for Promotion

John Mitchell was growing increasingly impatient. He had developed a close relationship with Mary Fagan, the president's secretary, and the two often had coffee together in the cafeteria in the basement of the TEXCORP office building. Mtichell found Mary a perceptive and intelligent girl, and soon he was discussing a wide range of company problems with her:

You know, if it weren't for Mary, I think I'd go nuts in the office. Today we talked about Kirk. She agreed with me that he's a brilliant engineer . . . but really out of sight when it comes to company politics. You know, he calls Mary from his engineering offices (located in North Carolina) just to find out what kind of a mood Abbott is in before calling him. And today he called me and asked who was meeting in the board room. He'd heard there was this big meeting and he wondered why he hadn't been invited.

The reorganization of TEXCORP into divisions had not, in Mitchell's opinion, straightened out the most serious company problems. Lines of authority were still unclear. Old, informal relationships still prevailed over the new (and as yet "unofficial") lines of communication. Abbott and Thompson continued to make most of the decisions. And overall marketing and sales objectives were left undefined. Mitchell became more and more disgusted with his situation:

I've decided that TEXCORP reminds me of a country club. Abbott and Thompson are both top golfers. They must spend $300 a month taking customers, friends, etc., golfing. And when it comes time to make a few decisions, they do it like they might select an iron. You know, squint down the fairway, laugh a little, say "What the hell," and blast away. I'm convinced there are three or four of our top executives who ought to be retired . . . permanently . . . but Abbott could no more do that than he could give up his booze or his golf . . . Yeah, I am depressed . . .

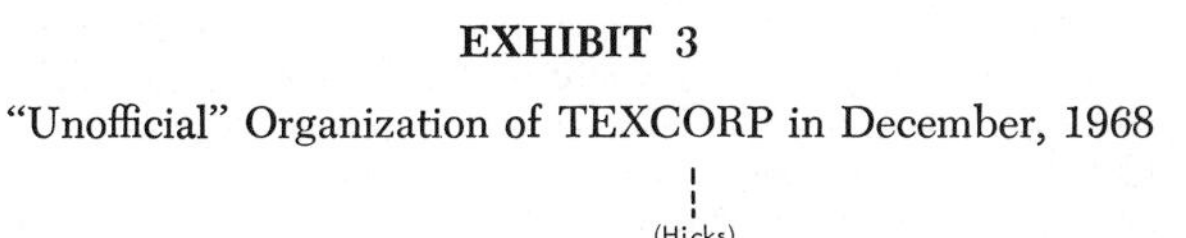

**EXHIBIT 3**

"Unofficial" Organization of TEXCORP in December, 1968

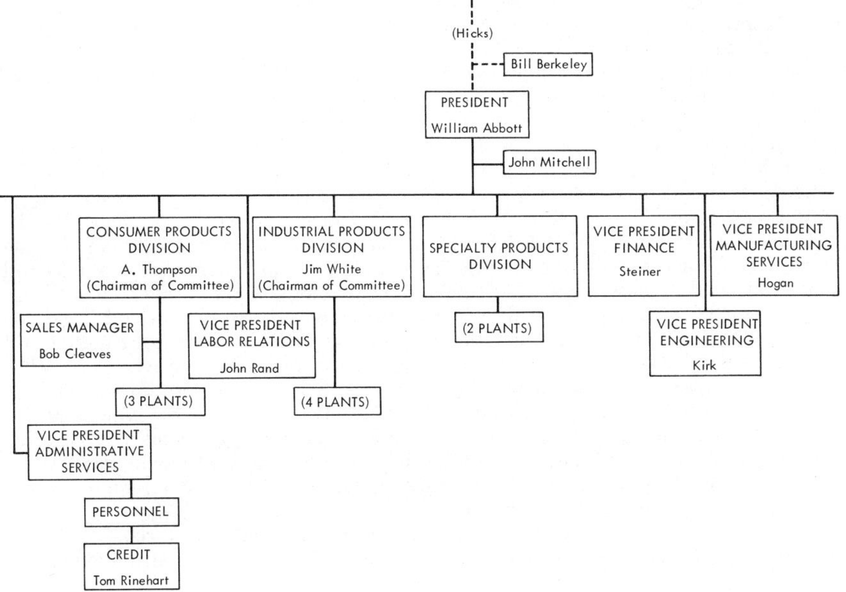

Prompted by his continued frustration and the company reorganization Mitchell decided to write Andrew Thompson a letter asking for a new job. He anticipated that Thompson would show the letter to William Abbott. It is reproduced as Exhibit 4.

**EXHIBIT 4**

John Mitchell's letter to
Andrew Thompson, dated January 13, 1969

Dear Andy,

I hope this note will help you understand my as yet unresolved anxieties concerning my future here in TEXCORP. I am putting this in writing to save your time and to facilitate any further discussions. Let me try and describe my perspective.

First, I see a lot of work to be done at all levels of the organization. Much of this work is a matter of analysis (data collection, organization, setting priorities, etc.). Systems must be set up, studies made, programs established and monitored, etc.

Second, I see a limited number of people with the background and training to accomplish all of the analytical work that has to be done.

Third, I see myself and my own selfish goals. I have spent all of my lengthy (four year) business career doing analytical staff work. I have developed a certain facility for this kind of work. But it no longer offers the challenge I desire. I want to assume more complete responsibilities. I want to be a boss. I want to be able to look back and say, "Look, I did that . . . that's my success." When I spoke to you earlier, I hoped you might have a line position for me in your division. I have been told—and I am forced to agree—that I lack the experience to be a line manager in Sales or in Manufacturing. Those are the only two lines at the divisional level.

Given what I see around me, I conclude that from the organization's point of view, I should be in a position where I could move freely about; conduct market studies in the divisions, assist Engineering in plant relocation studies, help establish systems and procedures, etc. (As William would say, "For Chrissake, John, we have so much to do, let's just do it!") I would need some source and position of authority that everyone saw as "legitimate" so that cooperation would be maximized. I guess my present status and title of "Assistant to the President" seems best suited to these organizational needs.

From a personal point of view, however, this role is less than ideal. William, I suspect, has never quite known what to do with me. I am always a little "in the way" or "under foot." My duties too often dissolve into those of a clerk-secretary-adding machine. I bear much responsibility for this, I will admit. I haven't tried to be "pushy" and I have avoided playing too many games with too many people. And I have paid a personal price: boredom. The frustration I can handle; the boredom slowly destroys me. All of this has been changing, but the deeper I get into the problems and the personalties, the less secure any "assistant to" position becomes. As your assistant, for example, a careful (and probably not very convincing) explanation would have to go out if I were to involve myself in the Industrial Products or Specialty divisions. I guess it comes down to the fact that I don't think being anyone's assistant will offer me the kinds of challenges I desire. (Man, this is sounding more and more presumptuous and egotistical every minute.) Anyway—from my own standpoint, I would like to be in the position of Vice President of Administrative Services. Here I would have the challenge of line responsibility and the opportunity to test myself. (Although I still wouldn't have the kind of "line" challenge and satisfaction you have when you sell a good fabric order, or a plant manager has when he reads the bottom line of his P&L statement.) In charge of administration I would still have both the time and the authority to conduct the needed analytical studies and services. I would be available to all departments—both informally and formally. In this position I would also be able to involve myself in those kinds of administrative tasks that do not require twenty years of experience in the textile business.

Before you laugh at my conceit, let me explain why I think it's a reasonable gamble from the organization's point of view. We all agreed some time ago that the job should

**EXHIBIT 4—*Continued***

be created. We knew that systems were needed and that a man was needed to supervise these tasks as well as Purchasing and Credit (neither of which involve close or imaginative supervision). Bill Berkeley can handle the job, and I've heard his name mentioned. But he has said "No" to both of us privately, and I doubt anyone will change his mind.

"NOW WAIT A MINUTE!! You really want me to say you can be VP of Administrative Services?!?!" Yes, I'm only 27 (But, just think! I'll be 28 in June!) Yes, I just started shaving last year. Yes, only six months in textiles . . . only six months in this company. I realize William is the man to talk to in the end. It's his ball game. But with your understanding and support, my feelings, expectations, and anxieties can be more carefully presented to him. Anyway, I've got enough guts to think I can do a better job there than anyone else we've got. And I don't think it's the kind of position that a new man would be able to take over. I'd be the lowest paid VP in the city, and that'll help our budgets.

I'd like to speak with you about this note and try to cover the 100 other questions that arise from my cocky, impertinent ambition before approaching William.

If and when you show this to William, remind him he once told me to stick around because "the way we are, there are plenty of opportunities to learn." Remind him he said that, and then ask him how he learned to catch a football.

John

Mitchell continued to work on his final marketing study. It was completed in February and focused on the declining profitability of the large Smith-Abbott Mill in Fitchburg. Using it as an excuse to talk to William Abbott, he tried to broach the subject of the unfilled position of administrative vice president. Mr. Abbott ignored Mitchell's casual inquiries, and at the end of February Mitchell's letter of January 11 still remained unanswered.

Well, scratch one effort. I guess they couldn't have made me any vice president. Who did I think I was . . . Oh well, it sounded good at the time. Here I am. A guy's who's supposed to be an expert in human relations. And I'm tied up in knots by a bunch of dumb playboys! I can't figure it out. One day I think I know why Hicks hasn't done anything. I see a little spark of hope for Abbott. And the next day I hear that Abbott has gone and wasted more money on a project that has no chance of success. You should hear the other executives talk about him. They're all losing confidence. And, you know, he hasn't called me into his office in almost three weeks now. Hell, he used to give me little odd jobs every day.

On February 1, 1969 Bill Berkeley resigned from the National Chemical Company. The day he left, he and John Mitchell had a long luncheon and Berkeley talked about National Chemical and Richard Hicks:

John, I've worked for that man longer than any of his previous assistants . . . and I still don't really know him. The "in fighting" at National is intense as hell nowadays. The president resigned last year and they still haven't filled the position. Hicks knows he's in line. I'm sure the lousy 1968 TEXCORP figures shook him up. Abbott keeps telling him "things will improve, things will improve," and I think he believes it! He won't listen to me. I've heard a lot of talk around the

Chemical company about Hicks and some of the other vice presidents. There's the "pro-Hicks" and the "anti-Hicks" factions . . .

Mitchell expressed his surprise at the extent of the office politics at National Chemical, but admitted that he knew Hicks must be under considerable pressure. Mitchell refrained from telling Berkeley that he believed that Berkeley could have prevented the "communications gap" between National Chemical and TEXCORP by being more frank with his boss.

### TEXCORP Management

Mitchell was also beginning to believe that everyone in TEXCORP and National Chemical was guilty of "playing politics." TEXCORP's plant managers operated with considerable independence. Martin Steiner, the VP of Finance, was the only home office executive who dealt with plant personnel on a continuing basis; yet, by January of 1969, he had been unable to implement a company-wide cost accounting system. The controller of Smith-Abbott Mills, for example, was very "secretive" with his cost information and Steiner received only token cooperation from him. On several occasions Steiner remarked to John Mitchell that "things were sure different when old Bob Ford was running the company."

In spite of Richard Hicks' attempts to restructure the TEXCORP organization, the old company loyalties and factions continued to function. William Abbott, Walter Hogan, and Andrew Thompson directed the Smith-Abbott plants; Jim White and Martin Steiner spent most of their time dealing with the North Carolina Mills plants; and John Rand and Sam Jarvis concerned themselves with the Carolina Cotton plant. As the profitability of this latter plant declined, both Rand and Jarvis tried to "mind their own business" and avoided discussions with TEXCORP executives of overall policies and problems.

Management meetings were held once a month in the TEXCORP board room. The members of the Management Committee were: William Abbott, Andrew Thompson, Walter Hogan, John Rand, Martin Steiner, George Kirk, Sam Jarvis, Bob Cleaves, and Richard Hicks. John Mitchell was invited to attend many of the meetings. His increasing concern over the company's viability and his interest in psychology prompted him to reflect upon the "patterns of communication" that emerged among the TEXCORP executives.

When Hicks attended the meetings, a business-like atmosphere prevailed. The management meeting was almost formal, and the men seemed "on their toes." Many even took notes as the National Chemical vice president asked his pointed questions. However, Hicks was unable to attend all of the meetings. In his absence William Abbott would usually begin by smiling and saying, "Well, what'll we talk about today?" Mitchell noticed that these meetings often degenerated into rambling discussions of the performance of the three family companies. Members of the Management Committee were constantly being called to the phone to "put out a fire," and little seemed to get accomplished. Mitchell soon realized that it was an "unwritten rule" that nobody paid much attention to Management Committee meetings or decisions made there, for William Abbott consulted afterwards with Thompson or Hogan and decided upon the actions to be taken.

To John Mitchell, the most confusing aspect of the TEXCORP management and communications system was the lack of objectivity. No matter what subject was raised—be it a question of buying a new loom or expanding a product line—everyone seemed to have a known and fixed position. TEXCORP executives *expected* Andrew Thompson to fight for increased expenditures for blended wool fabric capacity, and everyone *expected* Sam Jarvis to say that cotton prints were the best long-term investment for the company, and Mitchell observed that they were never disappointed. Since the members of the Management Committee were already "on record" as holding certain opinions, discussions were usually routine and (Mitchell thought) uninteresting. New facts were seldom presented. The voluminous industry-wide marketing statistics published by the Textile Trade Association were never cited. TEXCORP executives seemed to rely on their intuition and "gut feel" for the situation. The engineering studies of George Kirk were privately referred to as "worthless." Bob Cleaves and Martin Steiner confided to John Mitchell that on several occasions Kirk had changed his facts and figures to make the studies "come out the way Abbott wanted."

Mitchell tried to remain neutral as far as office politics were concerned, but this was often difficult:

> With a climate so politically sticky—I never pulled punches or played politics. This got me into trouble. When someone said, "How's it going?" I said, "Lousy." I was everyone's friend, and they (the execs) all wanted me for their assistant. All the division managers lacked management expertise.

Mitchell had tried to figure out why NCC was so reluctant to examine the situation at TEXCORP. He thought one reason might be the fact that the presidency of NCC had been unfilled for several months and a successor had not yet been chosen:

> Hicks may be mixed up in the hassle over who gets to be president of NCC. He wants to sweep TEXCORP under the rug because it's a bomb. They have lost at least five million in profits because of TEXCORP, and part of this is company politics. Bill Abbott is one of the largest single stockholders in NCC and he also knows Bill Scott (board chairman of NCC). So Abbott is formidable.

What really shocked Mitchell, however, were the day-to-day politics at TEXCORP:

The number-one priority here is personalities. The prime commodity people fight for is Abbott's time. I'm shocked at the amount of time spent on personalities. Eighty to 85 percent of people's time is spent warming up somebody or cooling off somebody or on other nontask conversation.

Another related commodity is information—facts about what's going on, who's taking to who, etc. But you can't get any data from the responsible people—the secretaries are the people to talk to if you want information. Everyone relies on rumor, and people here ask the secretaries to relate casual conversations they've overheard so they can figure out which way the wind is blowing. Mary Fagan even says that Abbott has asked her to spy on me!

Many people at TEXCORP used Mitchell as a confidant, and Mitchell felt he had to keep a delicate balance of discretion and candor. For instance, Martin Steiner would complain to Mitchell that he desperately needed a new accountant and this complaint would serve as a smokescreen if Steiner's department got behind in its work. Mitchell felt that George Kirk, the head engineer, was almost paranoid about authority. If Abbott requested that Kirk see him in his office, Kirk would call Mitchell first to find out what Abbott wanted.

In February an incident occurred that John Mitchell found to be almost humorous. Three new looms had been installed in Bill Davis' (North Carolina Mills) plant, and William Abbott sent Walter Hogan south to "supervise the breaking-in period" at the plant. Bill Davis was not informed and was upset when Hogan walked into his plant and began asking questions. Davis placed quick calls to Jim White and John Rand protesting Hogan's presence, and finally called William Abbott. The irate plant manager said he could handle any "breaking in." Abbott explained that Hogan was just "inspecting" the new looms and said that George Kirk had suggested that Hogan be present when they started operations.

John Mitchell became involved in the controversy when he had lunch with Kirk the day following Hogan's arrival at Bill Davis' plant. Kirk was furious. He did not respect Walter Hogan and said he "didn't particularly care for Bill Davis" either. But he stated that he had never suggested that Hogan be sent to Davis' plant; "Now Jim and Marty Steiner won't speak to me. They think I sicked Hogan on Davis. You should talk to them, John, and tell them what really happened. . . ." Mitchell discovered from Mary Fagan that Kirk had, in fact, written a memo about the looms to Abbott. When questioned by Abbott, the chief engineer had evidently agreed that Hogan might "supervise the looms for a few weeks." A few days later, Mitchell mentioned the matter to Bill Berkeley. The young National Chemical representative pointed out that George Kirk seldom disagreed with anything William Abbott suggested. The entire incident seemed ridiculous to John Mitchell, but Berkeley pointed out that such "misunderstandings" were common at TEXCORP.

### A Final Confrontation

Mitchell was becoming increasingly aware of his unique position in the TEXCORP organization. More and more often he was asked to listen to the problems of various company executives. Bob Cleaves confided in him almost daily. Cleaves' responsibilities had been reduced when TEXCORP was reorganized, and he constantly spoke of "retiring" or quitting. Walter Hogan was also expressing personal opinions to Mitchell. Hogan's new position as "manufacturing services manager" was a clear demotion. Hogan was 62 years old and admitted to Mitchell that he knew "his days were numbered." Martin Steiner and Jim White spoke to Mitchell in January about the financial and sales deficiencies they had observed at TEXCORP. They encouraged Mitchell to "speak to someone at National Chemical" to see if Abbott could be replaced and new talent recruited. Mitchell responded by speaking to Bill Berkeley, but advised both Steiner and White that they should be the ones to approach Hicks:

> I don't know, the atmosphere is geting thick as glue around TEXCORP nowadays. The company's going down hill. Abbott's spending more time on the links. Everyone comes to me with their problems. What am I supposed to do? Except Andy. . . . He and Abbott don't talk to me any more. I guess they know I think they're both doing a lousy job. But, hell, they're in charge. All guys like Cleaves and Jarvis and Steiner seem to be doing is bitching. . . .

During the months of February and March, Richard Hicks was out of New York City. This only added to John Mitchell's feelings of helplessness. He was now convinced, beyond doubt, that TEXCORP was being badly mismanaged. His personal future seemed to depend on the National Chemical Company: when and if it would step in and replace Abbott and his management "cronies." On March 2 he spoke with William Abbott and told him he was "thinking of quitting." Mr. Abbott reacted very calmly and remarked that it was "too bad," but that it was his (Mitchell's) own decision:

> Hell, he just sat there. The bastard. Didn't even bat an eye. I gave him the chance to try and talk me out of it. It was half a bluff anyway. Man, now I have to find another job! Wait 'till Hicks hears this. He's going to wonder what's been going on while he was away.

The following day, Mitchell told Bob Cleaves what he had done. Cleaves reacted emotionally and told Mitchell he was a fool. "The future of TEXCORP will rest with guys like you," he exclaimed. "You're throwing away a great opportunity. You know National Chemical will have to move in soon. And when they do, you will be the one who comes out on top!" Later on that day, William Abbott called Mitchell into his office and asked if he would "reconsider" his resignation. He said he could only reconsider if "major changes" were implemented at TEXCORP, but Mitchell agreed to spell them out in writing. Abbott said he would read what Mitchell wrote and "we can talk when I get back from Augusta."

Mitchell proceeded to write a three-page description of what he saw wrong with TEXCORP and what changes might be made. Excerpts from this letter to William Abbott are reproduced as Exhibit 5. When Abbott returned to New York, he asked Mitchell to have lunch with him at the Union League Club. During the lunch, it became clear to Mitchell that writing the letter was a mistake.

**EXHIBIT 5**

Excerpts from Mitchell's Letter to William Abbott,
Dated March 3, 1969

Mr. William A. Abbott
Augusta National Golf Club
Washington Road
Augusta, Georgia
William—

I am sorry to bother your golf, but all of this is important to me and I wanted you to have time to think about it. I have not gone into personal requests. If this letter makes sense to you, we can speak about my future when you return to New York.

. . . . .

I. Prerequisites for Success in Textiles
   1. Must have market specialization with a well-focused sales effort. This is the only way to avoid competition based on price alone.
   2. Must develop those services our key customer groups want (and will pay for).
   3. Must carefully control costs. Because of the competitive situation and the large capital investments involved, incremental profits derived from cost control are often the key to success.

II. Obstacles to TEXCORP success in the Market

. . . . .

We lack almost all of the above prerequisites.
We are trying to serve too many markets . . .
We are being forced to compete more and more on price alone . . . (cf. my Smith-Abbott study). Major product lines are declining in value and suffering heavy losses (cf. North Carolina Mills study).
We are unable or unwilling to specialize . . . our sales efforts are poorly directed . . . our cost controls are inadequate . . . Where are our budgets?

III. Organizing to Meet the Market
. . . must begin with the New York office.
Planning is critical . . . real planning and risk taking depend on some very simple things; rapid, clear communication, getting the right people together to make the right decisions, collecting the right kind of data in the fastest amount of time, getting quick and decisive answers to questions that can be answered quickly.
The office of the president can set the whole "organization" in motion . . . By demanding prompt decisions, by demanding facts (rather than feelings or opinions), and by demanding that standards be met, the office of the president can begin to make TEXCORP one company.
And this is impossible unless the example at the top is consistent with what is being asked of the rest of the organization . . . There are many decisions that I think can be made today . . .
While doing this housecleaning and planning, talent must be recruited . . .

**EXHIBIT 5—*Continued***

IV. Some Specific Examples
Bring talent into central office.
Redefine head office responsibilities. Much housecleaning is needed . . . Have you reviewed Andy Thompson's budgets? His plans? If the office of the president can't answer yes to these questions . . . then why not?
Reorganize the Engineering Group . . . Create budgets for all vital functions . . . change the layout of the head office . . . Establish a uniform cost accounting system for all of the plants . . . create a system of sales management . . . without reports and communication, how can we expect focus and direction?
If you were to consult others in TEXCORP, and if you could get honest responses, I am absolutely positive many other specific examples could be cited—examples of things that should *and can* be decided and implemented immediately. Your organization, William, will withhold information from you because they do not have confidence that the information will be used wisely.

. . . . .

In all honesty I must say that I really don't know if my leaving the company is a very good thing for TEXCORP or a very bad thing. Because, in the clutch, I guess none of the fancy degrees, and none of Harvard's "principles" count for much. And I've never been there in the clutch.

He was really upset. I mean, he had the letter with him. And he would read for a while then say, "You're right." Then he'd read on. He said he agreed with everything I said. He didn't even argue!! He didn't question anything I said. I know now it was a mistake. I've hurt him . . . he can't even read the words I wrote. If he *were* reading them, I know he would have disagreed with some of what I said.

After the lunch Abbott said he wanted to show the letter to Andrew Thompson. He said he would talk to Mitchell later that week.

John Mitchell was very discouraged. Word of his letter had spread around the TEXCORP offices and he spent the next several days answering questions about what he had said. His efforts to evade questions only added to the tension in the office and gave the entire incident "mysterious" overtones. Without exception, TEXCORP managers told Mitchell he was making a personal mistake to leave the company at this point in time, but they admired his "guts" and hoped his confrontation would force National Chemical into taking some action with respect to Abbott.

On March 11, Mitchell decided to speak to Hicks about TEXCORP and what he had done. Hicks was in Washington, D.C. and Mitchell flew to the capital city and spoke with Hicks for two hours. Hicks was disturbed that Mitchell had acted so precipitously and rebuked him for not having come sooner. Mitchell showed him a copy of the letter he had written Abbott and told him that it was "impossible" for him to have come to Hicks before. "I felt I should quit first . . . before telling you all of what I know about what's going on at TEXCORP. I guess it sounds hollow and self-righteous now, but it's how I feel." After Mitchell talked for a while about TEXCORP's problems, Hicks asked him to write a more detailed analysis of the textile company's prospects for success. The National Chemical Company vice president cautioned Mitchell to be "cool" and reasonable in this report: "Tell me what my alternatives are; tell me how much it will cost to make the changes you think should be made; and tell me what the risks are."

For the next month Mitchell worked on his report for Richard Hicks. William Abbott did not ask to see him, and Mitchell decided not to renew their Union League Club luncheon discussion. On April 10, the 1969 first quarter results were published. They showed that TEXCORP had lost over one million dollars after taxes during the first three months. TEXCORP executives now spoke openly of "moving to greener pastures" and the offices on Executive Row were usually empty. William Abbott took three- and four-day weekends; Walter Hogan, at Abbott's suggestion, spent all of his time at one of the large North Carolina Mills' plants in the South; Tom Rinehart seldom came into the office; and John Rand took a month's vacation.

John Mitchell, while researching and writing his report, was also actively searching for another job. He talked to his wife:

> This time I can forget about overseas work. How would you like to work in Denver? I've got a contact out there. No, I don't know if I'd stay at TEXCORP no matter what Hicks does. You never know when action might be taken. A couple of other National vice presidents have been calling Steiner and asking for some financial data, so I guess the word is finally out that all is not well with their new acquisition. But I've waited too long already. The way I see it, it'll be a year before that company's alive again. Just not worth waiting around for. . . . What do you think?

On April 17, as Mitchell was putting the finishing touches on his report, Jim White stopped in his office. White announced that he had just spoken to Hicks and that he had tried to communicate to the National vice president some of the facts concerning "how bad things were at TEXCORP." White smiled and said, "John, you just can't leave now. From what Hicks told me today, I'm sure we'll see big changes very soon. Really, this time I know it will happen. You've got to stay. We'll all be better off if you do!"

# Allied Food Company

On March 10, 1955, Mr. Nelson Anders, general sales manager of the Allied Food Co., presided at an all-day meeting of sales executives from the company's Eastern sales region. The meeting was held in a hotel conference room in New York City. Exhibit 1 presents a partial organization chart of the Allied Food Co., and Exhibit 2 indicates the name, title, and seating place of the executives at the meeting. The March 10 meeting had been called by Mr. Anders to make some final detailed plans prior to the institution of a major reorganization of the Eastern sales region scheduled to start in less than a month.

The Allied Food Co. was a large national company that produced and purchased for resale a fairly complete line of food products. The company had been growing rapidly since World War II, and its sales in 1954 were well over $100 million. In the latter half of 1954, the top sales executives decided after considerable study, to change the existing national sales organization from having a single sales force in a given sales territory to having a dual sales force. In other words, the company's products were to be split into two major groups, called groups A and B, and different salesmen were to sell each group of products. This change also called for a doubling of the number of people needed as territory sales managers (see Exhibit 3). It was decided to make this organizational change in the Eastern region first and, if it worked as expected, introduce it in time into the other sales regions. Prior to the March 10 meeting Mr. Anders had asked Mr. Butler, the Eastern regional sales manager, to request his district managers to nominate people for each of the newly created jobs of territory sales manager and to indicate how they would split their territorial sales forces. The resulting proposals for personnel changes in each district were available in advance in written form to all those attending the March 10 meeting.

The following account and excerpts of the March 10 meeting were prepared by a research man from the Harvard Business School who attended the meeting.

The discussion throughout the morning concerned such topics as the timing of the announcements of the new organizational plan, the problem of setting up appropriate sales quotas for the new sales territories, the problem of handling the customers who were now to be called on by two different representatives of the Allied Food Co., and several other problems related to the reorganization. Mr. Anders took an active part in these discussions. Mr. Butler was much less active and acted more as a moderator in calling on the different people who wanted to speak on the issue at hand. The problems that were raised seemed to be getting a very thorough discussion, and by and large, the group seemed to be agreeing on the ways that the different aspects of the change would be handled.

After lunch, by previous arrangement, Mr. Anders called the attention of the group to the problem of deciding on the specific people who would be given the new jobs of territorial sales managers and the question of making the related personnel shifts.

ANDERS: We have to approach this problem this afternoon by going through one district at a time looking at the nominations that have been put up by the district managers. I suggest we start by looking at those districts where there are relatively few problems involved so that we can get some of these out of the way before we tackle the districts where it will probably be a little more difficult to find the answers.

BUTLER: In that case, let's start with the Buffalo district.

The Buffalo district manager took about five minutes to explain the nominations he had made in the report he had prepared for the meeting. He had nominated one of his own men for each of the new jobs that were being created and spoke briefly of the qualities and personality attributes of the people he was proposing for those positions. After a couple of questions were asked him, everyone at the meeting seemed to agree with his proposals. Mr. Butler then asked the Baltimore district manager to present his report. The Baltimore manager also took about five or ten minutes to present his nominations, and these were very quickly accepted by the rest of the group.

The third district manager to report was Mr. Murdock from the New York district. He presented his nominations in much the same fashion as the previous two district managers. He then concluded his presentation:

MURDOCK: I am down now to the final territory and that is our Newark territory. This territory presents a problem and I need some help on it. I don't feel that I have a qualified man in my district to nominate for that new job in Newark. We're up against some pretty rough competition there. We need a very competent man to take over that territory. What I feel we need is an older man who has had plenty of sales experience with our company and who has handled some tough assignments. He has to be able to make a very good appearance and to really know what he is doing in order to do a good job with that territory. As I've said, I think I've got some very good men in my territory. I've moved a number of them up to take these new slots, and I think they'll do it well. But I don't feel I have another man who's ready to step into a job like this Newark one.

ANDERS: Does anyone have any suggestions for this problem?

EASTERN REGION SALES PERSONNEL MANAGER: I understand that the situation in our Boston district is somewhat related to the question that has been raised here about Newark. So why don't we take a look at the Boston picture and see if it doesn't help us settle this Newark problem in the New York district.

ANDERS: Fine, why don't you go ahead then.

Mr. Ranford, the Boston district manager, proceeded to give his proposed lineup for the new jobs as territory managers in the Boston district. After he had proceeded about halfway through this presentation he was interrupted.

ANDERS: I'm looking down here at the Hartford-Springfield territory [a territory in the Boston district]. I see you don't have a territory manager for Group B named there. How about this fellow Tompkins? Isn't he one of our senior salesmen in that territory?

RANFORD: Well—yes. We have considered Tompkins. We haven't recommended him for this job. All of the reports on him haven't been exactly good. I don't want to give the impression that he's not a good salesman because I think he is. Everybody says he's got a good record as a salesman, but the reports I get are that people aren't too sure he will work out as a territory manager, at least not right there in the Hartford-Springfield territory. I guess he's rubbed some people a little bit the wrong way, and I don't know if he would work out there. That's why we didn't put his name in as a nominee for a territory manager at this time. However, we do think he's a good man. I don't want you to think otherwise.

ANDERS: Well, what's the trouble, then?

MURDOCK: Maybe I'd better speak up here about the conversation I had with Ranford last night over cocktails. I was telling him about our problem down in Newark, and we came up with the idea that maybe this fellow Tompkins might be somebody we could move into this Newark job. I understand he's had some problems up there, but if we all have our eyes open on this, I'd be willing to take him for that Newark job.

ANDERS: Didn't I hear something about his having a pretty good-sized family?

RANFORD: That's right. I understand he has six kids.

ANDERS: And I thought I also heard he's recently bought himself a new home.

RANFORD: I think that's right. I think he did buy himself a home within the last few months.

ANDERS: Well, hadn't we better think about that? What's the move going to mean to him? If we push him into moving, is there a possibility we might lose him? It doesn't sound as if a move would be very easy for him.

EASTERN REGION SALES PERSONNEL MANAGER: I have had several chats with Tompkins about his personal situation and I might be able to add something here. Tompkins has been passed over twice for promotion to territory manager. This has upset him and if it happens again I predict that he will leave the company. But I don't think he wants to leave. And even though he stands to lose money on selling his house now, I think he would move to get a territory manager's job if he couldn't move up where he is.

RANFORD: I was sort of hoping it wouldn't be necessary to bring all this up at this meeting, but maybe I'd better tell a little bit more about the story on

**EXHIBIT 1**

Partial Organization Chart—Sales Department

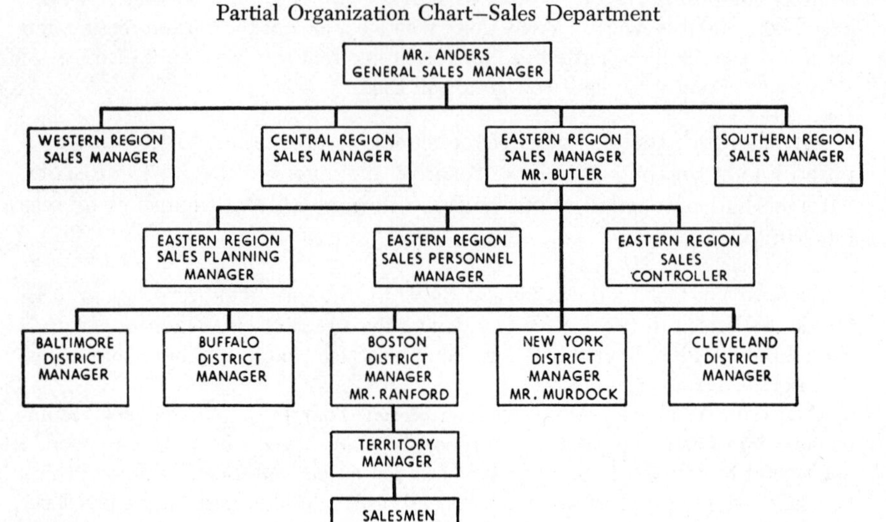


**EXHIBIT 2**

Seating Arrangement for Meeting, March 10, 1955

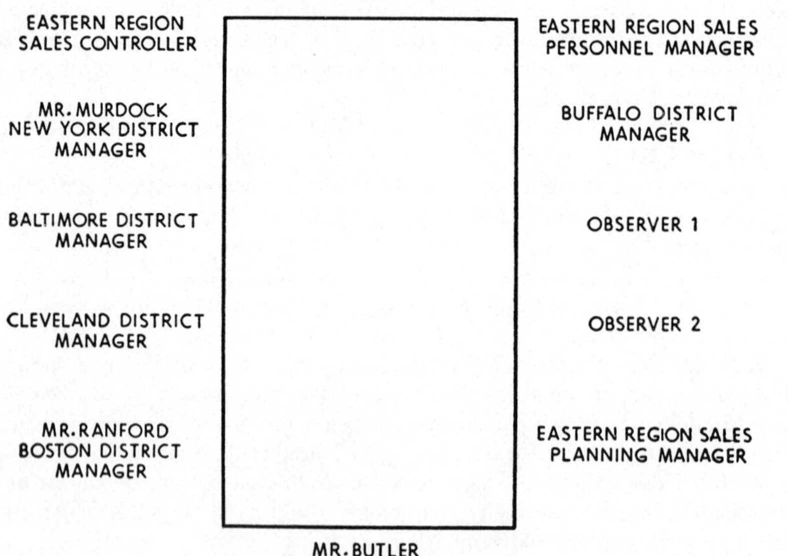

Tompkins. It's a little complicated, but what it amounts to is that Tompkins has been going around talking to quite a few people in our organization about his difficulties in the Hartford-Springfield territory. He's got a good sales record but he's been talking to different people in our organization about his troubles, and mostly they add up to the fact that he's running down his current boss, John Clements [manager of the Hartford-Springfield territory]. Needless to say, it hasn't made Clements happy to have Tompkins running around undercutting his position. Clements isn't one of our strongest men, but he is perfectly okay as a territory manager. You'll see that we have Clements slated for a transfer to Providence. Well, Tompkins is really giving him a bad time—going outside channels to make things tough for him. It's things of that kind that made us think that it wouldn't be wise to move Tompkins up to the job of manager in that territory. This idea of moving him down to Newark seemed to be a pretty good way to handle the whole thing.

ANDERS: Maybe we ought to think about firing Tompkins. What would you say to that?

RANFORD (*pause*): No, I wouldn't recommend that. He is certainly controversial, but on balance, I think he ought to be kept.

ANDERS: Have you or have any of your subordinates called in Tompkins to tell him exactly what you think of his talking about his boss outside of channels?

**EXHIBIT 3**

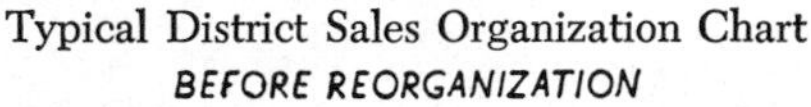

Typical District Sales Organization Chart

*BEFORE REORGANIZATION*

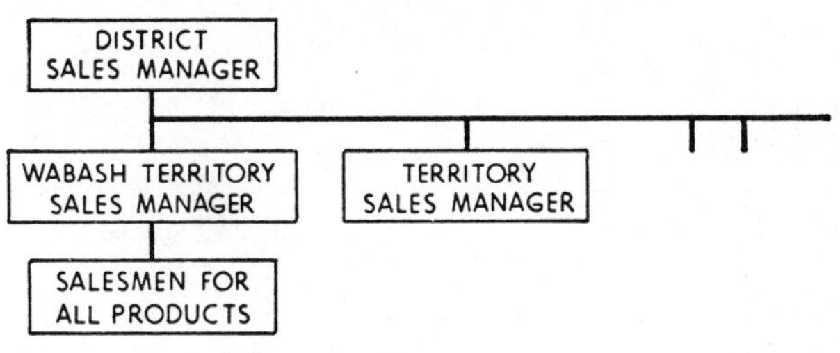


*AFTER REORGANIZATION*

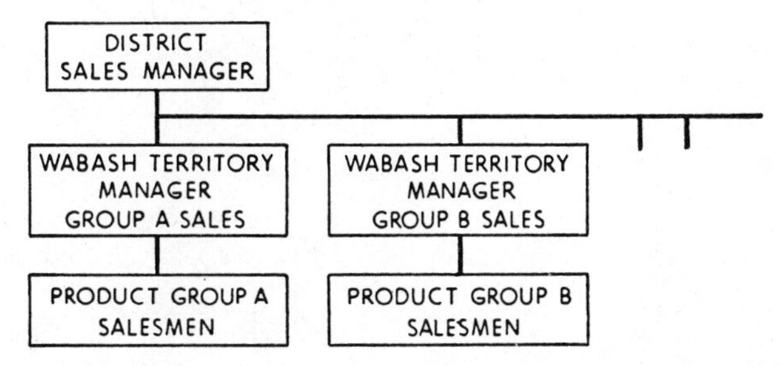

RANFORD: I don't think that is the kind of thing that you necessarily have to tell a man. He ought to know better. It is all spelled out in our company policies. Besides, he could have caught on to how people felt about this from the cold shoulder he has been getting when he peddled his stories. We thought he would straighten himself out. I've been hearing stories about this for quite a while, but it has been hard to pin down. It's not easy to know just how to approach Tompkins on a matter of this kind. It's something that I've talked about a bit with Clements and some of the other men who have stopped by that territory and have had a chance to hear some of these things from Tompkins. But it always comes in little pieces and it's hard to know just what to do about it.

ANDERS: I take it, then, you haven't talked to Tompkins about this.

RANFORD: That's right.

ANDERS (*pause*): Do you have any serious objection to promoting Tompkins to be a manager of the Hartford-Springfield territory?

RANFORD (*pause*): No, I wouldn't say I could put up any serious objections to such a promotion.

ANDERS: Well, in that case, why don't we go ahead on that. Now let's go back to the New York problem. This doesn't help on the Newark vacancy, does it? (*Laughs.*)

# Markham Instrument Company

In the spring of 1959, the management of the Markham Instrument Company was confronted with an impasse in pricing the latest addition to its line of scientific measuring instruments. Markham had two basic product groups, instruments for use in scientific laboratories (Laboratory Products), and industrial instruments for use in manufacturing processes (Industrial Products). The present problem centered around the Dual Sensitivity Level Instrument (DSL) which was intended for the more specialized scientific laboratory market.

## History of Development of the Laboratory Product Line

The line of scientific measuring devices which the Markham company introduced in 1924 was adversely affected by the business decline of the 1930's. In 1935, however, the potential for reversing this trend appeared in the form of a major product innovation. A company salesman discovered a young inventor who had developed an electronically controlled measuring device. Markham officials found from comparative tests with their own instrument that the "shoe box" (a name derived from the new instrument's dramatically reduced size) was superior in performance, and they purchased the rights to develop it.

No one at Markham understood the new machine sufficiently to complete its development. Just at this time, however, Alfred Reece (Markham's director of research in 1959) approached the company seeking part-time employment to support his doctoral studies. When he demonstrated a thorough understanding of vacuum tube technology, he was immediately hired. Working with Roger Finlay (representing sales and engineering) and Caleb Webster (mechanical engineering), he redesigned the shoe box until it met scientific and commercial standards.

Several competitors had already introduced comparable electronic devices to the scientific market, but they met considerable customer resistance. Dr. Markham pointed out in retrospect, "The change from electrical controls to a vacuum tube amplifier was a big one for Markham. Scientists and technicians were against it. We had advertised the electrically controlled version as the only reliable standard regulator, and this had become the general consensus among our customers. Radio types on the market had been widely criticized and we needed strong evidence to justify our change in attitude."

While Markham management believed their shoe box to be superior to competitors' electronic machines, they did not rely on this to overcome customer resistance. Instead they appealed to the customers' conservatism, which had been the major factor in blocking acceptance of competitors' machines. The new machine was designed to look and operate as much like the old machine as possible, even to the extent of compromising a few of the advantages of the electronic design. As Finlay said later, "Our customers distrusted the electronic devices which were already on the market, so there was nothing else to do but make ours look and act like the electrical one they were familiar with."

This strategy was successful. Dollar sales volume in 1936 doubled that of 1935, while the number of units actually tripled. Consistent with its past success, however, Markham continued to rely heavily on conscientious customer service to enhance its position in the scientific measurement field. Field sales offices and branch service agencies were set up throughout the country. Company salesmen, continuing their traditional practices, carried customer service to the extremes of repairing competitors' equipment, extending liberal credit and trade-in terms, and offering rapid emergency replacement service.

The next major change in these products occurred in 1946 when the company developed a chemical-sensitive paper, which among other improvements, eliminated the inconvenient use of recording inks. This development gave Markham a competitive advantage and simultaneously, due to sole control of the paper supply, provided an increase in profit margins. During this period a portable measuring device, long sought by scientific field workers, was also developed. Although these innovations gave Markham a technical lead, the company still depended on customer service for the basic maintenance of its market position.

During the early 1950s competitors began work on a machine which gave the scientist the option of measuring either of two sensitivity levels simply by throwing a switch. In 1957, the competitors' development work reached fruition, and these Dual Sensitivity Level (DSL) machines were introduced commercially. Markham was not disturbed by this new feature on competitive instruments, since potential applications for the additional sensitivity level were extremely limited. Furthermore, management's attention was diverted from this development by the addition to its own line of a transistorized portable, 40 percent lighter than any then available. This machine's compactness was expected to attract scientists engaged in field experiments, while its price, flexibility, and reliability were expected to make it also a replacement for most applications of the standard model.

Markham elected to push the transistorized model at the expense of the older, larger instrument, basing its decision on a prediction that customers would prefer the smaller machine. In adopting this strategy, management was confident that its ability to take the customers' viewpoint, a company strength over the years, still enabled it to judge what the scientists wanted. Markham had historically been able to lag in technological innovation with little risk, because when their new products were finally introduced, they surpassed competition in meeting customer needs. Markham managers believed that this intimate relationship with the market was as strong as ever.

Company executives were quite pleased when sales of the transistorized model surpassed expectations. They were surprised, however, by two trends. First, sales of the older machine did not decline as had been expected. Secondly, Markham salesmen began asking for DSL instruments such as competition was offering.

To determine the feasibility of producing a DSL while maintaining the basic strategy of promoting the transistorized instrument, exploration was begun on the redesign of the transistorized model. By the end of 1957, a tentative DSL design was developed, although two stubborn technical problems, peculiar to a transistorized DSL remained unresolved. Before devoting more time to the solution of these difficulties, top management decided to review the entire issue of producing a DSL machine. After some deliberation the DSL was dropped as being a short-lived fad rather than a long-term trend. It was felt that the difficulties in overcoming the remaining technical problems would not be worth the effort, in view of the limited applications the customers had for the DSL feature.

During 1958, requests from the field for a DSL became more frequent, and Herb Olson (sales vice president) began pressing for a reversal of a decision not to produce such a device. He pointed out that salesmen were becoming increasingly embarrassed by customer insistence on DSL features. In view of these increasing requests, Roger Finlay (president) became convinced in the fall of 1958 that Markham should add a DSL to its line, if only to satisfy the "gadget" appeal of such an innovation. Since the older standard machines were continuing to sell, and since the development of a transistorized DSL was still problematical, it was decided to proceed with a DSL redesign of the older machine.

Shortly after making the decision to go ahead with a DSL, Roger Finlay met with Herb Olson (vice president, sales), Alfred "Doc" Reece (director of R&D), Caleb Webster (in charge of mechanical design of the DSL), and Bill Reynolds (responsible for electronic design of the DSL). Finlay told the three R&D men that while he was anxious to get the new machine into production as quickly as possible, the company's reputation was also involved, so that it would be necessary to do the usual careful job. Reece asked if all the same features that were in the standard would be included in the DSL. Finlay replied that while the DSL was to be patterned after the standard model, he wanted all the latest features included. Herb Olson explained that although the DSL was to be offered at approximately the same price as the standard model, they would still have to maintain the traditional external appearance and features on the DSL. In response to a question from Doc Reece, Olson pointed out that they were not too concerned with the weight of the DSL, since it was not to be a portable. As the meeting ended, Reece indicated that they would have to do some careful planning to keep costs down, but he was sure it could be done. Webster and Reynolds agreed, stating that they thought the design could be completed by the end of the year.

In spite of this optimistic appraisal the members of the research and development department did not greet the decision to redesign the older machine with unrestrained enthusiasm. In the first place, they felt that completing the redesign of the transistorized machine would be ultimately feasible and would be more stimulating technically. Secondly, they had several other challenging ideas which they believed would place the company in the growing space and missile field. The redesign of the standard machine would cause them to put aside these more exciting projects for several months.

In spite of these reservations, design work went ahead on the DSL. Meanwhile, inquiries and complaints from the field about the delay in offering a DSL continued to come into the home office. While many sales personnel blamed R&D for the relay, Herb Olson explained the problem differently, "All these problems that the laboratory salesmen are having aren't just the fault of engineering. Top management simply didn't think the DSL was important. Well, this was a mistake. Of course, when this happens the people out in the field get to feeling sore and they come ask us why we don't have the equipment."

Ed Greene expressed a similar view: "Sollie (a formerly influential but now deceased member of R&D) was screaming four years ago for a DSL, but top management could see no need for it. Now all the machines on the market have this feature and we are breaking our neck trying to catch up."

### Pricing Meeting, March 6, 1959

The development work on the DSL machine was completed by the end of 1958 and late in January, 1959, production received the information it needed to establish production methods and estimate costs. By early March, cost estimates had been completed by the production department, and a meeting was arranged for the morning of March 6, to discuss the DSL selling price. The ten executives named in the seating chart, Exhibit 1, were all present when the meeting started, except Mr. Webster, who arrived later.

Willard Tierney, acting as chairman, opened the meeting by asking

Ed Greene to present his cost estimates. Greene's initial position (which he maintained throughout the meeting) was that the DSL was more expensive than had been expected. He concluded his presentation by saying, "You are going to have to sell this machine for a lot more than you thought. I think these figures are sound. If anything, we have been too loose in our estimates and the figures are too low. We can't lower them any more."

**EXHIBIT 1**

Seating Arrangement—Pricing Meeting, March 6, 1959

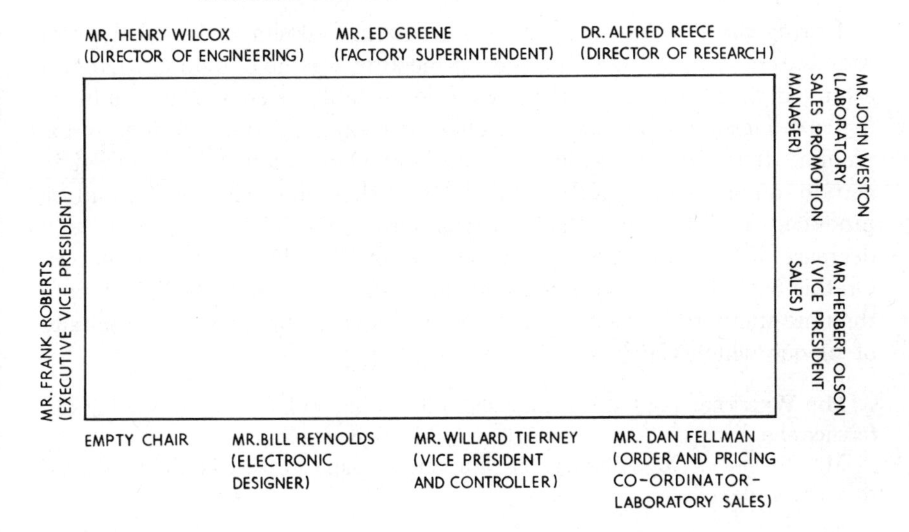


Herb Olson took a different position, maintaining that something had to be done to lower costs so the new machine could be sold at a realistic price. Represenative of his remarks is the following statement: "The fact that the figures are sound isn't going to help us meet competition. The way you [others at the meeting] are talking we would have to sell this machine for $1,000. If we did that our volume would go to hell in a hand basket."

Olson was not alone in finding the costs higher than expected. Caleb Webster remarked, "I am really surprised at these estimates. I didn't think they would be that high." Doc Reece also felt the estimates were higher than he had thought they would be. Bill Reynolds, on the other hand, found the estimates realistic as far as the electronic parts were concerned: "I'm not at all surprised at Ed's figures, because I knew what they would be from my design work."

Confronted with this impasse, Tierney summarized the situation at the end of the meeting: "I didn't think we could arrive at a decision today, and it doesn't look like we will, so why don't we adjourn and meet again next week? In the meanwhile Ed (Greene), Dan (Fellman), and Doc (Reece) can check over these costs to see if we can reduce them."

As the meeting broke up, Olson remarked, "If we can't do something about these costs, you guys can take it (the DSL) out in the field and give it to the salesmen yourselves. I won't do it."

### Pricing Meeting, March 13, 1959

During the next week, Reece, Greene, and Fellman reviewed the cost estimates, and on March 13 a second meeting was held. The participants arranged themselves around the conference table as shown in Exhibit 2. Willard Tierney again served as chairman, opening the meeting by explaining that Doc Reece, Ed Greene, and Dan Fellman had agreed to certain minor changes in the DSL and that they now felt that it could be produced at $110 more than the standard. (This figure represented a decrease of $35 from the highest figure quoted at the previous meeting.) On this basis Tierney proposed that the DSL be priced at $875, $90 more than the standard. After he completed his remarks there was a full minute of silence which Caleb Webster interrupted.

MR. WEBSTER: I still don't understand it. I'd like to know where the big differences lie, because I didn't think it would be that much.

MR. TIERNEY: Doc [Reece], can you itemize these so we will all know what they are in detail?

Reece and Greene then spent several minutes explaining the costs of various components, as well as the basis for their estimate of assembly costs. Webster, however, remained unconvinced. Tierney suggested that he and Greene work together to discover if further cost savings were possible. Greene replied.

MR. GREENE: I don't think there are many big changes we can make. It has been cut to the bone already.

MR. OLSON: Well, for example, look at that little trap door. It costs a lot of money.

Several minutes were devoted to the costs of the door which Roger Finlay had suggested to improve appearance and operating access. No on suggested changing the door, and the discussion then centered on the differences between the two models. Doc Reece concluded his explanation of the major causes for the difference.

Dr. Reece: Look, there is twice as much shop time for parts on the DSL as there is on the old one. That is a big part of the difference. (*Pauses*) Sitting around the table here we aren't going to remove Caleb's [Webster] doubts about the reasons for this big difference. He thought it would be less than $25 and it turns out to be between $90 and $120.

The meeting then divided into several conversations. Herb Olson and Frank Roberts talked together with John Weston listening; Doc Reece and Ed Greene carried on a conversation with Henry Wilcox listening. The others waited. After several minutes Roberts addressed the entire group.

Mr. Roberts: It appears to me that you aren't going to change the spots on the leopard. We have to fix a realistic price. You have all the estimates you can get.

In spite of this statement, discussion about cost differences continued with Reece and Greene furnishing more details about the costs of subassemblies to Webster. Roberts interrupted this discussion.

Mr. Roberts: We haven't heard from Herb [Olson]. He's probably got a lot to say.

**EXHIBIT 2**

Seating Arrangement–Pricing Meeting, March 13, 1959

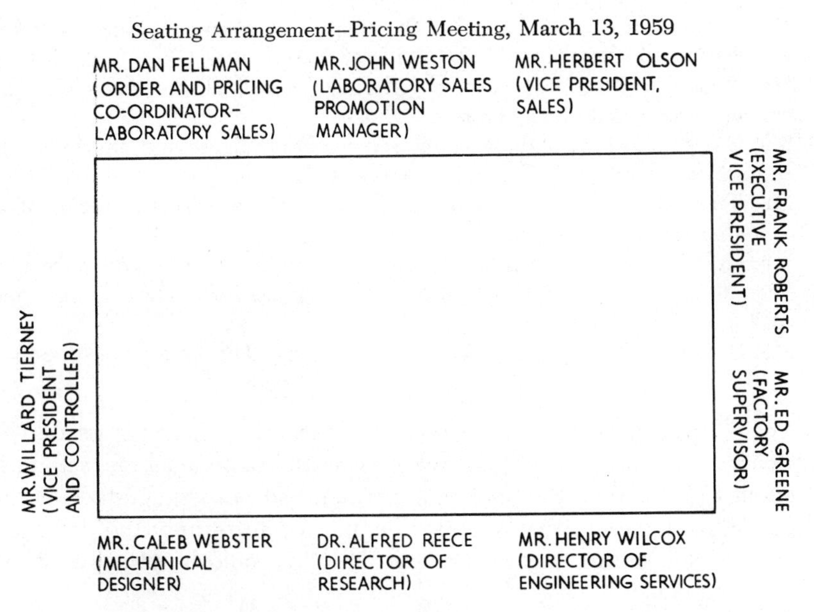


ABSENT: MR. BILL REYNOLDS (ELECTRONIC DESIGNER)

Mr. Olson joked with the group, and then began to discuss the competitive aspects of the situation.

MR. OLSON: We have to consider the selling price of this machine in comparison to competition. Competitors are selling their machines at between $440 and $460 to the dealers, which means they are about $800 at retail. Measuretech [a competitor] retails at $785, and their machine does everything ours does. Of course, they, like everyone else, offer discounts. Whatever we do, we have to be in the ball park on the initial list price. Perhaps controlling trade-ins will help some.

MR. ROBERTS: What do you think this price should be?

MR. OLSON: Oh, I suppose about $795, that's only $10 above the Standard Model.

Roberts, Wilcox, and Tierney then discussed the minimum DSL selling price. They agreed that using estimated costs, it would be necessary to price it at $875 to obtain the normal margin. Wilcox proposed that they set a target for cutting costs through redesigning the machine, because he thought cabinet and purchase part costs could be reduced in this manner. Olson supported this proposal, but Tierney disagreed.

MR. TIERNEY: I don't know what we can find. Ed [Greene] has made a careful estimate and there is still a $110 difference.

MR. ROBERTS: Well, maybe it is just being hopeful, but I think we should do what Henry [Wilcox] suggests.

DR. REECE: All Ed can control is the shop costs, shop time, and assembly time. I don't think there is much fat in any of these figures.

MR. WEBSTER: I still can't see why the machine should be that high. The mechanical costs should be much less.

MR. GREENE: Let him [Webster] go somewhere to figure and add them up. Then he'll see. Damned if I'll give him any of my figures.

MR. TIERNEY: You know, I still would feel more comfortable pricing it at $875. Otherwise I think we might be cutting it too close.

MR. OLSON: Competition is rough in this line, Will; $850 sounds much better than $875. Even at $850 we will have to work like hell to beat Asprey and some of the others.

MR. GREENE: I'll tell you this, I'd still rather build that Asprey machine than ours.

The relative merits of competitors' machines were then discussed. The consensus was that competition was making the same machine, selling it at about $75 less than the $875 figure which had been suggested for the DSL. Olson suggested that Webster be allowed to restudy the design to see if he could reduce the cost so that the DSL could be priced at $850. Tierney replied.

MR. TIERNEY: All right, maybe we should call this meeting off, and give Caleb [Webster] a chance to satisfy himself.

MR. ROBERTS: That's just a waste of time. Let's get this settled.

Greene and Wilcox also objected to further study and Tierney withdrew his proposal.

MR. TIERNEY: You're right. After all, we have never priced any instrument with as much information as we have on this one.

MR. OLSON: That really doesn't make any difference. We still have to get the price down where we can sell it.

Tierney then continued the discussion of competitors' machines and prices. There was general agreement that the Simpson Company had, at $785, the best DSL presently on the market. Olson expressed particular concern about the advantage competitors had because of the light weight of their machines.

**EXHIBIT 3**

Organization Chart—1959

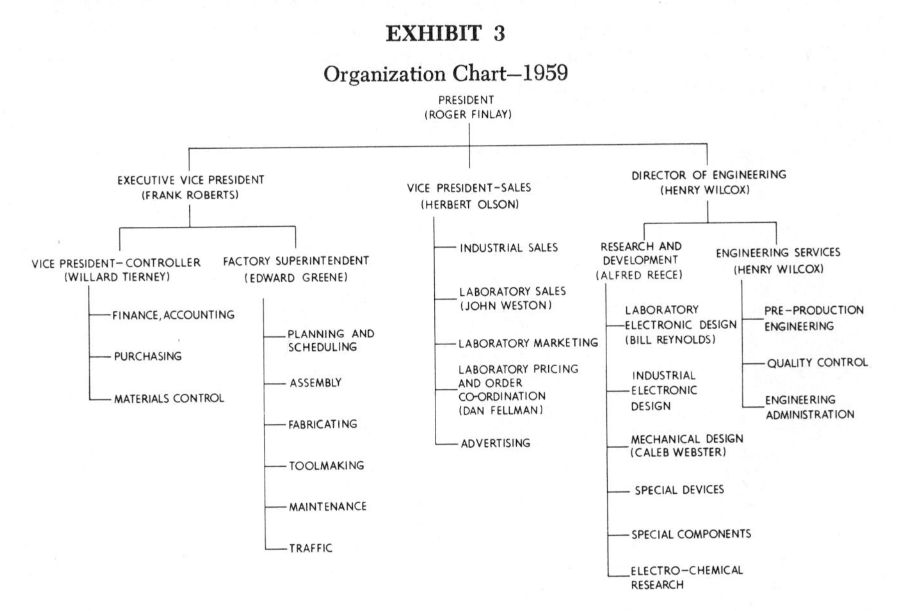


Note: Names are furnished only for persons mentioned in this case.

MR. OLSON: Look at these competitors' weights. Simpson's only weighs 20 pounds, while ours will be 34. Even Asprey's is 10 pounds less than ours. This is an important selling point and we can't ignore it.

DR. REECE: Damn it, don't start talking weights at this point. We were told from the start that they weren't important.

MR. TIERNEY: Herb [Olson], what do you think the end user pays for an Asprey?

MR. OLSON: Anywhere from $650 up. It depends entirely upon the deal and the trade-in. I was just wondering, though, if maybe we haven't got too many features on this machine. After all it is supposed to be sold as a general purpose machine.

DR. REECE: We designed it according to what Sales wanted. We have to go by what you fellows need. The trouble is that around here everybody wants everything with frosting on it.

MR. OLSON: Right, and then we price ourselves out of the market.

MR. TIERNEY: It seems to me that we had better change our whole official attitude if this is the way our market and our competition are acting.

MR. GREENE: O.K. Then we ought to start with an estimate of the market and the price and then design within that.

MR. OLSON: That's exactly what got us into this mess. The district managers are really going to be unhappy about this one. Finlay told them the DSL would be available at $800, and now you are talking about a minimum of $50 or $75 more than this. They aren't going to be happy about pushing this one. I still would like to see Caleb [Webster] take another crack at cutting the cost.

MR. ROBERTS: Doc, can you and the mechanic [Webster] take another shot at redesign after we get it into production? Maybe we can reduce costs then.

MR. TIERNEY: I think that is wishful thinking. We have to resolve this on the basis of the information we have.

# READINGS ON GROUP ISSUES

## The Individual in the Organization: A Systems View

JAY W. LORSCH
ALAN SHELDON

### INTRODUCTION

OUR PURPOSE is to develop a set of concepts which can aid the reader in thinking about and dealing with issues which arise in managing relatively small work groups in an organizational setting. Underlying the entire discussion will be the notion that the individual and the group of which he is a member can both be thought of as a system of interrelated parts. For example, in both a biological and psychological sense, the individual can be regarded as a system. Biologically, the individual is a complex hierarchy of systems ranging from the cells upward through tissues, organs, organ systems (e.g., nervous systems) to the whole. Psychologically, the individual is a system of thoughts, motives, and values which interact with external stimuli to produce the behavior we observe.

Socially the individual is a system and is, as well, a subsystem of larger social systems. The individual participates in many activities and many areas in his life. The most important of these are probably the family, work, and the group of activities called "social life." In each of these areas or systems, the individual has a part to play, his role. This role is in part determined by his own preferences and personality, and in part by the system in which he is an actor. Thus a man plays a part as father, manager, community leader, etc. His behavior may differ to varying degrees as he assumes different roles, but nevertheless the underlying consistency of his personality is present.

The demands that the various roles make upon the individual may be harmonious and consonant with each other, or may be in conflict. A conflict may be apparent and external; for example, a man may be a foreman on shift work which involves his being at work when his children are at home. Here his role in the family system as a father and his role as a manager are clearly in conflict. But such conflicts may be much more subtle. His role as manager may require him to be aggressive, determined, and exacting, while his family role as father requires him to be gentle, patient, and tolerant.

The manifestations of such conflict may be obvious to others or barely evident even to oneself. Furthermore, such conflict may turn up in unexpected places. And frequently conflict within a particular system which cannot be dealt with there can appear in other systems. Thus as a psychological defense, a man who for very good reasons finds it difficult to speak up to his boss may displace his resentments into his family life.

Up to this point we have dealt with the way that various systems interact upon the individual. But there may be more direct interaction between the systems to which a person belongs. In a small company town, it is difficult to avoid the group of people socially that one knows at work. Families often know as much or more about company gossip as the employees themselves know. Or, some types of interaction that may occur are attempts by the company to monitor and even influence areas of a man's life beyond his job.[1] A particular company might feel that the demands of the job are such that the man has to have an appropriate wife and family life, and therefore company management might not only make inquiries about these but also attempt to influence them. While it is important to recognize that the demands of membership in various systems can interact, our focus will be on how the work organization as a system, and particularly its smaller units (subsystems), affect the behavior of its members.

## THE ORGANIZATION AS A SYSTEM

Any work organization is an open system consisting of the patterned activities of a number of individuals and engaging in transactions with the surrounding environment. The system has a boundary which separates it from its environment, and most organizations having several subunits also have a number of internal boundaries. The organization takes in inputs from the environment and executes transformation processes which turn these inputs into outputs. Thus, a manufacturing company imports raw materials, converts them into products, and acquires a profit from selling the product. It also recruits employees, trains them, assigns them to jobs, and sooner or later exports them by resignation, retirement, or dismissal. It imports and consumes supplies and power. It also collects intelligence about its market and its competitors, analyzes this information, makes decisions about the quality, quantity, and price of the product, and

[1] William Whyte, *Organization Man* (London: Jonathan Cape, 1957).

issues communications of different kinds as a result of the decision made.[2]

The *environment* of the system is important in a number of ways. In the first place it is the source of the inputs and the market for the outputs. Second, other organizations also exist in this environment which may well be competing with the organization under consideration. Furthermore, the environment in general may influence the organization directly or indirectly, and in a way not connected with the major operating task of the organization. For example, in the last few years concern with the rights of black citizens has put pressure on organizations to hire more blacks.

In order to perform its task of converting inputs to outputs, an organization essentially engages in two types of processes: maintenance and task performing.[3] The *maintenance process* is essentially those activities which the organization engages in to remain viable. It must build and maintain staff, plant, etc., in order to perform any task at all. The second set of processes, *task performing*, are the actual activities by which raw materials are transformed into finished products. Finally, there are import and export processes across the organization boundary, as organization members gather resources and distribute products or services.

As an organization grows, efficacy requires that many activities which have to take place become divided, and the organization therefore develops subsystems. This process is called the division of labor, specialization, or task differentiation. Thus personnel departments, purchasing departments, service departments, etc., evolve while production departments attend to the process itself, and advertising and sales departments distribute the product to the customer. Although such specialization is efficient, as this specialization increases it causes problems of coordination or integration. Control of the various components in the system and the subsystem, as well as their linking together, become a major issue. A traditional method of control and coordination is that of the formal organization, with specific regulations and routines, and use of a management hierarchy. This formalized control is essentially a form of feedback. Feedback is the monitoring of output so that inputs can be changed to maintain a steady state in the system. Thus, if the performance of the task starts to deviate from acceptable limits, the supervisor may instruct the employee accordingly and rules may be enforced. More complex forms of feedback control include the development of specialized subsystems (e.g., quality control, production control) to perform a similar function.

We have thus far talked about the individual, specialized units, and the organization as systems in their own right as well as parts of a larger

---

[2] Kenneth F. Berrien, *General and Social Systems* (New Brunswick, N.J.: Rutgers University Press, 1968).

[3] Eric Miller and A. K. Rice, *Systems of Organizations* (London: Tavistock Publications, 1967).

system. Our major emphasis in the balance of this paper will be on subsystems which so far have been described essentially as specialized task units. However, usually an individual has face-to-face contact only with a portion of the work force engaged in such a subsystem and the term work group is usually reserved for this group. Since our concern is with the individual as an actor in the organization, we therefore want to focus here on such work groups as subsystems.

## SUBSYSTEMS IN OPERATION

How do such subsystems (work groups) operate? What produces the behavior we observe in a particular work group? Why are some work groups more productive than others? Why do some groups resist innovations in technology or organization while others welcome them? The answer to these and related questions are important for any manager. They not only enhance his understanding of his own behavior, but also that of peers, superiors, and subordinates.

To answer these questions we need to focus on the factors which determine the behavior of the members of a work group.[4] One reason people behave as they do in a work group is because of the functioning of their personality systems. We shall refer to this as *individual inputs,* since it is an input to the subsystem from the individual members of the unit. But this is only one of several forces which affect members' behavior. Two other clusters of factors which affect behavior in a subsystem are imposed from the larger organizational system. The first is the nature of the work assigned to the unit—what we shall call *task inputs.* The second is the formal organizational practices (supervisory arrangements, control systems, procedures, rules, etc.) which are usually defined by the management of the larger system. These we shall term *organizational inputs.* While we shall discuss each of these inputs in more detail below, two points about them require emphasis now.

First, these three factors are interdependent. They interact with each other. For example, an organizational input (personal selection procedures) may affect the kinds of individual inputs in the system. Similarly, the character of organizational inputs may be affected by the task inputs. When a highly routine task is to be performed, management may find it feasible and efficient to rely heavily on formal rules and procedures to regulate the work, but when a more uncertain or problem-solving task is to be performed, it may be impossible to rely on such predetermined

---

[4] The ideas which follow are derivations and modifications of those contained in John A. Seiler, *Systems Analysis in Organizational Behavior* (Homewood, Ill.: R. D. Irwin and the Dorsey Press, 1967).

procedures. Recognizing the interdependence of the inputs is crucial, because it means that when a manager thinks about altering one of them he should be aware of the effects on the other inputs if he is to keep the system operating effectively.

Inputs not only interact, but this interaction creates a fourth determinant of behavior in the work group—*the emergent social controls and structure*—which in turn interacts with the inputs to produce the behavior which emerges in the subsystem. By social controls we mean the traditional ground rules or *norms* about how members should behave which develop in a work group and which guide behavior, and the methods which develop within the group to enforce these norms through feedback. Social structure includes such factors as the status hierarchy which develops informally in any group, the established power relationship in the group, and the stable pattern of friendships which supports this pecking order.

Although social controls and structure are treated more fully below, it is helpful to illustrate the interdependence of this set of variables with the task, organizational, and individual inputs. One obvious example of this interdependence is provided by the degree of physical proximity of group members required by the task. If they must work in a confined space together, this is likely to result in more stringent norms about behavior, such as one should not talk loudly if it will disturb others. Organizational inputs, such as compensation schemes and measurement methods, can also affect the extent to which a group develops into a tightly knit subsystem with strong social controls and a well-defined social structure. In those situations where measurements and financial compensation emphasize group accomplishment, instead of individual output, stronger social controls are apt to develop. The interaction of individual inputs with social controls and structure is even more obvious. As an illustration, the needs, interests, and skills a member brings into the group and the way he is perceived by others will have a great deal to do with the position he ends up with in the group status hierarchy.

These examples are brief and oversimplified and are intended only to demonstrate what is meant by the interdependence of social controls and structures with the three sets of inputs. This interdependence is illustrated in Exhibit 1. Note that the relationship between behavior and these inputs and subsystem social controls and structure is diagrammed as a two-way relationship. We shall explain these feedback loops from behavior to the other variables shortly, but we first need to examine further the interdependence of these variables. As we do this, we shall define each set of variables more precisely and shall describe briefly some of the research which suggests a relationship among them and their impact on behavior. In this discussion we use the term "behavior" loosely to refer to both task

**EXHIBIT 1**

Interdependent Determinants of Behavior

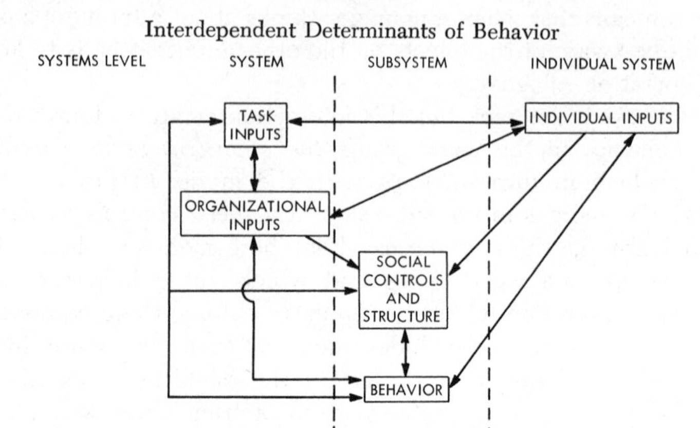


and subsystem maintenance activities. When we discuss social controls and structure more fully we will clarify this distinction.

## Organizational Inputs

Organizational inputs, as we shall use the term, consists of two sets of variables—the formal organizational practices imposed from the system level and the management style of managers supervising the subsystem. By formal organizational variables we mean such factors as the following:[5]

***Division of Work.*** This means the way work is divided among units and people within the unit. The work may be divided by product, by process, by time, or by geographic territory. Obviously, such organizational choices are closely related to the nature of the task inputs for the subsystem. For example, they define whether persons will work on a small portion of the total task or the whole task. The psychological consequences of such choices may be important also. Usually people working on a whole task get more satisfaction.[6] Similarly, these organizational choices

---

[5] William Evan, "Indices of Hierarchical Structure of Industrial Organizations," *Management Sciences,* September, 1963; Joan Woodward, *Management and Technology* (London: Her Majesty's Printing Office, 1958); Tom Burns and G. M. Stalker, *The Management of Innovation* (London: Tavistock Publications, 1961); R. H. Hall, "Intraorganizational Structural Variables," *Administrative Science Quarterly,* December, 1962; Paul R. Lawrence and Jay W. Lorsch, *Organization and Environment: Managing Differentiation and Integration.* (Homewood, Ill.: Richard D. Irwin, Inc., 1967). This list could also include other factors such as training, promotion criteria, etc. They have been omitted from the list because they will be considered more fully in Organizational Problems.

[6] A. K. Rice, *The Enterprise and Its Environment* (London: Tavistock Publications, 1963).

can determine whether people will work relatively independently or will have frequent contact with others.

***Span of Control.*** This is the number of subordinates reporting to a common boss. In some subsystems the span of control may be very narrow with few subordinates reporting to each supervisor while in others the span of control may be wider with many subordinates reporting to each supervisor.

***Hierarchy.*** This means the number of levels in the management hierarchy. As suggested above the principal function of the hierarchy is to provide a mechanism for coordinating the work of organization members. Through a network of common superiors the work of individual members can be coordinated. In this process information can move both up and down the chain of command.

***Rules and Procedures.*** This aspect of formal organization is concerned with the extent to which explicit rules and procedures about conduct (such as safety procedures) are imposed by higher management. In some situations rules and procedures can be so prolific and detailed as to cover every possible contingency. In others, formalized rules and procedures are nonexistent. The only rules are those norms which emerge within the subsystem itself.

***Measurement and Evaluation Practices.*** These formal practices are concerned with the measurement and evaluation of performance—both for the subsystem as an entity and for individual members. Such practices can vary from those which have many detailed criteria for performance evaluation to those which have only a few general criteria. Similarly, measurement and evaluation of performance can take place at frequent intervals or only infrequently. We should emphasize that these practices provide feedback to the individual, to the subsystem, and to upper management.

***Compensation.*** Financial remuneration has several parameters which can impact on behavior. First is the relative amount of compensation members are getting relative to other opportunities available to them. While recent research has indicated that high pay alone does not motivate people to work harder, it also suggests that people can become disenchanted with their situation if they feel their pay is inequitable given their level of self-esteem and their view of other opportunities.[7] A second parameter is the basis upon which payment is made. As we have already suggested, a group incentive plan can have one impact on people, while payment based on time or individual effort can have others. The third dimension of compensation which is important to consider is the range of

---

[7] Scott Meyers, "Who Are Your Motivated Workers?" *Harvard Business Review*, January-February, 1964; Elliott Jaques, *Measurement of Responsibility* (London: Tavistock Publications, 1956).

payments within the subsystem. The distribution of pay can be one important determinant of status in the subsystem social structure.

***Selection Criteria.*** Here we are concerned with the formally established criteria used to select new members for the subsystem. Characteristics such as skill, experience, age, psychological attributes (from tests) are frequently used to make selection decisions. While such criteria obviously will be affected by task requirements, if they are rigidly adhered to, they can have a significant effect on the individual inputs to the group. If these criteria are specific and many, they will create a group with members who are homogeneous in many characteristics. If the criteria are few and more general, they may lead to a more heterogenous collection of members.

**EXHIBIT 2**

Formality of Organizational Inputs

| | *High Formality* | *Low Formality* |
|---|---|---|
| Span of control | Narrow | Wide |
| Hierarchical levels | Many | Few |
| Rules and procedures | Many and specific | Few and general |
| Measurement and evaluation | Frequent and specific | General |
| Range of compensation in the subsystem | Wide | Narrow |
| Selection criteria | Specific and many | Broad and few |

With the exception of division of labor and the type and amount of compensation, these organizational inputs can be arranged on a continuum from high formality to low. (See Exhibit 2.) By formality we mean the extent to which the formal organization is intended to control behavior tightly. Recent research suggests that within many subsystems these variables tend to move in the same direction.[8] Thus, we can think of a subsystem as falling at some point along a continuum of formality of organizational inputs. As we shall see shortly, the formality of these organizational inputs can affect the attitudes of subsystem members about the organization, and partially determine the degree of autonomy they feel. These inputs are also closely related to the task inputs of the subsystem. But before we turn to task inputs, we want to touch on the second major type of organizational input—management style.

By style of management we mean the behavior pattern which is characteristic of the managers in the larger systems of which the subsystems are a part, as well as in the subsystem itself. Such behavior patterns have been

[8] Lawrence and Lorsch, *op. cit.;* Jay W. Lorsch and John J. Morse, *Individuals/-Organizations* (manuscript in progress).

characterized by different labels by a variety of theorists and researchers, but in essence most seem to be concerned with the extent to which managers are concerned with exercising unilateral control over subordinates versus the extent to which they foster a mutual influence process.[9] Since issues of leadership are dealt with in other papers in this book, the important points to be made here can be summarized briefly. First, management style obviously does interact with the other determinants of behavior to influence how a subsystem operates. Second, no one management style is appropriate for all situations. What style of management will facilitate subsystem performance depends on the other inputs to the system as well as its social controls and social structure.[10] Thus, as you consider your own management style you must be concerned not only with what is comfortable, given the dynamics of your personality, but also what fits the other variables in the subsystem to which you belong.

### Task Inputs

Our purpose now is to delineate certain characteristics of tasks, which research has shown are related to individual and organizational inputs and behavior. In discussing these task characteristics, it is useful to remember that in many work groups efficiency dictates that members perform similar tasks (e.g., all are purchasing agents).

The first task characteristic which is important is the relative certainty or uncertainty of the work. Several recent studies have amassed considerable evidence that there is a relationship between the certainty of a subsystem's task, its organizational inputs, and the effectiveness of the subsystem.[11] When the task is highly certain and predictable (e.g., an assembly line, turning out a standard product), the subsystem, if it is effective, will tend to have a highly formalized organization. Subsystems with more uncertain tasks (and again effective outputs) tend to have less formalized organizational inputs. An example of the latter situation might be found in a product management unit or a research laboratory.

The behavior of subsystem members also can vary with the task.[12] For example, in an effective research laboratory there is more autonomy of action among members and each member has more influence over his

---

[9] Fred E. Fiedler, *A Theory of Leadership Effectiveness* (New York: McGraw-Hill, 1967); Rensis Likert, *The Human Organization: Its Management and Value* (New York: McGraw-Hill, 1967); Robert R. Blake and Jane S. Mouton, *The Managerial Grid* (Houston: Gulf Publishing Company, 1964).

[10] This point is supported by the work of Fiedler, *op. cit.* and Tannenbaum and Schmidt, "How to Choose a Leadership Pattern," *HBR,* March-April, 1958.

[11] Edward Harvey, "Technology and the Structure of Organizations," *American Sociological Review,* April, 1968; Lawrence and Lorsch, *op. cit.;* Morse, *op. cit.,* Woodward, *op. cit.*

[12] Lorsch and Morse, *op. cit.*

own work. In a manufacturing plant there is often less freedom of action for individual members, and the amount of influence over activities tends to correspond closely to the formal hierarchical level of the member. The reasons for this interdependence between this task characteristic, organizational inputs and behavior and outputs are still being explored, but a promising explanation has to do with the fit between tasks and organizational variables. A good fit seems to have a motivational effect on subsystems members—providing them with a sense of competence in and mastery over their work.[13]

One problem with the concept of task certainty is that it is very broad and often difficult to apply to a specific task within a subsystem. A study by Turner and Lawrence, which is closely connected to those referred to above, suggests six more specific task attributes which were also found to be linked to formality of organization in a number of manufacturing plants. These are: (1) the amount of variety in prescribed activities; (2) the amount of discretion in job activities permitted and required of the job incumbent; (3) the frequency and diversity of interaction with others required by the job; (4) the amount of optional interaction possible; (5) the learning time required for job proficiency; and (6) the amount of responsibility assumed by incumbents as measured by the likelihood of serious error, the uncertainty about appropriate corrective action, and the length of time before feedback is received about the results of the work.[14] When jobs were rated low on these dimensions (e.g., little variety, limited discretion, little required interaction, etc.), it was found that the organizational inputs in the plant were more formalized. The organizations were less formalized in those situations where tasks scored higher on these dimensions. While there has been no empirical attempt to link these findings to those on certainty, it seems clear that jobs which score low on these dimensions are more likely to be highly certain.[15] We can therefore use these dimensions as more specific tools for analyzing and understanding the operation of subsystems.

That such task variables are related to behavior is demonstrated not only by the Turner and Lawrence study but also by Robert Blauner in his study of workers in the automobile, printing, and textile industries.[16] Blauner found that workers had varying attitudes toward work depending on the technology. Specifically, Blauner was interested in the extent to which workers felt alienated from their work. In the automobile industry

---

[13] *Ibid.*

[14] Arthur N. Turner and Paul R. Lawrence, *Industrial Jobs and the Worker* (Boston: Division of Research, Harvard Business School, 1965).

[15] That there can be exceptions to this conclusion is suggested, for example, by a task that is highly certain and still permits a high rate of interaction with others.

[16] Robert Blauner, *Alienation and Freedom* (Chicago: University of Chicago Press, 1964).

(which would be very certain and score low on the task attributes discussed above) workers were alienated from the company and its goals by an inability to influence the work situation, a loss of meaning in the work, a sense of being isolated, and a lack of self-involvement in the task. Textile workers, who had similar tasks to the automobile workers, did not feel the same way about their company. One reason was that they came from families in communities in which they were taught not to expect meaning in their work. These individual inputs plus organizational inputs, which were consistent with the values of the small communities in which the plants were located, caused these workers to be reasonably satisfied in spite of tasks which, in other circumstances, might lead to alienation. At the other extreme of task characteristics were the printing workers who engaged in a task which would score high on our job attributes and did not feel alienated from their work. The chemical workers, with a continuous process technology (but one which was changing and complex), felt responsible for controlling the process, had considerable autonomy, and felt they were members of cohesive teams. As a result, these workers felt integrated into the subsystem of their plant. Blauner's study, as this brief discussion implies, suggests not only that task attributes do have an impact on behavior but also that this impact cannot be fully understood without also considering individual and organization inputs.

In addition to task certainty and the task attributes identified by Turner and Lawrence, there are other task characteristics which can have an important impact on subsystem operations. One of these is the physical conditions in the work place. In manufacturing operations particularly, such factors as heat, odors, noise, and cleanliness can have an effect on the operation of the subsystem. For example, high noise levels can block oral communication and lead to feelings of isolation unless group members can find some way to communicate in spite of this constraint. Poor working conditions such as extreme heat, odors, etc., can often contribute to subsystem members drawing together in a more cohesive group. By banding together they gain a sense of support in the face of this hostile environment. While we tend to think of such factors as being relevant only in production settings and having a negative impact, it is worth noting that these factors are present in settings other than factories and can have a positive impact. Evidence of this is the time and money devoted to planning office environments so that they offer physical surroundings conducive to contemplative and problem-solving behavior.

Another important task variable is the spatial arrangement of the work place. As suggested above, whether subsystems members are close together or apart can have an important bearing on the amount of contact they have and how the group functions. Recent research by Allen suggests, for example, that the spatial layout of research laboratories can be an important determinant in getting scientists to interact with certain colleagues who had a particular capacity to bring new technical information into the laboratory.[17] Such interaction was important to the successful accomplishment of the laboratory's mission.

There is a final way in which task inputs affect subsystem operation, and it is perhaps the most obvious one. Since different tasks require different skills and interests, they are likely to attract personnel who have particular individual characteristics even if formal selection criteria are minimal. The reasons individuals select particular jobs are complex, and our knowledge in this area is far from complete. Yet there is mounting evidence that persons with particular needs are attracted to different job opportunities.[18] That this interaction of individual and task inputs can affect behavior is documented by Blauner's example of the textile workers mentioned above. Since these workers placed low value on the meaning of work, they adapted to the routine textile technology without the sense of alienation workers with other personality characteristics might feel. We will return to the issue of individual inputs in general shortly, but first want to make one final point about tasks.

In this discussion we have outlined a few of the task characteristics which affect behavior in subsystems. As with the other variables discussed in this paper, this cannot be a comprehensive discussion of the topic both because of space limitations and the fact that our knowledge about these matters is growing rapidly. Rather, we have suggested some of the important task characteristics and their relationship to other subsystem variables. As you apply the conceptual scheme outlined here, you will come to understand these and other relationships more fully. The essential points at this juncture are to recognize that these and other task characteristics can and do vary among subsystems; that these task inputs are interdependent with the other inputs and social control and structure; and that together these variables produce the behavior which you will be trying to understand and manage.

### Individual Inputs

Where organizational and task factors are inputs from the larger organizational system, the individual characteristics with which we are concerned are largely inputs from the personality system. Since personality issues are discussed in another volume in this series and because we will deal with individual inputs at length in considering social controls and structure, our discussion here will be limited to a few essential points.

---

[17] Thomas J. Allen and Stephen I. Cohen, "Information Flow in Research and Development Laboratories," *Administrative Science Quarterly*, March, 1969.

[18] Gene W. Dalton, Louis B. Barnes, and Abraham Zaleznik, *The Distribution of Authority in Formal Organizations* (Boston: Division of Research, Harvard Business School, 1968); Anne Roe, *The Psychology of Occupation* (New York: John Wiley and Sons, 1956).

Individuals bring to the subsystem a complex but balanced internal system of their own. In their role as subsystem members, they will behave in ways which are consistent with this internal balance. While the nature of the task and organization may attract people with somewhat similar characteristics, there will still be differences among members in terms of their particular internal balance and the factors which motivate them to work. This has an important impact upon the type of membership roles individuals seek in the subsystem.

But the way people behave in a group is not only a function of their internal needs in relation to task and organizational inputs, but also in relation to the ongoing social controls and structure present. One important implication of this fact is that one's role in a group is to a certain extent also a function of how other members perceive him in relation to their expectations of what a good group member shall be. These perceptions of a person are not only a function of how he behaves, given his personality, but also of certain *external characteristics* which a member brings to the subsystem. By *external* characteristics we mean such relatively visible factors as age, seniority, sex, ethnicity, skill level, and so on. As a very simple example take the case of a young MBA who, as his first job in a company, joins a top-level planning group whose other members are all long-service employees and older managers. He will certainly be treated differently than an older, more experienced manager joining the same group. We shall elaborate on this point in discussing social controls and structure.

### Social Controls and Structure

As pointed out earlier, social controls and structure are different from the other factors discussed above in that they develop within the subsystem out of the interaction of task, organizational, and individual inputs. Social controls refers to the norms about appropriate behavior for subsystems members which develop in a group and the mechanisms employed to gain compliance to these norms. Social structure is the hierarchy of membership positions which actually emerges in the subsystem.

The relationship between these social forces and behavior is highly interdependent and the distinction between them is very subtle. In fact the only way we can really track the social controls and structure which exist in a subsystem is by observing the behavior—interaction and activity patterns, feelings and attitudes expressed—over a period of time. This is so because social controls and structure represent relatively enduring subsystem-wide expectations about how members should behave collectively and individually. Actual behavior can and does deviate from these expectations, but in general the social controls constrain behavior so that it supports and reinforces structure. The connection between behavior and social controls and structure becomes clearer if we examine why and how the latter develop in a subsystem.

To do so, we need to answer the question, why do people become actively involved in work groups? After all, just because one is formally assigned or working in a subsystem is not sufficient reason to become involved in a process of social control. The answer to this question is simple enough—whether the subsystem we are talking about is defined on the organization chart or whether it just grows up in the organization without formal sanction. People become involved in work group activity because it meets certain of their needs. First, by joining a group, persons are often able to accomplish task objectives they cannot achieve alone. For formally established groups, this may be the solution of a complex problem one person could not solve alone or the manufacture of a complicated product. In such cases, the member is satisfying important ego needs for mastery or competence as well as meeting the task requirements of the larger system. Put another way, the needs of individuals and the primary task of the subsystem are consistent with the requirements of the larger system.[19]

But in other situations the group's primary task is not the same as the task inputs defined by management. For example, a group of workers who have developed a healthy distrust for management may implicitly define as their primary task protecting themselves from management pressure for higher productivity. By banding together, they can resist attempts to get them to work harder. Alone they could not accomplish this, but by coordinated activity, they can protect themselves from what they perceive to be a hostile environment.

Both these examples suggest the same essential fact—by joining into subsystem activity, members get things done which could not be accomplished alone. At the same time, they are also meeting important internal needs. By joining together to accomplish work, they can manage their drives for affection and aggression, can get reinforcement for their values, gain a sense of self-esteem from the acceptance by others, and so on.

As members work together on a task and satisfy their needs, the group as a whole develops certain expectations about what is appropriate behavior. In the second example above, for instance, the group might expect that members should not produce more than a certain number of units of output per day. Such shared expectations about behavior are what we mean by group norms. Variations in individual behavior from such work group norms can have major negative consequences for the group and the individual. First, it can prevent accomplishment of the task. Eventually, if a group ceased to fill such a major purpose, this could lead to its breakdown. Second, since people have needs which are being satisfied by group membership itself, as well as task accomplishment, they are reluctant to

---

[19] Rice, *op. cit.*

see this happen and they become involved in maintenance behavior aimed at controlling norm-breakers. This often painful sanction is what we mean by the process of social control.

Attempts at social control are a form of feedback about an individual's behavior and often consist of verbal sanctions—such as sarcasm, invectives, jokes, and the like. If these types of punishment don't work, the ultimate weapon is disregard or ostracism. Whether or not these controls will work on individual members depends upon the extent to which they value subsystem membership. If the group is an important source of need satisfaction for them, they will comply. If the group is not important to a member, he can safely disregard these sanctions. This point is closely connected to the formation of social structure, but before we discuss this, we want to make one other point about norms and social control.

In the discussion above of norms aimed at restricting productivity, we were, in effect, suggesting that the social controls of the subsystem would be operating in opposition to the organization and task inputs defined by the larger system. While this is often the case, social controls also often support organization objectives. An example of this is reported by Blau in his study of a government agency.[20] In this agency the group of investigating agents had developed a norm stipulating that the more competent agents should help the less competent ones when the latter were having difficulty. While this norm was contrary to a formal rule that agents should only confer with supervisors, Blau concluded that this interagent consultation improved the quality of agent decisions and contributed to the overall effectiveness of the agency. Obviously, the negative consequence of this norm was that it tended to weaken the authority of supervisors. However, the problem in this situation was not so much the norm but the rigid rules which seemed inconsistent with task requirements and social controls.

Turning now to the issue of social structure, we have already seen that different members may value subsystem membership to differing degrees. Similarly, certain individuals are more or less important to the group. This importance can take the form of contribution to task accomplishment or to their role in the maintenance of the group. For example, in Blau's group of agents the competent agent was an important member because of his ability to help others in task accomplishment. Simultaneously, the group was important to him because it fed his sense of self-esteem. These competent agents were high in the social structure of their group. In another situation a person might become a central member of a group because of his capacities to help maintain group cohesion at times of stress. For example, in a task force of managers working on a complex problem,

---

[20] Peter M. Blau, *The Dynamics of Bureaucracy* (Chicago: University of Chicago Press, 1955).

one of their number who was skillful at reducing tension through humor might become a valued member with high status. Also, as suggested in the discussion of human inputs, one's status in a social structure can also be determined by characteristics like age, skill, and the like. Which ones will be important depend on how task, organizational, and individual inputs interact with group norms to shape the attributes that group members value. What is essential to remember is that such hierarchies do develop and people's positions in them are related to their contribution to the group. At a minimum, such a contribution means adherence to group norms.

One way to illustrate these points is to describe four categories of group membership identified by Zaleznik, Christensen, and Roethlisberger.[21] The lowest of these on the totem pole is the *isolate,* a person who has been isolated from the group. This can happen because he has so little to offer the group that they isolate him and because the group is so unimportant to him that he chooses to stay out. In essence, he has signaled that group membership either is not important to him or he is not capable of meeting group expectations and the group, through its rejection, has indicated that he is not important to them. Next in lowest standing is the so-called *deviant.* He deviates from the expected patterns of behavior but is still tolerated by others. This tolerance may be because he is making some important contribution to the group in spite of his deviance or because other group members feel that there is still hope that he will conform to group behavior standards. In either case, a deviant can be identified because, instead of being ignored like the isolate, he will be the focus of much interaction directed at bringing his behavior back into line.

Next in line up the social structure is what these authors called the *regular.* As the name implies, such members are squarely in the group. They adhere to most, if not all, group expectations about behavior, so they are making the contributions expected of a good member. In exchange for this contribution they are rewarded by being included in the group. Finally, at the top of the pecking order are the *leaders.* These are the subsystem members who are seen by others as making the greatest contribution to the group. This may be the leader as defined by the formal organization, but they may also be another person. As a minimum contribution these members adhere to group norms. But beyond this, they make some special contribution which others value. It may be the contribution of helping others as in the case of the agents in Blau's study, or it may be a tension-reducing role like the task force example above. Whatever their contributions, the leaders can be identified because they will be at the center of the group in the receipt of interactions and in terms of

[21] Abraham Zaleznik, C. R. Christensen, and F. J. Roethlisberger, *The Motivation, Productivity, and Satisfaction of Workers* (Boston: Division of Research, Harvard Business School, 1958).

influence. In fact, this relationship between interaction and positions in the group can be seen throughout this discussion of membership roles. The more central a person is to the group in terms of his contribution, the more he is apt to be involved in positive interactions with others. This is another example of what we mean by the interdependence of behavior and social controls and structure.

Two other points need to be made about leadership in subsystems. First, throughout this discussion we have intentionally used the plural term leader*s*. The reason for this is that most subsystems often have a number of leaders playing slightly different roles. One very visible example of this point is in the top management subsystem of larger firms where two or three executives play different leadership roles based on their unique competences. Such an arrangement has been formalized in the office of the president in many companies. One executive may deal with external problems such as finance or marketing, while another devotes his efforts to internal issues of management development, organization, and so on. Such division of leadership is frequently agreed upon among the top group and is not necessarily officially recognized in titles or job descriptions. This is an example of the fact that in human organization of any size leadership must handle both task and maintenance functions. We should note in passing that for one individual to do both is often difficult.

The final point we wish to make about leadership has to do with the concept of authority. Too often we think of authority as coming from a formal position. This certainly is one basis of authority. But, as this discussion suggests, authority in organizations is also derived from the special contribution a leader makes to the subsystem of which he is a member. Often in management it is the particular competence a man demonstrates which makes him a valued group member whom others respect and are willing to follow. While this view of leadership and authority is more complicated than conventional ones, it is also more accurate. As a student of organizational phenomena who will be concerned with the use of power in organizations, it is important for the reader to recognize this complexity, and it is hoped that this discussion of subsystems in operation will help you to understand it. For leadership behavior like the behavior of any other subsystem member can only be understood in terms of the inputs and the issues of social control and structure.

To conclude this discussion, we want to consider one other facet of subsystems—their capacity to adapt and change. This is important because for many years students of organizations in general and groups in particular have thought of organization systems and subsystems as being more or less unchanging.[22] Such a view is contrary to the experience of many man-

[22] George C. Homans, *The Human Group* (New York: Harcourt, Brace and Company, 1950).

agers who live in changing organizations and who cause them to change. It is also contrary to more recent sociological theory which views organization systems as having the capacity to change.[23] We now want to examine briefly just how and why subsystems do adapt and change.

## ADAPTATION AND CHANGE IN SUBSYSTEMS

At the outset it is necessary to distinguish between the important processes of adaptation and change. The distinction between these is somewhat fuzzy; essentially change is an alteration in the state or level of some subsystem variable. For example, at one time it may be very easy to get unskilled labor as a human input to the organization, and because of economic changes at another time very difficult. This represents a change in the level of the human input to the system. Adaptation is the adjustment which the organization subsequently makes in order to accommodate the change in the level of such a variable. Thus, when the availability of unskilled labor drops, the organization has to do something about it. If it does this "something" effectively, this is called adaptation. If it fails to do this effectively, this is failure to adapt. In summary, adaptation is a second order change which enables the subsystem to maintain its balance in the new situation.

There is a tendency to think of change in organizations as being only such dramatic alterations as the introduction of automation or the formal reorganization of a company. But there are several kinds of change which we should at least touch upon that appear all the time in less evident ways. Most organizations are growing in size, just like the human organism, and this continual growth necessitates continual readjustments. For example, as an organization expands in size, it is apt to develop more subsystems which somehow must be linked. As subsystems grow in size they may be divided into separate units. A further "natural" and continuing change is the movement of people through an organization. People leave and are replaced by others. As new people join, they and the organization have to undergo adaptive processes so that the newcomers can become effective replacements for their predecessors. This process of socialization is part of the social control mechanisms described earlier. As the new member is socialized he learns the norms and expectations of the subsystem and the subsystem learns what it can expect from the individual. For a while during this period, deviant behavior on the part of the newcomer is tolerated as part of the learning process. This period may be as long as six months, but shortly thereafter organization members feel the newcomer has had time enough to learn and meet their norms and expectations.[24]

---

[23] Walter Buckley, *Sociology and Modern Systems Theory* (Englewood Cliffs, N.J.: Prentice-Hall, 1967).

[24] Robert S. Weiss, *Processes of Organization* (Ann Arbor: Institute for Social Research, University of Michigan, 1956).

It is also useful to make a distinction between change which originates outside the subsystem to which the subsystem must then adapt, and change which originates within the subsystem. As suggested above, most subsystems have a capacity to initiate change in themselves as well as in others.

Change may occur in any aspect of the system. For the organization as a whole, there may be changes in inputs so that the availability of raw materials, of financial support, or of appropriate personnel may vary; there may be changes in outputs so that the organization's position in the market changes; there may be changes in processes so that a new technology is developed (as, for example, the introduction of automation); lastly, there may be a change in the political environment, so, for example, the federal government may decide not to tolerate mergers. The changes of most concern to subsystem members are those which have to do with the nature of the task, the means by which the task is performed, or the way in which people are formally organized. A *task* may be changed, so that a work group will be asked to make book paper instead of writing paper; *technology* may change, so that instead of having machines to make paper which are run largely by hand, automated processes make the paper and fewer workers are involved in simpler tasks; or there may be the *reorganization* of a department and two groups which have hitherto worked separately may now be required to work together. In practice, because of the interdependence of subsystem variables, such changes rarely occur singly.

### Feedback

Before describing the dynamics of change and resistance to it, let us first relate change processes to the concept of feedback. By feedback we mean information received within the system or subsystem comparing actual events with expectations. Essentially feedback describes the comparison of actual output with expected output, and the linking of information back to modify the input-output process. In the strict cybernetic sense, negative feedback reduces discrepancies between actual and expected outputs, or variations from a norm, while positive feedback increases such discrepancies or variations. In popular usage, positive feedback describes information which supports a given direction or output, while negative feedback is critical of it. If the comparison is unfavorable in relation to the desired state of affairs, it is called negative feedback; if it is favorable it is defined as positive. The channels through which this information moves are feedback loops. One obvious example of feedback is the attempt by subsystem members to influence deviants to conform to group expectations. The feedback loop is between the subsystem and the deviant, with information moving in both directions. The deviant is receiving information about the consequences of his behavior; the rest of the system is learning whether or not their sanction is having an effect. Most changes in organizations or in subsystems occur because of information going through such feedback loops. Thus, if the environment changes, producing a market which is more competitive and therefore requiring a change in outputs, feedback loops conduct this intelligence through the marketing department to the production department. Here a series of decisions might be made depending on the situation: technology might require altering, people might require reorganizing, or costs may have to be reduced. As these internal adaptive changes are made the effects on output will be measured by the organization's capacity to compete in the market. Some feedback loops prompt alterations in the internal organization to improve its task performance and ability to compete in the external environment, while other feedback loops may stimulate organizational changes which are not related to such outputs. For example, an organization may be performing effectively, but its members may still feel that feedback from the internal environment demands change. Employees may be dissatisfied or alienated and so managers decide that an internal reorganization would increase their feelings of satisfaction with employment.

### Resistance to Change

When a change is made in any aspect of an organization, whether in technology, task, or the arrangement of people, such changes frequently are met by the people they affect with concern, if not active resistance. People have become very accustomed to doing certain things in certain ways and even if new ways are suggested which are in fact improvements, they will still be resisted. There are many reasons for this. A few examples are:

1. Any change involves the introduction of some uncertainty. What is affected and how is never entirely clear until it happens. Therefore, some individuals tend to prefer what is familiar.
2. Change usually involves the introduction of new things, and the dropping of old things. As a result a psychological sense of loss may be experienced, and this is uncomfortable.
3. Very often people's sense of competence at work is closely related to their having mastered a particular way of doing a task. When asked to change this, they may feel a lessened sense of competence.
4. Changes often also entail an alteration in valued interpersonal relationships. People may no longer have the same intensity of contacts with former associates or may be required to interact more intensively with strangers.
5. Finally, people may react to the way the change is introduced. If the change is imposed upon them unilaterally, persons who are accus-

tomed to having a voice in decisions may resist the change to counteract their feelings of powerlessness.

It should be stressed that these factors are not mutually exclusive, nor is this list exhaustive. Furthermore, in any given situation one particular reason for resisting change may be more important than others. This means that an important task for a manager engaged in making changes is to determine why his subordinates and associates are resisting a change. It is inevitable that people involved in a change will experience feelings such as those described above, but an effective manager can minimize the effects of these feelings.

The forms this resistance takes are many. Sometimes there is an explicit rejection of the new proposal. Sometimes indirect manifestations of behavior will indicate resistance such as an increase in people reporting sick or mistakes being made. After a period of initial resistance, there is usually a period of waiting and seeing. At this time people are often convinced that the change is going to be made but are not prepared to support it in case the effort fails. They do nothing to undermine it but also they will probably do nothing to help it. Finally, if the change persists, people will usually incorporate it as part of their everyday life and accept it.

### Managing Change

There are several important implications about change which stem from this systems view. First the manager must recognize the interdependency of all subsystem variables in producing behavior. Managers who rely on an overly simplistic view of human behavior instead of a systems view such as that presented here run great risks of selecting an inappropriate course of action. Understanding the functioning of a system cannot only guide the manager in working out his own behavior, given the constraints of the social forces and inputs facing him, but also can be crucial in determining which of the various inputs to alter. Such understanding may be the difference between the successful introduction of action in general and of change in particular.

A second major point for the manager to recognize is that an important element of the behavior which occurs in subsystems is the feelings of the members. As we have seen, the interaction of subsystem inputs and social mechanisms produces feelings among the people involved. It is these feelings which lead to the manifest behavior we call resistance to change. In thinking about action taking and change managers must recognize and deal in some way with these feelings because they are as real as the mechanical hardware on a factory floor.

The manager must also recognize that in groups, members work together to control their environment and to satisfy their own needs. A unilateral introduction of change can upset the members of the subsystem and can create negative feelings about a management action. It is therefore important to educate group members to the rationale and details of change and wherever feasible to foster their active participation in the planning and implementation of change. While a manager has the responsibility to make certain decisions, it is clear that the quality of these decisions and their implementation will be greatly enhanced if the manager is open to feedback from others in his subsystem. In fact, as a manager makes a diagnosis of the problems facing him, he is engaged in the process of collecting feedback about the current state of his subsystem. The more open he is to this feedback, the more adequate will be his diagnosis.

## CONCLUSIONS

This issue of an adequate diagnosis provides a useful way to close this paper because the set of concepts described are basically a set of diagnostic tools. With them a manager should be able to increase his understanding of the multiple factors which lead to the results he gets from his particular subsystem. However, even with a thorough understanding of these concepts, it is no simple matter to make an accurate analysis of the causes of behavior in an organization. The number of factors involved is large and they are related in complex ways. For the student using these concepts for the first time, they may seem too complicated and awkward. He may be inclined to revert to his own intuitions to explain what is happening in a particular situation. While such intuitive insights are often accurate, our experience indicates that the student who struggles to apply these concepts to case situations will soon find that he is achieving a more accurate understanding of human problems in organizations than he can from his own intuitive feel. This does not mean we should ignore intuitive hunches, but rather that they should be tested against the facts of the situation organized with a systemic perspective.

# The Foreman: Master and Victim of Double Talk*

FRITZ J. ROETHLISBERGER

## The Position of the Foreman

NOWHERE IN the industrial structure more than at the foreman level is there so great a discrepancy between what a position ought to be and what a position is. This may account in part for the wide range of names which foremen have been called—shall we say "informally"?—and the equally great variety of definitions which have been applied to them in a more strictly formal and legal sense. Some managements have been eloquent in citing the foremen's importance with such phrases as: "arms of management," "grass-roots level of management," "key men in production," "front-line personnel men," and the like. Not so definite is the status of foremen under the National Labor Relations Act, since they can be included under the definitions given both for "employers" and "employees." To many foremen themselves they are merely the "go-betweeners," the "forgotten men," the "stepchildren" of industry. And what some employees call some foremen we shall leave to the reader's imagination.

But even without this diversity of names, it is clear that from the point of view of the individual foreman the discrepancy between what he should be and what he is cannot fail to be disconcerting. At times it is likely to influence adversely what he actually does or does not do, communicates or does not communicate to his superiors, his associates, and his subordinates. For this reason let us try to understand better the foreman's position in the modern industrial scene.

It is in his streamlined social setting, far different from the "good old days," that we must learn to understand the modern foreman's anomalous position. The modern foreman has to get results—turn out production, maintain quality, hold costs down, keep his employees satisfied—under a

* Excerpts from the article of the same name. Reprinted with permission of author and publisher from *Harvard Business Review,* Spring, 1945, pp. 283–98.

set of technical conditions, social relations, and logical abstractions far different from those which existed 25 years ago.

### More Knowledge Required

For one thing, he has to "know" more than his old-time counterpart. Any cursory examination of modern foreman training programs will reveal that the modern foreman has to know (and understand) not only (1) the company's policies, rules, and regulations and (2) the company's cost system, payment system, manufacturing methods, and inspection regulations, in particular, but also frequently (3) something about the theories of production control, cost control, quality control, and time and motion study, in general. He also has to know (4) the labor laws of the United States, (5) the labor laws of the state in which the company operates, and (6) the specific labor contract which exists between his company and the local union. He has to know (7) how to induct, instruct, and train new workers; (8) how to handle and, where possible, prevent grievances; (9) how to improve conditions of safety; (10) how to correct workers and maintain discipline; (11) how never to lose his temper and always be "fair"; (12) how to get and obtain cooperation from the wide assortment of people with whom he has to deal; and, especially, (13) how to get along with the shop steward. And in some companies he is supposed to know (14) how to do the jobs he supervises better than the employees themselves. Indeed, as some foreman training programs seem to conceive the foreman's job, he has to be a manager, a cost accountant, an engineer, a lawyer, a teacher, a leader, an inspector, a disciplinarian, a counselor, a friend, and, above all, an "example."

One might expect that this superior knowledge would tend to make the modern foreman feel more secure as well as to be more effective. Unfortunately some things do not work out the way they are intended. Quite naturally the foreman is bewildered by the many different roles and functions he is supposed to fulfill. He is worried in particular by what the boss will think if he takes the time to do the many things his many training courses tell him to do. And in 99 cases out of 100 what the boss thinks, or what the foreman thinks the boss thinks, will determine what the foreman does. As a result, the foreman gives lip service in his courses to things which in the concrete shop situation he feels it would be suicidal to practice. In the shop, for the most part, he does his best to perform by hook or by crook the one function clearly left him, the one function for which there is no definite staff counterpart, the one function for which the boss is sure to hold him responsible; namely, getting the workers to turn the work out on time. And about this function he feels his courses do not say enough —given the particular conditions, technical, human, and organizational, under which he has to operate.

### Freedom of Action Restricted

Curiously enough, knowledge is not power for the modern foreman. Although he has to know a great deal about many things, he is no longer "the cock of the walk" he once was. Under modern conditions of operation, for example, there seems to be always somebody in the organization in a staff capacity who is supposed to know more than he does, and generally has more say, about almost every matter that comes up; somebody, in addition to his boss, with whom he is supposed to consult and sometimes to share responsibility; somebody by whom he is constantly advised and often even ordered.

To the foreman it seems as if he is being held responsible for functions over which he no longer has any real authority. For some time he has not been able to hire and fire and set production standards. And now he cannot even transfer employees, adjust the wage inequalities of his men, promote deserving men, develop better machines, methods, and processes, or plan the work of his department, with anything approaching complete freedom of action. All these matters for which he is completely or partially responsible have now become involved with other persons and groups, or they have become matters of company policy and union agreement. He is hedged in on all sides with cost standards, production standards, quality standards, standard methods and procedures, specifications, rules, regulations, policies, laws, contracts, and agreements; and most of them are formulated without his participation.

Far better than the old-timer of 25 years ago the modern foreman knows how much work should be done in what length of time; how much it is worth; what the best methods to be used are; what his material, labor, and burden costs should be; and what the tolerances are that his product should meet. But in the acquisition of all this untold wealth of knowledge, somehow something is missing. In some sense, not too clearly defined, he feels he has become less rather than more effective, less rather than more secure, less rather than more important, and has received less rather than more recognition.

### Interactions with Many People

Let us explore further this feeling of the modern foreman. Not only does he have to know more than his old-time counterpart about the "logics" of management, but also he has to relate himself to a wider range of people. In any mass production industry the foreman each day is likely to be interacting (1) with his boss, the man to whom he formally reports in the line organization; (2) with certain staff specialists, varying from one to a dozen people depending on the size and kind of organization—production control men, inspectors, standards men, efficiency engineers, safety engineers, maintenance and repair men, methods men, personnel men, counselors; (3) with the heads of other departments to which his department relates; (4) with his subordinates—subforemen, straw bosses, leadmen, group leaders, section chiefs; (5) with the workers directly, numbering anywhere from 10 to 300 people; and (6) in a union-organized plant, with the shop steward. Exploring the interdependence of each of these relationships as they impinge in toto upon the foreman makes it easier to understand how the modern foreman may feel in his everyday life. A diagram may help to make this clear (see Exhibit 1).

**EXHIBIT 1**

Forces Impinging upon the Foreman

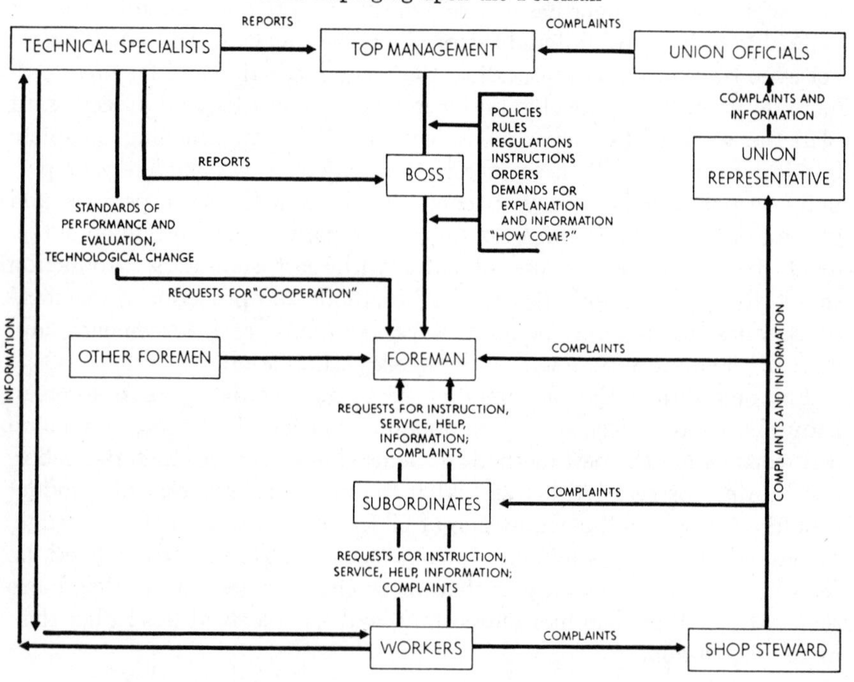


### The Foreman's Situation Summarized

The salient features of the foreman's situation should now be clear. In very broad outline—tentatively and approximately formulated—the failure on the part of top management, in mass production industries in particular, to understand the social implications of its way of doing "business" has resulted in the development of certain rigidities which do not make for cooperation in the industrial structure.

(1) At the bottom of the organization there are people called *employees* who are in general merely supposed to *conform* to *changes* which they do not originate. Too often the attitude is that employees are merely supposed to do what they are told and get paid for it. Directing them there is—

(2) A group of *supervisors* who again are merely supposed to *uphold*—"administer" is the popular word—the standards of performance and policies determined by other groups, one of which is—

(3) A group of *technical specialists* who are supposed to *originate* better ways and better standards through which the economic purpose of the organization can be better secured and more effectively controlled by—

(4) A group of *top management* men who in their *evaluation* of the workers' behavior assume that the major inducement they can offer to people to cooperate is financial (i.e., that they are merely providing a livelihood, rather than a way of life); that informal organization is either "bad" or not "present"; and that authority comes from the top, so that no attention has to be given to that authority which is a matter of individual decision and comes from the bottom. This group's whole explicit theory of human cooperation—but not necessarily the practice of it—dates back to the eighteenth century: (*a*) society is composed of a rabble of unorganized individuals; (*b*) these individuals are only interested in the pursuit of profit and pleasure; and (*c*) in the pursuit of these ends the individual is essentially logical.[1]

In this environment the foreman stands—victim, not monarch, of all he surveys. And what does he survey? On the one hand, a monument of technical achievement such as no civilization has seen before, and, on the other hand, what Elton Mayo likes to refer to as "the seamy side of progress," a bleak and arid human scene scorched dry by the babel of words and logics which have long ceased to have any power to motivate or fill with renewed hope and vigor the hearts of men. Separated from management and separated from his men, dependent and insecure in his relation to his superiors and uncertain in his relations to his men, asked to give cooperation but in turn receiving none, expected to be friendly but provided with tools which only allow him to be "fair"—in this situation of social deprivation our modern foreman is asked to deliver the goods.

---

1 These assumptions are taken from an unpublished paper written by Elton Mayo on "The Rabble Hypothesis," to be incorporated as a chapter in a book to be published shortly, *The Social Problems of an Industrial Civilization.*

# How to Choose a Leadership Pattern*

*Should a leader be democratic or autocratic in dealing with his subordinates—or something in between?*

ROBERT TANNENBAUM
WARREN H. SCHMIDT

I put most problems into my group's hands and leave it to them to carry the ball from there. I serve merely as a catalyst, mirroring back the people's thoughts and feelings so that they can better understand them.

It's foolish to make decisions oneself on matters that affect people. I always talk things over with my subordinates, but I make it clear to them that I'm the one who has to have the final say.

Once I have decided on a course of action, I do my best to sell my ideas to my employees.

I'm being paid to lead. If I let a lot of other people make the decisions I should be making, then I'm not worth my salt.

I believe in getting things done. I can't waste time calling meetings. Someone has to call the shots around here, and I think it should be me.

EACH OF THESE statements represents a point of view about "good leadership." Considerable experience, factual data, and theoretical principles could be cited to support each statement, even though they seem to be inconsistent when placed together. Such contradictions point up the dilemma in which the modern manager frequently finds himself.

## NEW PROBLEM

The problem of how the modern manager can be "democratic" in his relations with subordinates and at the same time maintain the necessary authority and control in the organization for which he is responsible has come into focus increasingly in recent years.

* Robert Tannenbaum and Warren H. Schmidt, "How to Choose a Leadership Pattern," *Harvard Business Review* (March-April, 1958). © 1958 by the President and Fellows of Harvard College; all rights reserved. Reproduced here with permission from the *Harvard Business Review*.

Earlier in the century this problem was not so acutely felt. The successful executive was generally pictured as possessing intelligence, imagination, initiative, the capacity to make rapid (and generally wise) decisions, and the ability to inspire subordinates. People tended to think of the world as being divided into "leaders" and "followers."

### New Focus

Gradually, however, from the social sciences emerged the concept of "group dynamics" with its focus on *members* of the group rather than solely on the leader. Research efforts of social scientists underscored the importance of employee involvement and participation in decision making. Evidence began to challenge the efficiency of highly directive leadership, and increasing attention was paid to problems of motivation and human relations.

Through training laboratories in group development that sprang up across the country, many of the newer notions of leadership began to exert an impact. These training laboratories were carefully designed to give people a first-hand experience in full participation and decision making. The designated "leaders" deliberately attempted to reduce their own power and to make group members as responsible as possible for setting their own goals and methods within the laboratory experience.

It was perhaps inevitable that some of the people who attended the training laboratories regarded this kind of leadership as being truly "democratic" and went home with the determination to build fully participative decision making into their own organizations. Whenever their bosses made a decision without convening a staff meeting, they tended to perceive this as authoritarian behavior. The true symbol of democratic leadership to some was the meeting—and the less directed from the top, the more democratic it was.

Some of the more enthusiastic alumni of these training laboratories began to get the habit of categorizing leader behavior as "democratic" *or* "authoritarian." The boss who made too many decisions himself was thought of as an authoritarian, and his directive behavior was often attributed solely to his personality.

### New Need

The net result of the research findings and of the human relations training based upon them has been to call into question the stereotype of an effective leader. Consequently, the modern manager often finds himself in an uncomfortable state of mind.

Often he is not quite sure how to behave; there are times when he is torn between exerting "strong" leadership and "permissive" leadership.

Sometimes new knowledge pushes him in one direction ("I should really get the group to help make this decision"), but at the same time his experience pushes him in another direction ("I really understand the problem better than the group and therefore I should make the decision"). He is not sure when a group decision is really appropriate or when holding a staff meeting serves merely as a device for avoiding his own decision-making responsibility.

The purpose of our article is to suggest a framework which managers may find useful in grappling with this dilemma. First we shall look at the different patterns of leadership behavior that the manager can choose from in relating himself to his subordinates. Then we shall turn to some of the questions suggested by this range of patterns. For instance, how important is it for a manager's subordinates to know what type of leadership he is using in a situation? What factors should he consider in deciding on a leadership pattern? What difference do his long-run objectives make as compared to his immediate objectives?

## RANGE OF BEHAVIOR

Exhibit 1 presents the continuum or range of possible leadership behavior available to a manager. Each type of action is related to the degree of authority used by the boss and to the amount of freedom available to his subordinates in reaching decisions. The actions seen on the extreme left characterize the manager who maintains a high degree of control while those seen on the extreme right characterize the manager who re-

**EXHIBIT 1**

Continuum of Leadership Behavior

BOSS-CENTERED LEADERSHIP

SUBORDINATE-CENTERED LEADERSHIP

USE OF AUTHORITY BY THE MANAGER

AREA OF FREEDOM FOR SUBORDINATES

MANAGER MAKES DECISION AND ANNOUNCES IT.

MANAGER "SELLS" DECISION.

MANAGER PRESENTS IDEAS AND INVITES QUESTIONS.

MANAGER PRESENTS TENTATIVE DECISION SUBJECT TO CHANGE.

MANAGER PRESENTS PROBLEM, GETS SUGGESTIONS, MAKES DECISION.

MANAGER DEFINES LIMITS; ASKS GROUP TO MAKE DECISION.

MANAGER PERMITS SUBORDINATES TO FUNCTION WITHIN LIMITS DEFINED BY SUPERIOR.

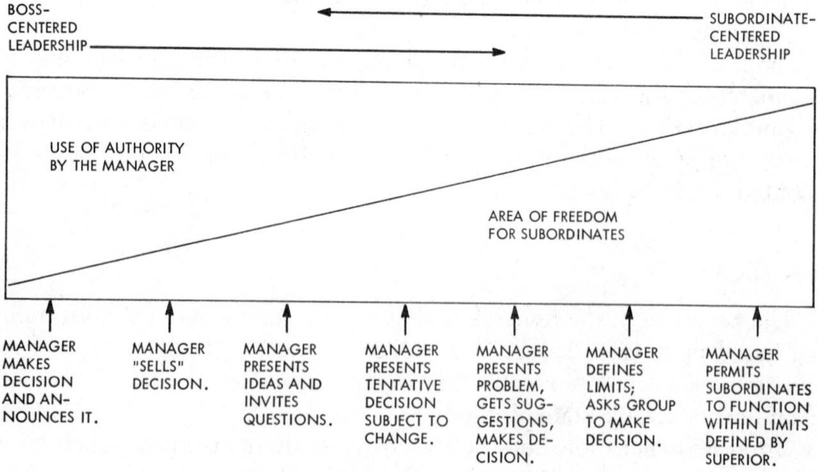

leases a high degree of control. Neither extreme is absolute; authority and freedom are never without their limitations.

Now let us look more closely at each of the behavior points occurring along this continuum:

*The manager makes the decision and announces it.*

In this case the boss identifies a problem, considers alternative solutions, chooses one of them, and then reports this decision to his subordinates for implementation. He may or may not give consideration to what he believes his subordinates will think or feel about his decision; in any case, he provides no opportunity for them to participate directly in the decision-making process. Coercion may or may not be used or implied.

*The manager "sells" his decision.*

Here the manager, as before, takes responsibility for identifying the problem and arriving at a decision. However, rather than simply announcing it, he takes the additional step of persuading his subordinates to accept it. In doing so, he recognizes the possibility of some resistance among those who will be faced with the decision, and seeks to reduce this resistance by indicating, for example, what the employees have to gain from his decision.

*The manager presents his ideas, invites questions.*

Here the boss who has arrived at a decision and who seeks acceptance of his ideas provides an opportunity for his subordinates to get a fuller explanation of his thinking and his intentions. After presenting the ideas, he invites questions so that his associates can better understand what he is trying to accomplish. This "give and take" also enables the manager and the subordinates to explore more fully the implications of the decision.

*The manager presents a tentative decision subject to change.*

This kind of behavior permits the subordinates to exert some influence on the decision. The initiative for identifying and diagnosing the problem remains with the boss. Before meeting with his staff, he has thought the problem through and arrived at a decision—but only a tentative one. Before finalizing it, he presents his proposed solution for the reaction of those who will be affected by it. He says in effect, "I'd like to hear what you have to say about this plan that I have developed. I'll appreciate your frank reactions, but will reserve for myself the final decision."

*The manager presents the problem, gets suggestions, and then makes his decision.*

Up to this point the boss has come before the group with a solution of his own. Not so in this case. The subordinates now get the first chance to suggest solutions. The manager's initial role involves identifying the problem. He might, for example, say something of this sort: "We are faced with a number of complaints from newspapers and the general public on our service policy. What is wrong here? What ideas do you have for coming to grips with this problem?"

The function of the group becomes one of increasing the manager's repertory of possible solutions to the problem. The purpose is to capitalize on the knowledge and experience of those who are on the "firing line." From the expanded list of alternatives developed by the manager and his subordinates, the manager then selects the solution that he regards as most promising.[1]

*The manager defines the limits and requests the group to make a decision.*

At this point the manager passes to the group (possibly including himself as a member) the right to make decisions. Before doing so, however, he defines the problem to be solved and the boundaries within which the decision must be made.

An example might be the handling of a parking problem at a plant. The boss decides that this is something that should be worked on by the people involved, so he calls them together and points up the existence of the problem. Then he tells them:

> There is the open field just north of the main plant which has been designated for additional employee parking. We can build underground or surface multilevel facilities as long as the cost does not exceed $100,000. Within these limits we are free to work out whatever solution makes sense to us. After we decide on a specific plan, the company will spend the available money in whatever way we indicate.

*The manager permits the group to make decisions within prescribed limits.*

This represents an extreme degree of group freedom only occasionally encountered in formal organizations, as, for instance, in many research groups. Here the team of managers or engineers undertakes the identification and diagnosis of the problem, develops alternative procedures for solving it, and decides on one or more of these alternative solutions. The only limits directly imposed on the group by the organization are those specified by the superior of the team's boss. If the boss participates in the decision-making process, he attempts to do so with no more authority than any other member of the group. He commits himself in advance to assist in implementing whatever decision the group makes.

---

[1] For a fuller explanation of this approach, see Leo Moore, "Too Much Management, Too Little Change," *HBR*, January–February, 1956, p. 41.

## KEY QUESTIONS

As the continuum in Exhibit 1 demonstrates, there are a number of alternative ways in which a manager can relate himself to the group or individuals he is supervising. At the extreme left of the range, the emphasis is on the manager—on what *he* is interested in, how *he* sees things, how *he* feels about them. As we move toward the subordinate-centered end of the continuum, however, the focus is increasingly on the subordinates—on what *they* are interested in, how *they* look at things, how *they* feel about them.

When business leadership is regarded in this way, a number of questions arise. Let us take four of especial importance:

*Can a boss ever relinquish his responsibility by delegating it to someone else?*

Our view is that the manager must expect to be held responsible by his superior for the quality of the decisions made, even though operationally these decisions may have been made on a group basis. He should, therefore, be ready to accept whatever risk is involved whenever he delegates decision-making power to his subordinates. Delegation is not a way of "passing the buck." Also, it should be emphasized that the amount of freedom the boss gives to his subordinates cannot be greater than the freedom which he himself has been given by his own superior.

*Should the manager participate with his subordinates once he has delegated responsibility to them?*

The manager should carefully think over this question and decide on his role prior to involving the subordinate group. He should ask if his presence will inhibit or facilitate the problem-solving process. There may be some instances when he should leave the group to let it solve the problem for itself. Typically, however, the boss has useful ideas to contribute, and should function as an additional member of the group. In the latter instance, it is important that he indicate clearly to the group that he sees himself in a *member* role rather than in an authority role.

*How important is it for the group to recognize what kind of leadership behavior the boss is using?*

It makes a great deal of difference. Many relationship problems between boss and subordinate occur because the boss fails to make clear how he plans to use his authority. If, for example, he actually intends to make a certain decision himself, but the subordinate group gets the impression that he has delegated this authority, considerable confusion and resentment are likely to follow. Problems may also occur when the boss uses a "democratic" façade to conceal the fact that he has already made a decision which he hopes the group will accept as its own. The attempt to "make them think it was their idea in the first place" is a risky one. We believe that it is highly important for the manager to be honest and clear in describing what authority he is keeping and what role he is asking his subordinates to assume in solving a particular problem.

*Can you tell how "democratic" a manager is by the number of decisions his subordinates make?*

The sheer *number* of decisions is not an accurate index of the amount of freedom that a subordinate group enjoys. More important is the *significance* of the decisions which the boss entrusts to his subordinates. Obviously a decision on how to arrange desks is of an entirely different order from a decision involving the introduction of new electronic data-processing equipment. Even though the widest possible limits are given in dealing with the first issue, the group will sense no particular degree of responsibility. For a boss to permit the group to decide equipment policy, even within rather narrow limits, would reflect a greater degree of confidence in them on his part.

## DECIDING HOW TO LEAD

Now let us turn from the types of leadership that are possible in a company situation to the question of what types are *practical* and *desirable*. What factors or forces should a manager consider in deciding how to manage? Three are of particular importance:

Forces in the manager.
Forces in the subordinates.
Forces in the situation.

We should like briefly to describe these elements and indicate how they might influence a manager's action in a decision-making situation.[2] The strength of each of them will, of course, vary from instance to instance, but the manager who is sensitive to them can better assess the problems which face him and determine which mode of leadership behavior is most appropriate for him.

### Forces in the Manager

The manager's behavior in any given instance will be influenced greatly by the many forces operating within his own personality. He will, of

[2] See also Robert Tannenbaum and Fred Massarik, "Participation by Subordinates in the Managerial Decision-Making Process," *Canadian Journal of Economics and Political Science,* August, 1950, pp. 413–18.

course, perceive his leadership problems in a unique way on the basis of his background, knowledge, and experience. Among the important internal forces affecting him will be the following:

(1) *His value system.* How strongly does he feel that individuals should have a share in making the decisions which affect them? Or, how convinced is he that the official who is paid to assume responsibility should personally carry the burden of decision making? The strength of his convictions on questions like these will tend to move the manager to one end or the other of the continuum shown in Exhibit 1. His behavior will also be influenced by the relative importance that he attaches to organizational efficiency, personal growth of subordinates, and company profits.[3]

(2) *His confidence in his subordinates.* Managers differ greatly in the amount of trust they have in other people generally, and this carries over to the particular employees they supervise at a given time. In viewing his particular group of subordinates, the manager is likely to consider their knowledge and competence with respect to the problem. A central question he might ask himself is: "Who is best qualified to deal with this problem?" Often he may, justifiably or not, have more confidence in his own capabilities than in those of his subordinates.

(3) *His own leadership inclinations.* There are some managers who seem to function more comfortably and naturally as highly directive leaders. Resolving problems and issuing orders come easily to them. Other managers seem to operate more comfortably in a team role, where they are continually sharing many of their functions with their subordinates.

(4) *His feelings of security in an uncertain situation.* The manager who releases control over the decision-making process thereby reduces the predictability of the outcome. Some managers have a greater need than others for predictability and stability in their environment. This "tolerance for ambiguity" is being viewed increasingly by psychologists as a key variable in a person's manner of dealing with problems.

The manager brings these and other highly personal variables to each situation he faces. If he can see them as forces which, consciously or unconsciously, influence his behavior, he can better understand what makes him prefer to act in a given way. And understanding this, he can often make himself more effective.

### Forces in the Subordinate

Before deciding how to lead a certain group, the manager will also want to consider a number of forces affecting his subordinates' behavior. He will want to remember that each employee, like himself, is influenced by many personality variables. In addition, each subordinate has a set of expectations about how the boss should act in relation to him (the phrase

---

[3] See Chris Argyris, "Top Management Dilemma: Company Needs vs. Individual Development," *Personnel*, September, 1955, pp. 123–34.

"expected behavior" is one we hear more and more often these days at discussions of leadership and teaching). The better the manager understands these factors, the more accurately he can determine what kind of behavior on his part will enable his subordinates to act most effectively.

Generally speaking, the manager can permit his subordinates greater freedom if the following essential conditions exist:

If the subordinates have relatively high needs for independence. (As we all know, people differ greatly in the amount of direction that they desire.)

If the subordinates have a readiness to assume responsibility for decision making. (Some see additional responsibility as a tribute to their ability; others see it as "passing the buck.")

If they have a relatively high tolerance for ambiguity. (Some employees prefer to have clear-cut directives given to them; others prefer a wider area of freedom.)

If they are interested in the problem and feel that it is important.

If they understand and identify with the goals of the organization.

If they have the necessary knowledge and experience to deal with the problem.

If they have learned to expect to share in decision making. (Persons who have come to expect strong leadership and are then suddenly confronted with the request to share more fully in decision making are often upset by this new experience. On the other hand, persons who have enjoyed a considerable amount of freedom resent the boss who begins to make all the decisions himself.)

The manager will probably tend to make fuller use of his own authority if the above conditions do *not* exist; at times there may be no realistic alternative to running a "one-man show."

The restrictive effect of many of the forces will, of course, be greatly modified by the general feeling of confidence which subordinates have in the boss. Where they have learned to respect and trust him, he is free to vary his behavior. He will feel certain that he will not be perceived as an authoritarian boss on those occasions when he makes decisions by himself. Similarly, he will not be seen as using staff meetings to avoid his decision-making responsibility. In a climate of mutual confidence and respect, people tend to feel less threatened by deviations from normal practice, which in turn makes possible a higher degree of flexibility in the whole relationship.

### Forces in the Situation

In addition to the forces which exist in the manager himself and in his subordinates, certain characteristics of the general situation will also affect the manager's behavior. Among the more critical environmental pressures that surround him are those which stem from the organization, the work group, the nature of the problem, and the pressures of time. Let us look briefly at each of these:

***Type of Organization.*** Like individuals, organizations have values and traditions which inevitably influence the behavior of the people who work in them. The manager who is a newcomer to a company quickly discovers that certain kinds of behavior are approved while others are not. He also discovers that to deviate radically from what is generally accepted is likely to create problems for him.

These values and traditions are communicated in many ways—through job descriptions, policy pronouncements, and public statements by top executives. Some organizations, for example, hold to the notion that the desirable executive is one who is dynamic, imaginative, decisive, and persuasive. Other organizations put more emphasis upon the importance of the executive's ability to work effectively with people—his human relations skills. The fact that his superiors have a defined concept of what the good executive should be will very likely push the manager toward one end or the other of the behavioral range.

In addition to the above, the amount of employee participation is influenced by such variables as the size of the working units, their geographical distribution, and the degree of inter- and intraorganizational security required to attain company goals. For example, the wide geographical dispersion of an organization may preclude a practical system of participative decision making, even though this would otherwise be desirable. Similarly, the size of the working units or the need for keeping plans confidential may make it necessary for the boss to exercise more control than would otherwise be the case. Factors like these may limit considerably the manager's ability to function flexibly on the continuum.

***Group Effectiveness.*** Before turning decision-making responsibility over to a subordinate group, the boss should consider how effectively its members work together as a unit.

One of the relevant factors here is the experience the group has had in working together. It can generally be expected that a group which has functioned for some time will have developed habits of cooperation and thus be able to tackle a problem more effectively than a new group. It can also be expected that a group of people with similar backgrounds and interests will work more quickly and easily than people with dissimilar backgrounds, because the communication problems are likely to be less complex.

The degree of confidence that the members have in their ability to solve problems as a group is also a key consideration. Finally, such group variables as cohesiveness, permissiveness, mutual acceptance, and commonality of purpose will exert subtle but powerful influence on the group's functioning.

***The Problem Itself.*** The nature of the problem may determine what degree of authority should be delegated by the manager to his subordinates. Obviously he will ask himself whether they have the kind of knowledge which is needed. It is possible to do them a real disservice by assigning a problem that their experience does not equip them to handle.

Since the problems faced in large or growing industries increasingly require knowledge of specialists from many different fields, it might be inferred that the more complex a problem, the more anxious a manager will be to get some assistance in solving it. However, this is not always the case. There will be times when the very complexity of the problem calls for one person to work it out. For example, if the manager has most of the background and factual data relevant to a given issue, it may be easier for him to think it through himself than to take the time to fill in his staff on all the pertinent background information.

The key question to ask, of course, is: "Have I heard the ideas of everyone who has the necessary knowledge to make a significant contribution to the solution of this problem?"

***The Pressure of Time.*** This is perhaps the most clearly felt pressure on the manager (in spite of the fact that it may sometimes be imagined). The more that he feels the need for an immediate decision, the more difficult it is to involve other people. In organizations which are in a constant state of "crisis" and "crash programming" one is likely to find managers personally using a high degree of authority with relatively little delegation to subordinates. When the time pressure is less intense, however, it becomes much more possible to bring subordinates in on the decision-making process.

These, then, are the principal forces that impinge on the manager in any given instance and that tend to determine his tactical behavior in relation to his subordinates. In each case his behavior ideally will be that which makes possible the most effective attainment of his immediate goal within the limits facing him.

## LONG-RUN STRATEGY

As the manager works with his organization on the problems that come up day by day, his choice of a leadership pattern is usually limited. He must take account of the forces just described and, within the restrictions they impose on him, do the best that he can. But as he looks ahead months or even years, he can shift his thinking from tactics to large-scale strategy. No longer need he be fettered by all of the forces mentioned, for he can view many of them as variables over which he has some control. He can, for example, gain new insights or skills for himself, supply training for individual subordinates, and provide participative experiences for his employee group.

In trying to bring about a change in these variables, however, he is faced with a challenging question: At which point along the continuum *should* he act?

### Attaining Objectives

The answer depends largely on what he wants to accomplish. Let us suppose that he is interested in the same objectives that most modern managers seek to attain when they can shift their attention from the pressure of immediate assignments:

1. To raise the level of employee motivation.
2. To increase the readiness of subordinates to accept change.
3. To improve the quality of all managerial decisions.
4. To develop teamwork and morale.
5. To further the individual development of employees.

In recent years the manager has been deluged with a flow of advice on how best to achieve these longer-run objectives. It is little wonder that he is often both bewildered and annoyed. However, there are some guidelines which he can usefully follow in making a decision.

Most research and much of the experience of recent years give a strong factual basis to the theory that a fairly high degree of subordinate-centered behavior is associated with the accomplishment of the five purposes mentioned.[4] This does not mean that a manager should always leave all decisions to his assistants. To provide the individual or the group with greater freedom than they are ready for at any given time may very well tend to generate anxieties and therefore inhibit rather than facilitate the attainment of desired objectives. But this should not keep the manager from making a continuing effort to confront his subordinates with the challenge of freedom.

## CONCLUSION

In summary, there are two implications in the basic thesis that we have been developing. The first is that the successful leader is one who is keenly aware of those forces which are most relevant to his behavior at any given time. He accurately understands himself, the individuals and group he is dealing with, and the company and broader social environment in which he operates. And certainly he is able to assess the present readiness for growth of his subordinates.

---

[4] For example, see Warren H. Schmidt and Paul C. Buchanan, *Techniques that Produce Teamwork* (New London: Arthur C. Croft Publications, 1954); and Morris S. Viteles, *Motivation and Morale in Industry* (New York: W. W. Norton & Company, Inc., 1953).

But this sensitivity or understanding is not enough, which brings us to the second implication. The successful leader is one who is able to behave appropriately in the light of these perceptions. If direction is in order, he is able to direct; if considerable participative freedom is called for, he is able to provide such freedom.

Thus, the successful manager of men can be primarily characterized neither as a strong leader nor as a permissive one. Rather, he is one who maintains a high batting average in accurately assessing the forces that determine what his most appropriate behavior at any given time should be and in actually being able to behave accordingly. Being both insightful and flexible, he is less likely to see the problems of leadership as a dilemma.

# Organizational Systems and Engineering Groups: A Comparative Study of Two Technical Groups in Industry

L. B. BARNES

THE RESEARCH reported by Barnes[1] compares two engineering groups in two different industrial organizations. Each group was an engineering department in a fairly large manufacturing company. The two departments are referred to as Departments A and B and their organizations as Companies A and B. Companies A and B formed the organizational systems within which Departments A and B functioned.

The research consisted of identifying and describing the organizational system for each department, then in exploring and comparing the relationship between each system and the backgrounds, behavior, performance, and satisfaction of each group's members. To aid in this task, the author proposed certain hypotheses and predictions to be tested with data from each department.

The research began in Company A. Its organizational system, within which Department A members worked, is described as a *relatively closed* system because Company A's management, including Supervisor A, tended to stress management controls and (1) relatively low member autonomy, (2) low opportunities for interaction, and (3) low upward influence. Addressing this relatively closed system, the author framed an initial hypothesis proposing that individual members would behave according to the values and norms of their dominant value system or reference group. It was predicted that individuals who identified themselves with either (1) their profession (Professionals), (2) the organization (Organizationals), or (3) familial-religious values (Socials) would behave according to that particular reference group's values and norms. Consequently, the hypothesis states that *an individual behaves in accord with the values and norms of his dominant reference group*. The predictions proposed that:

[1] L. B. Barnes, *Organizational Systems and Engineering Groups: A Comparative Study of Two Technical Groups in Industry* (Boston: Division of Research, Harvard Business School, Harvard University, 1960).

1. Professionals tend toward relatively low nonwork activities, low interactions, and low mutual friendships as they strive to attain the values of science, e.g., truth and knowledge.
2. Organizationals tend toward relatively high nonwork activities, high interactions, and high mutual friendships as they strive to attain the values of the organization, e.g., promotion, organizational prestige, and social acceptance.
3. Socials tend toward relatively high nonwork activities, high interactions, and low mutual friendships as they strive to attain the values of good group membership, e.g., popularity and acceptance by higher status groups.

The Department A findings showed that Professionals tended to rank low on nonwork activities, interactions, and mutual friendships. Organizationals ranked high. Socials (mostly technicians) tended to behave more according to age level than according to reference group affiliation. Younger Socials tended to behave more like Organizationals. Older Socials tended to behave more like Professionals.

Beyond these initial predictions, Professionals tended toward highest engineering performance and toward lowest satisfaction. Organizationals tended toward highest satisfaction, though ranking lower in job performance than Professionals. Socials tended toward higher satisfaction than Professionals, though their job performance was ranked lowest in the department, since most were technicians.

At this time the research moved beyond Department A hypothesis testing and toward more divergent explorations with several intriguing questions. These were:

1. What other factors besides an organizational system and its leadership help to explain Department A's polarized reference groups and social structure?
2. What would an engineering group look like in a more open organizational system? What hypotheses and predictions could be formulated for comparing relatively open and closed systems?

To answer the first question, the author explored the relationships between a department member's status characteristics and his reference group and social structure positions. To answer the second question, the author sought and found in Company B "a company which seemed to offer a more open organizational system. As we have noted already, it cannot be rigorously compared with Company A, but in this imperfect world, Company B was the closest we came to finding both a relatively open system and a roughly comparable organizational situation."

Before Company B was selected, however, six hypotheses were proposed comparing relatively open and relatively closed organizational systems. These hypotheses were each accompanied by specific predictions. The hypotheses read:

1. Dissimilar value emphases in a group are more apt to lead to polarization of reference group identification and accompanying behavior patterns in relatively closed than in relatively open organizational systems.
2. Job and social status positions are more apt to govern or dominate a person's behavior and job performance levels in relatively closed than in relatively open organizational systems.
3. The nature of an organizational system (i.e., relatively closed or relatively open) affects a group's social structure.
4. The nature of an organizational system affects a group's interaction patterns.
5. The nature of an organizational system affects the perceived job opportunities, job challenges, and satisfactions of group members.
6. Social structure position is less highly related to performance in relatively open than in relatively closed organizational systems.

These hypotheses and their accompanying predictions were designed to test some causes and consequences of a more open organizational system. Department B existed within an organizational system whose management and supervisor actively encouraged high autonomy, interactions beyond those required by the job, and *mutual* influence between status levels. At the same time, the company's vice president of manufacturing noted that:

> Department B does an excellent job of getting its work out. . . . I suppose that if there is any single group in the company that is working over their own heads, beyond their own capacities, it would be those people. That isn't bad either, of course, because they are in a position where they are reaching out for something, always trying to do a little more and a little better than their capabilities permit. It is the only way they can grow.

The research findings in Department B generally supported the hypotheses and predictions. The relatively open system apparently helped create a less rigid social structure, less status consciousness, and higher satisfaction. Though productivity patterns could not be compared with any real accuracy, management and customer productivity expectations were better met in Department B than in Department A.

In the final chapters of the book, the research explores other differences that emerged between Departments A and B. To begin with, formal education as a status factor differed in importance in the two departments. In addition, the research showed different degrees of status congruence in Departments A and B. Finally, the two organizational structures affected the ways in which individuals behaved and worked in each department. In all three cases, these factors tended to reinforce each department's organizational system.

# The Comparative Effectiveness of Groups and Individuals in Solving Problems

DOUGLAS R. BUNKER
GENE W. DALTON

FOR A NUMBER of years various researchers have been studying the problem-solving effectiveness of groups as compared with individuals working by themselves. A review of this literature suggests the carefully qualified conclusion that certain kinds of groups can be more effective than individuals in solving certain kinds of problems. This quibbling statement is derived from both the variety of substantive findings reported and a recognition of some of the methodological limitations of these studies in providing generalizable conclusions which apply to natural groups dealing with "real" problems.

## The Task as a Variable

It is characteristic of research on group-versus-individual problem solving for the experimenter to impose a task with clearly defined work rules and a standard, quantifiable criterion of success. The nature of the task is critical to the type of research results obtained. If its performance requires merely the pooling of additive bits of information until some fixed quantity is achieved, then groups will routinely do "better" than individuals. If, conversely, the task requires a division of labor in which the performances of all group members are linked in series, then the group can do no better than the performance of its poorest member—the weak-link phenomenon. Both types of studies are reported in the literature, but neither directly represents the work of a group *qua* group.

One early experiment reported by Thorndike[1] illustrates both the methods and typical results from research focusing on task differences. The principal hypothesis tested in this study was that greater group superiority will be associated with tasks which require greater range of

[1] R. L. Thorndike, "On What Type of Task Will a Group Do Well?" *Journal of Abnormal and Social Psychology,* Vol. 33 (1938), pp. 409–13.

responses. This tended to be confirmed across a series of different tests in which it was indicated that the superiority of groups increased as you moved from a task involving the choice of a response from among several given alternatives to a task requiring production of a free response to fit fixed criteria. One of Thorndike's tasks which did not directly fit with his other results confirming the hypothesis is independently illuminating. He found that groups were superior to individuals in *solving* a crossword puzzle, but that individuals were more efficient in *constructing* a crossword puzzle. In solving a puzzle, success is facilitated by the production of a profusion of alternative responses, for they can be immediately and objectively tested for fit, and while incorrect responses are sifted out, correct responses accumulate toward a complete solution. In constructing a puzzle, however, clear-cut, simple criteria of success are not available. Responses cannot simply accumulate toward a successful solution by a process of gradual confirmation. The task is more complex, requiring that many things be kept simultaneously in mind and developed as an integrated whole. The group product, Thorndike reports, "frequently amounted to nothing but the best individual performance of a member of the group, turned in for the group."

In making the point that the efficiency of groups for problem solving depends somewhat on the task, let us keep in mind that the types of tasks for which individual and group performance differences have been explored cover only a limited range of the types of work requirements which groups must meet in organizational settings. In experimental studies the group goal is generally given, while in real-life situations goal formation is an important and demanding aspect of group work. Continuing work groups also frame policy, develop strategies, solve technical problems, and devise tactics for the implementation of group decisions. Such work is qualitatively different from the purely intellectual process involved in solving or constructing crossword puzzles.

## Group Superiority—Majority Rule or Discussion

In a more recent experimental study Barnlund[2] not only compared the problem-solving abilities of individuals compared with groups, but also developed a number of clues as to what tends to enable experimental groups to secure superior results. Is it because the superior individual supplies the correct answer to the group, because the simple majority of the answers of individuals working alone provides a superior answer, or is it because of the problem-solving qualities of an open discussion within the group? To explore these questions, Barnlund used a complex intel-

[2] Dean C. Barnlund, "A Comparative Study of Individual, Majority, and Group Judgment," *Journal of Abnormal and Social Psychology,* Vol. 58, No. 1 (January, 1959).

lectual task involving the ability to draw logical conclusions from given arguments. Individuals receiving similar scores when working alone on the first half of the test were assigned to the same experimental groups so that the factor on individual differences in ability would be reduced to a minimum. The experimental group then, using discussion, worked out the second half of the test in the same amount of time allowed for the first half. This procedure allowed comparisons between three problem-solving methods: (1) individual work, (2) "group" results determined by mathematically tallying the majority decision of each experimental group's members working alone, and (3) group results under discussion conditions. The results indicated that:

1. Majority decisions, when deadlocks are evenly divided between right and wrong answers, are not significantly different from those made by the average individual and are inferior to those of the best member of the group working alone.
2. Group decisions, reached through cooperative deliberation, are significantly superior to decisions made by individual members working alone and to majority rule.

In order to throw additional light on these findings some of the group discussion sessions were recorded and analyzed for clues to the psychological factors affecting the high level of group performance. Barnlund reported that the following factors were contributing to group success:

*Membership in the experimental groups produced a higher level of interest in the successful completion of the task.* Members concentrated more intently on the assigned problems after being appointed to a group than they did when solving the problems individually. Group members found themselves more and more deeply involved as they proposed, and were forced to defend, their ideas. Participants identified with their own groups to such a degree that when some members became fatigued, others urged them to continue working.

*Membership in the experimental groups had an inhibiting as well as facilitating effect.* Knowledge that one's opinions were to be shared publicly made group members more cautious and deliberate in their own thinking. The necessity of explaining a conclusion forced many students to be more self-critical. Errors that might have been committed privately were checked before they were communicated to others.

*Groups had greater critical resources than did individuals working alone.* In spite of the uniform level of ability, group members saw different issues and a larger number of issues than did a single person working alone. A greater number of viewpoints increased the group's chances of selecting a valid one. Even the poorest members contributed significantly to the quality of the group product. Remarks that went no deeper than "I don't understand" or "That's absurd" often saved the group from error by forcing others to justify their opinions and in so doing disprove their own conclusions.

*A more objective view of the problem resulted from competition between the private prejudices of group members.* The test arguments were stated in loaded terms designed to make the choices between conclusions as difficult as possible. Each individual, however, brought a different set of values to his group. When arguments were stated so they appealed to persons of one persuasion, those in opposition were anxious to detect their error. In this way, liberals counteracted conservatives, Republicans offset Democrats, and "independents" guarded against critical lapses on the part of fraternity members. Groups were forced to become more objective, and this, of course, increased their chances of drawing valid conclusions. The significance of this one factor alone would be hard to overestimate.

Discussion of the test items also prevented other incidental mistakes from occurring. Some groups had to check their instructions several times because members had different interpretations of them. Discussion often led to a clarification of terms used in the test, and, where logical fallacies spring from ambiguous terms, this may account for some of the gains. A number of groups formulated general principles as they went along to help them avoid repeating errors in later problems.

What, then, prevented experimental groups from attaining even higher scores than they did? Analysis of the transcripts revealed two factors that together accounted for a majority of the group errors. The first was that group members agreed immediately and unanimously upon the wrong answer to a problem. Further study of the issue was then considered unnecessary and wasteful. . . . The virtue of disagreement and the possible function of a "No-Man" in group deliberations, needs further testing.

The second factor was that groups, when they reached a deadlock, were unable to use their differences of opinion for their own advantage. When conflicts became intense they were resolved by surrender of the less aggressive members or by compromising on a third solution which was almost always incorrect but served to protect the egos of the parties to the controversy. Apparently disagreement stimulates thought up to a point; beyond that point, groups may lack the patience and skill to exploit it.

### Effective Groups—Experimental versus Natural

The generalized issue of groups versus individuals as problem solvers must also include the point that groups differ in their capacity to deal effectively with problems. One important factor, of course, is the "life span" of the group.[3] Experimental groups are usually contrived, short-lived collectivities in stark contrast to working groups, which have continuity and meaningful identity as a group. While the experimental group does have the advantage of several disparate points of view, it does not have the necessary accompaniment of a set of relationships and mutually understood decision-making mechanisms to enable the members to utilize efficiently their varied resources.

---

[3] R. F. Bales and F. L. Strodtbeck, "Phases in Group Problem-Solving," in D. Cartwright and A. Zander, *Group Dynamics, Research and Theory* (Evanston, Ill.: Row Peterson, 1960).

But long-lived groups also vary greatly in their effectiveness. Shared experience, alone, is no guarantee of high performance. From the various studies of long-lived experimental groups and natural work groups, a number of attempts have been made to formulate those features which are characteristic of effective problem-solving groups.[4] Although the orientations of the investigators have varied, there are a few features which tend to be common to these formulations.

Central among these is the idea that effective problem-solving groups have worked out some mechanisms for (*a*) sharing and building on another's information and ideas, and (*b*) examining and resolving differences.

They are conscious of their own operations. For example, at some point there is an open discussion of the objective or task of the group until it is formulated in such a way that it is well understood and accepted by the members. Likewise, a balance is maintained between the task and emotional needs of the members of the group.

There is an open confrontation of differences. Disagreements are not suppressed or smoothed over before they are examined and understood. Criticism and attempts to influence are both overt and legitimate.

Decisions are made in some way which facilitates the examination and comparison of differences and alternatives. Some kind of consensus is reached which goes beyond simple majority voting or steam-rollering.

Finally, supportive relationships are established which provide a context in which differences can be confronted and new ideas tested. The members listen to one another. Divergent ideas are given a hearing. Ridicule is not utilized to suppress extreme ideas. Respect is shown for the point of view of others both in the way contributions are made and received.

---

[4] For examples, see Rensis Likert, *New Patterns of Management* (New York: McGraw-Hill Book Co., Inc., 1961); and D. Kretch, R. Crutchfield, and E. L. Ballachey, *Individual in Society* (New York: McGraw-Hill Book Co., Inc., 1962).

# CASES ON INTERGROUP ISSUES

## Belmont-White Company

Two months ago, at an operating committee meeting, the president of the Belmont-White Comany[1] asked Thornton Peet, the general sales manager, and Paul Robb, manager of the organization planning and procedures department, to get together and determine if better forecasts of sales and of inventory requirements could be made available in order to improve factory schedules, financial planning, and so on. Bert Kent and Charles Stevens, both of whom worked for Robb, and Robert Henry, Edwin Merrill, and David Spitz of the sales department, were assigned by Robb and Peet, respectively, to work on the problem. Stevens and Henry, being older and more experienced, and being regarded as rather senior men, immediately became the informal leaders of the work group. The five men worked out the technical problems to the satisfaction of both Stevens and Henry. The group attempted to consult with its immediate superiors as the work progressed.

After the study had been under way for some time, Henry told Stevens that he, Merrill, and Spitz seemed to be blocked by the opposition of the product division managers. Henry also told Stevens that he felt "he could not go over the division managers' heads" to Peet; and he asked Stevens to have his boss, Robb, inquire of the sales manager whether a conference might not be held to appraise the progress of the work. Stevens told Robb of Henry's request and the reason for it. Accordingly, Robb talked to Peet about the matter. Peet acquiesced, as he believed the problem ought to be solved as rapidly as possible. Peet invited the four product division managers, Robb, and the five-man working group to the conference and set the time for it. Peet told Henry to go ahead with Stevens and set up the presentation to be made at the conference.

As Henry and Stevens planned the conference, they decided that the group from the sales department—Henry, Merrill, and Spitz—were really

[1] A partial organization chart of the company is shown in Exhibit 1.

on the spot. The three men all agreed that in order not to embarrass themselves or their bosses, the presentation of the joint conclusions of the working group ought to be made by Stevens.

At the meeting, Peet, the four product division managers, and the three men from sales who worked on the study were present, as were Robb of the organization planning and procedures department and his two assistants, Stevens and Kent. When Peet asked who was going to report progress, Henry suggested that Stevens was the best man to present their findings. Peet asked Robb if that was O.K. When the latter agreed, Stevens

**EXHIBIT 1**

Partial Organization Chart

PRESIDENT
OTHER STAFF DEPARTMENTS
ORGANIZATION PLANNING AND PROCEDURES PAUL ROBB, MANAGER
SECTION 1
SECTION 2
SECTION 3
SECTION 4
SECTION 5
BERT KENT
CHARLES STEVENS
GENERAL SALES MANAGER THORNTON PEET
PRODUCTION MANAGER
OTHER LINE DEPARTMENTS
PRODUCT DIVISION A MANAGER
PRODUCT DIVISION B MANAGER
PRODUCT DIVISION C MANAGER
PRODUCT DIVISION D MANAGER
SECTION HEADS
OTHER SECTION HEADS
SECTION HEAD EDWIN MERRILL
OTHER SECTION HEADS
SECTION HEAD ROBERT HENRY
OTHER SECTION HEADS
SECTION HEAD DAVID SPITZ

used half an hour to outline the concept of their work; he stated that both groups had agreed upon details and believed their recommendations would work; they were prepared to take personal responsibility for them. Both Merrill and Spitz asked Henry to amplify certain points during the presentation. It seemed to Robb that they had in mind clarifying matters for their own bosses who might be opposed or might not understand.

Following Stevens' statement, the sales manager called upon his product division managers to give their reactions to the proposals. One of them gave the plan lukewarm support; the three others said it could not be accomplished. There was much discussion among the three who were opposed. Occasionally, Henry, Merrill, and Spitz tried to "get a word in edgewise," without much success. Once, Kent asked the Division B manager a question; the effect seemed to be mild anger at being interrupted.

Robb watched the whole proceeding with interest. He recalled that it had seemed to him that for the past two years, this same group of four product managers had opposed every step involving changes in methods or procedures. In his opinion, their "delaying tactics" had been costly to the company. Robb knew that the president expected him to break some of these bottlenecks. Robb was only a staff adviser, but he knew he "had the president's ear" whenever he needed it. He considered the sales manager to be progressive and thought Peet could not tolerate these conditions much longer. It seemed to Robb that Peet had line responsibility to get something done in this area. Robb liked these "old-line" product managers and did not want to hurt them if he could avoid it.

While Robb was in the midst of these musings, and after two hours of apparently fruitless discussion, Peet turned to him and said: "Robb, you have heard this whole discussion; what do you think we ought to do next?"

# Mayflower Paper Mills

JOHN CURTIS was anxious about the pace of technical innovations in the three paper mills for which he was general manager. The mills had their own technical staff but for more long-term development and more sophisticated work there was a small research department that the three mills under Curtis shared with the Mayflower Company's other four mills on the East Coast. "I am not really sure," he said, "that we have found the best way of organizing research and development work for the mills. The Research Department seems to work pretty well with most of the mills but there is really no cooperation with the mill at Quinault. In fact, the mill manager at Quinault thinks that Research is useless and I find it difficult at the moment to persuade him to cooperate with them when his mill is the most profitable in the group." (See Exhibits 1 and 2.)

Curtis added, however, that even though the Quinault mill was working at full capacity, the newsprint sheet produced there was only of medium quality. The quality of the paper produced depended on many variables, such as fiber length, pulp consistency, machine speed, temperature, and water flow. The manipulation of these variables determined weight, finish, thickness, softness, and moisture of the finished product. In the past the quality of the paper produced had depended entirely on the skill and experience of the machine operators as they adjusted the process variables. This dependence of human ability, though still important, was decreasing, however, as scientific knowledge about the factors influencing quality increased.

Curtis was mainly concerned about the lack of cooperation between the Quinault plant and the Research Department. "There is a real running battle between the Quinault mill manager, Tom Moe, and the director of research, Bob MacCaulay," he said, "and although I think it might be having some harmful effects on our operations long term, I don't know how to resolve the problem. I do think that the friction between Research and Quinault has had some bad effects on technical innovations in the mill, but I can't say that they are really significant. We should have something to gain if Research had full access to Quinault. But all the things we want Research to do up there have been solved by the mill technical people."

**EXHIBIT 1**

Part of Organization Chart of Paper Group

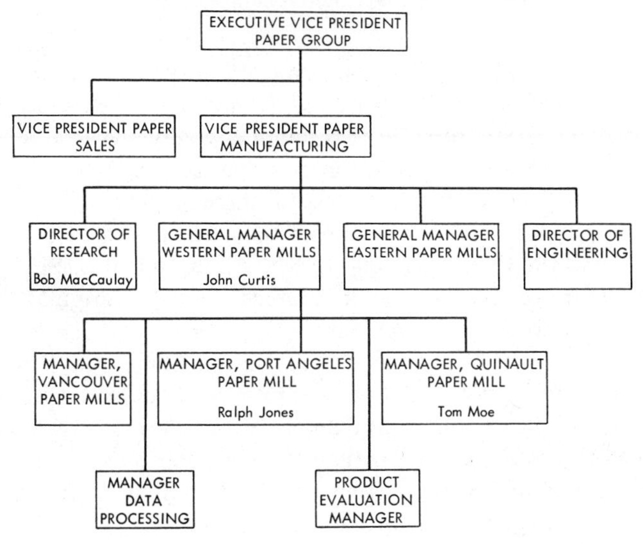


### The Mayflower Company

The three mills under John Curtis were part of a large and diversified "conglomerate" with sales of over one billion dollars in 1968. Mayflower corporate headquarters were located in Portland, Maine. The communications papers segment of the company's business, of which the paper mills were a part, contributed $130 million in sales and 13 percent of the company's profits in 1968.

. . . Mayflower paper mills produced 476,000 tons of communication papers during 1968 at seven locations. . . . Both the Quinault and Vancouver newsprint mills operated at peak capacity despite the general leveling of U.S. newsprint

**EXHIBIT 2**

Recent Operating Statistics for the Quinault Mill

| | *1966* | *1967* | *1968* | *1969 (6 mos.)* |
|---|---|---|---|---|
| Production (tons) | 218,548 | 239,915 | 239,949 | 130,410 |
| Net sales . . . . . . . | $28,582,436 | $31,896,698 | $32,520,552 | $17,928,430 |
| Income* . . . . . . . . | $7,791,053 | $7,880,985 | $7,732,235 | $4,844,880 |
| R.O.I.† . . . . . . . . . | 27.7% | 29.5% | 29.5% | 35.9% |

* Before GS&A and before tax

†R.O.I. $= \frac{\text{pretax income}}{\text{total investment}}$

demand that characterized the 1967–68 period. Newsprint accounts for just over half of Mayflower's communication paper production and is the largest single paper tonnage item produced by the company.

Of the seven mills in the communications papers group, the three western mills had originally been owned by the Washtenaw Pulp and Paper Company, either directly or through a wholly owned Canadian subsidiary. The Pulp and Paper Company was acquired by Mayflower in December, 1964. Its assets consisted of three papers mills, one at Port Angeles, Washington, one just across the straits at Vancouver, British Columbia, and the third one, 150 miles north at Quinault, British Columbia, and research facilities in Port Angeles. The four original Mayflower mills were located on the East Coast.

Among the paper companies in the United States Mayflower ranked about average for introduction of new products; compared to companies with an equal sales volume, Mayflower was below average. Curtis believed that this was because management of the ten-year-old company was more concerned with current earnings than with future earnings which might accrue from investment in research.

Curtis had been manager of one of the Mayflower company's East Coast mills before becoming general manager of the three western mills. He had worked in the industry ever since he had obtained his degree in Pulp and Paper Technology, except for two years spent with the U. S. Army. He attended the Program for Management Development at Harvard six months after taking up his new appointment as general manager of the western mills in May, 1967. Curtis maintained that a mill manager did not need to have a high degree of technical knowledge about paper making, but it was essential to have had some experience in the industry.

After the acquisition, the research laboratories at Port Angeles began to serve all seven of Mayflower's paper mills with the director of research reporting to the vice president of paper manufacturing. In January, 1969 the director of research was Bob MacCaulay. After receiving his Ph.D. in Chemical Engineering, MacCaulay had started work in the research laboratories of Washtenaw Pulp and Paper and subsequently became laboratory manager. Within a year of the acquisition of Pulp and Paper by Mayflower he was made director of research for the paper group.

Tom Moe, the Quinault Mill manager, had worked in the paper industry ever since he graduated as a chemical engineer in 1946. Early in his career he worked in Alberta in a newsprint mill and gradually worked his way up until he became technical director of the mill. When personal friction with some machine tenders in the mill caused him to resign, he joined another firm of paper manufacturers as a superintendent and was put in charge of starting up two new paper machines. Later on, when another company in British Columbia required an experienced man to start up a rebuilt paper machine he joined them as mill general superintendent and subsequently became mill manager. Some time later the problem of placing his children in a suitable school in a remote area caused him to look around for another job. He was appointed general superintendent of Mayflower's Vancouver Mill in December, 1964. Within a year he was promoted to mill manager and then in June, 1967 was appointed manager of the company's other Canadian paper mill at Quinault, British Columbia.

Tom Moe had become general superintendent of the Vancouver Mill on the day that the merger of Washtenaw Pulp and Paper with Mayflower was consummated.[1] Bob MacCaulay recollected that he was working on a problem with one of the pulp screens at Vancouver at the time that Moe was appointed. A small committee of technical and production people were discussing the screen problem and the question arose as to whether they should invite Tom Moe to the meeting. MacCaulay said he thought the new superintendent would be too busy settling into his new job and so Moe wasn't invited. MacCaulay recalled that when Moe had found out about this he was very resentful and had held a grudge against him ever since.

## Organization of the Paper Group

Exhibit 1 shows the formal positions of these two men in the management hierarchy of the paper group. The organization of the Mayflower Paper Group, comprising the seven mills and a number of service departments, was a complex one, involving differences in geography, product, nationality, technology, and date of acquisition. In financial terms, the paper mills were considered profit centers while the various service departments such as sales, research and engineering, were considered cost centers to the group. Both the Research Department and the Central Engineering Department received budget allocations from the vice president of paper manufacturing. Funds were also channeled from a particular mill to either of these departments if the project undertaken was specific to that mill only. For instance, when the Central Engineering Department did the design and commissioning for the rebuilding of a paper machine at the Quinault Mill the cost for this activity was charged against the mill. Similarly, when a mill manager requested that somebody in the Research Department carry out an investigation that was specific to his mill, the time spent by the Research Department was charged

[1] The general superintendent was responsible for the day-to-day operations of the mill's manufacturing departments and reports to the mill manager.

against the mill. A limit of 25 percent of the total time available to research personnel was to be used in this way, but this limit had never been reached.

The Research Department at Port Angeles was small, with assets of approximately $600,000 at replacement cost. Besides Bob MacCaulay, the director, there were nine professional engineers or chemists, including four Ph.D's and about 12 technicians and supporting staff members. In contrast, each of the seven paper mills represented an average investment of over $20 million and each employed between 400 and 800 men. In 1969 the budgeted net sales for the seven paper mills were $160 million, while budgeted expenditure of the Research Department was $360,000.

In the early part of 1969 there were 16 projects on which research personnel were working. Of these, six were applicable to all seven paper mills, four others were applicable to either three or four of them, and the remaining six were each relevant to one mill only. Some of the more important projects were concerned with increasing the yield of pulp, general explorations into the chemical and physical characteristics of pulp from different species of wood, the development of new or improved finishes, and the improvement of testing procedures for new grades of paper. Bob MacCaulay described the nature of some of these projects:

> Most of the work we do now is on a pretty short-term basis and involves no real risk. We aren't really doing any *new* developments. The Washtenaw Pulp and Paper management had a longer term outlook and in their research department some completely new products were developed. The Mayflower management are much more short-term oriented and although things look good at the moment I think we might suffer long term from some of the decisions that have been made. For instance, last year we dropped our membership in the Canadian research center of the Institute of Paper Chemistry because of the high cost of subscription.

Managers of the paper mills which used the Research Department were asked about their attitude toward the Research Department. Tom Jacobs, manager of the Vancouver Paper Mill, said:

> The people in the Eastern mills have a poor opinion of research, but the people here in my mill think highly of them. Charging for research time against the individual mill's profits doesn't affect or deter our use of them.

The manager of the Port Angeles Mill, Ralph Jones, said:

> We are working on three or four new grades with Research. We do a lot of work with them; in fact, I get a bill from them every month.

MacCaulay explained why it was that some of the paper mills used the Research Department more than others:

We do most of our work for the three mills here that used to be part of the old Pulp and Paper organization. At times our work with the mills over on the East Coast has been pretty small because of the distance, but relations with them are cordial and now our contacts with them seem to be increasing. Ralph Jones, the manager of the Port Angeles Mill, drives us crazy with requests to carry out investigations and we also do a fair amount of work for the Vancouver Mill. But Quinault people prefer to go their own way—they think the research people are spies. We got on fine with the people at Quinault when Ralph Jones was manager there, but when Tom Moe moved up there from Vancouver they cut us right out.

Tom Moe explained why:

My job as resident manager of the Quinault Mill is to run the mill, within the budget objectives and the goals set by top management, as a unit profit center. I see myself as a sort of team captain and I am trying to develop the people we have here so that the mill can be self-sufficient. If we haven't got enough people or we haven't got people with the specialized skills for a particular job, then we go outside: for instance, we might get people from the Central Engineering Department or hire some outside consultants. The tendency now in the corporation is to say that you should give Central Engineering preference over outside consultants because we are paying the overhead anyway and it is good training for the engineers in the corporations. Personally, I try to get my own people here in the mill to do as many of the jobs as possible so that they can learn from the experience and build up technical expertise. Anyway, the same concept that applies to the use of Central Engineering is supposed to apply to Research. So if we have a job up here that we don't have the expertise to handle I could go to Research and ask them to help us out. But they don't like working under that arrangement. Before Washtenaw Pulp and Paper was taken over by Mayflower quite a few research projects were started without consultation with the mills and so they have got used to doing jobs which the mill managers haven't asked them to do. I feel that the Research people want to run the mill technically and not accept the responsibility for it.

I am trying to achieve a balance of technical and practical skills for the mill superintendents and the mill technical staff. The mill superintendents are the people who should define research problems. No man can serve two masters; how can the superintendents be carrying out tests for Research and running the machines in the most profitable way for the mill?

I have never asked the Research people to do anything for us since I have been here. But I have got research questions ironed out by our suppliers; for instance, we get a lot of chemicals from Dow and they have helped us improve our utilization and reclamation of pulping chemicals. For other problems I will talk with my friends in other paper mills around the country. I know a lot of people in Canada through the paper industry associations and going to conventions and through working for different companies. We all try and help each other out as much as we can.

The Research Department here is on much too small a scale to be of any use.

The Research people have an 8 to 4 job and that's a pretty soft touch compared with the technical people at the mill. I reckon the Research people make work so that they can stick to their soft jobs.

The ill feelings between Bob and Tom, and between their respective subordinates, were well known around the organization. The manager of Data Processing described what happened when he worked on a job with the two men themselves.

We were setting up a new quality control system for the newsprint that we shipped from Quinault down to one of the large daily newspapers in California. Bob was involved because the Research Department collects quality data on the paper from all the mills so that it can do standard statistical tests and maintain standardized test procedures. They didn't get along very well together. Whenever Bob made a suggestion, Tom told him to stop telling him how to run his mill. One of the troubles is that Tom gets too involved with all the tiny details. When we were putting in that system we just couldn't have a meeting without Tom being there. He's a very hard-working guy but he just oversupervises. For instance, we had a small problem with data cards coming back which did not match the correct roles of newsprint. Tom insisted on going down and seeing the customer himself to sort out the problem. I don't think the mill manager should need to go and sort out these problems—they aren't important enough for him.

It's a funny thing, but Ralph Jones wants to get involved too much in the details as well and they are both Canadians. Perhaps this is one of the differences between Canadian and American managers?

Different people around the organization cited different factors as explaining the conflict between Research and Quinault. Besides the issue of nationality one of the popular explanations rested in the remoteness of the Quinault Mill from Port Angeles. The Research Department, the paper mill at Port Angeles, and the Vancouver Paper Mill were all within walking distance of each other, whereas the Quinault Mill was 150 miles north of Vancouver and occasionally, under bad weather conditions, it was impossible to get between the two places. Management personnel usually made the journey in a small company-owned plane and this was often grounded because of bad weather. To illustrate this point, it was not until the fourth day of his visit to Port Angeles in January, 1969 that conditions were suitable for the casewriter to be flown to Quinault to visit the mill. Such constraints also affected the travel plans of top management personnel of Mayflower so that their appearance at the Quinault Mill was extremely uncommon. In contrast, the facilities at Port Angeles and Vancouver were accessible by regular scheduled airlines.

The Quinault Mill differed from the other two western mills in other respects. Its three high-speed paper-making machines were given over to the continuous production of newsprint. One of the three machines in the Vancouver Mill made newsprint about 40 percent of the time and all the rest of its machine capacity was used for making specialty papers.[2] A further difference was that, at least during the financial year 1968, Quinault was the most profitable mill in the group. In fact, some of the managers in the group said that Quinault "prints money."

Bob MacCaulay put it this way:

> Because of the annual bonus system, which is related to the earnings per share of the total corporation, it is in my interest that the Quinault Mill makes more money, the same as it is for all the mills. The trouble is that they *are* making money so if you try to do any work there they think you are interfering.

The antagonism between the Research Department and the Quinault Mill was not confined to the two managers involved. The technical director of the Quinault Mill described how he dealt with technical problems.

> My department is involved in all the technical aspects of the mill. This includes production, shipping, quality control, testing, and even statistics on the supply of pulpwood. We would like to think that technically we are self-sufficient here. If a problem arises that is outside our scope, then I take it to the mill manager and he decides how it will be dealt with. The trouble with Research is that they feel the whole mill should be open for their investigation. We had some trouble with them recently over a screening improvement. We thought we had the expertise to deal with the problem and they thought they had more data available on which to base a decision. Well, anyway, we did the work on it and were able to successfully improve the process. Research shouldn't be involved with in-plant problems; they should be developing new processes and new products. Research should be technically ahead of the mills. The trouble is that they do not have the resources to do new product development.

A young chemist, with about three years' experience at the Quinault Mill, had this to say:

> When I first worked here as a summer student, there were people up here from Research working all the time. I worked with some of the guys from Research sometimes but I never really learned anything from them. Since I came here to work permanently two years ago the mill has become much more self-sufficient, from a technical point of view. If we get into trouble we usually talk to people we know in other paper mills and ask them how they solved the problem. It's a really friendly industry, the paper industry.

Typical of the views of the professional engineers and chemists from the Research Department was the following:

> We really have wonderful cooperation with the people in the mill here at Port Angeles but if we go up to Quinault we get the feeling that we are not wanted. Tom Moe has a technical background and he thinks he knows it all.

---

[2] Specialty papers are those papers which are further processed by the customer to make a finished product.

When they had a new technical director up there, at first he was quite okay but now he is as bad as the rest. We get better cooperation with the mills over on the East Coast than we do with Quinault. If they ever ask you anything they are just satisfied with a short-term answer and then they shut you off. Often they use our nationality as a justification for insulting us. They are all Canadians and there are no Canadians here in the Research Department.

One of the Ph.D.'s in the Research Department went on to describe an incident which he said showed the "bad way" in which they were treated by the people at Quinault. He had performed some tests at the Quinault Mill which involved staying there for three weeks. Usually anyone visiting Quinault stayed in the company staff house, provided there was room. When he arrived he was told that he had to stay in a motel in the town. As far as he could find out there were no people visiting the mill who would have been occupying the staff house during that period. The group of researchers suspected that this was just another case of "cussedness" on the part of the mill manager. In fact, the casewriter was able to ascertain from the staff house manager and the records in the guest register that at the particular period in question the staff house had been completely occupied by a party of important customers who were normally offered the facilities of the staff house for fishing trips at that time of the year.

Problems also arose between the two groups because of different outlooks towards tests that were carried out on the machines in the mills. The machine operators thought that Research people should be sure of the results of what they were going to do, while the Research people complained that this showed that the men in the mill had no understanding of what is meant to have a research orientation. A mill hand said: "Those guys from Research always muck us up when they do their tests," while the researchers accused the men in the mill of being resistant to change and unreceptive to new ideas.

Besides the research projects carried out in the laboratories and the consulting-type investigations requested by mill managers or their technical directors, the Research Department carried out other activities. One important activity of the Research Department was to standardize the tests used for assessing paper quality and to calibrate the instruments used to perform these tests. There were many nationally recognized standards for paper color, brightness, strength, porosity, opacity, moisture content, ash content, etc., that made it important to have consistent and reliable instruments to insure that the quality of the finished product from the mill met customers' requirements. Some of these tests had to be carried out in specially controlled conditions and often required the use of an air-conditioned room. The Quinault Mill was the only mill in the Paper Group which did not have an air-conditioned room for test purposes. Such a facility was estimated by the Research Department as costing approximately $10,000. The brightness tester at the Quinault Mill was made by a different manufacturer than those used in all the other mills. These factors were regarded by the Research personnel as being partly responsible for some of the disputes they had about product quality with Quinault Mill personnel. As Bob MacCaulay put it:

The basis of research is standardized conditions and procedures, and the people at Quinault don't use them. Our sales people are having a bad time getting tonnage for the newsprint mill that we are building in the South because of the poor quality of the Quinault newsprint. The reason why Quinault is full when other newsprint mills around the country are working on short time is that our sales people are building up the tonnage for when the new mill opens. Our two biggest newsprint customers say that our paper is the poorest for runability. Some time ago I sent Quinault a memo about runability and moisture content which they took offense at. They have been refusing to send me the summary of test results ever since as a punishment. They thought my memo was trying to tell them things that they knew. Well, everyone knows that runability and moisture content are related—the whole point is that they play it safe and don't use proper instruments. So they keep the moisture content too low and won't ease it up to the line.

The one function that the Research Department carried out which Quinault technical personnel agreed was useful was that of paying for a joint membership of the various industry and technical associations, thus reducing costs. Some of them also agreed that it would be useful to keep test equipment standardized through a central research department, while a smaller number maintained that Research should be concerned with developing marketable by-products and totally new grades of paper. Twice per year there was a meeting of all mill managers, mill technical directors, the director of research, and some of his professional staff. The mill managers received a monthly research report that described progress being made on current projects. Within the last year and a half technical directors at the mill had started sending monthly technical reports to the Research Department; Quinault was the last mill to adopt this practice. Bob MacCaulay said, "The technical report from Quinault was written by Tom Moe. You can't really call it a technical report because it contained no data—it was really just an essay from the manager's office."

In 1968 a major rebuild was completed on one of the paper machines at Quinault. This was the largest job that the western section of the Central Engineering Department had ever handled and the total contract involved 2.9 million dollars. The manager of the Central Engineering Department had this to say about the rebuild:

Tom Moe was skeptical to start with but the job worked out well. He respects technical competence. Nowadays I think Quinault is the best mill for cooperative effort.

The technical director at Quinault said that a few of the start-up problems after the rebuild could have been eliminated if they had been better informed and consulted by the Central Engineering Department. Tom Moe added, "We don't have any real problems in dealing with Central Engineering."

In January of 1969 the vice president of paper manufacturing, who was also concerned about the research organization, asked the paper mill managers, the two general managers, and the director of research and his assistant to submit their written comments on the following topics:

1. The guiding philosophy and basic objectives of research and development directed toward process improvement.
2. Increases, or other changes, in the personnel requirements of the Research Department and the technical departments at the mills.
3. Suggestions for suitable research projects to be carried out by the Research Department.
4. The best location of the facilities of the Research Department.

The suggestions made as a result of this request ranged from the establishment of a new research laboratory to serve the East Coast mills (made by a member of the Research Department) to the abolition of the Research Department (made by Tom Moe).

Curtis wanted to see the conflict between the Research Department and the Quinault Mill resolved. He felt that such a resolution was his responsibility. He knew that Quinault was the most profitable mill in the company and that this was due to some extent to Tom Moe's skill. He also felt that the Quinault Mill would not lose volume or profit when the company's new mill opened. Yet the long-term health of the mill and improvement of quality necessitated better relations between Research and Quinault. He summarized his problem this way:

> A lot of the problem is with Tom Moe, because of the way he is—his hang-ups. It's also Bob MacCaulay. He is quick, but somehow intense. So it's partly a personality clash. But it's mainly Tom, because he has problems with other people besides Bob.
>
> I think Tom must feel really insecure although he has no reason to. If he would work with staff groups to get the benefit of their knowledge and experience, he would be the best manager we have because he is without question the best paper man.

Curtis had discussed this problem on numerous occasions with John Dumont, vice president of paper manufacturing. At Dumont's suggestion, Curtis had also discussed the problem with Mayflower's new corporate director of personnel, Phil Hanson, who had recently acquired his Ph.D. in organizational behavior from the Stanford Business School. Hanson had offered to help with the problem in any way he could. Curtis there-

## EXHIBIT 3

Pulp and Paper
Canadian Domestic Supply, 1964–68

| | 1964 | | 1965 | | 1966 | | 1967 | | 1968 | |
|---|---|---|---|---|---|---|---|---|---|---|
| | 1* | 2† | 1* | 2† | 1* | 2† | 1* | 2† | 1* | 2† |
| 1. Manufacturers' shipments | 1984 | +10.6 | 2104 | + 6.0 | 2345 | +11.4 | 2356 | +0.5 | 2426 | + 2.8 |
| 2. Less exports | 1359 | +11.6 | 1432 | + 5.4 | 1576 | +10.0 | 1595 | +1.2 | 1718 | + 7.7 |
| | 625 | | 672 | | 769 | | 761 | | 708 | |
| 3. Add: imports | 65 | + 8.5 | 72 | +10.9 | 71 | − 2.1 | 70 | −0.6 | 78 | +10.5 |
| 4. Domestic supply | 690 | −17.4 | 744 | + 7.8 | 840 | +12.9 | 831 | −1.1 | 786 | − 6.4 |
| 5. Exports as a percentage of manufacturers' shipments (*B/A*) | 68.5 | | 68.1 | | 67.2 | | 67.7 | | 70.8 | |
| 6. Imports as a percentage of domestic supply (*C/D*) | 9.4 | | 9.7 | | 8.5 | | 8.4 | | 9.9 | |

* Value in $ million.
† Percent change over previous year.
Source: From a Report Issued by Toronto Dominion Bank on Paper and Allied Industries in Canada (includes pulp and paper, asphalt roofing, paper box and bag, and miscellaneous paper converters). Based on DBS figures.

fore wondered what he might do himself—or how he might involve Dumont and/or Hanson in solving the problem.

## CONCLUSION

The faster rise of wages, compared to industry selling prices, particularly in 1966 and 1967, no doubt accounts for the reduction in net earnings in those years. In addition, the increasing capital investment in 1964 and after also led to a substantial surplus of productive capacity in newsprint and chemical pulp. Signs are, however, that the current year will see better conditions, with improved exports. Mr. R. M. Fowler, president of the Canadian Pulp and Paper Association, in the annual speech in January, 1969, said, "Nevertheless, by the end of 1968 there were signs that some of the important problems that have plagued the industry for two years, problems of growth, really, were beginning to ease. In particular, world markets were considerably stronger, and for the immediate future, world demand for newsprint and pulps seems likely to increase more rapidly than productive capacity."

Newspaper reports have appeared that some of the larger pulp and paper companies expect improved profits this year, and newspaper reports also mention a probable rise in the price of pulp and paper products sometime this year.

# American Magnolite Company*

## PART 1[1]

IN LATE November of a recent year a group of the top executives of the Midtown branch of the American Magnolite Company met to make some critical decisions in regard to a new product development. The product in question was a radically new type of ignition control tube that two industrial engineers, Fred Fisher and George Ames, had been developing since the previous August. The project had reached the point where Russ Keller, the head of industrial engineering, had asked for a meeting to decide primarily whether the project should remain with the industrial engineers who started it or be turned over to the plant's regular staff of development engineers.

The American Magnolite Company was a leading producer of all types of electrical and electronic equipment. It operated manufacturing plants in many parts of the country; and each plant specialized in the manufacture and, in many instances, the marketing, of a related group of products.

The Midtown branch plant produced and sold a family of electronic tubes and control devices. The plant had been established only a few years earlier and had always placed heavy emphasis on new product development. In fact, 150 of the plant's 550 employees were engaged in some way in development engineering work in comparison with a production force of 250 people. Exhibit 1 presents a partial organization chart of the plant, showing the key people involved.

The new ignition control tube—or the "Amicon" tube, as it came to be called—had started as an idea of Fisher's in August. He thought that by a radically new design approach, it might be possible to replace the ignition control tube the plant was currently producing with a new one that would be superior in quality and production cost. Fisher had been looking for some kind of special project that would interest him, and the Amicon tube idea met these needs. As he expressed it: "I was par-

* This case is based on material from the book *Administering Changes: A Case Study of Human Relations in a Factory*, by H. O. Ronken and P. R. Lawrence (Boston: Division of Research, Harvard Business School, 1952). Data reproduced by permission.

[1] This is a sequential case. Your instructor may wish to have you discuss Part 1 of the case before reading subsequent parts.

ticularly displeased with our department's general position in the company and felt we didn't really have a chance to show what we could do. Everything we tried, we got held up on; and I was dying to get hold of a project that I could really get my teeth into."

Fisher talked to his boss, Keller, about his ideas for a new tube; and Keller, in turn, sounded out Larry Barnes on the subject. As Keller recalled it: "I mentioned the idea to Larry Barnes, and he immediately got enthusiastic about it. He suggested that I see if we couldn't make up a few tubes to see if they would work."

**EXHIBIT 1**

Partial Organization Chart of Midtown Plant

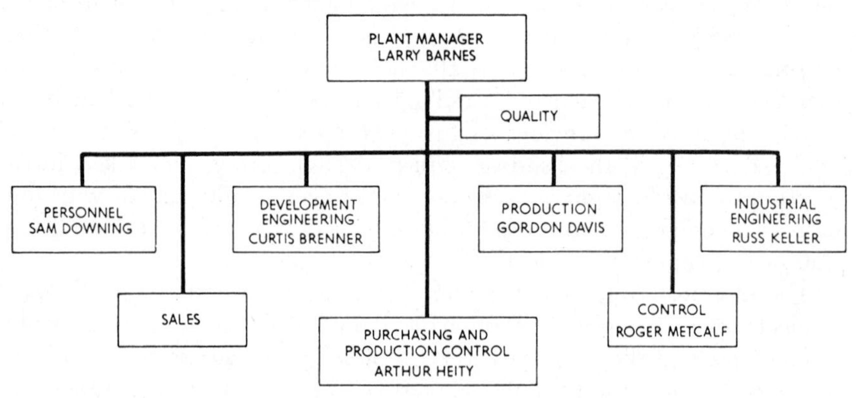


Fisher and Ames spent the months of September and October pretty well isolated in Fisher's office working on their ideas. Fisher gave an account of what they were doing and how they felt about the project:

Well, Ames and I got started working on it about last August. It really was a lot of fun. We used to try out every idea we got. We never assumed ahead of time that something wouldn't work until we tried it. We tried everything we could think of. For quite a while, we had this office set up as our experimental shop. We had a little engine lathe over there where we worked on the parts, and we had a test kit here where we tried them out. By starting from scratch on this problem, we learned a lot. A lot of the things we learned contradicted what everybody had previously thought about the problem.

Fisher went on to tell with enthusiasm how he enjoyed the work:

Those were great days! I never used to come to work later than 7 o'clock. A good many days, I would be working here so steadily that I wouldn't even notice it was time to quit until some time after 4:30. One day, I worked until 5:45 before I realized it was past quitting time. I always came in on Saturday and sometimes on Sunday. You know, I didn't get paid any overtime for those hours, either.

At the end of October, Fisher and Ames thought that their Amicon tube looked promising, and they were anxious to start making up more tubes for experimental purposes. The first thing they did in this direction was to secure approval for hiring two women to help them as experimental operators. During the first week in November, Sam Downing, the personnel director, hired two new employees, Claire Cochrane and Alice Nagle. These two girls went to work for Fisher and Ames, performing all the operations involved in making a limited quantity of experimental Amicon tubes.

During October and November the two men prepared specifications on the parts to be used in the new tube and on the processes to be used in producing and assembling these parts. These rough preliminary specifications were constantly being modified as the production experiments indicated improvements that could be made in design features and production operations.

Ames, with help from Fisher, converted an obsolete piece of equipment into an "envelope" machine to make the glass body cases for the new tube. This job took considerable time, since new parts had to be designed and built and then redesigned in order to get the "bugs" out of the machine. Ames always stood by this machine when it was in operation; and with many little adjustments and with the help of Claire and Alice, he could produce enough good-quality body cases in a few hours to keep the two girls supplied for several days.

Fisher and Ames also worked up some rough ideas for a semi-automatic machine for swaging the positive terminal. Karl Vronska, one of the industrial engineers' skilled machinists, was assigned the job of working out the design details and making the parts for this new piece of equipment. He spent considerable time conferring with the two men about the problems he was encountering in doing this job.

The results obtained from these activities were encouraging to the industrial engineers.

RUSS KELLER: In November, we started trying to put out these tubes on a regular basis, at least 20 or 30 a day. Fred and George were still making a lot of changes in the design of the tube and in the processes used. They were getting some very good results, though. The results were much better than what was being obtained on the old ignition control tube line.

One of the encouraging signs during this time was the relatively small number of Amicon tubes that proved to be defective. Only 200 Amicon tubes were assembled during November, but this was about what was expected. Of these 200 units, about 20 percent were defective. This compared favorably with the regular ignition control tube; during the corresponding period, about one half of these tubes proved to be defective. In addition, it looked to the industrial engineers as if the Amicon tube could be produced with fewer operations and less labor than was needed for the production of the regular tube.

Barnes heard about these events through Keller, and he had some additional reasons of his own to be encouraged by these developments. As he commented later:

> Our ignition control business at the time amounted to about 10 percent of the entire business of the plant. With the old ignition control tube, we knew we could never reach the potential market. That tube wasn't properly designed for low-cost mass production. The parts were too expensive, and they couldn't be assembled on automatic equipment. We tried one thing after another in an attempt to get the cost of that product down. I guess we spent about a year at it before it began to dawn on us that we weren't going to get much further with that type of design. We needed something quite radically new. Those were the conditions when we first started talking about the Amicon tube and thinking we might develop it as a substitute for the old tube.

In spite of these encouraging signs, Keller began to have some reservations about the way the project was developing. He commented: "I began to think we were getting in a little over our heads. What we were doing was really development engineering work, and that was supposed to be done by Brenner's people." Keller was not concerned with the ability of Fisher and Ames to master the technical problems. He was concerned with the organizational problems that might arise. Keller was also aware of the complication that Curt Brenner had only been with the company for two months. With these questions in mind, Keller went to Barnes, who suggested that he call a meeting of the key people involved to help decide on the proper handling of the project. In addition to Keller, Barnes invited Brenner, Gordon Davis, Roger Metcalf, and Art Heity to the meeting. While Barnes wanted the advice of all these men on the subject, he knew he would have to take responsibility for the consequences of the decision.

## PART 2

At the management meeting on November 23,[2] it was decided to leave the Amicon tube project in the hands of the industrial engineers. Keller summarized the meeting by saying: "Even before Larry suggested it, Brenner volunteered the suggestion that I continue to work on the project. He said that he didn't have any men he could assign to it right away, and

[2] See American Magnolite Company, Part 1, for further details.

we had already made some progress and certainly had some good ideas and a lot of enthusiasm for the work. So we agreed to do it that way. I was glad to do it because we were all interested in trying to get it worked out." Art Heity commented: "Everyone agreed that the industrial engineers should go ahead with their work, even though this was a slightly irregular procedure. Brenner said that his development engineers would stay out of it unless the industrial engineers got into trouble—in that case, they would help out."

During the next seven months the project moved through several additional stages—Fisher, Ames, and their two girl assistants continued to make progress on the tube during December and January. In January the decision was made to put the product into regular production as of February 1. Keller and Fisher urged that this transfer be postponed, but their objections were overruled. Going into regular production meant bringing in a production supervisor and setting some specific output goals. Barnes set the goal of getting the product into full-scale, low-cost production by July. This meant getting up to an output of 100,000 units per month at per unit cost substantially below that of the old ignition control tube. In order to reach this goal, a number of complex steps needed to be taken. The most critical of these are listed below:

Product Design:

Eliminate quality "bugs" in the design of the product.

Personnel:

Train the new foreman in the technical ins and outs of the new product.

Assemble and train a considerable work force: 20 to 30 people.

Equipment and Supplies:

Finish designing and produce or purchase the equipment needed to get production started: several test kits, an adequate envelope machine, a new etching device, an adequate swaging machine, and several subassembly devices.

Design and produce supplementary jigs and fixtures to speed up the production process: test kit holding fixtures, acid sinks, etc.

Lay out and set up a new production workplace.

Work the "bugs" out of the new equipment and fixtures.

Develop adequate sources of supply for a large volume of high-quality, low-cost purchased parts.

Design and secure more fully automatic equipment for a later stage of high-speed production: automatic envelope machine, etc.

The very nature of these jobs to be done required the cooperative efforts of many people from several functional groups, especially the production people, the industrial engineers, and the development engineers. A number of episodes are described below that exemplify the way these three key functional groups worked with each other in the months that followed.

**Industrial Engineers and Development Engineers**

***December.*** One of the design problems on the Amicon tube was getting a good solder joint between the body case and the terminal. Brenner suggested plating these parts prior to soldering to solve the problem. He assigned one of his development engineers, Dick Gantos, to trying out his idea. Gantos brought his plated parts to Fisher, who tried assembling tubes with them but decided that they did not work satisfactorily.

***February.*** Another design problem involved the process for preparing the grids for the negative terminal assembly. Fisher and Ames had been experimenting with a heat-treating process and felt encouraged by the results. When Brenner heard about this, he felt this was a development engineering problem and assigned one of his men, Wally Parent, to test the new heat-treating process on grids. On February 24, Brenner reported the results of the test at one of the regular management meetings. He said that the test indicated that the heat-treated grids were not so good as the grids processed in the routine fashion. Fisher began to say something to the group about why he thought the test had turned out as it did. Brenner precluded further discussion of the topic by saying that in the future, all experiments and tests on grids should be conducted by his group, in accordance with a memorandum to that effect issued by Barnes.

After the meeting, Fisher told how he felt about this entire incident:

> I was plenty sore when Parent had that report presented to the team about his poor results on the test with heat-treated grids. You know, you can utter a falsehood without actually telling a specific lie simply by leaving out a lot of pertinent information. He ran one test with heat-treated grids; and because it did not turn out well, he wrote a report that seemed to condemn the whole process. When he ran that test, I pointed out to him that in the process of working on the terminals, they had become corroded in some peculiar way that might give them trouble. He did not pay any attention to this. I reworked some of that same batch of heat-treated grids he was working on and got 25 perfect units out of it in 25 tries. It seems to me it would be more constructive to try to make a new idea work than to try to prove that it won't work by simply running one test.

***March.*** In spite of Fisher's negative report on plating prior to soldering, Brenner instructed Gantos to continue his experiments with the method on a part-time basis. During January and February, he ran different experiments in the development engineers' chemical laboratory on these soldering problems. By the third of March, Gantos had made some plated tube parts that he wanted to try soldering together on the regular testing kit set up on the production line. The following is the researcher's description of what happened when Gantos arrived at the production line to run his test:

Dick Gantos brought some of his plated terminals over to the production line to see if Alice[3] could make a good solder joint with them while maintaining the proper electrical characteristics. He and Lou[4] stood by while Alice went to work with the new terminals. She first attached the grids to one batch of terminals. She etched the taper on the positive terminals and then sat down at her test kit and assembled three units in succession. Each of these units turned out to be defective, since in the process of soldering they lost the proper electrical readings. It seemed to the researcher that Alice was not handling the parts with her usual care. As she finished each unit, she handed it to Lou, who passed it without comment to Dick.

Dick tried to explain the failures on the grounds that he had not been familiar with the method of etching the tapers. Lou replied that the method was written into the specifications.

Dick made some comment about trying a cleaning operation, and then both he and Lou were called away for a moment. While they were gone, Fred Fisher walked up to where Alice was working. Alice said: "Take a look at these units I made with Gantos' parts. They all turned out bad."

It seemed to the researcher that she had a sort of "I-guess-we-told-them-so" tone in her voice as she told the story to Fred.

At this point, Dick came back, and he and Fred watched Alice assemble three more tubes with the plated parts. They, too, were defective. Gantos said he thought the trouble might be caused by the way Alice was applying the flux, but Fred denied it. Gantos then mentioned his doubts about the effect of the etching operation. Fred replied that the etching operation had never caused any trouble before. Dick finally walked away toward his laboratory, saying something about running some more experiments. Fred commented: "We tried to use those plated terminals before, and they didn't work. Gantos can't seem to get it through his head that we have to get good electrical readings on these units as well as good solder joints."

After this event, Gantos and Parent set up their own test kit in the laboratory in order to be independent of the regular line in doing their work on the Amicon tube. Gantos continued to work on the plating idea but never again asked the industrial engineers or production people to try out his ideas.

***April–June.*** During these months, Parent and Gantos spent considerable time working on the project. Gantos, with help from Parent, continued to experiment in his laboratory with ways of improving the soldering of the Amicon tube. Parent, at specified time intervals, supervised the running of performance tests on samples of the tubes that were being produced, and he regularly reported the results of these tests at the team meetings. These two men ran a controlled experiment in April to test the relative usefulness of the industrial engineers' method of etching tapers

[3] One of the original two girls on the project.

[4] Lou Corriveau, the production foreman assigned to the Amicon tube in February.

and the regular method used for the old control tube. Parent periodically worked at keeping the design specifications on the Amicon tube up to date. These two men helped on the design of one part of the new etching equipment and experimented with new types of chemical solutions to be used in this process. In almost every instance, their evaluative reports indicated that the Amicon tube was not adequately meeting performance standards and that the industrial engineers' processes were inferior to other processes.

Meanwhile, the industrial engineers were performing a number of activities involving these same matters. In addition to working with Lou Corriveau on the production equipment, Fisher and Ames started again in April to experiment with new ways of securing a more satisfactory way of soldering the Amicon tube. They did most of the design work and supervised the construction of the new etching apparatus. When the etching apparatus was completed, they supervised its installation in the production line and worked to eliminate some of the "bugs" in the equipment and the process.

In spite of these overlapping activities, the two groups of engineers had virtually no face-to-face contact with each other during these months. From the first part of March until the middle of June the researchers neither observed directly nor heard of any occasion on which Fisher and Ames talked with Parent and Gantos outside of the regular meetings they were all required to attend. In June, Fisher said: "I get along with Gantos simply by leaving him alone."

During the December–June period the key members of the two engineering groups developed some strong negative feelings about each other and the state of the Amicon project, as indicated by the following comments to the researcher:

FRED FISHER: We haven't made any progress for the past month. It's certainly discouraging. They are still trying to make a good solder joint in the laboratory. I can't get it through Gantos' head that we don't just need a good solder joint, but we need electrical readings, too. . . . I have never been so close to exploding in my whole life. If they (the development engineers) are trying to kill our product, why don't they say so? That's what they're really doing, you know. You can always find something wrong with a product if you put it to extreme tests. There is nothing mechanical that you can't break if you try hard enough. You ought to see the performance tests they are running on the tubes. Ames was telling me something about them today. They're just trying to prove it won't work. . . . Things aren't coming at all well. We aren't getting anything done around here. We've got a couple of ideas for some equipment we want some day, but nothing much is getting done. We're still talking about the same things we were two months ago. We're still fighting the same old fights about plating or not plating.

I feel completely frustrated on this work now. It's terribly discouraging. I get blocked no matter what direction I go. By the time I have finished a day around here, I am all tied up in knots. My stomach feels like a lead weight. My wife notices it and asks me what's wrong when I get home. There are just too many people involved in this thing now—too many cooks—everybody has to get into the act. Everybody expresses his opinion, but nothing gets done.

DICK GANTOS: The Amicon tube project got started all wrong. We're going to have a hell of a time getting it straightened out. That product shouldn't have been turned over to the industrial engineers when it first started. Some Joe Doaks on the line gets an idea, so Barnes says to him go ahead and engineer the product. Joe can think and may get good ideas, but it is a different story to try and work out a finished product. That takes experience and engineering know-how. Even before we heard anything about the project, industrial engineering was getting it into production. When we saw what they had done, we knew they were going to have trouble. They just didn't listen to us.

WALLY PARENT: We resented having the industrial engineers doing the design work on the Amicon tube. It just wasn't right. It isn't so much the fact that they are doing it as the way they are doing it. The whole thing makes us look bad.

The industrial engineers and the development engineers accomplished very little together during this period. The one thing that these groups worked out jointly was the new etching apparatus, which was modestly successful. At no time, however, did they work out together any new design feature or process change that made an appreciable improvement in the product in terms of cost, quality, or output volume. This was in sharp contrast to the earlier design period, when new ideas for the product were being put into use at a rapid rate.

From February through June the development engineers also ran periodic performance tests of different kinds on the Amicon tubes. They tested both the final product and some of the production processes. In the latter part of June the development engineers tested a sample of the tubes that had been produced several months earlier. The results of this "life" test showed that a number of the tubes had "gone bad" electrically while in storage.

The statistical results of these tests were interpreted by the development engineers to mean that the product was essentially unsound.

GANTOS: They just aren't making the product right. Too much of their production fails when it is just sitting on a shelf for a couple of months.

Fisher gave these same statistics a different interpretation. He concluded from Parent's performance test reports that the development engineers were trying to prove the product no good by setting impossible standards. In late June, Fisher recognized that the product still had its shortcomings, but he believed they could be easily remedied.

FISHER: If the Amicon tube works, and we know it will work, then there are only a few problems to iron out, and they are mostly "manufactured" problems. We made good Amicon tubes once; and we know they can be made again, if they will just let us iron out a few problems.

### Industrial Engineers and Production

On February 1, Lou Corriveau, as the new foreman of the Amicon tube line, was given formal responsibility for production and made the supervisor of Alice and Claire, the two girls who had been helping Fisher and Ames. Corriveau was a relatively young supervisor who had been given a wide variety of production assignments. At the time he was given the Amicon tube job, he was told it was his "big chance." He expressed his reactions to the new job thus:

> You know, I have been transferred seven times in the last three years. I just get one operation started when they move me again. They've never really given me a chance to complete a job. They've sort of promised me if I get the Amicon tube rolling, I can count on it as a regular job. I certainly hope that's true, because I want to do a good job, and I want to see some results. I figure that if they give me a job like this, they must have some reasons for doing so. I told Davis if he thought I could do the job, he should give me enough time and a chance to do things my own way. If they don't give me a decent chance this time, I'll probably have to leave the company.

In the first few days after this transfer, Fisher went about his work on the project with no noticeable change. As he put it, he considered the formal transfer merely a "paper change." He continued to spend a high percentage of his time working with the two girls, Claire and Alice, on the little technical details of making tubes with their experimental equipment. He frequently sat down at the equipment to try his hand at making good tubes. He discussed with the girls all the details of the difficulties they were having.

Meanwhile, Corriveau was spending relatively little time around the Amicon tube work. He continued to spend most of his time in the lithotron section, where he still had some supervisory responsibilities. However, during these few days, he observed that he was being ignored by the industrial engineers in their work with the girls. He commented: "Fred and George are always stirring up the girls. Fred sits down with Claire, and they run all sorts of little experiments, changing things on the tubes and trying different ways of doing things without telling me what's going on."

Corriveau complained in this vein to Davis, and Davis apparently agreed with him, because a few days after the transfer Davis called Fisher into his office. The latter reported this incident to the researchers.

> FISHER: Davis called me into his office and told me, in effect, to stay away from the Amicon tube girls. He said it was all right for me to go around and

watch the work; but if I had any orders to give, I should talk to Lou, and no one but Lou should give any orders to the girls. I try; but you know, it's almost impossible to work that way.

A few days later, Fisher made statements about Corriveau that indicated his resentment about the way the latter was acting.

FISHER: Take this matter of Corriveau. He didn't know anything about making Amicon tubes when he was put in charge of producing them. Now he is having to learn everything over again, but the hard way. He goes right back through a lot of trial-and-error steps we've already been through. And he isn't too anxious to take our advice on these things.

Meanwhile, Corriveau was disturbed because the industrial engineers did not seem to be giving him adequate help on the matters he wanted help on. He went to Fisher with a request for a change in the job classification assigned to a key job in the new line, and he received a "book" answer as to why it could not be done. He kept experiencing one delay after another in getting delivery of the various pieces of production equipment that the industrial engineers were supposed to design and build for him. After a few days, Corriveau commented:

I'm not getting anywhere. I can't get anything done. We talk about everything, but no one does anything about it. When Davis tells me to do something by Friday, I have to have it done by Friday. He won't take Monday for an answer. But I can't get it through if I don't have the equipment. . . .

When I first came on this line, I had a meeting downstairs with Keller and Davis and some of those people. They promised me certain things in the way of equipment that they said were all ready to go. I was supposed to start production with them. I took over on Monday. At the end of the week, I still didn't have the equipment, so I wrote a report to Davis. How could I do what they asked me if I didn't have anything to work with? And if I didn't tell them I didn't have it, they would never know. It would look bad for me. Well, the industrial engineers talked as though I was attacking them or something.

After a few weeks, in the face of what seemed to him the engineers' indifference, Corriveau tried to force them to keep their promises.

CORRIVEAU: I don't like keeping after them, but it's the only way I can get anything done. Like Karl.[5] I have to check him in the morning, check him at noon, check him at night. I don't like that, either. At least, I am more tactful than they are. I don't just tell them to do something. I have tried to go up and ask them if they need any help or anything. I'm going to start blasting if things don't move pretty soon.

Vronska, in turn, resented this pressure.

[5] Karl Vronska, a machinist who was working with Fisher and Ames, making some of the production equipment.

KARL VRONSKA: I'm not worried about this die. I know that if I can just have enough time, sooner or later I'll find out what's causing the trouble; and my boss knows it, too. It's guys putting pressure on you all the time that make me mad. I get so sick of Lou. I'm going to push his teeth down his throat some day. I said to him one day: "You get out of here quick. When this is ready, I'll turn it over to you; but until then, it's none of your business. I'm going to do my work myself without any interference from you."

An incident that occurred around the envelope machine in mid-April exemplified the nature of the relationship. The envelope machine was an old piece of semiautomatic equipment that Fisher and Ames had salvaged and rebuilt to form the body cases for the tube. When the Amicon tube was put into production, this machine was working, but only sporadically. One of Ames's jobs was to keep it in running condition and to try to make it a dependable piece of equipment. This job involved Ames spending many hours making adjustments on the machine and periodically redesigning and rebuilding parts of it. As time went on, Ames and the machinist Vronska, who occasionally helped him in this job, grew tired of the assignment. They wanted to turn all responsibility for the machine over to Corriveau. But whenever the machine got in trouble, Corriveau went to Ames to get it fixed. Everyone concerned began to get irritated and impatient. Ames accused Corriveau of not operating the machine properly, and the latter countered that the industrial engineers did not get it fixed right.

On the fourteenth of April, Ames and Vronska had spent the morning working on the envelope machine. About 11:00 o'clock, Corriveau joined the group and entered into their discussions. At the time the researcher appeared, the men had decided that the pins on which the parts were loaded were too long and were discussing how much to shorten them. Ames held several sample pins which he was measuring while Corriveau looked over his shoulder. Corriveau's gestures suggested that he was with difficulty refraining from taking the scaler and making the measurements himself. Before Ames spoke, Corriveau suggested cutting off $3/32$ of an inch, adding that the job could be done on a machine in the salvage section.

VRONSKA: That machine isn't accurate enough.

LOU CORRIVEAU: It's close enough.

VRONSKA (*standing up as if to leave*): Well, we're off. If you're going to run this, you don't need us.

CORRIVEAU: What do you mean? This hasn't anything to do with me. I didn't mean that.

VRONSKA: Go ahead and do it your way. It's all yours.

CORRIVEAU: Why, this machine isn't in production yet. When you can run a couple of hundred on it and have them O.K., I'll take it over.

VRONSKA: Well, if you want a machine that'll work, you've gotta have things the proper length. If something is supposed to be a certain size, it's gotta be exactly that size. Then you know what you're dealing with.

After considerable discussion, Ames suggested that each pin be cut to a length of $^{19}/_{32}$ of an inch. No further comment was made on where the cutting was to be done. Vronska remained standing where he was, measuring some bushings. Presently, he called Corriveau over and told him that they varied a good deal in length.

VRONSKA: You need some new bushings.

CORRIVEAU: Those are new. We just used them on the last two hundred envelopes we made.

VRONSKA: That makes no difference. They're different lengths. Some of them vary by almost .025.

CORRIVEAU: Karl, I can't throw them out. Do you know what they cost?

VRONSKA: It doesn't make any difference what they cost. We're only trying to see where the trouble comes from. If we reduce the tolerance in all these places where we know there is variation, we might be able to get it straightened out. I don't care how new these are. If they're different lengths, they're no good.

CORRIVEAU: You mean we have to throw out the bushings every time we make a couple of hundred envelopes?

VRONSKA: If you want good body cases, you'll have to.

CORRIVEAU: Why, Karl, these cost me $18 a hundred.

VRONSKA: So what? What's $18?

CORRIVEAU: I'm going to be over my budget. Do you know how much that die[6] cost me? Ninety dollars.

VRONSKA: You're not going to get that die, either.

CORRIVEAU: What do you mean?

VRONSKA: You can't make good terminals with it. Somebody told me you said that. If you can't make good terminals on it, I'm not going to give it to you. I'll fix it so you can't use it, if that's the way you feel about it.

CORRIVEAU: Who told you that? Huh? Who told you I said that? Fred again!

VRONSKA: Just somebody told me you said it was no good.

CORRIVEAU: I didn't say that. I never said anything of the sort. The only thing I ever said was to ask a question about whether you could make good terminals with it. I wanted to know whether it was ready. If people go around stirring up trouble like that, no wonder we never get anywhere. You better go back to the person who told you that and ask him what I really said.

At that moment a bell rang, indicating that it was Vronska's lunch period, and he left without comment. Corriveau turned to Ames; his voice dropped; his shoulders sagged slightly.

CORRIVEAU: Well, if that is the way it's going to be, I'll just have to run the machine using only the heads that happen to be working. But I know one thing—

[6] The die concerned was one that Vronska had built and was trying to perfect to do a delicate swaging operation on the positive terminal.

they better make up their minds that they can forget about the production schedules. They're too idealistic.

GEORGE AMES: Well, I'll go see about cutting the pins.

CORRIVEAU: If you need any new pins, I have some. But you better not tell Karl about it; it might hurt his feelings.

During this period (February–June), the results secured by production and the industrial engineers on the Amicon tube fell far short of their February goals and were disappointing to all concerned.

In February, 198 Amicon tubes of acceptable quality were produced. In March, there were approximately 800 tubes produced as against an original schedule of 7,500. In April, approximately 2,500 tubes were produced as against an original (February) schedule of 20,000 and a revised schedule of 7,000. During May, production went up to about 5,000 tubes but dropped again in June to about 3,000. It will be recalled that the February plans called for production at the rate of 100,000 tubes per month by the end of June.

During this time, relatively little progress was made toward securing and perfecting the production equipment. The envelope machine was improved but was still not completely dependable. Vronska's swaging die was not in shape to be used for production purposes. A new high-volume etching apparatus had been built but was not performing consistently. At no time had the industrial engineers and production collaborated on eliminating any of the design "bugs" in the product.

The people involved in the project recognized these poor results; and each, in his own way, expressed his disappointment:

FISHER: The tube is no further along than it was a couple of months ago. There has even been some retrogression. The readings, for instance, are not nearly so high on the units being produced now as they were on those we made early in the developmental stage.

. . . . . . . . . . . . . . . . . . . . .

AMES: That's right. Nobody seems to be interested in it now. Nobody cares whether school keeps or not. Sure, people still go to the team meetings, but then everybody goes away and forgets it, so that at the next meeting, they have to start all over again. This Amicon tube could have been in full production right now if this sort of thing wasn't happening all the time. They could have been saving $10,000 to $12,000 a month. They could have turned out twice the production with half the number of girls working on the old control tube line.

. . . . . . . . . . . . . . . . . . . . .

CORRIVEAU: It's getting so you can't even ask a question around here without hurting someone's feelings. I'm getting tired of this. I try, but I don't get any cooperation. . . . I'm not getting anywhere. I can't get anything done. We talk about everything, but no one does anything about it.

. . . . . . . . . . . . . . . . . . . . .

The higher management of the Midtown plant was gravely concerned in late June with the state of the Amicon tube project. The top group concerned had experienced two important personnel changes in May. Barnes had left the company, and Metcalf had succeeded him as plant manager. Davis had been transferred; and Jim Hurtig, a general foreman, had taken over as production manager. These two men were joined by Keller, Brenner, and Heity in a meeting on July 1 to review the status of the Amicon tube project. Hurtig had instigated the meeting because he was upset with the poor production results. He was proposing that the tube be taken completely out of production and turned over to the development engineers for further basic engineering work. Keller felt this step was too drastic. Brenner doubted that the industrial engineers were technically competent to solve the tube's problems. Heity was discouraged about the entire project. Metcalf was simply anxious to come up with an answer that would make it possible to stop the losses and start making some profits on the Amicon tube.

## PART 3

At the conclusion of the top management meeting on July 1, Metcalf made the following two decisions: (1) The Amicon tube section was to be taken out of a production status and put under the supervision of the development engineers until such time as the quality difficulties of the product were eliminated and the production processes and equipment were under control; (2) the industrial engineers were to have nothing to do with the design of the product.

## PART 4

The development engineers were pleased with the new arrangements set up by the July 1 meeting.

PARENT: This is the sort of thing that should have been done a long time ago.

They went right to work on all aspects of the Amicon tube. By the first part of August, Parent reported that they were getting promising results in several ways.

PARENT: Things look a lot better. It looks like we've got this soldering problem licked. . . . It's encouraging to be getting these things licked.

During July, Corriveau had his doubts about the benefits of the development engineers' work. He and the operators continued producing tubes on the line as they had before. Corriveau saw relatively little of the development engineers, who were doing most of their work in the laboratory. By the middle of August, however, he was attending short daily meetings with the development engineers to discuss their progress and the details of the day's work. The development engineers were beginning to introduce some innovations in the line that were helpful to Corriveau.

CORRIVEAU: I'm getting better results from the changes the development engineers are introducing. They have reduced the number of defective units an awful lot.

Parent gave the researchers a description of the way he and the other development engineers worked with production on the day-to-day technical problems during this time.

PARENT: We've got a good group working on this. The first thing every morning, all of us get together to discuss what we accomplished the previous day and what needs to be done the coming day. We take the problems one day at a time and work them out. We have a different man working on each aspect of the problem.

The results of the development engineers' program were so encouraging that they hoped to turn the production line back to a straight production status by the middle of September. As this date was approached, however, the development engineers found themselves with a new problem on their hands. The envelopes started cracking during the final soldering operation. No sooner had this problem been solved in October than they started having trouble with the leads coming off the negative terminals. During this time, both the development engineers and Corriveau became very discouraged with the project. For several weeks the production line was completely shut down. But throughout this difficult time, Corriveau was in daily contact with the development engineers, and they were always working on the hundreds of details involved in improving the product and getting it produced. Finally, in January, they were able to begin turning out tubes of fairly consistent high quality, and the production rate began to climb. There had been no dramatic changes in the basic design of the Amicon tube, but many little things were working better technically.

In the following months the Amicon tube work gradually shifted to a more routine production basis. The development engineers spent less and less of their time on the project. Corriveau put increasing emphasis on meeting his higher production quotas and on lowering his unit costs. The Amicon tubes were being sold as a premium-quality product at a premium price. In the late spring the Amicon tube project began to show a monthly operating profit for the first time; and from that date, it became a consistently profitable product.

The following excerpts from interviews with Parent and Fisher several months after the July 1 decision indicate the state of their relationship at the time.

PARENT (*after explaining to the researcher some of the latest technical developments*): We're now getting into the second stage of operations. It's sort of an interim period between pilot production and full-scale production. For the next few months, we're going to have to coordinate more with the work that is being done by industrial engineering and production.

RESEARCHER: Won't that be a rather critical stage?

PARENT: Oh, I guess not any more than any other stage. Things can go wrong anywhere along the line. We're going to start tomorrow holding meetings to keep everything coordinated. People from industrial engineering and production will be coming to those meetings. Things will be going kind of slowly. It takes time.

RESEARCHER: You mean you'll have to be patient about getting results?

PARENT: No, you can't be patient. I'm going to have to keep pushing things along.

RESEARCHER: You'll be doing a lot of follow-up work, then?

PARENT: Yes, I'll be checking to see that we make headway. Then I'll be reporting to Brenner about how we're doing and keeping him informed. I'll be talking with him about the technical problems we're having and even some of the problems of personnel and our problems about getting along with production and things like that. Of course, these meetings will just be concerned with the immediate problems we're running into. We won't be discussing any big overall plans, as we did in the old meetings. These meetings will be different.

Well, as I said, we're now getting into a rather critical stage of having to refine our production methods and reduce shrinkage. The industrial engineers have just worked out a comprehensive program for getting in some good production equipment.

RESEARCHER: How do their plans look to you?

PARENT: I haven't had a chance to go over them in much detail; but it looks like a very good, vigorous program. It looks like the sort of thing we need. I'm glad to see them going at it this way. There has really been a big change in the way the industrial engineering group works around here. They're concentrating on production methods now and are willing to accept our design specifications. Of course, I don't want to give you the idea that I think the industrial engineers didn't make a big contribution to the Amicon tube. Actually, we wouldn't have had an Amicon tube if they hadn't done the work on it. They developed a good mechanical design. They just ran into trouble because of the problems of chemistry and metallurgy involved. They really couldn't have been expected to solve those problems. You couldn't tell there was anything wrong with it by looking at it. You can sort of see how the whole thing happened.

This project has helped me a lot to understand the point of view of the industrial engineers and the production people. I used to think those people were just dumb, stupid, and no good. Now I can really understand their point of view. I think they have changed, too. You know, if you can't work in some way with the others on a project, then you just can't get anything done. Of course, I want you to understand, I don't entirely agree with everything that industrial engineers and production people believe in. I still don't see eye to eye with them. But now I can discuss problems with them without thinking they're dopes. I can understand their ideas, even if I don't agree with them.

Then Fisher has changed a lot, and we're working along with him fine now. Fred has been bringing his men down here and showing them what we're doing. I don't want to give you the impression that everything is rosy and that we're not going to have any more problems. It's going to take time to get this thing into full-scale production.

. . . . . . . . . . . . . . . . . . .

Fisher: Speaking of relationships, you know for a long time I was having a hard time with Lou. There has been a tremendous change just lately. Now we're getting along swell. It's no trouble at all. He's all the time coming to me for help and advice, and I try to do the best I can to help him. It's been a big change. . . .

I am terribly encouraged about the way things are going. Everything seems to be breaking at once. We have our program for the Amicon tubes all mapped out now. We have arranged to get in a lot of new equipment to do that job. That's working with the present specifications that were drawn up by the development engineers, too. We're sticking by our promise not to try and change those specifications. . . .

You know, I can understand now why the development engineers acted the way they did. They didn't like our doing their job. If I'd been in their shoes, I guess I would have acted the same way. . . .

You know, I think the way you have to get along in an organization is by being willing to give away your pet ideas and gain satisfactions from your job in other ways. . . .

I've decided that if I just concentrate my attention on getting along with other people around here that I work with, and on helping them out as much as possible, my own personal progress in the organization will probably come along automatically. It'll probably come along faster and better than it would if I worried about it directly. . . .

The situation has improved an awful lot in the last few months. Take the relations between our industrial engineering department and the development engineers. We really understand and appreciate what each group's function is, and we're beginning to go to each other for help instead of working at cross purposes. Roger Metcalf is helping a lot to work this thing out. I am perfectly aware it isn't enough to define responsibility on a piece of paper. You've got to clarify those responsibilities right in the heads of the people who are doing the work. They have to learn what their own job is in respect to the function of other engineers. I personally think it's quite amazing the way our relations with the development engineers have improved. We are closer right now than any other two groups in the plant. You will remember how bitter I was about that group a few months ago. I thought they were no good at all and couldn't find enough horrible names to call them. In a way, we sort of took the initiative by agreeing to stay out of their bailiwick. They've done an awful lot to help the situation, though.

# United Diesel Corporation

United Diesel Corporation was one of a few large-scale manufacturers of diesel engines for locomotives and other heavy equipment. For many years, the heavy manufacturing investment required to break into the industry had restricted the entry of new competition, while the rate of market growth had kept prices at a level profitable for existing manufacturers. More recently, however, competing forms of power generation began to challenge the positions of the large diesel manufacturers. At the time of this case, price competition among diesel manufacturers had become severe.

United Diesel management was eagerly seeking ways to reduce manufacturing costs, delivery lead times, and customer maintenance problems. Because nearly every United Diesel engine was uniquely constructed to customer specifications, its engineering department had been assigned projects which on the one hand would increase the degree of engine standardization and on the other would simplify and increase the efficiency of its engines.

The organization of the engineering department, including indications of work flow through the department, is diagrammed in Exhibit 1. Typically, preliminary design and cost estimates were discussed by sales engineers with customers (1).[1] As the prospect developed, sales called in product design engineering (2) which acted throughout the project as technical liaison between the customer and United Diesel (3). With the help of specialist design groups (4), product design engineering submitted a concrete proposal to the customer. If the proposal were accepted, product design then administered the project by stimulating the statement of firm requirements by specialist design groups (5) [which worked directly with subelement draftsmen (6)], [as did product design (7)] by using specialist and subelement data to instruct the work of general engine layout draftsmen (8) [who also worked directly with their subelement colleagues (9)] and by consultation with members of manufacturing planning (10) in which planning voiced its constraints and became informed of project development [much of this information flow passing directly

[1] The numbers in parentheses correspond to numerical designations appearing in Exhibit 1. These numbers designate the sequence of relationships necessary to obtain and fulfill a customer contract.

**EXHIBIT 1**

Engineering Department Organization and Work Flow

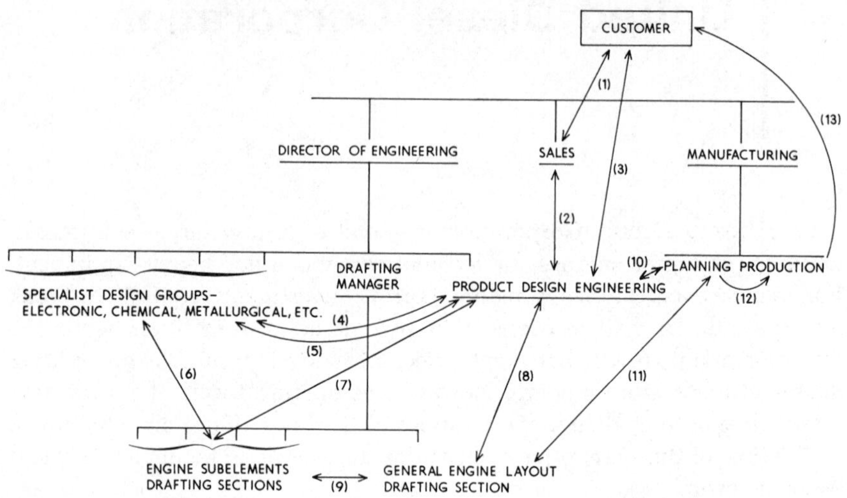


between planners and draftsmen (11)]. As blueprints were completed, planning converted them into production instructions (12) by which production built the engines which were then custom installed in customer equipment (13). At any time in this work-flow cycle, product design engineering was on call to "shoot trouble" and, if necessary, initiate further negotiations with the customer.

A researcher from the Harvard Business School became interested in studying behavior in United Diesel's engineering department when he learned that United Diesel management was increasingly concerned by the mounting costs, diminishing speed, and apparent lack of creativity in its drafting rooms. Preliminary observations indicated that general engine layout drafting displayed behavior typical of other drafting sections and that the relationship between this section and product design engineering formed a kind of nerve center in the department. He secured permission to study these two groups and their relationship.

Product design engineering was composed of nine engineers and a manager. Two engineers specialized in customer liaison, two in manufacturing liaison, and five were assigned overall responsibility for specific projects. All were graduate engineers. Three senior men were in their forties and had been with United Diesel for at least fifteen years. The rest were in their late twenties or early thirties with no more than five years seniority. The senior engineers were all committed either to pure design activity or to a combination of design and engineering administration. The junior men tended to be somewhat less certain of their goals,

**EXHIBIT 2**

General Engine Layout Drafting Section Organization

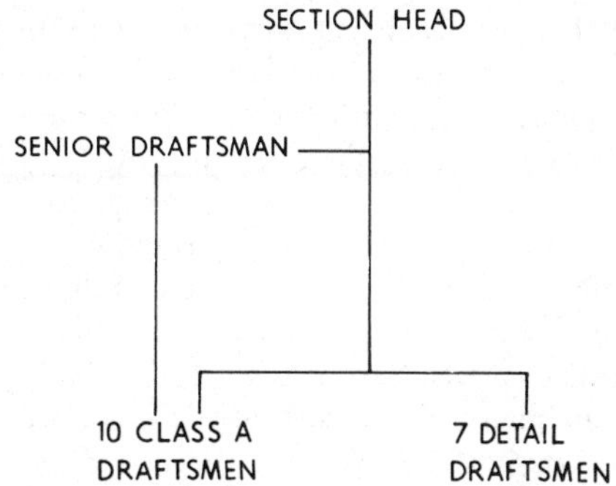


which ranged from sales engineering to pure design to manufacturing engineering. The older men could remember when a national technical union had narrowly missed winning the right to represent United Diesel engineers.

General engine layout drafting's organization is shown in Exhibit 2. The section head assigned work to the men of his section. The senior draftsman was responsible for working through major design problems with engineers and for technical supervision of the Class A draftsmen. Each Class A draftsman was responsible for a project, though the youngest of these often worked under the supervision of those more senior. Detail draftsmen were assigned by the section head to make detailed working drawings from the master layout of a particular project or to work on routine changes in old drawings. All of these men except the section head were union members. One of the senior Class A draftsmen was president of the union local. Another was union steward for the section.

During the period of his orientation to these engineers and draftsmen, the researcher was busying himself studying company background material at a desk in the engineering office, when he overheard two engineers talking.

RALPH BURKE: Jim, one guy you want to steer clear of is Parker.[2] You know what he just did to me? I was in a meeting on that Crafts job. The customer's not happy, so Parker got everybody together who's been in on it. He didn't like the design, and I admit he had some points. But do you know, he criticized engineering's judgment right in front of the drawing office people! Why couldn't he have talked with the engineers first so we could have headed this thing off before it got to a public demonstration? But no, he had to pull out our dirty

[2] Philip Parker was a sales executive in the company.

linen right in front of a lot of drafting people. Parker's supposed to be interested in improving the communication line between the customer and the draftsman, but all he's doing is making the drawing office lose faith in engineering judgment. It was all I could do to sit there while he questioned my design ability, with those drafting people sitting back and taking it all in. We had to rush those Craft designs too much and I admit they were not red hot. But now Parker's got the draftsmen thinking I'm incompetent.

JIM PACKARD: Yeah, I know how you feel. One meeting like that can really set us back. We spend a hell of a lot of time figuring jobs in detail before passing them on to the drafting boys so they can trust our judgment that everything is going to fit together and work properly. Then some chump like Parker puts his foot in it, and the draftsmen don't know what's up. You and I both know how important it is to a draftsman to know just what's expected of him and how he's supposed to develop a design. This is what they need and want to know. But without some faith in us, they won't know where to turn. Someone ought to set Parker straight.

The researcher also had a number of opportunities to talk with draftsmen about their jobs and their working conditions, and especially about their relationships with the design engineers.

One old-time design draftsman, regarded by the engineers as "a plodder," told the researcher:

All the motivation to do good, creative designing has been lost around here. Take a chemist or a teacher. He doesn't care about money all the time; it's his work that he's interested in. It's what he can do. It used to be that way before, but not any more. Nowadays, nobody has any interest in what he's doing. They just tell you to draw some lines, and you draw them. In the old days, you would work on it with the engineer, you'd make your own layout, you would even do your own detailing, and you would work with the guys in the shop. Everything. In those days, you had responsibility for a whole job, for a whole engine; and you were interested in what you were doing, and you knew your work, and you were good at it. I could design a whole engine in the old days. There isn't a guy here in the whole department that could do that now.

I'm not surprised that nobody's got any incentive or wants any responsibility. In the old days, I would be so wrapped up in the job that I'd go out to the woods at night, my hands clenched so tight they bled, and scream with frustration because I couldn't figure something out on a design. Nowadays, it's all I can do to stay awake. I'm not interested any more. I could go to work any place. I'm a trained draftsman, not a line drawer. I'm a layout man. I could work in automatic machinery, electronics, or any place.

A little later, the researcher talked to Henry Nelson, a senior design draftsman who was respected by the other draftsmen. He said:

I came to United Diesel in 1923 with a background of six years of drafting experience with several concerns. Why had I chosen drafting? As a technical school student, I worked two summers in a drafting room and became quite impressed with the prestige the draftsmen enjoyed, so the die was cast.

Soon after starting with United, I had the opportunity to do more and more work of an engineering nature, so I did considerable home study to qualify for a transfer to engineering. It finally came at the end of six years and lasted about three years until the depression came, along with a new department manager. Because I had no college degree, I was transferred back to drafting.

This brings up the point that United has a barrier which cannot be passed by a draftsman unless he possesses a degree; whereas in the automobile plants and many other plants, a man can go as far as his abilities can take him.

Another point is the fact that if a man is exceptionally good at a given job, he finds himself pegged and often bypassed from promotion in favor of someone who may be less capable in the job he is holding. This means we have in some cases "eunuchs" who tell you what to do, even though they cannot do the job themselves.

The draftsman in United no longer enjoys the prestige of years past. Now he is considered a necessary evil or burden. While it is true that the draftsman is to a certain degree dependent on and guided by the engineer, he nevertheless has to interpret and execute the necessary working drawings for production of the design.

. . . A few years ago, I asked for a wage increase; and after six months or more, I was told that my name was on the list. In an interview with my supervisor, I was told that the reason the raise was delayed was that quite often I would design to suit myself rather than follow the engineer's wish. My reply was that I first followed the engineer's instructions; and then, to avoid sitting around thumb-twiddling, waiting for the engineer, I would try to work up other possible solutions. About six months later, I did get my increase, which actually was two years overdue.

The ironical part is that about one year later, "Value Analysis Seminars" were held for two large groups in two sessions of about five weeks' duration. One of the points stressed was that there was probably a better way of doing the job; consequently, all ideas should be studied, not immediately rejected, as is too often the case when they differ "from the way it has already been done for years."

A younger draftsman, regarded by the engineers as "something of a problem," explained: "A good draftsman is one who will take responsibility. Most of the men around here would do it if they only had more information. As it is now, nobody knows what's expected, so all he does is just exactly what is required."

Another old-timer designer at the next board, who was something of a social leader in the group, heard this last comment and chimed in:

They always say the engineer doesn't know what we're doing, anyway, but he's got to act as though he does. So when you show him a drawing, he'll say, "Change this radius here," when the radius doesn't have any significance at all. They should respect our feeling for a problem and not always give an answer when they come in "cold" on something we know a lot about. Of course, they see a lot out in the field that leads them to infer that there are problems, but they shouldn't feel they always have to have an answer.

A middle-aged designer, about whose ability the engineers were sharply divided, joined the group. He said:

Yeah, engineers always want to make changes in your designs. I don't have any trouble with Richardson (a senior design engineer). He always approves my work, but Burke has to play the game. He didn't use to check my work. Then, he made a stink over a new idea I put in, and now he does. He has to go over and over it and make suggestions; but nine times out of ten, he comes back to my original design.

And an older designer, evaluated by the engineers as "outstanding," added:

The tendency of an engineer is to get unhappy when a designer puts his own ideas in and goes beyond the engineers. I've never felt I had anything extra to contribute from a design point of view. I give them what they want and express my own thoughts and ideas when I've got them, but not very forcefully. Mostly, the design ideas are a matter of detail (like wall thickness or contour or something). It's never a very big thing because we always work on about the same kind of designs. So what I have to offer is always going to be equal to whatever the engineer wants.

. . . . . . . . . . . . . . . . . . .

Several days later the researcher posted himself in the drawing office, his eyes open for contacts between draftsmen and engineers. At 8:30 A.M., Henry Nelson, whose comments were quoted above, invited the researcher to join him in a visit with Ralph Burke[3] in the engineering office. As the two men walked the few hundred feet between offices, Nelson described the reason for his call on Burke.

Ralph came down to my drawing board a few days ago in a rush to get going on the packaging design[4] for the Proxmire job. I had already done a crude layout of the package over a month ago, but it had to be put aside because we didn't have the final "specs." I was just finishing another project when Ralph told me he had the Proxmire data, finally, and was most anxious to get under way. So I've been pushing hard to complete the job I had on my board, and now I'm free to go ahead with Burke.

It turned out that Burke was temporarily out of the office, so Nelson left him a note. Back at his drawing board, Nelson made further sketches, outlining his ideas for the Proxmire package. Whenever someone walked by his workplace, he glanced up, as if expecting Burke. On several occasions, Burke came into the drawing office to consult with other draftsmen, but he did not approach Nelson. The latter remarked to

---

[3] Ralph Burke was one of the older junior men in product design. His work habits, level of competence, and outlook on life appeared to be typical of most engineers in his section.

[4] The housing in which the diesel would be enclosed.

the researcher that he could not understand the delay, in view of Burke's previous insistence on getting the job started.

At 4:00 P.M. a clerk informed Nelson that Burke was ready to see him. Nelson gathered his sketches and, again accompanied by the researcher, walked to Burke's office. On Burke's desk was a copy of the preliminary package layout which Nelson had drawn. It became the focus of their conversation.

BURKE: Henry, you won't have to build the package as high as it's drawn here. The latest information indicates that a shorter package will allow sufficient maintenance access.

NELSON: All right. Do you know yet just how the package will connect with the customer's installation for it?

BURKE: Specific details on their installation aren't necessary for this job. If you keep the height to a minimum, there should be no problem of fitting the engine into the machine. Now, you'll want to use a corner radius of four inches on this size job.

NELSON: Four inches—just the radius for all the other jobs of this type.

BURKE: That's right. Just follow the ideas on previous layouts.

NELSON: What ideas did the customer give you about designing the package so it can be taken apart whenever repairs to the engine have to be made?

BURKE (*after several minutes' silent study of the drawings*): I don't think any changes over what we knew before have been made in their "specs" on that aspect of the job.

NELSON: Well, we could handle the disassembly in a number of different ways; and as I recall, no specific choice has been made up to now.

Burke sat back and again silently studied the drawing. After several minutes, Nelson assumed that Burke was not going to respond to his question. He pulled the sketch sheets he had been working on out of his pocket and spread them on top of the layout drawing.

NELSON: Here are some sketches I've been working on which seem to be flexible enough to take care of all possible repair contingencies, but I don't think the design would be so complex as to be uneconomical. You see, the panel on this end could be broken out to allow for this section of the engine to be removed without disassembling the whole package.

BURKE (*with a brief glance at Nelson's sketches*): The chances are that if anything breaks down, it will be this section over here. That would require taking the whole package apart, anyway. Your end-panel idea would probably be used so seldom that it wouldn't be worth including. No, just design the package the way you've done similar ones.

NELSON: Well, if that's all, then, I'll get started on the final layout. What drawings should I look at to base this design on?

BURKE: It would be the XYZ job, but you'll have to look up the drawings. I wouldn't know which ones would be relevant. And you might as well take this layout drawing with you. I have no use for it.

NELSON: I'll get started on this as soon as I can.

. . . . . . . . . . . . . . . . . . . .

After the meeting with Burke, the researcher asked Nelson what his reaction to it had been.

NELSON: Well, I was surprised that Ralph knew so little more than he had known before. I guess he's trying to keep things open so he can change his mind later. A lot of the engineers seem to work that way, particularly the young ones. They put up a front, as though they didn't have anything left to learn. They're afraid we'll find out how green they are. It hurts their pride to have a mere draftsman giving them answers or ideas. Well, I guess I can junk these sketches and do it his way. I won't bother him again with my ideas. My mistake was thinking that he wanted some help in the first place. For a guy who's been around here a long time, I can be pretty dumb sometimes.

Not long after the meeting between Nelson and Burke, the researcher found an opportunity to ask Burke what qualities in a draftsman he most highly valued.

BURKE: A draftsman should have good visual imagination and be able to create things. He should be able to give you what you want the first time you ask for it. Of course, that means you have to explain what you want and how you want it done, clearly and in detail. The trouble is that too many draftsmen spend valuable time putting extraneous ideas into the design. You have to keep a tight check on their work to make sure they haven't fouled up the machine. It's O.K. if they do something on their own *after* they've done what you've asked them to do.

Take Henry Nelson, for example. You were there the other day when we went over the Proxmire job. That's an important order, and we're way behind schedule on it. Henry knew it had to be completed quickly. And yet, he wanted to play around with some fancy ideas that weren't necessary and might well have weakened the overall design. If he had spent the time he put into those sketches digging out background material from other jobs to build the basic design on, he'd be living up to my idea of how a good draftsman should behave.

. . . . . . . . . . . . . . . . . . . .

A short time later the researcher talked with the director of engineering of United Diesel, Mr. Buckley. Buckley was responsible for all design and preproduction activities throughout the entire company. He said:

I don't understand it. Men just don't seem to want to work hard any more. Why, I can remember when we were smaller and I was a design engineer, we'd work till 2:00 or 3:00 o'clock in the morning, night after night, when we were trying to solve a difficult design problem. It was an enormous challenge to try to solve problems which we had no idea how to deal with. All of us had to learn a tremendous amount, and we thirsted for the knowledge and experience that would help us.

But today, all the men seem to be interested in is the money they make and their leisure time to enjoy it. They want job security, too—but the challenge of the job itself is gone. That's particularly true of the draftsmen. You know, those fellows like to think of themselves as sort of "engineers," and they get very sensitive about their status and prerogatives. But then they turn around and just barely work hard enough to get by. You have to keep after them all the time. Now, that's no way for a professional man to act. If they want recognition, why don't they earn it by hard, creative work?

# Interview with Tom Craig

Prior to starting his second year of M.B.A. training, Tom Craig dropped by the office of one of his first-year professors to talk with him about his summer job experience. After listening to Craig for about five minutes, the professor asked if he could record the discussion on a tape recorder. Craig agreed and the conversation proceeded without notes or preparation. A major segment of the interview is transcribed below.

Tom Craig completed his first M.B.A. year in June, 1966. Before that he had worked for four and one-half years as a general foreman, production foreman, and plant engineering supervisor in two plants of a chemical company in Massachusetts. He also served three and one-half years in the Navy as an engineering officer on two destroyers. Craig majored in philosophy at Amherst. At the time of the interview, he was 30 years old, married, and had two children. According to Craig, his decision to attend a business school was part of an "overall plan which hopefully would lead to a rapid rise in general management."

The first five minutes of the interview (not included below) were devoted to a brief description of how Craig obtained his job and the company where he worked. He was hired, along with five other M.B.A. candidates, to work at the Beverly, Massachusetts plant of the United Shoe Machinery Company. Prior to arriving at the plant, he was assigned to the company's Harmonic Drive Division and given four projects to work on; Craig indicated that his primary interest was in a "computer project designed to speed up the processing of sales orders," because it sounded like an area to become "better informed about" and which "sounded important to the company's future." He reported to the controller of the Harmonic Drive Division, Charles F. Terrell.

Craig explained that the Harmonic Drive Division had been in existence for only one year but that it had already experienced a rapid growth in sales. It specialized in servo-mechanism devices, such as gear reducers, which were in heavy demand by the aerospace industry. In Craig's opinion, the division was a "self-contained," though "marketing oriented," organization that lacked only in manufacturing facilities. All production operations were performed by the United Shoe's main plant, which was located a short distance from the division's offices. Craig described the main plant as a "huge job shop designed primarily to produce large machines for manufacturing shoes." The plant manufactured products for other United Shoe Divisions, such as Harmonic Drive, as a way of making up for a slackening demand in shoe machines.

PROFESSOR: Could you tell me something about your first few days there and what struck you and made an impression on you, and so on?

CRAIG: Well, I walked into the office and everybody was very nice, and they were all interested in telling me that they had a lot of problems, and I thought that this was kind of unusual that they should want to open up their . . . let me know what all their problems are at the beginning. But it turned out that the problems that they were opening up weren't their problems, they were problems of the factory. I described the factory as separate from this division, which is principally a marketing division as it sits right now. It receives orders and it places them with the factory, and then it deals with the customer and then the factory ships out the order. Now, it also has pricing problems and it has a few inventory problems, but it doesn't carry its own inventory, it doesn't determine how much inventory to carry. Then, in a second area, in the area of government contracts and special products, they have a great deal to do with an engineering department that tries to design these products. And then once the factory has built the parts, or the components that are required, they assemble the products. This is only in special areas. In the standard product line the factory does all this . . . the engineering, the inventory of parts, the assembly, everything is . . . ordering of raw materials . . . everything is done by the factory.

PROFESSOR: You said you were surprised that people were telling you about their troubles. You just walked in and . . . did they ask you to go around and see people . . . to find out about? . . .

CRAIG: Yes, what I did was I started out by getting involved in the sales order system and I went around trying to follow an order through the system. And I got to see a lot of people and to get a pretty good knowledge of how the company worked in a mechanical sense of the term.

PROFESSOR: Did you decide to do this yourself—to follow something around?

CRAIG: Well, yes, I had the choice of four projects. I looked at this one and thought it would be a good place to start because it would get me out and get me to know a lot of people. As I started around asking embarrassing questions, I was surprised at the answers. Most of the answers were in terms of: "Well, the factory can't do this for us, and we don't get any of that from the factory and we never know when the factory is going to ship the product." And what looked to be problems from their side . . . then I went over to the factory and got almost the opposite view from the factory. They were all talking about: "The problem is the people over in Harmonic Drive never tell us anything. We never know what to do and we're always three weeks late before we get started with an order" . . . Well, I was able somehow to keep an open mind through this a little bit and also I think . . . .

PROFESSOR: You don't think the factory people saw you as a spy?

CRAIG: No, and I think this was one of the important things that I . . . I'm not quite sure how I did this but I managed to make everybody think that I was a little bit on their side. I wasn't deceitful about it, I didn't go around with two faces. But I was very careful not to criticize either side too much and to try and understand the problems of people I was talking to. If I was talking to the manufacturing people, I would try to see their view and try to understand what troubles they were having, rather than try to say: "Well, the Marketing people can't live with this." I wasn't criticizing either side, I was trying to take the positive view of "What's your problem and how can it be done." And in a lot of cases I think . . . just in the beginning . . . they began to see from the questions that I was asking that they had problems that didn't . . . that they hadn't thought about it, because they were blaming them . . . it was very easy to pass the buck to the other side.

PROFESSOR: What kinds of questions were you asking them?

CRAIG: Well, I was asking sort of . . . I was just trying to get deeper and deeper into the system as it worked. I tried to find out how the particulars that they were talking about . . . an order that was placed too soon . . . I was trying to find out how they thought the order got placed and what they did with it after they got the order and then just try and, I suppose, follow it through as logically as I could to what would happen. And I tried also, I think, tried specifically to avoid drawing conclusions but tried to let them draw the conclusions.

PROFESSOR: What did these people know about you, you know, in terms of what they heard ahead of time . . . Had there been any announcement, was it word of mouth . . . ?

CRAIG: There was a letter sent around to the department heads in the Harmonic Drive Division explaining the four projects, that I was a summer project student from the Harvard Business School, and the four projects that I was to work on. That was all, none of the people under them knew and most of the people I was dealing with were under them, at least in the beginning, were under the department head level, and none of them knew who I was until I arrived on the scene and I was introduced as a summer student who was working on the sales order system. Over in the factory they knew even less. They hadn't been told . . . the department heads . . . no one had been told of my existence, and I arrived on the scene with the same spiel about being a summer student and tried to put across the fact that I wasn't there to tell them how to run their organization, which would have been silly, but to try and find out what the organization was, and then see if there was anything I could see from an outsider's point of view that might be different.

PROFESSOR: Did they know you had access to anyone who might be able to do anything about their problems?

CRAIG: There were perhaps only two ways . . . they knew I worked for Charlie Terrell and he's the controller of the company and he's a pretty influential guy in the division that he works for. The second thing was that, . . . the first day that I arrived and every Monday thereafter, except well it wasn't always Monday but it was supposed to be Monday, there was a department heads meeting and I went to most of those meetings. I'm sure that people noticed this and that may have been some indication, but those were the only things that I can think of that would have indicated really where I stood in the organization. It didn't show, except, . . . well, I had an office and not everybody had an office. I suppose there was a little status there. But that was . . . the people in the factory didn't know that much.

PROFESSOR: So one of the impressions that you got from going around was this blaming between the factory and Harmonic Drive. . . .

CRAIG: There was tremendous buck-passing involved.

PROFESSOR: What were some of your other initial impressions of the place?

CRAIG: Some of my other impressions were that the company was behind the times in terms of . . . well they used a full cost system that sort of hid a lot of what I thought were the relevant costs in the projects. They didn't do very much planning, advanced thinking. They were talking about the computer, but nowhere in the company did they seem to have a computer really operating, except to pay people. Production control was very loose; inventory control, however, was very good. And then just the very fact that they had these two organizations which, there was quite a bit of repetition. It was production . . . in Harmonic Drive it was called Production Coordination, in the factory it was called Production Control, Production Scheduling. But these people were doing the same job twice and any planning that was done was done twice because nobody in the factory got any benefit from the planning that was done in the Harmonic Drive Division and vice versa. So that I had the feeling that they were pretty far behind in terms of an organization that's ready to move out on a new product. This was a new product, it was only about 18 months old and really it only had about a year of sales on it, a few samples were out for the first six months, but it was just barely beginning to build a volume and . . . .

PROFESSOR: Did you get the impression that people there were concerned about the same things you were, or did people seem pretty self-satisfied?

CRAIG: No, I got the impression that the one thing that really made the organization click was that they knew they were, that they had some work to do to catch up, or maybe catch up isn't the right term, but to get moving. And they were all very anxious to do it. They didn't all have the same ideas of what had to be done, and because they didn't get together, they were perhaps all going in different directions. I think one of my biggest values for the summer was the fact that I served as a link between a lot of different groups, between the group at the factory and the group in the Harmonic Drive Division. I think that's the biggest and most obvious one. But I also served as a link between Marketing and Engineering, Production Coordination and Marketing. Just by being or appearing to be a neutral, people would come to me and say: "Gee, you know, I wish we could get those guys over there to understand this." And these weren't solicitations. I hadn't said: "Well, come to me with your problems," because I didn't really feel that was my job.

PROFESSOR: How did you feel about being in this sort of neutral role, or trying to be in it . . . is this something you had been in before and were accustomed to?

CRAIG: No, it was certainly not something I had been in before. I had always been, I think just by my nature I tend to be a . . . very partisan. I tend to side or associate myself with a group that I'm involved with very strongly and any challenge that comes to the group I take personally. So this was certainly not the situation . . . before, for instance, when I worked for Dewey and

Almy in Manufacturing, probably some of these same problems existed, but I'm sure that my blinders were on just as much as the blinders were on some of these fellows. I wasn't about to take criticism about the Manufacturing area as opposed to the Engineering area or some other area. On the other hand, I was, I think, a little more open about my thoughts in the Manufacturing area. In other words, I wouldn't hesitate to criticize myself or someone else in the Manufacturing area among, so to speak, among the group. If the challenge came from some other group, then I was the first one to toot the horn. But if the challenge came within the group, then I might have been a little more objective. But the idea of being a sort of a neutral with no home was unusual for me, that's for sure.

PROFESSOR: Did it bother you, or did you enjoy it?

CRAIG: It bothered me at first but I think perhaps I got to enjoy it more and more as I found that it worked. When a guy came to me with a problem and I'd listen . . . I think that one thing that is in my nature is that I tend to listen, perhaps too much, when someone comes to me with a problem I get interested in it, and sometimes this means that I just don't have time to do what I was doing before they came in. But getting interested in it and doing something about it in terms of just passing this information on to somebody else and seeing that, by golly, you know, the other guy listened as well. And I knew that he, in some cases, I knew that he was listening when he wouldn't have listened to the guy who was first bringing it up because there were lots of closed minds in this organization. And if somebody from Marketing came in to tell the Production Coordination group what to do, or the Production Control group, or even the Engineering group, it was automatically wrong because it was thought of by Marketing. I didn't mean to single out Marketing, this was true of a lot of the groups. So my position of being a neutral was very important, I think, in getting the information across the lines. I'd like to think that later on in the summer, as a result of some of the things that I had passed back and forth, these guys understood a little bit more about what the other half was doing and were a little more willing to talk about it, but at the beginning it was very surprising to have a guy come up to me and . . . you know, he's been working in this business for a while. . . . In fact, most of the guys that were involved had been out in business for fifteen years or so at least, and they would come into me and without any real reason, they just sort of appeared at the door and would want to talk and they'd sit down and talk. I'm afraid that this idea sort of snowballed because they found it . . . that this was a tool that they could use because it did get results sometimes. So more and more there'd be people appearing at the door with. . . . And I was surprised . . . you know, sitting down working with the sales order systems. It was very interesting but it was unusual to me.

PROFESSOR: What happened as you begin to put, get this information. . . . I noticed this from some of your materials that you put together some reports.

CRAIG: Yes, I started working on the sales order system and probably being very analytical in trying to create a flow chart and I was reading a book on the side about computers and there was a guy in the factory that had some computer experience and I'd done some talking with him. So that I was really looking at this as a computer problem, very analytical, very dry . . . probably to me at least it was getting very boring. And it did, however, provide me with a lot of information to start out with and as I . . . I guess I had one other thing that really helped and that was a set of financial statements or financial reports that come out every month. And I spent a few hours in the first week trying to play with this as if it were a case and see what kind of things I could make out of it in terms of finance, in terms of marketing . . . I was just playing around because I really didn't know where to go or what problems were really important and what problems weren't. After playing around with this information for awhile, I have a pretty . . . I found later, although I didn't really know at the time, I had a pretty good picture of what was really going on in the company. One of the . . . I guess it was the second department head meeting that I was in, it struck me particularly that the manufacturing manager and the marketing manager were talking about two different things. One of them was saying that: "Gee, he was just getting out all the sales that he could think of getting and it was too bad we weren't making money," and the other guy was saying: "Gee, they were selling all they could, it's too bad they weren't producing enough so that they could make money." And I sort of sat quietly in the meeting and thought about this and then when I got out of the meeting I talked to my boss about it, and I tried to point out a couple of things that I had seen in the numbers that I had, and he got very interested in it and asked me to follow it up a little bit. The result was that we made several different tries at trying to explain this problem in terms of numbers because. . . .

PROFESSOR: What was the problem?

CRAIG: The problem was that they just, the factory, was unable to produce the products that Marketing required. The reason behind this was probably that Marketing hadn't asked for them long enough in advance so that the factory could plan and get the equipment ready, get the capacity ready. I don't think that the company now has the capacity to meet its sales requirements and that its sales are growing very fast. It's getting worse and worse, and it was hard to show this to a general manager who had been looking at sales figures going down every month. They were going down because the backlog of orders was building up behind them and they were trying, . . . they were shuffling around, instead of building a hundred units all one size, they'd build five units of that size and then have to shift to another size because another customer needed it badly, and they were just locked into a situation where sales were bound to level off or even in fact go down. And I was trying to pinpoint this and nobody in the organization had made, really made the distinction to themselves. . . . The difference between a product shipped out the door and a product sold in terms of the customer calling up and placing an order. So I started talking about shipments and orders as if they were different things, and it didn't, just didn't make much sense to them but it gradually began to sink in.

PROFESSOR: You got the interest of your boss?

CRAIG: Yes, I got that right away and there were several times during the first few weeks when I was worried because we weren't involved at all in the projects that we said we were going to be working on. But I guess three different times during that period I went back to him and said: "Now look, we're not doing what we said we were going to be doing, I think what we're doing is important but I want to be sure that you understand that we're not working on the sales order system, any of these projects, this is something different." And in my reports which I was making at the beginning of the year, or the summer. Every week I tried to make some report . . . I don't know whether it was for me to collect my thoughts or to pass on to him, or what. It just seemed like a good idea. And in my reports I tried to make it obvious that I had shifted my emphasis and I was working on something that was entirely different from which we started out with.

PROFESSOR: How did he respond to this?

CRAIG: Well he responded . . . he was worried he said, that I wouldn't have something concrete to hang my hat on at the end of the summer. He wanted me to be able to say: "Well, I went to work for United Shoe and I did this, and here it is." And he was worried that there might not be something like this at the end of the summer. But he was, I guess he was willing to take the chance for a while in order to get something that he thought was worthwhile. And as it grew, it became obvious that this was something that you could hang your hat on very easily; in fact, to me it seemed a great deal more important than the sales order system or any of the other projects.

PROFESSOR: Now the "this" that you could hang your hat on, is trying to . . . around the sales order shipment?

CRAIG: The shipments and orders, yes. Well, the first problem was to make this distinction so that people could understand that there was a difference. And the second problem seemed to be, from both sides, to determine how much we could ship in a month, or whatever period, and the second problem was to try to determine how much we were selling. And it sort of . . . so we could say: "All right, we're not getting what we need." Then from that we went on to produce a forecast which would show what we, what the people in the organization thought could be sold in the future, and from that, once again to follow it up, we tried to make a schedule of what equipment we needed, what size of a factory we needed, did we have enough plant? We didn't know the answer when we started out. Now do we need three. . . . So we tried to determine the kind of equipment that we needed, and all the implications that we could think of along the way. And this kind of helped me a little bit in my neutral plan too, because I became an oracle of information from both sides, so that lots of times people found that they didn't have . . . I wasn't just a middle man . . . I had the answer. Perhaps they were better answers than had been around before. None of the stuff that I had was original, though, I didn't go out and do marketing research, and I didn't go out in the plant and study how, make a time study on how much time it took to do any operations. I took information that was already there in some form and changed it into another form that looked usable, and then tried to point out to people how it could be used, and this was the result. One of the final results was that we came to the conclusion that we didn't really have enough information . . . enough capacity to meet our forecasts for this year. And for next year it was going to be worse and for the year after that it was going to be worse. We actually set up a plan where we were going to try and make several steps of it and move to a new plant eventually. We worked with the facilities, the equipment, the people that we'd need. We took a really whole broad range of what we would do, to set up when we got through a new company or a new separate, autonomous division.

PROFESSOR: Now, who is the "we" here? How were you working. . . ?

CRAIG: Well, as I told you before that I rapidly associated with the people I worked with. The *we*, I guess, is the Harmonic Drive Division, but it's not the Harmonic Drive Division that exists now. It includes the manufacturing manager who works for the factory, it includes the production scheduling clerk who works in the factory, it included the foreman, the manufacturing engineer, as well as my boss, the marketing department. . . .

PROFESSOR: Were you meeting with these people as a group or were you going around to each individually and sort of gradually bringing them to some consensus around what needs to be done or. . . ?

CRAIG: Well, mostly, we took it step by step. In other words, we . . . I started out with the marketing problems of trying to forecast what sales would be in the future and as we went through that the word got out that this kind of information was available and the people came looking for it, and that's when I got involved with the manufacturing manager who was newly appointed to the job and very anxious to find out what my information was going to say and what he should be doing about it, and the second half of the summer was almost exclusively spent in the area of facilities planning . . . . how to determine what kind of facilities and what kind of organization we'd like to have in the future.

PROFESSOR: This planning . . . was it all going on sort of informally . . . . and were you doing the major bulk of it and then shoving out your ideas to these people. . . ?

CRAIG: I was asking questions and then taking their answers and trying to work it into something that looked feasible.

PROFESSOR: Did you write a report on what looked feasible?

CRAIG: I didn't write a report but I produced a forecast for ten years in terms of sales and broke it down into different areas. Then I produced a . . . and these were a, you know, a table or a chart or something like this . . . was usually what came out of it, and we also produced a report trying to show how many hours of work would be required on each number of machines in the different years involved. How much floor space we needed, how many people, and we developed charts for all of these that were used later in a presentation to top management in order to implement things, the plan. But the planning itself . . . we didn't have a meeting and say: "O.K. We're going to have a planning meeting today." It came from moving from one step to another and I guess I was the one who produced the format in terms of what steps should we go to next. And then I picked it up and would go and talk to somebody and try to find out some answers. He might not particularly know where I was going or why I was going there, although I tried to let them know as much as I could about the background involved. But sometimes I didn't know myself until I got back and looked over what I had and knew where I was going. It involved a lot of duplication . . . If I sat down and thought very carefully just exactly where I wanted to go I might have been able to go into one guy and ask him a series of questions and come up with a series of answers, and then go to the next guy and the next guy and never go back. But the way I did it, I think, produced two results, or maybe three. First of all, I wasn't tied to a procedure that, perhaps, could have locked me into an answer that I didn't like, or not that I didn't like but an answer that wasn't the best one as I saw it at the end. The second thing was, it got them interested in what I was doing, got them some knowledge of what I was doing so that the answers they gave me weren't just pat answers, they were interested in doing this. They were interested in giving me answers that were worthwhile. Several times they'd come back and say: "Gee, I've been thinking about that . . . I think there's a better answer, or there's a better way to answer it, and we should look at it this way or that way." And the other thing, of course, was that I got almost all my ideas from them, by talking with them and trying to find out how they thought the situation worked. Then I'd go back and think about it and then I might come back to ask another question or check to make sure if this, "Is really what you meant . . . Now, does this, you know, this seems to imply that we don't have enough product? Is that really what you meant? Did you really mean that we could do it this way?" I can't think of a specific example right now. Well, I guess in the government sales forecasting area the government marketing manager had given me a forecast for two years and then for five years and ten years . . . he had given me 1, 2, 5, and 10. And he had given me a forecast one way for one and two and another way for five and ten. And when I was trying to figure, when I was trying to develop the different categories involved, I found that I had categories for one year here and then I didn't have anything in that category for 5 and 10 years, but I had other categories for 5 and 10. So I thought about them and tried to relate them, tried to relate the two categories and had to go back and say: "Is this really what . . . if you meant this in this category, it seems as if you must have meant it this way in another category." And I tried to get him to agree . . . all the way along the line I tried to do this, especially in the Marketing area, to get them to agree that these are the numbers that they like the best. In fact, it got so that they were coming to me for these numbers because they had given them to me in one form and I'd spread them out into several forms and they knew this . . . they knew what the form was so they'd come back and say: "Hey, you've got that number . . . I've been looking for a number and I think you've got it somewhere in there." So the information we had was really getting used because people knew where it was and they knew what it was . . . and then, go ahead.

PROFESSOR: I was just going to say, could you tell me where this finally jelled around . . . you mentioned a report to top management, and I'm getting sort of interested in its final, its impact as it begins to come into some form?

CRAIG: Sure, we had a . . . what we developed and a lot of people were pushing this . . . the factory was pushing it and the Harmonic Drive Division was pushing it, and we would . . . and when I say "we" now, I think I mean myself and the manufacturing manager at this point, because we were talking about a new facility. And we would each talk with the people, and some of the people that would have a hand in a decision on this matter and go in with our ideas and they'd ask questions and we'd come back out and we'd say: "Yeah, that's a good question . . . we should have thought of that before and we'd work that out." And finally we came up with a plan that both the factory and the Harmonic Drive Division was behind, and the general manager of the Harmonic Drive Division and the plant manager of the factory went to the . . . well, he doesn't really, he's the president of a company which is really a division of the holding, the major company, and made a presentation to him, using our charts and our numbers, asking that we get the money to make this plan work.

# Product Management at United Brands (A)

THEY ARE the chosen few . . . the MBA Club. They've got the fastest timetables in the company.

They're a bunch of young, bright, and terribly egotistical guys.

They're very smart . . . *shrewd* is a better word.

It's the Momma's-chicken-soup syndrome. These guys *assume* they know how to do it best.

What they call creative thinking would be called B.S. any other place.

They're bringing people in from the outside all the time; because they don't know their own business. They can't develop their own people; they promote them instead.

They have charisma. They are always great personalities . . . a bunch of actors . . . a superior race. They're the prestigious group, the comers.

All these statements are about product managers. They were made by people in the various departments of the Butternut Division of United Brands, Inc. Only the last statement was made by a product manager.

## THE DEVELOPMENT OF PRODUCT MANAGEMENT AT UNITED BRANDS

Established in the late 1920s through the merger and acquisition of a number of independent packaged food producers, United Brands was one of the United States' first multiproduct packaged food marketers. United Brands was also a pioneer in the use of the product management form of organization.

Originally, at United Brands, as in most companies, each function—production, research, marketing, and financial services—played a specialized role in the total operation of the company. The general manager of a division coordinated the work of the functions in implementing the corporate strategy. However, as the number of products each division produced and sold increased, the job of coordination became increasingly complex. The product management type of organization was United Brand's response to this complexity in coordinating the functional departments in the development, production, and marketing of a large number of products.

The product management organization was superimposed over the traditional functional organization, cutting across functional lines, as shown in the matrix below:

| | MARKET RESEARCH | SALES | PRODUCTION | ACCOUNTING AND CONTROL | PRODUCT RESEARCH |
|---|---|---|---|---|---|
| PRODUCT GROUP A | | | | | |
| PRODUCT GROUP B | | | | | |
| PRODUCT GROUP C | | | | | |
| PRODUCT GROUP D | | | | | |
| PRODUCT GROUP E | | | | | |

Each product manager played a role similar to that of the division general manager, coordinating the work of people in the functional departments, in implementing the strategy for the product (or products) for which he was responsible. An important difference, however, was that he had little structural authority over the people whose work he coordinated, as did the general manager. In fact, a product manager had to sometimes compete with other product managers for the services of the functional departments. For example, in the Butternut Division of United Brands, the same sales force handled all the products of all five product groups. In other departments, such as financial services and, to some extent, market research, employees were assigned to work with particular product groups, while at the same time working for their superiors within the function.

In 1970, United Brands marketed a wide range of packaged food products in the United States through four operating divisions, each of which was treated as a relatively autonomous unit.

## THE BUTTERNUT DIVISION

The Butternut Division of United Brands maintained its own production facilities, sales organization, product management section, marketing research group, research and development organization, raw foodstuffs purchasing group, and personnel and controllership functions. (See organization chart and division headquarters floor plan, Exhibits 1 and 2.) Its products included peanut butter, jams and jellies, honey and maple syrup.

According to Mr. Lee Edwards, Butternut's marketing manager, the Butternut Division had traditionally been United Brands' largest division and the backbone of the company in terms of sales and contribution. In 1970, the Butternut Division accounted for 37 percent of domestic sales.

However, although Butternut sales had continued to steadily increase over the past five years, their share of United Brands' total and domestic sales had decreased over the same period, due to a leveling off of the market for their group of products, United Brands' renewed acquisition program, and United Brands' increased activity in the institutional and international markets.

According to United Brands' 1970 annual report, the business of the Butternut Division would "remain a dependable and profitable business, but will account for a relatively smaller share of overall sales and earnings as other areas of the company grow more rapidly."

## PRODUCT MANAGEMENT IN THE BUTTERNUT DIVISION

According to Mr. Edwards, Butternut's marketing manager, the product manager's was a key role in the operations of the division. Characterizing them as "little general managers," he described how the product managers are central to the planning and execution of marketing strategies:

> The product groups, with the advice of the various functional departments, formulate the marketing strategies and then pass them up the line of management for modification and/or concurrence. When agreement on the strategy is finally achieved, responsibility for the execution of the strategy rests with the product manager. This approach keeps senior management in control of policy and strategy, but it puts the burden of "managing" on the product manager. It also serves as a built-in manpower development program, as the product manager must constantly think up solutions to business problems and accomplish their successful execution.

The casewriter discovered that product management in the Butternut Division had traditionally been the route to top management positions in the company. The chairman and the president of United Brands and 12 of the corporation's 16 top nonproduction operating officers[1] were once product managers in the Butternut Division.

On the whole, people in the product management group were younger and more highly paid than their counterparts in the other departments of the division Most of them had MBA's.

## WHAT THE JOB ENTAILED

The product manager's work in implementing the product strategy could be divided into two broad categories:

***1. The Administration of Trade Discounts on Current Products.*** Butter-

---

[1] Division managers, marketing managers, national sales managers, advertising and merchandising managers.

**EXHIBIT 1**

**Butternut Division Organization Chart**

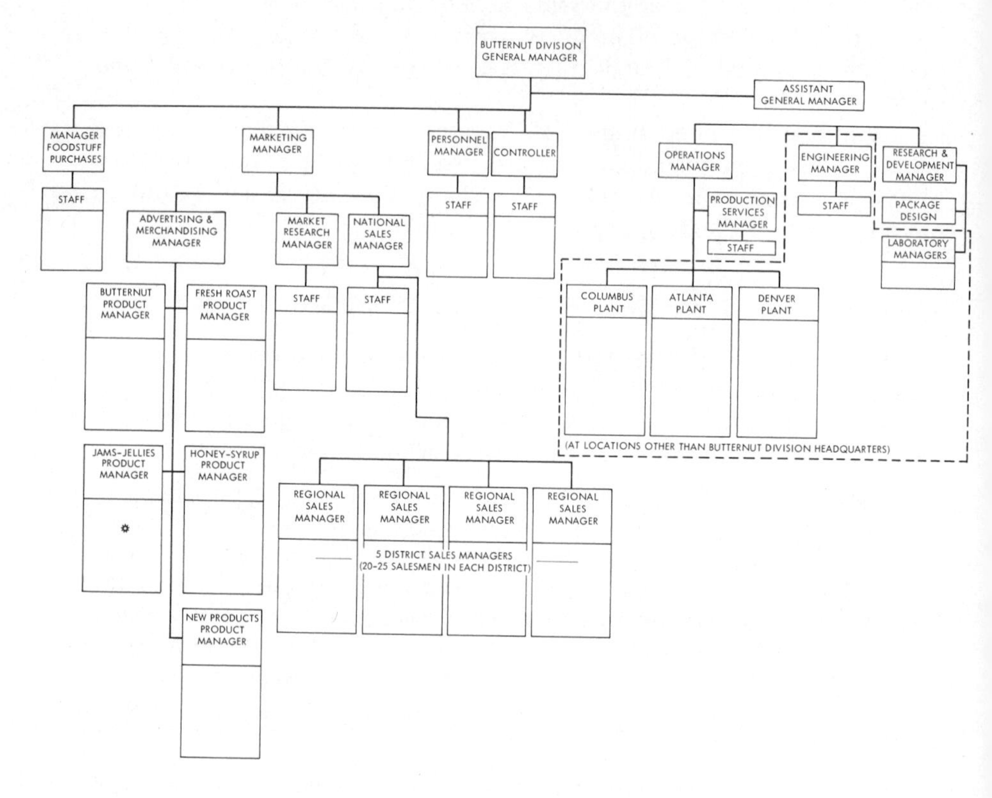


* Each product group was made up of a product manager and, usually, two associate product managers and two assistant product managers.

nut management considered most of their products to be commodities in the packaged food business. Therefore, in terms of marketing expenditures, the division's marketing emphasis was on price competition. Three fourths of the division's marketing expenditures were spent on trade deals.[2] Trade deals were administered on a district by district basis over the 20

[2] Trade deals were promotional expenditures aimed at distributors and retailers, rather than directly at the customer. They included discounts off regular trade prices and allowances to retailers for running special newspaper advertising and retail coupon offers. These expenditures were often made with the intent that price reductions be passed on to the consumer. Sometimes trade discounts or dealer promotions required action by the retailer before the money was turned over; sometimes they did not. Trade deals did not include consumer promotions, such as sweepstakes contests, merchandise send-ins, and the like.

**EXHIBIT 2**

Floor Plan of Butternut Division Headquarters*

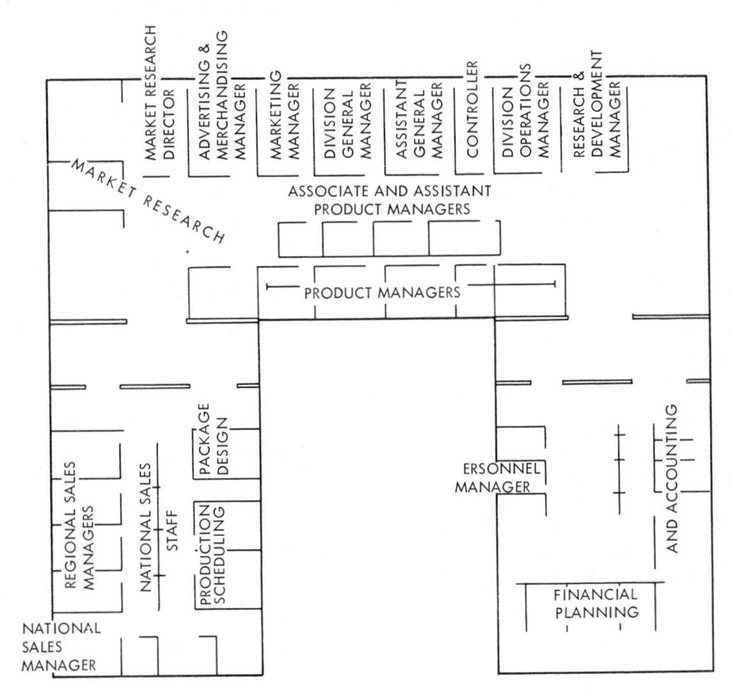


* The production plants and research laboratory were at separate facilities.

sales districts. (The four regional sales managers each had five district sales managers working for them, who in turn each had 20–25 salesmen.) Managing trade deals required negotiating the types and amounts of the trade deals for each district with the regional sales managers and coordinating the volume requirements with production. In the negotiations with the regional sales manager, the product manager had the final say as to how and where the marketing money would be spent; he controlled the purse strings.

***2. Managing Advertising and Product Changes.*** This could entail introducing a new product, changing a current product, or changing its advertising. These activities required working together with the product research group, the market researchers, the product group's advertising agency, Sales, and Production. An extremely simplified example of the process follows: Product Management and Market Research determined what could sell. This had to be reconciled with what Product Research could create and what Production could produce within cost limits. Production was then established on a limited basis. Product Management, Market Research, and the advertising agency then developed selling concepts and introduced them through the sales force to test market the product. Test market data were evaluated and decisions were then made on a final strategy. The controller was involved in financial analysis throughout the complete process.

While this example was sequential, in actuality, all the different functional departments were involved in the process at all points along the way to some degree. A large number of unforeseen problems would come up in coordinating the work of the functional departments; and much of the product manager's job involved getting these cross-functional conflicts resolved and getting decisions made, so that schedules and objectives could be met. The product group served as the focal point of most coordination and decision making.

When the casewriter asked Mr. Edwards, the division marketing manager, the basis on which product managers were evaluated, he answered, "On how well they did their job." He was reluctant to be more specific, explaining that, even though a product manager had met all the financial and market objectives of his product strategy, he could still be judged as performing poorly because of other circumstances, such as momentum in the product before his arrival, or his ineffectiveness in dealing with others.

A successful product manager, he pointed out, must be able to not only coordinate the work of others, but must also be able to get good ideas from them and motivate them to carry out the decisions he ultimately makes, following the timetable he establishes.

## PRODUCT MANAGEMENT AS SEEN BY THE OTHER DEPARTMENTS

The casewriter arranged to talk with people in each of the functional departments and with representatives of the advertising agency, with whom the product managers came in contact. His intent was to find out what constituted "effective dealings" with each of the groups. The casewriter asked these people two questions: (1) What are the basic conflicts between your department and Product Management? (2) In terms of helping you do your own job more effectively, what constitutes a good product manager and what constitutes a poor product manager?

Representative answers to the two questions appear below:

QUESTION NO. 1: *What are the basic conflicts between your department and Product Management?*

### Advertising Agency

The thing that's always bothered me about Butternut is, where their businesses are so huge and the funds are there, they don't try new approaches to advertising enough. They spend too much time on the day-to-day operations, making sure the deals are effective, making sure they meet their monthly share objectives. Product Management simply does not experiment enough.

### Production

Plants are basically big thick machines. Product Management is constantly thinking of ways to market the product that don't fit those big machines, that require a significant amount of change. These big machines don't like to get changed. So this basic plant wish—in an ideal world, to run everything in a one-pound jar—is basically at odds with Product Management, who are trying to make up exotic things to sell, exotic ways to make products, and exotic ways to package it.

. . . . . . . . . . . . . . . . . . .

The Product Management people seem to continually come up with new ideas that the plant cannot do.

. . . . . . . . . . . . . . . . . . .

One conflict is the speed with which Product Management would like to react. Once they have an idea, our cycling times to get that idea from a drawing board into a package is usually far too long for Product Management; and they try their damndest to get us somehow to commit to a date that's unrealistic.

### Market Research

What keeps competent people in the department is the opportunity for being personally creative, the opportunity to develop new market research techniques. Too often Product Management gets in the way of that. They're constantly sending us out to put out brush fires—little projects, the same kinds of things all the time. What's worse is when they ignore your results, because they don't fit the product manager's preconceived conclusions.

### Controllership

Our main job is helping them project the results of their programs and then tracking what they've done and determining how successful it's been. They've got so many programs going at the same time—and these programs overlap—that it makes our job very difficult. And there's always something new and different that doesn't fit our ways of doing it. It's really a can of worms. But, then, that's what we're paid for. I shouldn't really complain about that.

. . . . . . . . . . . . . . . . . . .

Product Management has traditionally not paid close enough attention to profits and has emphasized market share. They have rationalized that they were buying future profits; but until recently they haven't tried to cash in on their past investment. That's beginning to change now. Mr. Parkes, the new division manager, is putting increasing emphasis on the profitability of brand strategy; and the product managers are catching on. But it is still something of a problem.

### Sales

Some of the product managers are inexperienced. They don't know what the hell they're talking about. For the most part, they're trained to think profits and how to increase profits and spend the least amount of money. Or maybe it's the reverse—spend the least amount of money and, therefore, get more profits. Unfortunately it doesn't work out that way.

. . . . . . . . . . . . . . . . . . .

Product Management's job is to make sure the consumer wants our product. Sales' job is to make sure the products are there. That means Sales has to know what is the best way to present it to the trade, which is the key execution in getting the product to the shelf.

Every market is different. But our salesmen are in each and every market. So we know our customers' needs; we have accumulated knowledge of those markets. Given our intimate knowledge of each of these markets, we can recommend to the Product Management people how they should spend their promotion money. Sometimes they follow our recommendation; sometimes they won't. When they don't, then there's conflict.

. . . . . . . . . . . . . . . . . . .

The major complaint in Sales is that we don't handle the money. Product Management has complete control of the purse strings. We try to get X amount of dollars from the product group for a program we feel will be beneficial to the division. They may not give it to us. And they have the final say.

### Product Research

The overriding basic conflict is we can't make what they want as cheaply as they want it. And they don't want what we can make. Of course that's an overexaggeration. But the conflict is there.

. . . . . . . . . . . . . . . . . . .

There's a tendency on the part of the Product Management people to theorize and postulate, etc. They see themselves as being very creative. They'd much rather argue than go out and try to get the information, to run the experiment. They shouldn't be creative to the point that they neglect facts. There's too great a tendency, I think, to fly by the seat of their pants, and not to get the facts.

QUESTION NO. 2: *In terms of helping you do your own job more effectively, what constitutes a good product manager and what constitutes a poor product manager?*

### Advertising Agency

A good product manager doesn't use me just for working up copy. He includes me in on the full range of marketing strategy formulation. That makes it very satisfying for me personally. It also insures that what we're thinking at the agency is in sync with what's brewing here. And, occasionally, I'm able to contribute something valuable that may have been overlooked by the product management people.

### Production

A good product manager is a guy who understands the production function. So when we are unable to meet some of his timetables, he better understands the situation. He should be a guy who's quite openminded, quite willing to listen, and perhaps give some part of his day, or some importance, to Production.

. . . . . . . . . . . . . . . . . . .

Some Product Management people are honest and aboveboard. They tell you what they want, their reasons, and the impact on the company if they get it and if they don't get it. Others, you feel they're not really being honest with you. Their objective is to make short-term heroes out of themselves at the expense of long-term gains. They are in such competition with each other. There's a lot of backbiting.

A Manufacturing guy will bust his rear end to get something for a Product guy if he knows it's in the interests of the division or the corporation. But if they think it's just to make the guy look like a hero, they're not going to.

. . . . . . . . . . . . . . . . . . .

A good product manager is willing to make a decision and stand by it.

### Marketing Research

He will ask the staff to make recommendations on how best to solve a problem. He will *not* tell them what test to use, what kind of sample, and so on. Instead, he will allow the market researcher to do his job and make recommendations. Of course, he has the right to question the program—you know . . . "Is this question really answered?" But he won't tell you what to do; he will define the problem and then await your recommendations.

. . . . . . . . . . . . . . . . . . .

A good product manager gives us the opportunity to be directly involved in the formulation of marketing strategy, the chance to make and defend our own recommendations.

. . . . . . . . . . . . . . . . . . .

What I don't like in a product manager is indecisiveness. If I work out a program with a product manager, and he likes it and has bought it, I think he should support me in his recommendations to senior management. If there are points of conflict, he should be willing to let the market researcher into the discussion, where senior management is present, and let him defend it, too.

### Controllership

The man who fails as a product manager is the one who is not able to meet schedules and timetables.

. . . . . . . . . . . . . . . . . . .

The good product manager is not only good at dictating, he's also a good listener.

### Sales

A good product manager has to have a good personality—almost a sales-type personality. He has to be able to come down like he has just stepped out of the shower, and give an amusing, enlightened presentation to the sales force. He has got to be an extrovert, to be able to project a good image.

I have never seen a negative, or introverted, or nasty dispositioned product manager make it.

. . . . . . . . . . . . . . . . . . .

A good product manager will come right out and tell it like it is. "Here's how much I have. I'm sorry I can't give you more," rather than "We feel this strategy would be better for you."

My bag is tell me what your story is and, if you don't have the funds, I can sit down with my guys and explain that to them. But I can't tell my guys we didn't get X promotion dollars because Product Management didn't think we were right. Because we know we were right!

. . . . . . . . . . . . . . . . . . .

You've got to have people to deal with who will act, who will make decisions, not the ones who think "If I don't do anything, it will go away."

. . . . . . . . . . . . . . . . . . .

A good product manager can develop a strong point of view, articulate it correctly, and stand up to his superior with it.

### Product Research

The poor product managers tend to look down on people in the other departments—like "you're my lackey."

. . . . . . . . . . . . . . . . . . .

A product manager must be able to speak the languages of the people he deals with, which is quite different from technical research, operations, or financial people.

He must have a basic desire to communicate with the different functions and be sympathetic to their needs as they relate to the total business. Not to their gripes, but to really try to understand and appreciate the problems a guy is trying to explain. He must be willing to give up valuable time to communicate to these people what he is trying to do and the reasons why.

## PRODUCT MANAGEMENT AS SEEN BY SUBORDINATES OF THE PRODUCT MANAGERS

Another group each product manager dealt with was his own subordinates. The casewriter asked several junior members of the Product Management group what kind of product manager they preferred working for. Some of their answers appear below:

A good product manager will give his subordinates new chances to develop their skills and new types of things to work on. I don't want to stay on one thing for too long after I've learned it. Then I'm just wasting time. I want to move on and up in the business. To do that I've got to learn all aspects of the business. A good product manager won't hold me back.

. . . . . . . . . . . . . . . . . . . .

A good boss will always be ready to help you out with a problem; but he won't hover so closely over you that you can't grow through overcoming the difficulties of the problem yourself. He'll be there when you want him.

. . . . . . . . . . . . . . . . . . . .

He'll include me in on what's happening in the Product Group, beyond the particular project I'm working on; so I know where my work fits in.

## PRODUCT MANAGEMENT AS SEEN BY PRODUCT MANAGERS

The casewriter also asked two product managers to describe what they thought differentiated the successful product manager from his less successful counterpart:

### Product Manager No. 1

The most difficult part of the job is to get the uninvolved, the not-interested people to be involved and interested in the business, like the production and packaging guys, the nine-to-five's, the people who have no future in their jobs. A good product manager can do that.

You have to understand what the guy needs—a kick in the ass or a pat on the back. Some fellows like to be loved. So you ask "How's your dog today? Did your wife sleep well last night?" He'll think "Hey, there's a nice guy. I'm going to take care of him next time." If you're sending pen and pencil sets to retailers as a promotion gimmick, you send him one. So he feels he's part of the brand. Others you have to lean on, get tough with, threaten. It depends on the guy.

Let me give you an example—the purchaser in the Production department. If you don't get his attention, and you miss your target date, you may have the best program, but without glass to pack the product in, you don't have *any* program. And he is the guy who orders glass. He is the guy who can make Supply work extra hard for you. But he works for five Product groups, seven brands, and 30 different sizes. If he doesn't like you, you're in trouble.

So it's a function of how you show your respect for him, and how you communicate with him, how you build up this rapport.

If you need to get something done in three weeks, and the book says it takes four to six weeks to get it done, but you know if he wants to help you he can do it in three weeks, then it's that critical area of whether he's going to help you that makes or breaks you, or makes you look good.

That's why it's important to know how to deal with each of these guys.

There are other things too, of course. If a guy can't handle the complexity of many things going at the same time, he'll never make it.

Also, there are some guys who have great ideas, but can't sell them. They're just poor salesmen. They will yield right away when the boss gives them the pressure treatment, even if it's just to test them. They don't last.

There's another type that is extremely competent, but won't succeed because they can't live within the system; they won't observe all the protocols, they won't follow the procedures. If you want to succeed, you can step out of bounds only once in a while to show you're a tiger. You can be sort of a bastard; but not much, just sort of. You step on people's toes only once in a while to show you're a tiger.

The organization demands that its people be good Christian soldiers. That also means that you may stay in a position longer than you should, or take a job that you don't want; but you don't say no, you say "Yes, but." You have to strike the right balance between independence and compliance.

### Product Manager No. 2

To become a product manager, you have to be smart, aggressive, and creative. The smarter you are, the better. By aggressive, I'm referring to a people-oriented aggressiveness. To get ahead and succeed as a product manager, that aggressiveness must be attached to a commitment to get things done. Creativity is very important; but it's not necessary that the guy be creative himself with new and appropriate ideas. It's more important that he be able to recognize appropriate creativity in others when he sees it. He should continually be running across things others do with the reaction, "Gee, I wish I'd thought of that." The important thing is that the fact that he didn't come up with it doesn't bother him—that he is delighted to accept an idea someone else has.

To get ahead as a product manager, a fellow has to have a commitment to the results rather than to a particular technique or to a personality or to the source of the ideas. He has to show aggressiveness and a toughness, a tenacity that doesn't stop when somebody says "No, you can't do it." He'll try to figure out another way to do it.

Another thing a fellow needs to get ahead in Product Management is the broadest scope view of the job possible—that means he goes beyond the requirements of his own job. There are three kinds of people who start off in Product Management: (1) Those who look upon the job as a crappy job; that go through the motions, not wanting to do it. The job suffers. (2) Those who manage to do the job adequately; that are committed to it; that want to do it well, so they can move on to something else more fun and exciting. (3) Those who do the job adequately and have the time—no, make the time—to do other things as well, that they think are important. They are the ones who go beyond their jobs. They are the ones who will succeed in Product Management.

Another important factor is what I call public relations (the cynic would probably call it politics). The fact that someone is using a great new idea in his work doesn't do any good unless the right people know about it. That is the job of the product manager. I am continually sending things up just to keep them posted as to what guys in my Product Group are doing that is good.

Finally, a little humility goes a long way. That's trying to know as much as you possibly can without flaunting it. The guy who says "I've been in this business 20 years, so I ought to know more about it than you do"—that's categorically wrong. He knows more about his job; but I know more about how his job related to what I'm trying to do—which is what we're sitting down to talk about.

So his attitude is wrong, if that's his attitude. But making him see that does not move the ball ahead. Playing got-cha is sometimes satisfying; but it doesn't help much.

# Product Management at United Brands (B)

DAVID ALPERT was the product manager for Butternut Peanut Butter in the Butternut Division of United Brands, Inc. (See organization chart, Exhibit 1, Product Management at United Brands (A).) A year ago—five years after receiving his MBA degree—he had assumed responsibility for Butternut Peanut Butter, one of United Brands' top selling products. (Over the previous five years, Butternut sales and profits had been 9.1 percent and 15.4 percent or corporate sales and profits, respectively.)

## EVALUATION OF DAVID ALPERT AS A PRODUCT MANAGER

As far as the casewriter could tell, David Alpert was doing well in his work as product manager. Lee Edwards, Butternut Division marketing manager, had referred Alpert to the casewriter as a good example of a strong, effective product manager. Other people from the various functional areas in the division described Mr. Alpert in the following terms: ". . . Flexible . . . prompt . . . decisive . . . a decision maker (Sales); receptive to different ways of looking at the business (Control); sympathetic to problems we might have in accomplishing our task . . . tries to understand . . . a good communicator (Product Research); very fair-minded person . . . generally given to listening to all sides of a thing, given to letting people express their opinions . . . parochial in terms of pushing for his brand's priorities, but easy to work with (Market Research); excellent . . . a good listener . . . keeps us informed as to how we fit into the overall picture (Production)."

## DAVID ALPERT'S EVALUATION OF THE JOB

David Alpert told the casewriter he liked his job. He listed a number of reasons why:

First, I like the responsibility the job entails and I like the fact that I can measure my accomplishments. There are measures like market share targets and return on investment. There is also a certain measurement in the sense that we deal with programs that can be completed. We've just completed a successful program that involved spending an awful lot of money. It had a lot of little

**EXHIBIT 1**

Butternut Division Organization Chart

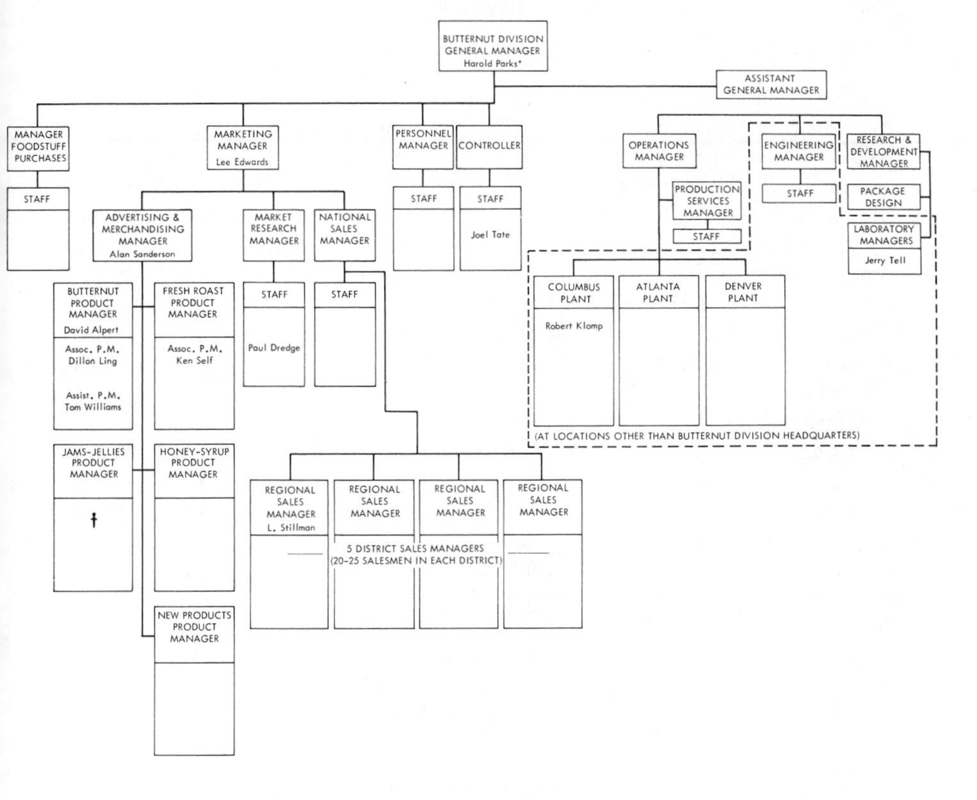


* Only names mentioned in the case are given.

† Each product group was made up of a product manager and, usually, two associate product managers and two assistant product managers.

pieces to it. It was a real executional nightmare. It was satisfying to fit all these pieces together.

Second, I find a lot of personal satisfaction in being responsible for the expenditure of a lot of money and spending it well. I guess beneath that is the fact that I like to be looked upon as a guy who has things under control. It means something to me to have that reputation in the company.

Another thing about project work that is fairly appealing to me is the fact that on no given Tuesday do I have the same thing to do from week to week. There are no routines in the work.

Then I guess that I would have to say that there are people that I like to work with. First, there are those outside the Product Group. I find a great deal of satisfaction in cranking these people up to get a job done. Secondly, within the product group I have four people working for me, and I think I'm relatively good at getting them to progress—getting them to feel they are progressing.

There are two aspects to this. The first one is the training aspect. I enjoy working with my people and helping them to develop along the lines that I think are important for product manager types to have.

David then paused for a moment before he went on.

The second aspect you might call the public relations job. I like to insure that my people will have their day in court and be exposed in the way that will help them to get promoted. I think I'm pretty good at that.

Finally, the material rewards—the money—are, of course, very important. It's strange how you are consistently able to live just beyond your income; so that you're looking forward to each raise as it comes. I guess that's very much the American way of life. In any case, my salary progression has been fairly dramatic. My salary has increased fourfold since coming to United Brands. I am making in the high 30's now; and that's pretty damned important. Especially when it comes by doing something I like—that I'm making progress by doing things I enjoy doing.

Of course, he added, it's not all a bed of roses.

It's aggravating to any product manager who wants to get the job done to sit and listen to somebody else tell you about their problems. If they didn't have problems they wouldn't have a job; and because they've got problems, they become one of your problems. On the other hand, if reciting their problems to you helps to solve their problems through some ego satisfaction or whatever, and your job is to solve their problems, then you are doing your job by listening to them talk about it.

But that's really not the most important part of our job—listening to somebody create a problem before your very eyes, which he will then proceed to solve and be a great big hero. When they do that, it's a fairly obvious ploy.

## DAVID ALPERT'S DEALINGS WITH OTHERS IN THE BUTTERNUT DIVISION

The casewriter spent three days with David Alpert, recording his dealings with others in the Butternut Division. Later he asked David to comment on these exchanges.

### Monday—Task Force Meeting

David Alpert headed a task force, formed to make up the five-year plan for the two peanut butter brands sold by the Butternut Division. Alpert represented Butternut Peanut Butter, United Brand's popularly priced line. Representing Fresh Roast Peanut Butter, United Brand's premium brand, was Ken Self, an associate product manager in the Fresh Roast Product Group. Other members of the task force representing other groups in the division were:

Robert Klomp, Production
Joel Tate, Control

Larry Stillman, Sales
Paul Dredge, Market Research
Jerry Tell, Product Research
Ned Ashby, Advertising Agency Representative

Below are excerpts from one of the task force meetings (the Control and Sales representatives were absent):

The meeting began at 9:00 A.M. Jerry Tell (Product Research) summarized to the group the results of a meeting with higher management on task force objectives. He had attended the meeting representing David Alpert, who had been on vacation. Fifteen minutes into the presentation, Ned Ashby, the advertising agency representative, walked into the meeting late. He made a short apology and excuse and took a seat.

David Alpert answered his apology:

ALPERT: I told the secretaries there were two things we were missing—Ned Ashby and the coffee—and I wasn't sure which we were missing most.

ASHBY: You're being polite. (*Everybody laughed.*)

The meeting then continued. Jerry Tell (Product Research) finished his summary with a comment on the use of market research in the division:

TELL: The next issue was that, in a business that is as consumer oriented as ours is, we are not spending really enough time, money, effort on trying to improve our ability to communicate with and to the consumer in the way of basic marketing research. The comment was generally made that there should be a great deal more effort in this area.

ALPERT: Did you make the comment or did higher management?

TELL: I did. That's a personal thing I've been carrying around for quite a while. . .

ALPERT (joking tone): You got that off your chest?

TELL: Yes, I felt a lot better. I slept very well that night.

Later, the discussion turned to looking into areas of peanut products other than peanut butter, such as peanut candy bars, peanut cake frosting mixes. Several possibilities got batted around by the group in an animated discussion for about ten minutes. During that time, David Alpert remained silent. He then cut the discussion off, saying that what they were discussing were areas for the division to look into, but they were probably more appropriate for the New Products Group—that the Peanut Butter Group would not have to worry about them.

Alpert then went through the five-year plan point by point with the group. All members of the task force participated freely in the discussion.

Robert Klomp (Production) raised the question of whether changes in taste preferences were going to come about in the next ten years, or whether it had been assumed that tastes would stay the same. Klomp suggested that it should be possible to project future changes in taste preferences on the basis of changes over the past ten years. Alpert answered him in a roundabout way:

ALPERT: Well, you've gotta have some givens—you've got to establish some base objectives. And the easiest ones to establish are markets and margins. You just can't cope with all the variables. You have no control or relatively no control over what the market's gonna be. We hope we can expand it, but we made the best guess we can.

Jerry Tell (Product Research) joined in the discussion.

TELL: With our share of market, we have more control than I think we tend to exercise.

ALPERT: Well, we don't know how to exercise it.

TELL: But with margins . . .

ALPERT: Yes, we've gotten some control over margins. But if the cost of peanuts is 70 percent of cost of goods sold, a . . . Fred (the raw foodstuffs buyer) doesn't know what the cost of peanuts is one day to the next, let alone one week or month to the next.

ALPERT: All you can do is assume you will take active pricing action and adjust it as you go along.

The casewriter noticed that during the meeting, Ken Self, the associate product manager from the Fresh Roast Group, challenged David Alpert a number of times on points such as use of merchandising methods, perceptions of the consumer, and advertisability of the brands. Each time, when Alpert answered his challenge with a milder response, Self backed off.

The meeting concluded at 12:15 P.M.

After the task force meeting was over, the casewriter asked David Alpert about aspects of the meeting that intrigued him:

#### Rivalry and Competition among Product Managers

CASEWRITER: I thought what I saw going on between you and Ken Self was friendly rivalry. Was it?

ALPERT: No, it wasn't. I haven't been in a position to develop a lot of respect for his talent. The guys he works with think he's pretty good. I just haven't seen it. He hasn't really been any help on the task force. I thought it was nit-picking.

CASEWRITER: How did you try to handle it?

ALPERT: Just as briefly as possible without being rude. Because, obviously, any obvious dissension between product manager and associate product manager in a group like that would be picked up by the other functions. Probably with some relish; even though they are pretty mature people. There was nothing there to call for his being put down. In meetings like that, when somebody like Ken brings up something, I just tend to lose interest in the conversation. I let it wander around for a while, then pick it up again after a few minutes.

CASEWRITER: But, still, it looked like rivalry. Is there much competition among the product management people?

ALPERT: Not really. I can't think of any. There is no reason to be. United Brands needs all the good product managers it can get.

### Use of Humor

CASEWRITER: Let's turn to something else in the meeting. I noticed you used humor a number of times.

ALPERT: Humor goes a long way.

CASEWRITER: Like when you asked Jerry Tell if it felt good to have it off his chest, after his analysis of the marketing situation. It seemed to me he wanted to get involved in marketing decisions.

### Dealings with Product Research

ALPERT: Nearly everyone does. That's where they think the action is. It's where the status is.

Jerry Tell is very easy to work with. He is far and away the most competent man at the laboratory from my standpoint. He thinks more like a manager than a technician. He evaluates a proposal on rational return on investment criteria rather than on whether it would be technically fun. He is a delight to talk to, a real breath of fresh air in the organization. But there are others who don't act that way. Really, he is the exception.

CASEWRITER: How do you deal with others in Product Research?

ALPERT: Those are the kind of guys you coddle. They have just as much education as you do. But they need experience on the job before they become effective. We spring full blown from business school as "marketing experts." They don't; so our counterparts there are generally older than we are. Therefore, we tend to exclaim loudly and make a terribly big fuss over their accomplishments.

For example, I'll call a guy down in the bowels of the laboratory someplace and congratulate him, and make it very clear that a product improvement was his accomplishment. Which it was.

### Dealings with Production

CASEWRITER: How about the Production man, Robert Klomp? His major contribution was some speculations on the probability of taste preferences changing. It seemed he wanted to play marketer too, perhaps.

ALPERT: Could be. He was really here primarily so the Production people would feel included, although there could be some things come up where I could use his knowledge.

I've simply learned that bridges built to the plant will pay innumerable dividends. Primarily the junior product managers deal with them; but I try to keep in touch because they can screw us up so bad.

And those are the kinds of people that, if they want to, will ruin an entire plan just to prove that they're right and you're wrong. And they can do it.

I have no idea what goes on down there in the plants. And most of it, I suspect, would horrify me if I did. But that's not really important, so long as I can get them to do what needs doing for us. And change is by definition bad at the plants. So it's very important that I win them over to my side. It is important that they feel that they can come into my office and tell me that they are not able to do what I want them to do. If they don't come, but shove the problem under the rug, we can't work things out before it's too late. So the key there is communications—direct and easy communication and access. When they come to me with a problem, we sit down and try to figure out what we can do to overcome the problem.

### Dealings with Market Research

CASEWRITER: What about Paul Dredge, the market researcher?

ALPERT: He is a bit parochial, but that's what he's paid to be. When he says he'll go away and think about ways we can incorporate research into our presentation and make it a little more research oriented, he'll probably be back in here first thing Tuesday morning with a bunch of ideas about how to do it. He's a good man. I've got few worries in that department. I was the market research director for four months before I got this position. Now they're convinced true or false that I know enough of what's going on down there that they can't fool me. The key there is to keep them informed about the business so that they can keep their research program up to date. They don't need a lot of guidance.

CASEWRITER: Your Sales and Control people were not at the meeting.

ALPERT: They are both out of town. I'll be meeting with Joel Tate, the accounting guy, tomorrow morning to discuss ROI calculations. I have to find out how United Brands does it before the next task force meeting. Our Sales representative is a very good man for this job. He worked in product management for a while and has a broader view of things than most of those guys.

### Dealings with Sales

CASEWRITER: Tell me about your dealings.

ALPERT: The day-to-day dealings are handled almost exclusively by our junior people in Product Management. I usually get involved when they can't get a problem worked out.

The Sales people resent us. And yet maybe they are the most crucial people we have to work with. That whole relationship is a difficult one from their point of view. The regional sales manager sees you as younger and less experienced than him (which we are). And yet as his volume and sales promotion planners, his success depends on our ability to get him his share of the total dollars for promotion and spending. So I can certainly understand the resentment—particularly against the people who don't do well at it.

We treat them with a combination of deference—because they are a little older, and particularly when we are junior—and candor. Candor is the key to the thing. They like to deal with decision makers. It's good for their own self image, plus it saves time—which is an important commodity for any guy.

When they make a request for a program that they think is necessary, they would far prefer they be told that we don't have enough money to do it. Whether it's a good idea or a bad idea, it's wasting time to debate it when you don't have the funds.

But if *you* don't think it is a good idea and you can convince the sales manager yourself, that can take you miles. If you can disagree and give him your reasons and really communicate, so that you end up working out something that you agree to, or at least he can understand your position, then that's very good. There's a lot of respect built in that kind of relationship. Say "I can't afford it" when you can't afford it, and say "I don't agree" when you don't agree.

#### Tuesday—Meeting with Control

The next morning, Alpert had a short meeting with Joel Tate, the Control representative to the task force, to talk about ROI calculations for the five-year plan. Alpert needed the material for a meeting with his superiors, Alan Sanderson, the advertising and merchandising manager, and Lee Edwards, the marketing manager.

ALPERT: Where are your ROI calculations for the five-year plan? I've got to get some by Thursday. I need at least one, and perhaps several exhibits on that subject. Because that's probably the most important numbers—at least the second most important after share—that we'll talk about. And I can't just go say to Edwards it ought to be approximately 35 percent.

TATE: I'll have to do some work on it. I'm not too sure I can have all the data and all the . . . a . . . things together by Thursday.

ALPERT: I mean we've got something, haven't we, we've got . . .

TATE (*cuts in*): Oh, I have the actual of how we came up with fiscal '70—the 35 percent.

ALPERT (*acts impatient*): Well . . .

TATE: And, and I just got pieces for the other years.

ALPERT (*speaking firmly*): I'd like to see what those pieces are.

TATE: O.K. . . . as far as projections. We can maintain, I'm sure we can . . . . We should say that minimum is 35 percent.

ALPERT (*more impatient*): I mean over the last three years, can I see the calculations?

TATE: Sure . . . I'll bring them in. (*Tate leaves.*)

After Tate had left, Alpert turned to the casewriter and volunteered:

ALPERT: You needn't worry about stifling creative ideas that the elves down in accounting may have; because they don't have any. I think the secret with those guys is that you not deal with them at the middle management level, that is Tate's level. Because I think that the truth of that department is that they occasionally get lucky and hire somebody that's good. But they can't keep them long enough to promote them through the ranks to get them to Tate's position. It's only the relative dullards, like Joel, that stay. I suppose he is a capable guy in his own right. He is not really stupid. He's not awfully smart; he can add a column of figures. But he is not going to become treasurer of the corporation or controller of the division or anything else.

The best way to get real performance there is to latch on to a young guy who's aggressive and good and very junior in the organization and just have him working his ass off for you.

We've got a financial analyst under Joel who's assigned directly to Butternut. He is very good. He's the guy through whom we get things done. He is practically a member of the Product Group. A very, very junior member; because he doesn't create anything, he just does what he is told. But he is a tremendous help.

### Tuesday—Meeting with Subordinates

Later that same day, Alpert met with Dillon Ling and Tom Williams, associate and assistant product managers on Butternut, about a test market they were proposing in Atlanta. Ling was Chinese; Williams was a black. Alpert listened quietly to the presentation, now and then probing their assumptions, asking extra questions to see how well they had thought things out. After Williams finished his last points, Alpert spoke.

ALPERT: That's a very thorough way to go about analyzing what it ought to be. . . . The only question I have. . . . We've traditionally gone from a Northeastern test market like Albany south and west without any compunctions. If it tested well in Albany, Syracuse, or Indianapolis, we'd take it South. We haven't got any experience with anything testing it in the South and taking it North.

LING: We don't?

ALPERT: I don't see any radical differences. But we don't want to get ourselves into situations where we've selected test markets that rationally people would think okay, but when it comes right down to it, they won't accept it emotionally—

They discussed that issue. Ling pushed for Atlanta, citing advantages with media and outlet control.

ALPERT: O.K., let's assume it will be Atlanta. In the meantime, I'll do a little spade work across the hall with the advertising and merchandising manager and the marketing manager and see if that makes people uncomfortable. Because I think it clearly is the best market. But I think we ought to be pragmatic about it. We want it, not because it's Atlanta, but because it's the best way we can think of to test our product.

WILLIAMS: We had a couple minor positives and negatives to going into Atlanta.

ALPERT: O.K., I'm convinced.

WILLIAMS: I think you want to hear these, though. One thing, a positive, is I'd go to the Hiatt House; I've never seen it.

Another, a negative one, it's not a great area for minority groups to take their field trips. (*Williams laughs cautiously.*)

ALPERT: Well, Atlanta's all right; but I'm not so sure about eastern Tennessee. (*Everyone laughs.*)

LING: Johnny Cash is the spokesman for Nashville.

ALPERT: Yes. For eastern Tennessee, you want to send your white Anglo-Saxon Protestants; and we ain't got any of those kind of people.

WILLIAMS: Buy somebody some cut-off Levi's and get him a rope to tie 'em up and a T-shirt, and send him to eastern Tennessee. (*Everyone laughs.*)

LING: The introductory promotion in March could be a shotgun; then for 50 cents you can get the shot and shoot the revenuer. (*Laughter.*)

ALPERT: Make the ammunition the continuity. (*Laughter.*)

After the meeting, the casewriter asked Alpert about his dealings with the subordinates in his product group.

CASEWRITER: How do you train your people?

ALPERT: A lot of the training is in your expectations. Junior product managers are, in their individual ways, terribly anxious to please. You don't have to give them orders, you just have to make known simply what you want and be clear about what it is you want done, and then stay out of their way. Because they will go to great lengths and work terribly hard to get it done just the way they think you would want it done. That's a characteristic of the good product manager. The thing that separates the good ones from the excellent ones is that the good ones get it done just the way they think you want it done, and the excellent ones will get it done that way, unless they think there might be a better way—and they'll stop and think about it. I think my people know about the distinction, because we've discussed it and will continue to discuss it. The key is initiative. You tell them something and they do it—that's awfully important. There are not a whole lot of people that can do exactly what they are told effectively. On the other hand, if you tell them something, and they come back to you and say, "I heard you, but this is a better idea," that's sort of a step beyond.

The most important thing is getting the job done, achieving the objectives. I don't have a lot of pride of authorship. I'm not really creative in bringing up new ideas of my own. I'm better at being able to take other people's ideas and adapting things that have been done before to problems that we have now.

### Wednesday—Meeting with Superiors

On the morning of the third day, Alpert met with his two immediate superiors, Alan Sanderson (advertising and merchandising manager) and Lee Edwards (marketing manager), to discuss the final stages of the five-year plan. Alpert was concise in his remarks and candid in his presentation. Several times the marketing manager disagreed with market assumptions he had made. Alpert defended his ideas, saying that he thought the issues were more complicated than the marketing manager perceived them. He suggested that they look into them further.

After the meeting, the casewriter commented on Alpert's skill in making a persuasive, concise presentation. Alpert replied.

ALPERT: I've learned most of that from Alan (the advertising and merchandising manager). He's a very good businessman and he's hard nosed. And he doesn't like to beat around the bush. If you start to give him something in a roundabout sort of fashion, he's very good at cutting right through to the meat of it. And, he will do it disapprovingly, because he doesn't like you to be wasting his time telling him something in five sentences when you should be able to tell him in one. He doesn't like you to take five minutes on justification when one minute will do. He's a terribly busy guy. He has an incredibly time-consuming job. He can't afford the luxury of people who can't afford to talk straight, and his style is blunt enough; he'll tell you if you're wasting his time.

CASEWRITER: You were pretty candid in the meeting yourself.

ALPERT: Ed and Alan encourage that. They encourage opposition. They're open enough so that if they don't agree with you, and you tell them you think they're wrong, they'll very quickly admit it if they agree with you. Alan, in particular. He'll sometimes test you to see whether you've thought things out. He'll ask for five reasons you feel the way you do, and very often, he will cut you off after reason No. 2 and say "O.K."

That starts, of course, with the general manager—to tell people what you think. That's Harold Parks' style.

# READINGS ON INTERGROUP ISSUES

## Interdepartmental Conflict and Cooperation: Two Contrasting Studies*

JOHN M. DUTTON
RICHARD E. WALTON

THIS REPORT compares and contrasts emergent behavioral patterns in two district organizations. It focuses on how personnel of functionally interdependent departments enter into the process of joint decision making and otherwise relate to each other. The study is based on data gathered through field observations and interviews. The analytical approach is to describe behavior in tactical terms, characterizing the participants in these two lateral relationships as behaving instrumentally and adaptively, albeit not always effectively.

Although the organizational literature on lateral relationships is meager when compared with the studies on leadership and authority, both M. Dalton and G. Strauss have published insightful accounts of tactical patterns in lateral relationships in several firms they have studied.[1] Dalton's studies have focused upon relations between production and

* Reproduced by permission of the authors.

[1] M. Dalton, *Men Who Manage* (New York: Wiley, 1959). G. Strauss, "Tactics of Lateral Relationship: The Purchasing Agent," *Administrative Science Quarterly,* VII (September, 1962), 161–86; "Work-Flow Frictions, Interfunctional Rivalry, and Professionalism: A Case Study of Purchasing Agents," *Human Organization,* XXIII (Summer, 1964), 137–49.

Other notable treatments of lateral relations are: E. R. Chapple and L. Sayles, *The Measure of Management* (New York: Macmillan, 1961); H. A. Landsberger, "The Horizontal Dimension in a Bureaucracy," *Administrative Science Quarterly,* VI (December, 1961), 298–332; and J. A. Seiler, "Diagnosing Interdepartmental Conflict," *Harvard Business Review,* XLI (September-October, 1963), 121–32.

R. E. Walton, "Theory of Conflict in Lateral Organizational Relationships," *Proceedings of the International Conference on Operational Research and Social Sciences,* Cambridge, England, September, 1964 presents a theory of lateral relationships which the authors are testing in a comparative field study of six or more plants. In the six-plant study relatively fewer variables are subjected to statistical treatment. In the present study we subject two more comprehensive cases to intensive clinical analysis.

maintenance and between "line and staff." Strauss analyzes the tactical patterns of purchasing agents in their relations with other departments. This article adds another account of conflict in the lateral relations between another pair of departments—sales and production. In the organizations reported upon here, sales and production represented the two most important functions and both were "line" departments. Moreover, their interdependence was intense, frequent, and central to the core activities of both departments.

The two case studies of conflict and collaboration presented here are especially fruitful objects of analysis because they are placed in the same general technological, economic, and market context and within the same overall organizational structure. The two company districts had the same basic task. Within each district, production and sales tasks included independent and interdependent aspects. Yet the two emergent relationships differed dramatically. In the Elgin district, production and sales each adopted a narrow, exclusive goal structure and engaged in reciprocal organizational strategies and tactics of conflict. In sharp contrast, each of the two parties at Bowie adopted goals that embraced the other's operating objectives and pursued strategies of collaboration.

The discussion first analyzes the technological and economic interdependencies of the production and sales departments. Subsequently the relationship syndrome is described point by point in each district. The discussion then turns to the stabilizing processes in each relationship; the factors which may account for the different patterns in the two districts; and the consequences of these patterns for the participants and for the larger organization.

## AREAS OF INTERDEPENDENCE BETWEEN PRODUCTION AND SALES

Peerless was a large manufacturer which owned and operated more than a dozen widely dispersed plants.[2] The company produced a wide line of metal windows, doors, and sashes for sale to industrial customers and to the building industry. Products ranged from simple metal frames to complex all-weather doors and sashes and included both standard industry items and products made to customer order specifications. Individual order quantities varied from a few dozen to several thousand items. Items were produced only upon receipt of firm customer orders.

Each company plant was a relatively self-sufficient unit, dependent on its own resources for obtaining and producing customer orders in a profitable manner within its geographical area. Each district consisted of a production plant and a sales area. Responsibility for company field oper-

[2] Company data are disguised for protection of the firm and of individual employees. The essential elements of the lateral relationships discussed have been preserved while names, places, and setting have been altered.

ations was divided at the home office between a general sales manager and a general production manager. Several regional production managers and several regional sales managers provided a link between the home office and the subordinate managers in the various districts. Especially important for the study was the fact that no position of overall general management responsibility was established for any of the districts or regions. Thus, coordination between sales and production was largely an *ad hoc* arrangement in each district.

Important areas of interdependence which called for some degree of joint decision making between production and sales at Peerless metal fabricating plants included acceptance of new orders, scheduling, and quality control.

### Order Acceptance

Obtaining orders was a responsibility of the district sales personnel. New orders required designing and cost estimating, and often involved hard negotiating with customers on price and terms of delivery. Decisions which affected both production and sales were frequently made in day-to-day order procurement activities. Salesmen would have liked, essentially, to sell any and all orders they could. The buyer's market they faced inclined them to let customers exercise great influence over product design. However, some orders were less profitable for production than others. Given the plant's staff and equipment, some were technically only marginally feasible. Others were feasible but not economical. The potential participants in decisions regarding new designs and order acceptance included: (1) the sales manager, salesman, service manager, and product designer; and (2) the production manager, plant superintendent, production control manager, and shipping manager.

Top management's expectations were that designs and order acceptance would be decided on the basis of a full search for alternatives and a balanced examination of the implications for both departments. Beyond this, sales could seek orders to balance production facilities. Similarly, production, by experimenting with new, initially costly orders, could assist in building profitable sales volume in the company's competitive market.

### Scheduling Decisions

Production was a rapid and complex operation. Each day many different standard and specialty orders passed through several fast-moving stages of fabrication and assembly work to the shipping department for direct delivery to customers.

Both sales and production had a strong interest in scheduling. Responsibility for scheduling orders for production was assigned to the production manager. The sequence of orders produced was important to sales, however, because lead time was short between order receipt and the delivery date required. Consequently, sales officials were concerned that the sequence of orders through the plant reflect their customer priorities.

Production's stake in scheduling decisions was equally important. A large number of scheduling sequences was technically possible for a set of current orders, but widely varying costs were attached to these sequences.

Coordination between sales and production was also required in the handling of customer requests for revision of delivery dates and order quantities, and in resolving the problems arising from plant congestion and equipment breakdowns. Changes in the production schedule which resulted from these problems placed special potential strain on the sales-production relationship.

The formal organizational plan called upon sales and production personnel to balance customer priority on the one hand and production cost and inconvenience on the other hand. Ideally they would share accurate information relevant to these considerations, collaboratively weight the factors, and reach a decision through consensus.

### Quality Control

Opportunities for quality errors were numerous because of the nature of company operations. Sales was responsible for securing complete and correct order specifications. Production was responsible for producing orders free from defects and in the quantity stipulated. Each party possessed information of value to the other. Production possessed information on defective and marginal orders which it could reveal or conceal. Sales was in a position to ascertain whether a customer could accept an order of marginal quality; also sales was frequently the first to be informed by the customer of an error or defect and could conceal or reveal this knowledge. Sales officials felt the threat of losing customers by failing to maintain quality in a competitive market. Production appreciated the need to maintain minimum standards in the area of product quality but was subject to production performance criteria, including raw material waste control and machine and labor utilization, which sometimes competed with quality considerations. Moreover, once a quality error or loss occurred, the expense was charged against either sales or production. Thus, both had an incentive to avoid unnecessary bad marks on their respective records, and each had reason to be less concerned about those defects charged against the other department. Notwithstanding these divisive incentives, both parties were ultimately dependent—for sales and production volume—upon an acceptable level of quality.

Analysis of the organizational setting thus revealed a potential toward both collaboration and conflict at the district level. Sales was more sensitive than production to volume, and production more concerned than sales with cost factors. In addition, the fact that plant production and district sales did not report to a common superior allowed each to choose to concentrate on its separate functions to the exclusion of the other's interests.

## THE ELGIN PLANT—A CONFLICT RELATIONSHIP

The Elgin plant was the largest and one of the oldest plants in the company, with many employees of long-time service. Plant layout and equipment were typical and posed no particular problems, save in shipping, where space was cramped.

### Bargaining and Other Dynamics of the Conflict Relationship

Maintenance of a bargaining approach to joint decision making imposed particular requirements on the social system, as well as on the process of information handling and exchange in joint decisions. Each party required a conflict-oriented frame of reference consistent with a bargaining approach to joint decisions. Bargaining also imposed a need for particular, supporting patterns of attitudes and interaction. These Elgin behavior patterns can be analyzed in terms of strategy and tactics employed to implement a bargaining relationship.

### Goals and Orientation to Decision Making

Officials in each of the two departments adopted narrowly defined objectives for their own department. That each department perceived the other as adopting divisive rather than unifying objectives can be seen in the comments of Elgin sales versus production officials.

> SALES OFFICIALS: Sales is customer oriented. Production is interested only in cost. . . . Production only sees plant waste in costly orders and low output. . . . Sales' job is service—delivery when the customer wants it. . . . Sales' main job is to build volume in customer orders.
>
> PRODUCTION OFFICIALS: Our goal is to run orders efficiently. Many opportunities arise to reduce costs . . . but the salesmen don't know enough about production to recognize these things. . . . New items often give us problems. . . . Many times the salesmen try to sell ideas that cannot be produced economically or even at all!

These statements go beyond superficial confirmation of the departmental division of labor intended by top management. The two parties were aware of the existence of larger, overall district goals. But they chose not to adopt district goals as superordinate and not to coordinate their departments in the maximum interest of these goals.

### Information Handling

Lack of understanding of each other's department problems characterized the approach to joint decision making at Elgin. The parties also failed to communicate, or delayed communicating, relevant information to each other. These conditions at Elgin were legitimatized by the viewpoint of each party which saw problems of the other as "their problem, not ours."

Scheduling decisions, for example, were subject to mutual influence but were arrived at through demand-counterdemand, exaggeration, pressure maneuvers, and so on. Padding of needs for prompt and urgent handling of customer orders by sales officials was at the heart of the bargaining process. Production personnel, however, privately discounted sales requests as "obviously padded." On the other hand, production would exaggerate the difficulty it anticipated with a given request, whereas sales would assume that production constraints were more fanciful than real.

Quality control decisions exhibited the same bargaining pattern, including deliberate distortion and concealment. Sales engaged in overstatement of quality needs and production discounted sales quality requests.

The withholding of information stemmed in part from fear of raising future performance expectations and from fear of home office sanctions. If production (or sales) was too accommodating in scheduling decisions, they might create high expectations and, therefore, future problems for themselves. Similarly, full disclosure of quality defects might bring home office sanctions.

Because each department usually possessed more flexibility than it was willing to admit, it limited the number and type of contacts with the other, thus reducing the risk of revealing the true facts to the other.

### Freedom of Movement

At Elgin each party sought to gain maximum freedom for itself and to limit the other's freedom. On the one hand, each party attempted to fix future performance obligations and to establish jurisdictional limits *for* the other. On the other hand, each party engaged in tactical violations of limits imposed *by* the other.

Elgin sales was particularly active in circumventing formal procedures. Sales found production lacking in understanding, consideration, and competence and therefore attempted to take direct, unilateral action on their problems even when this violated procedures and usurped jurisdictional authority from production. This type of behavior is succinctly summarized in a sales official's comments:

> When production refuses, we have to act to satisfy customers. For instance, production often claims not to have material to produce an order. So we get on the phone to locate and purchase material. Production then, of course, claims

that we are not within our rights. But we can't solve our problems by turning customers away.

To counteract this behavior, and to satisfy its generally felt need for caution and certainty in the conflict bargaining process, production further emphasized jurisdictional limits, restricted interaction, and formalized decision-rules to govern interdepartmental relations. The resulting oscillation between emphasis on rigid rules on the one hand, and unilateral action on the other, heightened the dilemma for each party of either choosing dependence on a reluctant peer or risking independent action. These tendencies are shown in the following comments by members of both units.

Problems are resolved on a jurisdictional basis: "You take care of your part and we'll take care of ours." Each group decides who's responsible for what part of the problem and then goes its separate way; each party tries to hold out for the least possible action on his part.

The relationship between sales and production doesn't permit very much innovation on new orders. Production tends to resist, saying "Do it the old way," and finding lots of reasons not to try new ideas. However, sales needs new designs and depends on production for help. But if sales goes ahead with a new design alone, production feels their rights are infringed on.

The difficulties in joint decisions on scheduling resulted in a supreme attempt to formalize relationships between the parties on the handling of this problem. The parties at Elgin negotiated a written agreement which stipulated procedures for scheduling customer orders. The new scheduling agreement established the minimum production lead time on customer orders, and the plant capacity, and set forth a detailed plan of organization and procedures for scheduling customer orders. Under the plan two new expediters, plus the production control manager and service manager, were to constitute the sole contacts between sales, the production office, and the plant production floor.

This remarkably formal and explicit signed agreement was an expression of the two-unit relationship at Elgin. Its twofold significance was that it was produced by the bargaining relationship and that it was widely heralded at the plant as a forward step. Apparently the agreement controlled the tension and conflict between the departments. It strengthened tendencies already present to limit interaction between sales and production. Since members of the units found these exchanges both punitive and unrewarding, the plan provided welcome relief. The agreement delegated the scheduling problem to a small group and, as a consequence, numerous persons were able to withdraw from an uncomfortable relationship.

Sales was inclined to initiate more contacts than production. While the agreement tended to restrict interaction in scheduling, sales remained active in other areas, such as quality control. Here sales employed the tactic of circumventing formal procedures by exploiting special relationships with a person in production. Contrary to policy, this official permitted sales people into the plant to check on customer complaints.

Both parties frequently used pressure tactics to achieve their ends. The two types commonly employed were hierarchical relationships and "commitment tactics." At Elgin both sales and production turned to their regional and home office superiors as a means of resolving differences. For example, both managers frequently refused to accept responsibility for a given quality error. As a result disagreements were carried all the way up to the home office general sales and general production managers for a decision.

Another type of behavior, referred to in bargaining theory as "commitment tactics," was tactical to the conflict approach. One manager would attempt to influence a joint decision by structuring the situation so as to be seen by the other as irrevocably or maximally committed to his preferred position. For example, a sales official would often call the production planning manager to get a promise on delivery while holding the customer on another telephone line in order to "put the pressure on" production.

Production also used commitment tactics, sometimes by presenting sales with a *fait accompli*. This was not uncommon when an order cancellation or delay by the customer would be inconvenient to production. A sales official commented:

> Production will try to get a customer to take an order when the latter wants to cancel. Production has sometimes waited until the order was in production or has asked us to tell the customer the order was already in process.
>
> Production will also ship ahead of time when they have an order completed before the planned delivery date. They will do this even when they *know* the customer does not want the order early and has no place to store it.

Blaming was also tactically used both as a form of punishment and as a means of avoiding responsibility for failures in performance. The conflict about who was to blame for errors, losses, and delays was especially intense. The sales manager commented:

> Recently a customer received an order with oversize frames in it. He was willing to sort out the bad items himself if we could give him credit. But the production manager wouldn't do it. He wouldn't take the loss in production.
>
> We finally had to take the credit as sales expense. However, we delayed so long that the customer lost patience and we got the whole order back to rehandle ourselves.

At Elgin this pattern was often carried to the point of attributing every problem or negative result to the other fellow. Moreover, not only was the other party perceived as responsible for what was bad, but he was also seen as erroneously accepting credit for what was good! For example, production personnel charged that sales people took a lot of credit for work on new designs done in production.

### Attitudes

The attitudes of the parties supported the bargaining approach to joint decision making. Each department used the terms "we" and "they" to distinguish between the two groups and to compare "good" and "bad" motives. Each found occasion to report unfavorable attributes of the other, such as the lack of integrity of a plant foreman who expected personal gifts for helping a salesman. Also, each saw the other as lacking in understanding and competence. Vindictiveness was revealed in anecdotes in which one party expressed satisfaction at making the other "squirm."

The atmosphere at Elgin went beyond the use of stereotypes and obstructive behavior. Attitudes approached resignation and despair, and a lack of hope that any accommodation could be reached that would permit interdepartmental problem solving. Efforts which had been made to improve relationships had failed. The service manager reported:

> The production planner and I tried business lunches together. But we quit after a while. We weren't getting anywhere. We also tried customer service meetings. These didn't work either. People's feelings got involved. There were personality conflicts. Production felt they weren't getting a hearing. They started to make these meetings gripe sessions against sales.

There was little or no interaction that was not related to work, and when members of sales and production did meet, the atmosphere was cautious and hostile. It was apparent at these meetings that the parties were holding back information. It was also apparent that each party brought up topics and made statements that were designed to make the other party feel uncomfortable. For instance, one party would point out errors and oversights by the other or would verbally reprimand the other for withholding information.

## THE BOWIE PLANT—A COLLABORATIVE RELATIONSHIP

The Bowie plant had been acquired by the company within the past ten years. It had been purchased complete with equipment from its former owners, and many of the plant personnel had remained after the purchase. Bowie was somewhat smaller than the average plant but was fully equipped and could produce the company's complete product line.

### Problem Solving and Other Dynamics of the Collaborative Relationship

At Bowie members of the two groups interacted frequently to resolve problems that arose in the course of their work. They enjoyed these contacts, as the following scene indicates:

> The production manager burst into the sales manager's office and handed him a sample of a new part. "Try that," he said.
>
> "It certainly seems stronger," the sales manager replied. He tried to twist the sample in his hand and also tried to bend it under his foot. "It certainly is!" he exclaimed.
>
> "We'll run a trial on this in the plant and see how it works out," said the production manager, and then left.
>
> The sales manager explained the incident, saying, "We were having trouble with this part. Frank, the production manager, got an idea from a toy he got for his kids and came to see me about it. He gave the idea to Tom, the designer, who worked it over to make it easier to produce. We think it is a very good idea."

In this incident a production man and a sales person cooperated with each other to develop an idea for an improved product. They saw the problem as a joint task for both sales and production and provided social support for each other in their attempts to solve the problem.

At Bowie problem solving was the approach to joint decision making used in all areas of interdependence, including new designs, scheduling, and quality control. Maintenance of this approach required a collaborative orientation from each party and a supporting pattern of interaction.

### Goals and Orientation to Decision Making

Members of the Bowie organization tended to define objectives for themselves which embraced both production and marketing functions. The sales manager's comment was especially direct in this respect.

> You build a plant to make a certain product mix. Then you have to try to go out and sell this mix.
>
> In planning sales we try to develop a program to obtain business to keep all machines in the plant operating. There's a big capital investment out there and you can get terrible imbalances among departments if you don't exercise control.
>
> You also, however, have to sell what's there in the market. You can't tool up to produce what isn't there. The ideal is a balance between the market and the production setup.

The production manager had a similar view. For example, he indicated sufficient concern about missed deliveries that his remarks could have been confused with those emanating from sales.

**Information Handling**

In contrast with Elgin, both Bowie departments evidenced an understanding of the other's problems. For instance, the scheduling task at Bowie, as at Elgin, contained conflict potential: Customers tended to give short lead time and initiated requests for revised delivery dates; production officials had reasons peculiar to their task for preferring one schedule over another; breakdowns in bottleneck equipment occurred, etc. Distortion or rationing in the handling of information, however, did not develop. For example, the "padding" of sales requests which marked the scheduling process at Elgin occurred at Bowie only in a minor way, if at all. The salesmen at Bowie were more inclined than at Elgin to probe for the customer's real needs so that unnecessary demands were not passed on to production. The following salesman's comments are indicative of this understanding and consideration:

> The customers are educated not to expect delivery within a certain period of time. There are exceptions, but why foul up production scheduling to accommodate customers who don't anticipate their own needs?
>
> You do have to take the customer's needs into account. You can't be late. We have established an understanding with production. If our minimum delivery rule doesn't satisfy customers, then we contact production through the service manager.

Each party tried to anticipate problems, not only for itself but also for the other. Recall that at Elgin production was reluctant to inform sales of errors or slightly defective product runs. At Bowie, production people were encouraged to go to the service manager and tell him about an error. Sales would then phone to see if the customer was willing to accept the product anyway. The customer frequently cooperated if he was approached this way. The production manager commented on other areas in which he was benefited by sales:

> We have few problems in avoiding uneconomical or unprofitable orders. The sales manager is good about this. He gives me a look-see on possible problem orders insofar as cost is concerned. We look at these together and compare revenue and cost considerations.
>
> I also go to sales to *ask* for certain types of business. We may need finishing work of a particular type, for instance.

This degree of understanding at Bowie had not always existed. In the past salesmen had obtained every order they could. Certain current steps were being taken to further increase salesmen's understanding of production problems, including giving young salesmen firsthand experience in production.

Constraints at Bowie limited the degree to which the parties could be helpful to one another in jointly solving problems. One constraint was a lack of relevant cost information. The sales manager cited specific orders for small lots and complex items which were of doubtful profitability, but in the absence of cost information he could not be certain. This situation was viewed as a mutual problem rather than an intergroup issue, however.

### Freedom of Movement

At Bowie the parties generally tried to increase freedom of movement. Cooperation and procedures were adequate enough so that there was little or no incentive to circumvent the rules or formal procedures. Where deviations did exist, they did not present an issue. A member of the production organization said:

> Sales people are not supposed to come out on the floor but sometimes they do. I don't think there's anything wrong with it as long as the salesmen don't stop and talk to the machine operators. And they don't do this as far as I know.

There was flexibility in decision-making rules. No arrangement existed at Bowie comparable to the Elgin scheduling agreement. No minimum delivery rule was established. It was generally understood that quick delivery promises were risky, but the service manager was delegated authority by both parties to "play-it-by-ear."

In more general terms, there was a complete absence of attempts by either party to fix future performance for the other party or to force commitments from the other that would limit its future freedom. This freedom was accompanied by a relatively open interaction pattern. The sales and production managers met daily several times, as did their office subordinates, the service manager, and production control manager. There were few restrictions on the movements of any member of the plant organization.

Although Bowie's interaction system was more open than Elgin's, there were certain restrictions in selected decision areas at Bowie. These limits were, however, pursuant to the collaboration pattern rather than exceptions to it. Limited interaction was especially notable in day-to-day scheduling decisions, as shown by a sales official's comment:

> People are generally free to come and go in the plant and office. However, we don't want salesmen to try to persuade the foremen to get their orders. By the same token we don't want foremen to ask salesmen for changes in orders. We do have lines of communication on scheduling matters through the service manager.
>
> We confine our scheduling contacts with production to the service manager. As soon as you have a number of people doing it, you lose control.

These comments indicated conditions where limited interaction could be beneficial to the collaborative relationship. Successful collaboration on scheduling required both cooperative criteria and adequate decision-rules.

Scheduling was an extremely complex cognitive task. Limited interaction was beneficial to the scheduling system for the following reasons: First, it enabled the service manager to reject untimely distractions for the production scheduler when the latter was involved in the intricate task of constructing a schedule. Second, it kept the information on scheduling channeled through the position where cooperative criteria were applied. Influence exerted in a noncontrolled pattern was often suboptimal in effect; for instance, when a salesman operated with incomplete data and inadequate rules in seeking to persuade a foreman to give preference to a particular order.

Closely related to open interaction patterns and freedom of movement was flexibility at Bowie in the establishment of positions and the performance of tasks. The leading instance of flexibility was a quality control plan. This plan, which had been devised at the Bowie plant and was unique within the company, employed a quality control man who rotated continuously through all departments in the plant watching for errors. Although the system contained the normal instances of laxness, and although this person, in performing his difficult task, encountered instances of friction from individuals, he was generally supported by both departments.

Another instance of organizational innovation was the establishment of the office of general manager serving both sales and production personnel. Home office approval had been secured for this move but the plant had taken the initiative on this change. The appointed official, the service manager, had extensive experience in production control as well as sales service and, in this smaller plant with its collaborative patterns, was well qualified for an overall coordinating position.

Bowie presented a further contrast to Elgin in searching for solutions in lieu of using pressure tactics. Whereas at Elgin the sales official held the customer on the phone while making requests of production, in order to increase his own commitment to this request, at Bowie the sales official did not need this leverage to find out what production could or could not do. Therefore, he was free to try to influence the customer—or at least to test the customer's real needs.

> Because production tells us in advance that we will not make our schedule on a particular order, we can call the customer and ask for an extra few days. You find that 90 percent of the time if you call him first, you can get extra time. It's when he has to call you that you get in trouble. The customer is apt to wait until about 4 P.M. on the promised delivery date and then call and say, "Where are you?" If he learns then that no delivery is to be made, he loses confidence. If you call him, he will go to bat for you. If you don't, you embarrass him; he may not need the order but his attitude will be that he does!

There were hierarchical appeals within the plant. But it appeared that the issues which were bucked up raised appropriate questions for plant officials. They were not cases where power was needed to accomplish the obvious, as was the tendency at Elgin. Similarly, extra-plant relations were largely used to implement the *jointly* developed policies of the sales and production managers. By working closely with the home office, the sales and production managers had jointly secured transfer orders from other districts to level production through low periods and had obtained home office approval for the production of certain items for inventory, also a unique arrangement within the company.

Regional and home office sales and production officials were not used as courts of appeal. Superiors set budget goals and cost controls and established payoffs for performance but they were not feared or seen as arbitrators. The sales manager stated:

> I have little contact with the regional manager and the home office. We don't depend on them. There is very little contact, on my part at least, and I feel there is little contact by the production manager.

The production manager's views on the use of the regional manager were similar to those of sales. He was a younger manager in training; nevertheless, he acknowledged the importance of working with sales, perhaps at some cost to his training relationship. He said:

> I don't use the regional manager as a court of appeal. The regional manager is training me. But it has never reached the point where I can't work out any problems with the sales manager. We feel we can reach an equitable solution together.

The tendency at Bowie was to attempt to diagnose problems regarding defective joint decision rules rather than to find a "scapegoat" or to place blame on the other party. This pattern contrasted sharply with that at Elgin. Although much less energy was dissipated over the question of who was to blame, this was not because there was no penalty associated with accepting responsibility. There was as much penalty at Bowie as at Elgin.

The sales manager opposed pinpointing responsibility for errors because of the defensive atmosphere created by this procedure.

> We have a company quality control program. Its aim is to pinpoint losses. This aim can work against you because your people then try to avoid getting pinned for the error. However, we're not so interested in who created the problem as in what practices created the problem and how to correct these practices.

Not all officials wholly agreed with this position. The production manager was more inclined to support formal home office procedure—but for internal control purposes, not as an interdepartmental weapon. The quality control manager was still more favorably disposed to this procedure as an additional support for him in his task of maintaining quality. He also provided the researchers with information which, while it didn't change the general impression reported above, did confirm that the departments at Bowie were not always successful in avoiding the question of "blame."

### Attitudes

The attitudes of both sales and production at Bowie have already been seen to support the problem-solving approach used in joint decision making. Statements of members of the Bowie plant-district organization indicated that production and sales got along well. Personal relationships developed from work relationships. Members shared an interest in one another's affairs and saw each other off the job. Instances were revealed where members went out of their way to help another person.

The fact that liaison members at Bowie showed less strain than at Elgin was perhaps an indication of the differences in attitudes at the two plants. The Bowie service manager was well aware of the differences and potential conflict between sales and production in his district. However, he found his situation quite tolerable. And the quality control manager, who would be caught in the interdepartmental cross-pressure if anyone was, expressed the desire for *more* informal contacts.

Thus, the attitudes supporting the blurring of departmental lines; encouraged trust and support between the two parties, and avoidance of punishing contacts; and furthered attempts to integrate the two units.

## STRATEGY AND TACTICS: A COMPARATIVE SUMMARY

The patterns of behavior at Bowie were in sharp contrast with those at Elgin. Elgin employed a bargaining, and Bowie a problem-solving, approach to joint decisions. The patterns of goal orientation, information handling, interaction and attitudinal structure strategical to these contrasting approaches are summarized in Table 1.

The above comparative summary sharpens our understanding of the patterns of behavior which were strategical and tactical to the interdepartmental conflict at Elgin. How general are these particular patterns of interdepartmental conflict?

It is interesting to note certain contrasts and similarities in our observations and those of Strauss.[3] Whereas striving for status and authority seemed to be a major aspect of the strategic conflict engaged in by Strauss's purchasing agents, status was neither an objective nor a preoccupation underlying the conflict behavior of the sales and production managers in the present study. These managers were merely intent upon doing well in their assigned task (narrowly defined). Several possible reasons for these differences can be offered: First, the sales and production

[3] G. Strauss, *op. cit.* (1962).

**TABLE 1**

Summary of Two Contrasting Approaches to Interdepartmental Relations

| | *Elgin: A Bargaining Approach* | *Bowie: A Problem-Solving Approach* |
|---|---|---|
| 1. Goals and orientation to decision making | 1. With regard to respective goals and orientation to decision making, each department emphasized the requirements of its own particular task, rather than the combined task of the plant sales district as a whole. | 1. Each department stressed common goals whenever possible and otherwise sought to balance goals. Each party perceived the potentials for interdepartmental conflict in the separate task structures but nevertheless stressed the existence of superordinate district goals and the benefits of full collaboration for each party. Each saw the relationship as cooperative. |
| 2. Information handling | 2. With respect to the strategic question of information exchange, each department (*a*) minimized the other's problems or tended to ignore such considerations as it did recognize; and (*b*) attempted to minimize or distort certain kinds of information communicated. | 2. Each department (*a*) sought to understand the other's problems and to give consideration to problems of immediate concern to the other; and (*b*) endeavored to provide the other with full, timely, and accurate information relevant to joint decisions. |
| 3. Freedom of movement | 3. Several tactics were employed which related to the strategic question of freedom of movement. Each department sought to gain maximum freedom for itself and to limit the degrees of freedom for the other by the use of the following tactics: (*a*) attempting to circumvent formal procedures when advantageous; (*b*) emphasizing jurisdictional rules; (*c*) attempting to fix the other's future performance obligations; (*d*) attempting to restrict interaction patterns; (*e*) employing pressure tactics—hierarchical appeals and commitment tactics—whenever possible; (*f*) blaming the other for past failures in performance.<br>Relations were laden with threats, hostility, and the desire for retaliation. Interdepartmental interactions were experienced as punishing by both sides. Contacts were limited to a few formal channels, and behavior within these channels | 3. Each department explored ways it could increase its freedom of movement toward its goals with the following behavior: (*a*) accepting informal procedures which facilitated the task; (*b*) blurring the division between production and sales in tasks and positions; (*c*) refraining from attempts to fix the other's future performance; (*d*) structuring relatively open interaction patterns; (*e*) searching for solutions rather than employing pressure tactics; (*f*) attempting to diagnose defects in rules for decision making rather than worrying about placing blame.<br>Relations were characterized by mutual support. Department officials were independent of higher authority. Home office was asked to support initiatives of joint proposals from the plant. |

**TABLE 1—Continued**

| | *Elgin: A Bargaining Approach* | *Bowie: A Problem-Solving Approach* |
|---|---|---|
| | circumscribed by a rigid rule structure. Department officials depended on higher authority. Home-office managers were called upon to resolve opposing views, to suggest solutions, and to support one party against the other. | |
| 4. Attitudes | 4. Each department developed attitudes in support of the above bargaining strategy and tactics. | 4. Each department adopted positive inclusive and trusting attitudes regarding the other. |

managers were relatively high status; second, unlike the purchasing agents, who could attract the notice of higher management only by enlarging their responsibilities, assuming new initiative, etc., the sales and production managers were measured by higher management in terms of their routine performance; third, the sales and production managers, within their functional areas, had opportunities for upward mobility not available to the purchasing agents.

Despite these strategic differences, certain important similarities are noted in the implementing tactics used to pursue conflict in the two settings; namely, increase in formality, fixing of obligations, appeal to superiors, and selective circumvention of procedures.

There are fewer similarities between the conflict behavior patterns reported here and those described by Dalton.[4] The present study involved two dominant actors in a bipolar district organization, whereas Dalton's participants were in a multiperson and multigroup field; hence, the importance of bargaining strategies (information control, decision-rule framework, etc.) in this study and the importance of coalition strategies (alliances, favors, cliques, etc.) in Dalton's work. Nevertheless, many tactics such as blaming, hierarchical appeals, and formalization were often common to both bargaining and coalition strategies.

## STABILITY IN LATERAL RELATIONSHIPS

How were these contrasting patterns maintained at Elgin and Bowie, respectively? Apart from whatever forces might explain the emergence of either relationship, each pattern achieved added stability because it was self-reinforcing, reciprocal, and regenerative.

---

[4] M. Dalton, *op. cit.*

### Self-Reinforcing Process

There were important self-reinforcing processes within the orientation and behavioral patterns of a given party to a relationship. Perception of divisive goals by production (or sales) led to a bargaining orientation at Elgin. Bargaining called for the use of tactics such as concealment, distortion, threat. Implementing these tactics, in turn, required circumscribed interaction patterns and negative attitudes toward the other party. However, once adopted, each of these tactical patterns had a feedback effect reinforcing the others and the basic orientation to goals. That is, for example, unfriendly and suspicious attitudes reinforced the tendency to circumscribe interactions, to distort information, and to attend to divisive goals.

Precisely the same type of feedback and reinforcement tendencies existed within superordinate goal orientation, the problem-solving approach, full information exchange, open interaction patterns, and positive attitudes at Bowie.

The effect of these feedback and reinforcement processes within either approach to a relationship (once these components had achieved the apparent internal consistency found in these two cases) was to create some momentum and stability for the relationship itself. Because many elements of the total behavioral pattern would have to change together in order to achieve stability at some other point on the conflict-collaboration continuum, forces toward change greater than those which established the relationship in the first place would have to be brought to bear.

### Reciprocal Patterns

In a given plant the pattern was reciprocal for the two parties. At Elgin, where one department adopted a narrow goal structure, the other did likewise. Where one party rationed or distorted information, the other did also. Where one attempted to limit the activities of the other, both did. Where one expressed antagonistic feelings, the other, too, reciprocated. Perhaps the pattern could not have been otherwise for long, because for one party to have been free and candid in providing information and in accommodating the other's needs without assurances of reciprocal treatment would have been even more self-defeating than to pursue a defensive bargaining relationship.

The elements of the pattern at Bowie—which were the opposite of those just described—were also reciprocated. Although there were temptations to "cheat" on these patterns (for the temporary benefit that might accrue), both sides appreciated the fact that they enjoyed the larger benefits of collaboration precisely because there was reciprocity. This reciprocal nature of the emergent pattern was facilitated by the degree of symmetry which existed in the underlying structure of their interdependence: Each party had substantial initiative and ability to make the effective decision in one or more of the areas of decision making vital to both departments. Especially important for the maintenance of a collaborative pattern is an allowance for both parties to be equally and similarly rewarded by the benefits of collaboration.

### Regenerative Relations

Relations were also regenerative at each plant. The experience of older hands was communicated to new members. Only in exceptional cases did individuals resist the conditioning effect of the prevailing plant culture. Within each department existing patterns of behavior were encouraged and alternative patterns discouraged. Except for a single plant official at Elgin who cooperated with sales, the other sporadic attempts to achieve an element of collaboration between sales and production invariably collapsed in failure. The converse, and of equal significance, was Bowie's tendency to resist bargaining. Occasional attempts by Bowie individuals at concealment, threat, and division were greeted with stern and prompt disapproval. Sanctions at each plant thus supported the present behavior patterns and rejected the major alternative.

## ANTECEDENTS TO LATERAL RELATIONSHIPS

What factors explain the emergence of the divergent patterns in these two districts of the same company? Conflict relationships are sometimes explained in terms of contextual factors, such as payoff structure or difficulty of the task, and sometimes attributed to the personal characteristics of the principals in the relationship.

It has already been noted that the formal organizational plan in Peerless contained forces toward both conflict and collaboration at the district level. But at Elgin the parties acted on the conflict potential and ignored the collaboration potential. At Bowie the reverse was true. Why? Although to date we have not collected systematic data to test the many explanatory hypotheses we believe plausible, this intensive investigation is suggestive of the effect of certain factors.

### Contextual Factors

Although the same types of contextual forces may have been acting on the principals in both districts, the magnitude of these forces may have been different—and even subtle differences in the two districts may explain the contrasting responses.

For example, although the districts operated under a common formal plan (including performance criteria and reward structure), the plan could be interpreted differently by the several regional managers who supervised the Elgin and Bowie districts. That is, one or both of the regional production and sales managers responsible for supervising the Elgin district managers may have placed relatively more emphasis on performance of the separate sales (or production) department.

Similar differences were possible in the nature of the task. Although each pair of sales and production departments performed basically similar functions for the total system, slight differences here might have made great differences in the stress and strain on the production and sales interaction. Two circumstances of this nature can be cited which may have influenced the relationship.

First, compared to Elgin, Bowie seemed to enjoy a relatively large degree of home office support, particularly in terms of achieving a balanced plant load. Extensive arrangements had been made via the home office for providing orders for Bowie production during the slow season by transferring orders from other plants. It was not wholly clear whether this arrangement was possible because of the plant's reputation at the home office or because of the collaborative relationship at Bowie. It was clear, however, that the resulting arrangement was perceived as highly advantageous by Bowie production and that Bowie production gave credit for the plan both to Bowie sales and to the home office.

Secondly, compared to Bowie, Elgin was an older plant and was handicapped by lack of space, especially in shipping. Significantly, perhaps, this plant experienced problems of congestion and errors in delivery not mentioned at Bowie. In addition, Elgin operated a special department which produced a unique product for the whole firm. This utilized space, time, materials, and labor at Elgin in such a way as to restrict the amount of the plant's resources available to Elgin sales. This technological limitation on production's ability to respond to the needs or demands of sales could have been a factor promoting conflict.

### Personal Characteristics

There was an important comparability in the Elgin and Bowie situations in terms of the work background of the sales managers. At both districts the sales managers possessed production as well as sales experience. In neither case, however, did the production managers have experience in sales.

Direct familiarity with another department's operations—the problems, the possibilities, and the performance criteria involved—increases one's ability to initiate a collaborative pattern beneficial to both departments. For example, the first party is able to differentiate among those demands he would make on the other in terms of how much inconvenience would be involved for the latter. Similarly, he may be able to identify the relatively important task demands of the other and respond selectively to them. Also, the first party may possess emotional empathy for the other, which affects the timing and manner of presenting his requests or demands on the other.

Thus, in terms of background and experience, the sales managers in both districts were in a position to take the initiative in developing a collaborative pattern. Structurally—in terms of the work flow—sales was also advantageously situated to play an initiative role. With few exceptions, production produced only to customer order, and action by sales preceded action by production much of the time. Another precondition—and our final similarity—was that the Elgin sales manager, like the one at Bowie, had shown some personal interest in working toward a collaborative pattern.

But the differences between the personal characteristics of the principals in the two districts may help explain why a collaborative pattern developed in one but not the other. There were differences in the personal styles of the two sales managers; differences in the cognitive and interpersonal skills of the two production managers; and differences in the degree of status congruity within the two relationships.

First, we can present a brief summary statement about Bowie for use as a benchmark for examining the same factors at Elgin. At Bowie the sales manager was markedly senior to the newly promoted Bowie production manager "in training." The young Bowie production manager was eager to learn, both trusted and took direction from his sales counterpart, appeared to be relatively skilled in interpersonal relations, and was willing to experiment. The Bowie sales manager was also skilled in interpersonal relations and used a permissive, albeit somewhat paternal, approach in dealings with his younger production counterpart.

The Elgin sales manager had been promoted to his position fairly recently. Although his background included several years of work in production, his primary orientation was toward sales. He found resourceful use for his production knowledge in the pursuit of sales goals; believed that production as well as sales should seek innovative new products; and was convinced that greater customer service was required to cope with prevailing competitive market conditions. His leadership style was forceful and he aggressively sought ways to achieve sales goals. He was similarly action-oriented in his dealings with production.

The background and personality of the Elgin production manager were quite different from those of the sales manager. He was a veteran of long service (all in production work) with the company. During his early years of company experience, the industry's products were in great demand and industry capacity was short. He spoke with nostalgia of these earlier times:

I remember when customers took anything. During the war we doled out orders to customers. They felt you were doing them a favor to promise delivery in two months. I can remember how we allocated so many items to each customer.

The Elgin manager apparently found the current demands upon production increasingly difficult to cope with. In the past two years he had steadily gained weight, become increasingly defensive, and sought to substitute outside activities for painful plant relationships. Another member of the plant organization spoke about the production manager, saying:

The production manager has changed. He was relaxed when he first came here. Since he came, however, he has become more and more suspicious. People have become more and more afraid of him. He dresses down his production control manager terribly. He is stubborn and just won't cooperate.

A possible explanation for his worsening problem was his limited range of cognitive skills. Clues to these factors were contained in his comments on past events and in his methods of handling the relationship with sales. His perception of the district management problem was limited to a rigid view of plant costs as a function of customer order input.

In addition to inherent cognitive difficulties, the plant manager experienced interpersonal problems. The behavior he exhibited in this particular relationship may reflect a more general personal style for resolving problems in lateral relations where goal conflict exists. He seemed to have two approaches, either open conflict with the adversary or collusion with members of the other side. He related anecdotes regarding his style in dealing with the union that were of a collusive pattern.

The Elgin production manager may also have experienced much that was socially incongruent in the current situation. An older man, and accustomed to being in a position where production was dominant, he was increasingly required to act in response to the demands of a younger man whose goals and demands for an involved and tension-filled relationship ran counter to his own experience and desires. The corrosive effect of this situation on his physical and mental well-being may have been an apparent result.

Thus, at Bowie, a young and open production manager was being guided by a nondirective, senior sales manager with an overall production-sales district outlook; whereas at Elgin, an older, conservative, reticent production manager was being "pushed" by a younger ambitious sales manager with a dominantly sales point of view.

## CONFLICT IN LATERAL RELATIONSHIPS

### Consequences for Organizational Performance

Negative consequences of conflict for performance were widespread and pronounced in all areas of interdependence in the lateral relationship.

Conflict was accompanied by relatively fewer new designs, more frequent acceptance of unprofitable orders, loss of profitable orders, greater plant congestion, poorer customer delivery service, dismissal of crews for lack of work, refusal of overtime when customer orders were unfinished, shipment of orders of marginal and substandard quality to customers, and return of defective orders by customers. Some of these consequences were attributable rather directly to a competitive orientation to decision making. Other consequences, such as the acceptance of new, unprofitable orders resulting from a lack of information exchange on prospective new designs, stemmed from behavior tactical to the maintenance of competitive goal orientation. Still other consequences were the result of behavior that was retaliatory. Attempts by sales, for example, to blame production for quality defects led production to refuse to accept customer inspection for defects. Loss of orders and extra charges for return freight were the result.

This apparently wholesale indictment of the conflict pattern must be qualified. Conflict is sometimes exhilarating and motivating, sometimes debilitating and discouraging.[5] Conflict had the latter effect in the conflict plant studied here, in part because of the severity of the pattern, and in part because of the particular configuration of interdependencies in the two tasks involved. It is possible that a more moderate conflict pattern would have had high motivational effects; and that a different type of task interdependence would have greatly reduced the negative effects of the conflict tactics described here, or indeed have involved different, more innocuous tactics.

### Consequences for Individuals

Conflict had apparent psychological and professional consequences for the principals and their leading subordinates. Participants in the conflict relationship showed greater anxiety and frustration. Such reaction may well be a function of individual tolerance for conflict and deserves further study.

Professional consequences also appeared to stem from the relationship. Participants in the conflict relationship were criticized by their superiors both at the plant and at the home office, and during interviews a number reported contemplating leaving the company. By contrast, at the integrative plant a number of persons commented on their prospects for being moved to more responsible company positions in the future.

### Organizational "Hotspots" with Interdependent Tasks

Some positions were especially sensitive to conflict. The plant scheduling task seemed a position where severe, day-to-day crosscurrents were

[5] See J. A. Seiler, *op. cit.*

encountered. While both plants limited interaction in this area, their solutions were sharply different. At Bowie, the sales and production managers were kept in close contact with the problem. The service manager played a central role and employed cooperative criteria in scheduling. Moreover, his problems were widely recognized and he was insulated from damaging forays by the avoidance of unilateral action on scheduling. At Elgin, on the other hand, the parties had negotiated a highly formal solution which kept the principals as remote from the scheduling activity as possible. The two new expediter positions which were created served to "referee" scheduling problems for the parties. A competitive game continued, for high stakes, despite the existence of the scheduling agreement. Neither the principals nor the schedulers or expediters were protected from the bargaining practices of the parties. At Elgin considerable turnover and shifting characterized these scheduling positions.

Three tentative conclusions could be drawn from these comparisons: (1) Some task positions in organizations can be structurally sensitive to stress. (2) It is possible to protect members of the organization from the consequences of such inherently stressful tasks. (3) Lateral relationships dominated by conflict and competition do not provide such safeguards.

## SUMMARY

The comparative summary of the behavioral syndromes at Elgin and Bowie given in Table 1 shows sharply contrasting interdepartmental relations at the two plants. Both of these contrasting syndromes were deemed to be stable and resistant to change. The stability of each relationship was insured by reinforcement, where one element of a strategy was held in place by all the other elements; by reciprocation, where each party confirmed the appropriateness of the strategy of the other; by regeneration, where tradition and social pressure ensured that new members would maintain the prevailing pattern.

Analysis of these contrasting cases indicated that such contextual factors as more task facilitation from the home office for Bowie and less adequate equipment at Elgin might have contributed to the different degrees of conflict in the emergent relationships. Also contributing—in the same direction—were a more aggressive personal style of influence on the part of the Elgin sales manager; less adequate cognitive and interpersonal skills on the part of the Elgin production manager; and more status incongruity in the relationship between sales manager and production manager at Elgin.

Finally, the analysis indicated that the conflict relationship at Elgin had numerous and important negative effects on overall performance. However, it is apparent that sound judgments as to the effect of a generally competitive or conflictful relationship can be made only on the basis of an analysis of the specific elements of the relationship patterns and an analysis of the task, especially with regard to the interdependence of subtasks. It is also apparent that a conflict relationship can have significant negative effects for individual personal and professional well-being.

# Diagnosing Interdepartmental Conflict*

JOHN A. SEILER

## Traditional Explanations

WHY ARE some interdepartmental relationships successful and others not? Managers typically find themselves advancing one or the other of these explanations:

One popular opinion is the "personality clash" theory, which holds that stubborn prejudices and differences in ingrained personal styles (none of which are actuated by organizational influences) are behind nonproductive relations. As compelling as this explanation often seems to be, it fails to account for the fact that we seldom, if ever, encounter a group composed of people with identical or even closely similar personalities. Lacking evidence of such group identity, it is difficult to imagine an intergroup conflict between two "group personalities." This reasoning also fails to account for interdepartmental relations which are characterized by high productivity *and* some degree of personal antagonism. While personality differences undoubtedly play a part, they alone comprise an inadequate explanation of productive and nonproductive relations.

Another view holds that failure in interdepartmental relations is the result of "conflicting ideas." This theory asserts that nonproductive relations occur between groups whose respective memberships are so different in terms of skills, training, job activities, personal aspirations, and so on that they cannot possibly find a common area in which to communicate. While this explanation seems to apply to some nonproductive relations, it is not unheard of to find an advanced research group which works quite effectively with a nontechnical, highly consumer-oriented sales group. Seemingly, at least, groups can differ on many counts without a breakdown occurring in their relations. Furthermore, it is not unusual to find groups with remarkably similar points of view which seem to go out of their way to make trouble for each other. Something in addition to different points of view must be playing a part in forming the character of these relationships.

A third popular explanation for nonproductivity puts the blame on competition between groups for authority, power, and influence. Breakdowns occur because each department operates from an entrenched position which, if compromised, will bring the group nothing but defeat and loss of influence.

* This reading has been selected from an article of the above title by John A. Seiler, *Harvard Business Review,* September–October, 1963.

Many nonproductive relationships seem to display characteristics of this kind. But if this theory is to be sufficient unto itself, the only productive relationship would be one in which either or both of the groups had no desire or opportunity for influence over the other. Under these conditions, passivity would seem to be a requirement for productivity. Yet the most highly productive relations appear to take place between aggressive, confident, and high-achievement departments. Apparently other determinants, in addition to competition for prestige and power, must be operating to make interdepartmental relations successful or unsuccessful.

While no one of these theories is a sufficient explanation of why group relationships turn out the way they do, each has enough sense behind it to make it attractive. Consequently, what is needed is some way of pulling them together into a new and more useful way of thinking about interdepartmental conflicts. Let's begin this process by examining several actual cases of interdepartmental behavior.

## I. PRODUCTIVE FOCUS ON TASK[1]

Company A developed and manufactured ethical pharmaceuticals. The activities required to transform a product idea into a marketable item were performed in sequence by subunits of the research, engineering, and production departments. An idea would first take form in a research department test tube. It would then be evaluated by research chemists and chemical engineers in the pilot plant. Next, new process equipment would be designed by mechanical engineers and job designs laid out around the equipment by industrial engineers. Actual plant construction and placement of equipment were accomplished by construction engineers, and, finally, production responsibility was assumed by production chemists. The members of these formal units agreed that research had the highest prestige of all the work groups and that the relative prestige of the other units declined in the order in which each became actively involved in the new product sequence.

The engineering and research departments were housed in their own buildings some distance from each other and from the plant. The chemical engineers worked most closely with the research chemists—sharing many ideas with them because of the similarity in their training, their work, and their aspirations. The chemical engineers also worked closely with the mechanical engineers in the pilot plant and in process equipment design. The chemical and mechanical groups shared a number of ideas, though the mechanical engineers and research chemists thought quite differently about most things. The mechanical engineers worked closely with the in-

[1] The cases cited in this article have been taken from the case and project research files of the Harvard Business School and are reproduced by permission of the President and Fellows of Harvard College.

dustrial and construction engineers, who in turn were in close contact with factory personnel. These four latter groups shared similarities in background and in ideas.

Company A had an outstanding reputation for important production innovations and rapid development of ideas into mass-production items. Nevertheless, there was frequent argument among research, engineering, and production as to who should take responsibility for the product at what point in the development sequence. Engineering wanted control at the pilot plant. Production wanted control from the time the product entered its physical domain. Research wanted control, as one of its members put it, "until the actual factory yield reaches the theoretical yield."

The boundaries of control were actually somewhat difficult to pinpoint. Research was in command until factory problems seriously affecting quality were solved, except that research decisions were subject to engineering veto (in turn subject to top-management arbitration) anywhere beyond the pilot plant. In spite of continual argument about control jurisdiction, there were few engineering vetoes that ever reached arbitration.

The physical, mental, and emotional energies of these departments appeared to be devoted to the work at hand to a very high degree. While not absent from their relationships, conflicts took the form of tension between the inherently opposing values of quality and economy. The result was a competitive balance between the extremes of both. Why was conflict not destructive in this situation? There are basically three reasons:

1. Each of the three departments represented a social unit in which members could find not only satisfaction for their needs to belong, but also job interest, promotion opportunity, and so on. No one of these departments suffered from internal fragmentation.

2. At each point of significant interdepartmental contact, the members of the interacting groups agreed on certain important ideas as to how work should be accomplished. Wherever technical interdependence required intergroup contact, the groups tended to view each other and their common work with a markedly similar appreciation.

3. The hierarchy of authority among the departments was identical to the informally agreed-upon prestige hierarchy among these departments. This hierarchy was determined by the technical work limits set by one department for another, and by the initiation of activity by one department for another. The work done by research, for example, limited what the chemical engineers could work on but, at the same time, was the impetus which set the chemical engineers to work on each new product. The same was true of relationships down through the development sequence.

Very simply, then, when a man (or a group) told another what to do and when to do it, he did so as a member of a group of superior prestige, as agreed on by both groups. We might say that the orders which passed from one group to another were "legitimate," since most workers feel that it is legitimate in our society for a person of higher prestige to direct the activities of someone with less prestige, while it is illegitimate for the opposite to occur.

Thus, in the Company A situation, departmental energies were not consumed by internal activities designed to make the department a socially satisfactory place to live nor by struggles to communicate across abysses of viewpoint differences. Because authority was being exerted by socially legitimate persons and groups, little if any energy was wasted in jockeying for prestige positions. There was an abundance of group energy left for work and for contest over the organizationally desirable balance of quality and economy. Furthermore, since the work itself was intrinsically rewarding and since supervisory practices encouraged work satisfactions, Company A's interdepartmental relations were highly productive, despite continual battles over quality versus economy.

The three elements—*internal social stability, external value sharing,* and *legitimate authority hierarchy*—comprise a triumvirate of measures which indicate the extent to which departmental energy will tend to be freed for productive work. These factors can be thought of as minimum requirements for interdepartmental effectiveness. For, in their absence, it is highly unlikely that either intrinsically interesting work or encouragement from supervision will achieve much in the way of productivity increases.

## II. WASTEFUL CONFLICTS OF IDEAS

Company B designed, manufactured, and sold precision electronic instruments to scientific laboratories and industrial firms. The sales department was composed primarily of long-service, socially prestigious men (including the president) who had been instrumental in establishing what was referred to as a "family atmosphere" in the company. The sales department was the center of the dominant ideas in the company about how employees should behave.

During the manpower disruptions of World War II, the production department attracted a group of men who had started as workmen and had worked their way up the management ladder, often by transferring from one company to another. These men were perceived by the rest of the company (and even by themselves) as "rough diamonds." Their ideas about personal comportment were very different from those held dear in the sales department.

At the close of the war, certain irregularities in the behavior of top-level, old-line production management were laid bare by the rough diamonds. When the culprits were discharged, they left the rough diamonds in control of production.

At the same time, however, certain checks and balances—in reaction to the ease with which the wartime irregularities were committed—were built into the organization at the expense of production's jurisdiction over such functions as purchasing and stock control. These restrictions were highly resented by the new production regime which felt it was being punished by the "family" school, some of whose members (the discharged old-line production men) were the real culprits. This "injustice" widened an already considerable gap between sales' and production's views of "how things ought to be."

Sales and production came in contact primarily when the quarterly production schedule was being set and whenever sales initiated changes in the schedule within quarters. On these occasions tempers flared, walkouts occurred, and the services of the vice president—controller were required for mediation. Sales' concern for meeting customers' special desires was pitted against production's concern for uninterrupted runs of each instrument in the company's catalog.

Unlike the Company A situation where a balance was struck between quality and economy, in Company B the contest between customer satisfaction and economical production resulted in a breakdown of relations. Furthermore, the production department became an armed camp in which each junior member of the group was strictly warned against dealing with the sales department lest the latter influence production activities at less than the top hierarchical level of the department.

To make sure that sales could not infiltrate production, top production executives allowed the bulk of production's members little influence over internal production affairs. For its part, sales spent a great deal of time devising power plays to force production to deviate from set schedules. Top sales officials wasted hours personally exerting their authority in production offices to obtain schedule deviations. Retributions in the form of ultimatums and unprofitable scheduling "trades" of one instrument for another resulted. Sales' two subsections, scientific and industrial, vied with each other to see who could get the best production deal in the schedule, often at each other's and the company's expense.

In Company B, while the work itself was challenging and although supervision circumscribed that interest only to a modest degree (by removing purchasing and stock control from production's jurisdiction), relationships were relatively nonproductive between sales and production. Minimal standards of performance were met only by the intervention of a vice president in routine sales-production affairs. Energies were not absorbed in an effort to right an illegitimate authority sequence, for sales' commands were legitimated by sales' superior prestige, but in dealing with the breach of communication between two groups whose backgrounds and ideas were diametrically opposed in many important ways.

In turn, each department's internal relations, used as a means of combating the outgroup, absorbed a great deal of effort. Production kept a tight hold on its members, which caused subordinate frustrations, while sales was constantly patching the relations between its own two subgroups. Any work accomplished between the two groups was based on the question, "Will this effort strengthen our position in the battle with the other department?" Almost never could the two groups be said to agree that their combined efforts were satisfying to both, or even to one, of the parties.

The nonproductive conflict between these two departments can be viewed as the result of energies consumed by attempts to right an irreconcilably imbalanced trade.[2] By sales' values, sales' ideas should have dominated, tempered only by "practical" economic considerations. (In other words, production should have provided information on which sales could base its decisions.)

By production's values, however, production ideas received too little weight, if, indeed, they were accorded any weight at all. Production believed that sales' information should be added to production information and the decision should then be a cooperative one. For sales to achieve its idea of balance, production had to forfeit its idea of balance, and vice versa. So the conflict was irreconcilable. As the mathematicians put it, the two departments were playing a zero-sum game. One's gain was the other's loss, because their different ideas of what was "right" made it so.

## III. ILLEGITIMATE AUTHORITY CONFLICTS

Company B's production department was engaged in another, but quite different, cross-departmental relationship of nonproductive character. The production engineering department (formally considered a peer of the production department) took research designs and translated them into parts lists, production drawings, and fabrication and assembly specifications, and in addition processed engineering change orders (ECOs). Much of production's work—both its content and its timing—depended on production engineering's efforts, since Company B's product designs were constantly changing.

Thus, production engineering was seen by production as telling production what to do and when to do it. On the other hand, production engineering was composed of men with skills no greater than, in fact, quite similar to, those possessed by production members. Production felt itself capable of performing not only production engineering's tasks but the more important tasks of job design and methods work which were within production's jurisdiction but outside production engineering's.

The two departments had almost no face-to-face contact. Communication between them was conducted through memos carried by lowly messengers. Production managers spent an inordinate amount of time checking for consistency among the various items produced by production engineering. When errors were discovered (as they seldom were), a cry

[2] For further development of this concept, see Alvin Gouldner, "The Norm of Reciprocity: A Preliminary Statement," *American Sociological Review,* April, 1960, pp. 161–78.

of victory would ring out across the production office. A messenger would quickly be dispatched to carry the offending material back to production engineering, amply armed with a message elaborately outlining the stupidity which had produced such an error. The lack of direct contact between the two departments (other than this aggressive kind) made it impossible for technically desirable accommodations between the two departments to be made. The most common topic of production conversation centered about "those goddam ECOs," in spite of the fact that production originated as many ECOs (making changes for its own convenience) as did any other department.

In this case, energies were heavily focused on the impropriety of a low-prestige department like production engineering calling the tune for an equally prestigious or even superior department like production. Production devoted its energies to rebalancing trade between the two departments. In other words, production's prestige could be maintained only by calling more tunes than it danced. This rebalancing process had little to do with accomplishing any work. Yet it consumed vast amounts of production management time (particularly that of the factory superintendent who, of all people, checked every drawing); and, in the last analysis it failed its purpose, since the tide was too great to be stemmed, no matter how much energy was devoted to the effort.

## IV. VALUE AND AUTHORITY CLASHES

Company C designed, manufactured, and distributed a large variety of electronic tubes of advanced design. One of its most rapidly selling tubes had a poor cost record—primarily, it was finally agreed, because of design inadequacies. In the process of trying to reduce costs through fabrication and assembly changes, the industrial engineering department had generated an idea for basic tube redesign. Several industrial engineers experimented informally with the new idea and achieved favorable results. When the matter was brought to the attention of the research department, it found its full schedule would not permit it to take over and develop the new idea. The industrial engineering inventors were given authority to continue development of the new tube. A development schedule was set and a development budget assigned to the industrial engineers.

For a time, progress was satisfactory. Then, when some metallurgical problems developed, the research department stepped in to make tests in an attempt to solve the problem. Conflict immediately developed. The industrial engineers maintained that the research department was unfair to the new tube because of the unrealistic way it conducted its tests. Research found it could get no cooperation in its desire to use industrial engineering equipment to conduct part of its investigation. Contact between the two groups dropped to zero, and investigations were conducted in parallel, though each group technically required the other's resources. Development schedules became a farce as one date after another passed without expected accomplishment.

The industrial engineers had become engaged in the project in the first place because, as one of its members put it, "I was particularly displeased with our department's general position in the company and felt we didn't really have a chance to show what we could do." One of the members of research mentioned that he thought of the industrial engineers as "just dumb, stupid, and no good." There was no meeting ground on the value which the two groups could bring to a common project. Nevertheless, there was general agreement that the research people possessed considerably greater prestige than did the industrial engineers.

In Company C, interdepartmental conflict became so energy-consuming that relationships were broken off entirely, to the detriment of the project at hand. Normally, research would have held the authority position—and legitimately so, according to its superior prestige. Pressured by scheduling circumstances and by the different points of view concerning what industrial engineering's role should be, the normal authority sequence was turned topsy-turvy. Industrial engineering did the prestige work of invention, directing research to carry out routine tests.

Suddenly, each group attempted to behave in such a way that its own view of a proper relationship would predominate. Research criticized industrial engineering's work and tried to force the industrial engineers back into the subordinate role of helping with tests. Industrial engineering, which always had been eager for a chance to get its "teeth into something," was enjoying the fruits of its initial invention (which, incidentally, later proved to be basically sound). Feeling that its desires were being violated, it tried to keep control of the prestige activities and went out of its way to "prove" that research was barking up the wrong tree.

None of these activities had any necessary relationship to developing a new tube. All energies were devoted to forcing one group's values on the other and maintaining what were believed to be legitimate prestige positions. The two departments were playing another zero-sum game in which what seemed positive trading for one was inevitably interpreted as negative trading by the other.

## Varying Viewpoints

In each of these four cases, the forces siphoning energy away from productive work have been of a particular kind. In each instance, relationships within groups were at least socially satisfactory. (In Company B, the production group did enforce limits on member influence, but this discipline, because it was viewed as group defense, did not lessen cohesion within the department.) The work of the various groups was intrinsically interesting to group members. Supervision was relatively permissive in allowing group members to "complicate" their lives about the work itself. Obviously, these elements are not always present in organized situations. Equally obvious from our cases is the fact that these elements, by themselves, do not result in effective interdepartmental relations, though they may be considered to contribute to such relations if other conditions are also met.

***Focal Points.*** What the above cases focus on are the troubles caused by differences in point of view and legitimacy of authority. What these cases teach about group conflicts arising from these two trouble sources is just as true for our understanding of the interrelationships of individuals, for intergroup problems are only special cases of interpersonal issues. The only difference between them is the complexity of dealing with the problem, since the individual persons in our cases are representatives of social groups. Thus, their behavior cannot be modified by actions which are based on the assumption that groups respond exactly as do individuals. In short, the causes of conflict are similar, but the remedies are different.

**EXHIBIT 1**

Dominant Influences in Interdepartmental Relations

| | WHERE POINTS OF VIEW ARE CLOSELY ALLIED | WHERE POINTS OF VIEW ARE IN CONFLICT |
|---|---|---|
| WHERE AUTHORITY* IS CONSISTENT WITH PRESTIGE DIFFERENCES | WE WILL TEND TO FIND.... ....COLLABORATION AND PRODUCTIVE CONFLICT. | WE WILL TEND TO FIND.... ....ENGERGIES ABSORBED BY EFFORTS TO FORCE POINTS OF VIEW ON OTHER GROUPS. RELATIONS WILL BE FORMAL AND OFTEN ARBITRATED BY OUTSIDERS. |
| WHERE AUTHORITY IS INCONSISTENT WITH PRESTIGE DIFFERENCES | WE WILL TEND TO FIND.... ....ENERGIES DEVOTED TO REGAINING A "PROPER" AUTHORITY RELATIONSHIP. RELATIONS WILL USUALLY BE DISTANT AND BETWEEN LOW HIERARCHICAL LEVELS OF THE TWO GROUPS (e.g., messengers). | WE WILL TEND TO FIND.... ....ENERGIES INITIALLY EXPENDED ON FORCING POINTS OF VIEW AND RIGHTING AUTHORITY RELATIONS, BUT THE TASK WILL BE SO PATENTLY FRUITLESS THAT THE GROUPS WILL BREAK OFF CONTACT RATHER THAN EXPOSE THEMSELVES TO FURTHER THREAT. |

* As indicated by work flow.

What happens when groups suffer from authority and viewpoint conflicts is summarized in Exhibit 1. Like any diagram dealing with a limited number of factors, Exhibit 1 runs the danger of implying that these cause-and-effect tendencies represent all that need be known about interdepartmental relations. Such an implication, were it intended, would, of course, be fatuous. Research in the area of interdepartmental problems has scarcely begun. Furthermore, we have already noted that other factors can be expected to intervene and render the exhibit's hypotheses as they should be called, inoperative. Three of these factors have been emphasized—group cohesion, job interest, and supervisory practices.

Once we allow for these mitigating factors, however, we will find it useful to conceive of interdepartmental relations as though they were subject to the dominant influences cited in the diagram. The manager can make this concept more relevant personally if he reviews his own observations of interdepartmental conflict to see how they compare with the kind of analysis described here.

### Plan for Action

The question inevitably arises, "Suppose some sense can be made of interdepartmental difficulties by this kind of thinking; what then do we do with this understanding, even if it does prove to be accurate? How would we go about applying it to lessen interdepartmental conflicts in our company?" Let's look at some action ideas which stem from what has already been said.

***Stop, Look, and Listen.*** As frustrating as it might seem, the first suggestion is to stop to see if action is required and, if it is, whether it is feasible. It often may be wise to heed the admonishment (in reverse of the usual form), "Don't just do something, stand there!" The basis for this wisdom lies in the fact that formal organizations often display some of the characteristics of a biological organism, particularly insofar as the latter has some capacity to heal itself. The administrator, if this contention be true, may find the role of the modern physician attractive. He attempts to control the environment so that natural healing processes can take place unhindered within the human body. Here are some examples of where such inaction might be appropriate:

Take the case of Company A. Should something be done to alter jurisdictions among Company A's departments? Or are the natural tensions between these departments, the energies to expand jurisdiction, operating in precisely the most beneficial way for the organization? The best advice in this case seems to be to keep an eye on that tension. Watch that it does not degenerate subtly into another Company C situation. If it moves too far in that direction, then action is required.

This example helps clarify an issue which we have been flirting with throughout this article: the problem of distinguishing productive from nonproductive conflicts. It may not suffice to say that conflict is productive if the parties to it end up satisfied and get there under their own steam. In any particular case, in the heat of a tight scheduling situation, many an administrator has interpreted *any* disagreement as nonproductive and has succumbed to the temptation to interfere. If schedules then have to be junked, the blame is thrown on the groups in disagreement. Had the administrator satisfied himself about the basic conditions within which the fighting groups were working, and listened carefully to see if the fights were *working* or *warring* arguments, he might have saved himself and his organization much trouble.

A case more dramatic than that cited above, and one where action seemed inappropriate, takes us back to the Company B organization. The production department, as might be suspected from what we already know about it, was striving to enlarge its domain to conform to its own ideas about production's importance. This striving provoked a potential clash with the research department when the frequency of special orders began to increase rapidly. Special orders required research design but not production engineering attention, the work of the latter group being devoted to mass-production items. Thus, research would naturally be required to deal directly with production in the case of special orders. Inevitably, production—as isolated historical instances had convinced research—would attempt to dominate these relationships whenever it could.

To avoid this eventuality, research developed a small production unit of its own, though production was fully capable of doing special work. This "organizational invention" of the research department, stepping into work for which it was neither intended nor formally responsible, eliminated the need for contact with production and sidestepped the inevitably nonproductive conflict which would have resulted. The invention was costly in many ways, particularly in terms of valuable research time and space. But on balance it appeared to be the most adequate short-term resolution to a basic interdepartmental problem.

There are a host of other examples of this kind of self-regulation. Many of these measures are rather simple and expedient, if not conducive to removal of the basic causes of nonproductive conflict. Chief among these is the use of what may be called "expendable linkers" as go-betweens in conflicted interdepartmental relations. For example, a production department was observed to assign to its least important member the task of liaison between itself and other departments, where such expediting connoted the use of illegitimate authority. The expediter himself threatened no one, and adopted a most passive demeanor. Communication then took place not between main contenders who could only lose by such contact but through a neutral intermediary. The cursing went unheard by those for whom a damaging response would have been required.

Other examples involve the use of formal procedures or instruments such as the production schedule, fought over maybe once a quarter, but exerting independent authority between times and keeping sales and production away from each other's throats. None of these is an ideal solution to interdepartmental problems, but each is likely to emerge as a practical expedient in a difficult situation. The administrator may find his short-run problems solved if he is aware of the importance of these often unnoticed "inventions." Furthermore, if he wants to do away with these sometimes awkward mechanisms, he had better make sure he has something with which to replace them.

## Types of Resolution

Our cases (and there are unlimited examples like them) have shown that some interdepartmental difficulties go beyond the capacity of the groups to resolve them at anything but a survival level, if that. That level may well be, and often is, intolerable for the organization as a whole. Let us look at the two alternative types of resolution.

First are the resolutions which arise in response to conflicts of authority. In such cases the work flow designed into the organization (e.g., the passage of blueprints from production engineering to production) violates the notions of the organization's members as to who legitimately should, by right of superior prestige, tell whom what to do. Although such problems are not restricted to particular hierarchical levels of the organization, they do tend to become more intense wherever prestige relations are ambiguous or under threat. The higher one goes in many organizations, the more these conditions tend to apply. There are several ways of resolving such problems:

1. An obvious solution is to take whatever steps are available to reduce prestige ambiguity and threat. For example, if Company B's management had realized how pertinent production's resentment at being rated "second class" was to the interdepartmental problems in which it was involved, investigation might have produced ways of clarifying production's status and of enriching its participation in important decisions. Instead, the factory superintendent was the last to be admitted to the executive council and was not accorded vice presidential rank, as were most other department managers. Management failed to take these steps because it feared domination by the superintendent. Yet more careful diagnosis might have revealed that the superintendent's striving for dominance was a result of his impression that management thought him unworthy of participation in decisions for which his expertise was, in fact, badly needed. The circle was vicious.

2. Another step in reducing the amount of nonproductivity in illegitimate authority relations is to reorganize subunits of the organization in such a way that authority and prestige become consistent. In Company B's production engineering and production relationship, such reorganization could have taken the form of incorporating production engineering into production's domain, much as was done in Company A, where the chemical engineers had been removed from research and placed in the engineering department. With production engineering subject to production's control, yet sharing many ideas with both research and production, a mingling of points of view could have been achieved and authority questions dealt with from within.

The very same kind of potential authority difficulty was avoided in Company B because scheduling was incorporated within production's jurisdiction. Another way of justifying such a resolution of conflict is to note that production's technical functions, as well as those of production engineering, were so closely allied and overlapping that to separate them was to form a barrier across which required contact was extremely difficult and at times impossible. Unfortunately, once again Company B's management so feared production dominance that its inclination was much more to reduce production's domain than to enlarge it.

3. Another extremely clear example of how structural reorganization can resolve not only the authority legitimacy problem, but also have side effects in bringing clashing points of view into sufficient harmony for communication

to recommence, is contained in the actual resolution of the Company C difficulty reported above. The obvious solution was to take the research initiative away from the industrial engineers and put it back where prestige relations said it belonged, with research. The solution appeared obvious only because the breakdown between the two departments was so catastrophic.

Equally obvious before that breakdown was the apparently logical belief that the people who invent something should continue to develop it, both because the inventors would logically appear to be most expert in understanding the invention and because it is only fair that productive effort should be rewarded by continuing responsibility and credit. In fact, change was not instituted until the industrial engineers became so thoroughly frustrated by their continuing design failures that they could entertain the idea that their "baby" might be reorganized into more "proper" channels. Although costly in some ways and probably unconscious, management's decision to do nothing at first to set the interdepartmental relations back into the normal work pattern allowed industrial engineering to become receptive to such a change when it finally was made.

This crucial aspect of conflict resolution—receptivity to change—brings us to the second major strategy for helping departmental energies engage in constructive action instead of working against members of another department. This strategy involves what might be called intergroup counseling, therapy, or training. Conflicts in points of view are susceptible only to this strategy, short of complete personnel turnover in one or the other of the warring departments. And, because authority illegitimacy must inevitably engender conflict of viewpoint, it too can be mitigated, if only partially, by intergroup training. Several aspects of this strategy are worthy of attention, though the subject is a difficult and complex one.

Some studies show that intergroup conflict resolution hinges on a particular type of training which seeks an integration of viewpoints by making warring groups realize they are dependent on one another.[3] Such a strategy tends to work more readily when both groups fear some external threat to both of them. This idea is not greatly different from the idea contained in the observation that members of families may fight viciously with one another but when an outsider attacks one of the family, the family abandons its differences to fight together against the intruder. It seems obvious from the analysis presented in this article, however, that this strategy is operable only when prestige-authority issues are not present.

A number of researchers, teachers, and managers have begun to explore more direct methods for reducing point-of-view conflict. Some have pointed out that bringing group representatives together to explore their

---

[3] See *Intergroup Relations and Leadership,* edited by Muzafer Sherif (New York: John Wiley & Sons, Inc., 1962).

differences is usually doomed to failure since representatives, if they are to remain such, must be loyal to their respective groups.[4] Simple measures to increase contact also appear fruitless, because negative stereotypes end up simply becoming reinforced by the contact.

Other measures have proved more effective. Although they vary in form, almost all of these contain the following basic element: *the groups in conflict must be brought together as totalities under special conditions.*[5] The goal of all of these conditions is to reduce individual and group anxieties sufficiently so that a point of view cannot only be made explicit but can be heard by those who do not share it. This procedure requires not only considerable candor between groups, but also candor within each group and within the individual himself. Naturally, sessions in which such training is supposed to take place can be extremely threatening and should be mediated by an external agent to keep threat within manageable bounds and help guide the groups into explorative rather than recriminative behavior.[6]

(EDITORS' NOTE: See Reading 4 in this section of the book for further development of these ideas for reducing conflict.)

## Conclusion

Seldom, if ever, do problems of nonproductive conflict exist in isolation. It is extremely likely that wherever such conflict is found it has been engendered by organizational and emotional maladjustments, each of which has fed upon the other. It would make sense, then, to attack interdepartmental problems while fully realizing that they may be spun into the warp and woof of the organization's fabric. Such an attack has far-reaching consequences for the organization. It means, for example, that the goals of the organization must be critically examined, since these tend to influence the way in which the work of the organization has been divided up and division of labor is at the core of interdepartmental problems.

Because goals, in turn, are heavily influenced by the organization's environment and by the way in which that environment is interpreted by executives and directors, the environment and the process by which it is interpreted also must come under scrutiny. Do those in control have a clear idea of their company's relation to its market? If not, why not?

---

[4] See Robert Blake and Jane S. Mouton, *Group Dynamics—Key to Decision Making* (Houston, Texas: Gulf Publishing Co., 1961).

[5] See Herbert R. Shepard and Robert R. Blake, "Changing Behavior through Cognitive Change," *Human Organization*, Summer, 1962, p. 88.

[6] See Chris Argyris, *Interpersonal Competence and Organizational Effectiveness* (Homewood, Ill.: Irwin–Dorsey Press, 1962).

Have they made clear to the other members of the company the job to be done and what that job requires of each subelement in the organization?[7]

These questions are fundamental to the building of an organization. Without answers to these questions, any attempt to resolve an illegitimate authority problem usually is a patch-up job, likely to create as many problems as it cures. Furthermore, without these answers, the members of the organization cannot avoid feeling that their relationships to each other are ambiguous—and aimless ambiguity is a breeding ground for insecurity, defensive behavior, and sapped energy.

Involving the members of an organization in the pursuit of clarifying the organization's goals—in establishing a meaningful identity for the firm—is, perhaps, the soundest process for tapping into the wells of productive energy.[8] Such a pursuit, carried on openly and sincerely, cannot help but raise issues of interdepartmental ambiguity, illegitimacy, and conflicting points of view to a level where they can be reexamined and dealt with. An easy process? No. But as "old wives' tales" have told us, no remedy is without pain.

---

[7] See Wilfred Brown, *Exploration in Management* (London: William Heinemann Ltd., 1960).

[8] Alfred Kenneth Rice, *The Enterprise and Its Environment* (London: Tavistock Publications, 1963).

# The Role of the Norm of Reciprocity in Social Stabilization

Alvin Gouldner, in an article entitled "The Norm of Reciprocity: A Preliminary Statement,"[1] delineates the characteristics of social exchange between groups and individuals as a significant influence upon the stability of social systems in general. Although the utility of this concept is not restricted to analysis of intergroup behavior, it is particularly apropos of such diagnosis and is being included in this section of the book for that reason.

"There is no duty more indispensable than that of returning a kindness; . . . all men distrust one forgetful of a benefit." So Gouldner quotes Cicero, to begin his argument that a universal rule governs the social exchange[2] between men and groups of men in every culture on earth. Gouldner interprets reciprocity within the broader framework of sociological functionalism, quoting Merton: ". . . Analysis must begin with the identification of some problematic pattern of human behavior, some institution, role, or shared pattern of belief. 'The central orientation of functionalism is expressed in the practice of interpreting data by establishing their consequences for larger structures in which they are implicated.' "[3]

Gouldner holds that the concept of reciprocity is tacitly assumed as a basic component of functional analysis, since a foundation concept of functional analysis is the interdependence between social units. Often, the survival of a social unit (a production group, for example) is explained by the reasoning that that social unit's behavior is functional (provides a service) for the maintenance and development of other social units. Gouldner points out that such reasoning is sound only when the service provided by the one unit is, in fact, reciprocated and contingent

---

[1] *American Sociological Review,* Vol. XXV, No. 2 (April, 1960), pp. 161–78.

[2] Social exchange, lest the reader suspect that reference is here being made only to transactions of tangible character, involves the widest assortment of goods. Love, friendship, help, advice, emotional support, and similar commodities are as relevant here as money or concrete goods.

[3] R. K. Merton, *Social Theory and Social Structure* (Revised and enlarged ed.; Glencoe, Ill.: Free Press, 1957), pp. 46–47.

upon service from other units. In other words, for one unit to survive and prosper because of the service it provides to others, those others must, by definition, be supplying a return service. However, such a relationship does not imply that *equality* of exchange will always exist between social units. Power differences and unequal alternate sources of supply may well result in an imbalance in the social commodities which pass between groups or individuals. In such cases, Gouldner cites the existence of "compensatory arrangements that may provide means of controlling the resultant tensions, thereby enabling the problematic pattern to remain stable." He opens up the now value-laden concept of "exploitation" as a source of study for discovering the nature of these compensatory mechanisms. He points out, however, that the word *exploitation* is value laden because it represents violation of certain pervasive values, among them the *norm of reciprocal rights and duties.*

By reciprocity, Gouldner means that a right of A against B implies a duty of A to B and, similarly, that a duty of A to B implies a right of A against B. "In short, reciprocity connotes that *each* party has rights *and* duties" not just that "one's rights are another's obligations, and vice versa." Reciprocity he states as an empirical generalization, citing Malinowski, who observed "that people *owe obligations to each other* and that, therefore, conformity with norms is something they *give to each other.*" The rules for social exchange are governed, according to Malinowski, by a "presentiment of the consequences of reciprocity and of its breakdown."[4] Those rules, Gouldner points out, are based on a "higher level moral norm: you *should* give benefits to those who give you benefits." But, though obligations are closely linked to the intrinsic character of benefits exchanged, they "may vary with the status of the participants within a society." Nevertheless, the transaction in its totality, including, as part of the exchange, status and other factors which differentiate the interacting parties, is asserted to be "roughly equivalent."

Gouldner then turns to the function of the generalized norm of reciprocity as a stabilizer of social systems. First, he says, the norm acts as a force for social equilibrium because it accomplishes shared expectations of behavior among the members of the system. Further, "the norm of reciprocity . . . engenders motives for returning benefits even when power differences might invite exploitation." From Malinowski, again, comes the observation that social indebtedness tends to persist over time, "a time, then, when men are morally constrained to manifest their gratitude toward, or at least to maintain peace with, their benefactors." (Similar forces for stability are those obligations which have already been

---

[4] Bronislaw Malinowski, *Crime and Custom in Savage Society* (London: Paul, Trench, Trubner, 1932).

given compliance in the past.) Says Gouldner: "If this conclusion is correct, . . . . we should expect to find mechanisms which induce people to *remain* socially indebted to each other and which *inhibit* their complete repayment. This suggests a function performed by the requirement of only *rough* equivalence of repayment . . . , for it induces a certain amount of ambiguity as to whether indebtedness has been repaid and, over time, generates uncertainty about who is in whose debt."

Gouldner adds that the reciprocity norm is indeterminate rather than specific in its rules for conduct so that it "can be applied to countless ad hoc transactions, thus providing a flexible moral sanction for transactions which might not otherwise be regulated by specific status obligations. . . . Even when these are present and well established . . . the norm . . . provides a further source of motivation and an additional moral sanction for conforming with specific status obligations. . . . In this manner, the sentiment of gratitude joins forces with the sentiment of rectitude and adds a safety-margin in the motivation to conformity."

Gouldner makes the point, however, that as well as a "stabilizing mechanism," the norm of reciprocity may also be conceived as a "starting mechanism." As an example, he cites two individuals or groups which each have valuables sought by the other. Each feels that the other is motivated by self-gratification; and each, in turn, hopes to receive the other's valuables without relinquishing his own. Each suspects the other of precisely this intention and views the impending exchange as dangerous. Each takes the position, "You first!" "When internalized in both parties, the norm *obliges* the one who has first received a benefit to repay it at some time. . . . Consequently, there may be less hesitancy in being the first and a greater facility with which the exchange and the social relation can get underway."

In concluding, Gouldner emphasizes that he has limited his discussion to the functional aspects of the norm of reciprocity. He points out that it undoubtedly has dysfunctions around conflicts arising because of differences of judgment over the *ability* to repay and over the sufficiency of repayment. More important, the norm may be dysfunctional for human welfare in that it leads to the formation of relationships between parties who are able to repay, to the neglect of the needs of those unable to do so.

Gouldner's concept of the norm of reciprocity gives the observer of organizational behavior an opportunity to describe the relationships between groups in terms of the nature of the social transactions between them, the intergroup balance or imbalance of trade, and the compensatory mechanisms which arise to maintain stability among them. When one group violates the norm, the student can look for a breakdown in shared expectations, an exploitation of power, and a failure of self-starting relationships between groups. He can also expect to find significant social mechanisms which will come into existence to bring the violating group into conformity with the norm and which will also, in the meantime, work in the direction of providing stabilizing influences for the organizational system as a whole.[5]

---

[5] Sanctions imposed upon those who fail to reciprocate usually involve negative social goods such as hatred, enmity, ostracism, destructionism, and the like. In a very real sense, applying these sanctions tends to rebalance the relationship by meeting a failure to repay a favor with damage to the offender, damage in amount roughly commensurate with the value of the original favor.

# Understanding and Managing Intergroup Conflict

ERIC H. NEILSEN

ONE OF THE important advantages of large complex organizations is that they are capable of coordinating the labors of many different groups of men, working simultaneously on different tasks and in different places, in the service of some superordinate goal. A by-product of this condition, however, is that the groups involved, though subunits of the same organization, enjoy contrasting experiences which lead their members to view the world in different ways. Such differences can often lead to intergroup conflict at the social interfaces where the work of the different groups is coordinated, and they always represent the potential for conflict.

Whether one views intergroup conflict as good or bad, desirable in some cases or at best a necessary evil, the fact remains that it is ubiquitous in large organizations and thus comprises a salient phenomenon with which managers must deal. This article avoids the issue of the value of intergroup conflict and attempts instead to present a way of thinking about this phenomenon and some of the methods available for coping with it which will enable the manager to predict the consequences of his actions more accurately and to choose those tactics which are best suited to his particular objectives in a given situation, objectives which he deems appropriate based on his own experience. In doing so, the author does not suggest that his own way of thinking about intergroup conflict is value free, but rather that he values a contextual analysis where as many as possible of the relevant issues and their interdependencies are taken into account before action is taken.

## SOURCES OF INTERGROUP CONFLICT

There are four basic ways in which membership in different groups can create conflict; each involves a different aspect of the social structure and norms of a group. Membership in different groups may mean that individuals will (1) identify different personal characteristics as inherently attractive or unattractive; (2) see as legitimate different equations for determining how much reward—either in terms of status or goods—a person should have; (3) feel that different kinds of procedures and different interpretations of the same data make the most sense in performing a given task; and (4) feel that other persons' or groups' control over certain resources will be detrimental to their own group's interests. Of these issues only the latter seems always to promote a conflictual situation. The others may or may not depending upon whether the relations between the groups involved make them salient. This is most likely to occur whenever agreement on one or more of these issues is necessary for effective cooperation. For this requires that members of at least one group change their definitions of them, something they are not likely to want to do for fear of betraying their own long-term interests. Conformity to a given set of viewpoints is the payment men make for the emotional and material rewards their groups give them.

In the following sections we will elaborate on each of these factors and give some examples of how conflict is most likely to erupt because of them.

### Differences in Reference Groups

The members of any group tend to hold in common a series of definitions of what they ideally would most and least like their group and themselves as its members to be like. Such definitions may involve any combination of attributes, skills, and objects, real or fictitious that the mind is capable of imagining. The organizational units with which these definitions or images are associated in members' minds are commonly called reference groups, because, by evaluating their current group in terms of them, members are able to place their progress toward their ideal and away from its opposite. In the terminology of psychoanalytic theory, conceptions of reference groups comprise an important part of members' superegos. Feelings of progress toward the group ideal are inherently positive, those away from it inherently negative.

Progress toward the group ideal involves conformity to group norms and the development of goals consistent with group values. It also involves attempts to associate with other live groups whose characteristics are seen by group members as more like those of their group ideal than their own group's characteristics presently are. Likewise, it involves attempts to dissociate from other groups and individuals whose characteristics are more antithetical to the group ideal than members believe the characteristics of their own group to be.

These attempts at selective association and disassociation form probably the most basic source of conflict in society. When the members of one group see those of another as possessing traits antithetical to their ideal, there is little way to create true cooperation between them other than through some process of resocialization. The basic paradigm encompasses all forms of prejudice from racism to competitive social climbing. The intensity of feelings may vary, but they all have one thing in common. They are rooted in unconscious predispositions which individuals are not very capable of changing quickly, or of recognizing the need to change in the first place.

### Distributive Justice

Numerous writers on organizational behavior, especially those who have studied workers at the blue collar and clerical levels, have observed that work group status hierarchies are based on notions of distributive justice, i.e., that each man's status is allocated according to his past and present performance along a number of criteria commonly valued by group members.[1] In some groups age, seniority, and ethnic background are especially important. In others education and skill are. Any set of criteria is possible. This phenomenon can be a second major source of intergroup conflict when those appointed to coordinate or control the activities of two or more groups are identified by the members of at least one of them as not worthy of such status in terms of their group's equation for granting it. Typically, a new coordinator will meet the criteria laid down by one group, the one from which he came, but not those adhered to by the others.

The author has observed a good example of conflict stemming from this source at the management level in a small firm undergoing reorganization.[2] The firm in question had been operating in a highly stable industry and had relied for many years on field representatives to sell its products. Product development decisions had been in the hands of the engineering and production departments throughout the firm's history. Following a decision by top management to broaden the firm's market and seek new uses for its technology, a five-man marketing team was recruited and some of its members were given complete control over product development decisions heretofore held by the production and engineering groups. The marketing personnel given these powers had previously worked in firms where they controlled similar decisions and felt that their years of experience in the area and their educational backgrounds made them highly qualified for their jobs. The chief executives of the firm as well as the other marketing men expressed similar opinions.

The engineering and production personnel, on the other hand, felt that their control had been unduly usurped. As they saw it, long years

---

[1] See for instance: George C. Homans, "Status among Clerical Workers," *Human Organization*, Vol. 12, 1953; A Zaleznik, C. R. Christensen, F. J. Roethlisberger, *The Motivation, Satisfaction, and Productivity of Workers: A Prediction Study* (Boston: Division of Research, Harvard Business School, 1958).

[2] Eric H. Neilsen, *Contingency Theory Applied to Small Business Organizations*, unpublished doctoral thesis, Department of Social Relations, Harvard University, 1970.

of experience with their firm's particular products and ways of doing things were important criteria for possessing such control. Conflict between themselves and the newly appointed marketing personnel continued throughout the author's research.

### Differences in Task Orientation and Experience

Men who spend many years performing a given kind of task tend to become accustomed to organizing their work, to orienting themselves to time deadlines, to basic personal goals, and to each other as individuals, in ways that help them perform that task in an effective manner. But current research suggests that different kinds of tasks, involving the management of different levels of certainty, require different work orientations and norms.[3] Tasks that are highly certain, e.g., production tasks, can be done best through the use of steep, multileveled control hierarchies, directive supervision, and planning in terms of short-term deadlines. Tasks that are highly uncertain, e.g., research tasks, can be done best with flat, one- or two-level hierarchies, participative supervision, and planning in terms of long-term deadlines. When men who have become accustomed to working on tasks with different levels of certainty start to work together on some joint project, conflict can arise due to these internalized differences in their work orientations. The way the other fellow does it may simply not make sense. In fact, it may seem highly detrimental to the success of the joint task.

For example, men used to working on highly certain tasks tend to check with their superiors on most of the task decisions they make. This is useful in these settings because superiors here tend to have access to more of the relevant information than their subordinates and single decisions are likely to affect the chances for the whole unit's success. On the other hand, men used to working on highly uncertain tasks often do not check with their superiors before making task decisions. In these settings, so much information can be relevant to the task of the unit as a whole that superiors are incapable of assimilating all of the data and must rely on the subordinates who are closest to a given problem to make a decision related to it. Moreover, many single decisions are less crucial for the success of the unit as a whole. Thus, in cases such as these, it makes sense for subordinates to make decisions on their own.

When performers of certain and uncertain tasks get together, and men used to checking with their superiors deal with those who see no reason to do so, each side looks to the other as if it's doing things the wrong way.

---

[3] Paul R. Lawrence and Jay W. Lorsch, *Organization and Environment: Managing Differentiation and Integration* (Homewood, Ill.: Richard D. Irwin, Inc., 1967).

Differences in time horizons in the planning process create very similar effects.

Besides these kinds of orientations, which have developed over long periods of time, one can classify disagreements due to the possession of different information and its interpretation in different ways under this heading. The two go hand in hand. Men working on different tasks tend to seek out different kinds of data and to attach different levels of importance to the same events. A change in a delivery schedule may require little effort from a marketing manager, perhaps a little extra paper work. In the eyes of a production superintendent, however, such a change might mean a great deal of work—rearranging work assignments, overtime schedules, machine use priorities. While one man is tempted to treat the phenomenon cavalierly and use it as a small favor in his dealings with customers, the other sees it as a major problem to be avoided when at all possible.

### Competition for Scarce Resources

A fourth major source of conflict involves competition between two or more groups for what their members identify as a finite set of scarce resources. The resources may be rewards the individual members desire or the materials they think they need for performing their tasks. They may be tangible—money, facilities—or nontangible—prestige, popularity, influence. Whatever they are they contribute to conflict when the men involved feel, realistically or unrealistically, that their availability is limited and that any gain in control over them by other groups represents a loss for their own.[4] (See Figure 1.)

Conflict over scarce resources has been studied extensively in laboratory settings. Subjects have been given games to play in which options are open for both helping and hindering each other, and the proportion of hindering moves has been shown to vary directly with the extent to which a win-lose orientation has been built into the reward structure. Still other experiments have been run in which the reward structure itself depends upon the extent to which the participants are willing to cooperate with or hinder one another, and the proportion of hindering moves here has been shown to vary with initial levels of trust, opportunities for communication, psychological predispositions toward agression and affection, and other relevant variables.[5]

---

[4] Louis R. Pondy's article, "Budgeting and Intergroup Conflict in Organizations," *Pittsburgh Business Review,* April 1964, deals specifically with this source of conflict as it relates to the creation and use of budgets.

[5] Phillip S. Gallo, Jr. and Charles G. McClintock, "Cooperative and Competitive Behavior in Mixed-Motive Games," *Journal of Conflict Resolution,* Vol. XI, No. 1, 1967.

## METHODS OF CONFLICT RESOLUTION

Thus far we have identified what appear to be the four major sources of conflict, based on the available research literature. Let us now consider some of the tactics which can be used for coping with conflict.[6] There are literally an infinite number of ways in which one might go about stopping or reducing a particular pattern of intergroup conflict, but they all probably can be placed at some point along a continuum which represents different combinations of two basic approaches—halting the conflictful behavior itself without regard to changes in attitude, on the one hand, and changing the attitudes of the protagonists so that they no longer see anything to fight about, on the other. (See Figure 1.)

**FIGURE 1**

Strategies for Resolving Intergroup Conflict

*Behavioral Solution*

*Attitudinal Change Solution*

1 2 3 4 5 6 7

1. Separate the groups physically, reducing conflict by reducing the opportunity to interact.
2. Allow interaction on issues where superordinate goals prevail and decision-making rules have been agreed to beforehand.
3. Keep groups separated but use as integrators individuals who are seen by both groups as justifying high status for the job, possessing personal attributes consistent with both groups' ideals, and having the expertise necessary for understanding each group's problems.
4. Hold direct negotiations between representatives from each group on all conflictful issues, in the presence of individuals who are seen as neutral to the conflict and who have personal attributes and expertise valued by both groups.
5. Hold direct negotiations between representatives from each group without third-party consultants present.
6. Exchange some group personnel for varying periods of time, so that contrasting perceptions and the rationales for them are clarified through day-to-day interaction and increased familiarity with the other group's activities, and then attempt direct negotiations after returning members have reported to their groups.
7. Require intense interaction between the conflicting groups under conditions where each group's failure to cooperate is more costly to itself than continuing to fight, regardless of how the other group behaves.

### Physical Separation

Physically separating the conflicting groups has the distinct advantages of preventing more damage from being done and of preventing the crea-

[6] Richard E. Walton, "Purposive Behavior in the Confrontation of Differences," Harvard Business School course note adapted from material reported by the same author in *Interpersonal Peacemaking: Confrontation and Third Party Consultation* (Reading, Mass.: Addison-Wesley Publishing Company, Inc., 1969). Reprinted by permission.

tion of further rationales for fighting based on what happens in combat itself. If the intervening party is sufficiently strong, it is something which can be done quickly. The tactic may be especially helpful where the groups in conflict are not highly interdependent or where the intervening party does not rely on their active cooperation with each other in order to secure some desired output. One of the tactic's disadvantages is that it may require continuous surveillance to keep the parties separate, especially if tempers are hot and energy levels high. Also, the tactic does not encourage the members of the conflicting groups to change their attitudes toward one another. On the contrary, lack of new objective information about an opponent encourages a group's members to reinforce their negative attitudes through unchecked fantasy building. Most important, the tactic is of little use to those who rely on the active cooperation between the conflicting groups for getting some job done. For them it is at best a stopgap measure, a way of preventing further damage until some other tactic can be devised.

### Limited Interaction

Reducing interaction to issues where superordinate goals exist and where decision-making rules have been agreed to, offers the advantage of getting some joint work done, but its utility depends upon whether the areas in which the protagonists are willing to cooperate, if any, are of any use to those in a position to impose this solution. Continued surveillance is also likely to be necessary, since the protagonists might easily make use of the available opportunities for communication for further attacks. The tactic may be of considerable use in situations where the interdependence between the two groups is clearly defined and stable over time, and where the joint decisions involved are generally routine. The tactic is least advantageous where the groups need to cooperate on a variety of issues or where areas requiring cooperation shift frequently and new decision-making procedures must continuously be established. Like the first tactic discussed, this one does little to encourage attitudinal change either, so that the basic motivation to fight may remain indefinitely or be redirected in a more damaging direction.

### Using Integrators

Using as integrators individuals who are seen by both groups as possessing high legitimate status, high expertise, and a constellation of personal attributes consistent with group ideals, creates the advantage of allowing the conflicting parties to coordinate each other's activities on a variety of issues while making it unnecessary for them to interact with each other directly. Thus it can be used in conjunction with a policy of physical separation, or with a policy where some interaction is permitted on routine issues. Lawrence and Lorsch have shown that this tactic is typically used by firms which need to maintain high levels of coordination among functional groups with clearly different work orientations.[7] For instance, in some segments of the plastics industry, the production task is highly certain, the research task highly uncertain. As discussed earlier, this kind of situation promotes intergroup conflict. These authors found that in organizations where the men who were assigned the task of coordinating the research and production units were rated high by both in terms of expertise and legitimate power, the quality of relations between these groups was better and their firms on the whole economically more effective than in those firms where the integrators did not have these characteristics. Some research done by this author indicates that the possession by integrators of commonly valued personal attributes—education, business background, personal style—can play a similarly important role.[8] While studying relations among departments in two small firms, he found that coordination between pairs of departments was considerably better where the integrators possessed personal attributes valued by both groups, even in cases where ratings of power and expertise would have indicated no differences in their quality of integration.

One major difficulty in executing this tactic is finding the golden men who fit all the requirements. Many firms simply may not have the resources or the sophistication to do so. Also, as with the previous two tactics discussed, this approach does not encourage attitudinal change. In some cases—where job demands require differences in orientation—this may be an important advantage. Where this is not the case, though, the tactic is obviously less desirable.

### Third-Party Consultants

One tactic which represents something of a balance between attempts at attitudinal change on the one hand and the direct stopping of conflict behavior on the other, involves the use of direct negotiations between representatives of the warring parties in the presence of a third-party consultant whose advice and actions are valued by both groups.

The negotiating activity itself encourages the clarification of assumptions and the exploration of each party's motives—in essence a clear confrontation of differences. Thus, it sets the stage for new learning to take place. The presence of the third party, if the latter's opinions and counsel are sufficiently valued, inhibits lapses into name calling or other emotional outbursts and, in general, acts as a deterrent against further overt conflict behavior. If the third party is sufficiently skilled, he can also guide the negotiations in ways that tend to create the best results, e.g., sequencing

---

[7] Lawrence and Lorsch, *op. cit.*

[8] Neilsen, *op. cit.*

differentiation and integration phases, keeping tensions at a moderate level, lending his status to a weaker party so that a balance of power is obtained and issues of ultimate influence do not get in the way of the confrontation process.[9]

### Negotiations without Consultants

Bringing representatives together for negotiations without a third party present involves greater risk of further conflict. There is no one there to keep tempers under control. But one can argue that if the need to resolve differences is sufficiently important to both parties, the agreements under this condition might involve even more attitudinal change and acceptance. The participants are doing all the work themselves and thus the experience is more intense. The key to making this tactic work, of course, is one of making the motivation to resolve the conflict so strong that the negotiators are willing to work their way through the issues in spite of the mistakes they are likely to make without a third party present. One method for creating such motivation is to make the need to cooperate crucial for each negotiator, regardless of what the other party does. For instance, if each negotiator's failure to cooperate is likely to result in losses either to himself or his group that are nearly equal or slightly greater than anything the other party can do to him, cooperation in and of itself becomes important and he is likely to be more flexible in his demands. An example of this would be a situation in which both groups were in danger of being dispersed or reorganized by a powerful third party, e.g., top management, if their fighting continued, and thereby of suffering the same fate either one would if it were to lose control over its activities to the other. The relative strengths of the need to cooperate on the one hand and the need to meet group demands on the other must not be too disparate; otherwise agreements might be made simply for the sake of survival and no real differences aired. But if this disparity can be prevented, the tension created by attempting to serve two needs simultaneously can result in considerable attitudinal change.

### Exchanging Members

One problem with negotiations of the sort where only representatives of the protagonists are involved is that agreements made at the bargaining table may be interpreted as a betrayal by those group members who have not taken part in the negotiations and who therefore have not been subjected directly to the strains of having to come to an agreement. Even where notions of betrayal do not arise, members may interpret a new agreement as a behavioral requisite only, caused by prevailing circum-

[9] For a more thorough analysis of this approach, see Walton, *op. cit.*

stances, and not encouraging them to change their minds about anything. One way of setting the stage for more pervasive attitudinal change is to have the warring groups exchange some of their members for sufficient lengths of time to let them become familiar with how the other group operates, what kinds of problems it faces on a day-to-day basis, and how its rank and file explain their own ideals, statuses, norms, and the like.

The exchanged individuals then return to their own groups and, as accepted members who have not been working under the strain of negotiations, are possibly in a better position to communicate these data to their cohorts than would potentially suspect representatives. These data can then be used both during and following negotiations to evaluate the agreements made and encourage greater acceptance of them.

The tactic has some noteworthy disadvantages. It takes time, perhaps more than an intervening party thinks he can afford. It takes sophistication since an astute social analysis is a prerequisite. It requires the voluntary cooperation of both parties. Each group must be willing to give up some of its members. The exchanged members must be encouraged to gather their data objectively. Temporary outsiders must be responded to positively and provided with honest discussions of how one's group works and what its members actually believe. A visiting individual who is isolated or given poor data will probably hinder successful negotiations at a later date. Finally, the data visitors gain, even if honest and accurate, may possibly serve to convince one or more of the groups that they really do want to fight with the other or that agreements made later do not represent a change in attitude. Thus, a major risk is involved.

On the positive side, exchange of this sort can clear up important misconceptions, indicate to each party where the most fruitful negotiations might take place, and ultimately result in permanent attitude change so that the sources of conflict cease to exist. If the latter occurs, the intervening party or anyone relying on cooperation between the two groups no longer has to worry about the possibility of conflict or continue to invest his energies in preventing its occurrence.

Because of its disadvantages, this tactic is rarely used, if ever, in connection with major institutional disputes, such as those between labor and management. But it is used by firms to prevent or reduce conflict between members of different functional departments. For instance, numerous firms in industries that require close coordination between production and applied research departments require newcomers in each department to work for a time in the other to gain a greater familiarity with the problems the members of the latter face.

### Multilevel Interaction

At the other end of the continuum from the reduction of conflict through physical separation is the encouragement of intense interaction among many or all of the members of opposing groups. Like the previous two tactics, an essential ingredient in its use is the development of a set of conditions under which the failure of each group to cooperate will result in major costs to itself, regardless of what the other group does. This situation, if an intervening party can create it, ideally forces an open confrontation of differences followed by basic attitudinal change. Besides the fact that, like all negotiations, it takes time, the main disadvantage of this tactic is that the requisite conditions may be hard to create and to maintain for the period it takes for the issues to be resolved. Whole groups are involved and not just a few negotiators whose behavior and status can be closely surveyed. Members of opposing forces are likely to start out by making peace in terms of norms of action while maintaining their negative attitudes. In some cases, only time and shared experience can open up the way for the development of positive emotional bonds. If the intervening party is unable to maintain the reward structure as described above on a continuous basis, even if the lapse in these conditions is only momentary, one or both of the protagonists might seize the opportunity to attack and set the process back several steps. The possibility also exists that, if differences are strong enough, some of the protagonists may choose to incur the cost of refusing to cooperate and resolve the situation by leaving the group or being forced to leave. The intervening party has to accept this possibility and take into account his manpower needs and resources in the process.

## THE MANAGER'S VALUES

Whether a manager uses a given tactic to resolve intergroup conflict should depend on at least four factors: (1) his ability to execute the tactic, (2) the costs he might incur in using it in comparison to those he might incur in using another, (3) the tactic's appropriateness for creating the degree of attitudinal and/or behavioral change he desires, and (4) his own personal values. The importance of the first three of these factors should be evident from the foregoing analysis. We have said little so far, however, about a manager's personal values in the conflict resolution process. We would argue that the more deeply rooted a conflict is in the personalities and life-styles of the protagonists, the more carefully must a manager evaluate his actions in light of his own values, especially if he choses to try to resolve the conflict through attitudinal change. The four sources of conflict we discussed earlier appear to fall along their own continuum in this respect.

Conflict due to differences in reference groups appears to be the most deeply rooted in group members' personalities. A reference group is part of a man's superego. His conceptions of an ideal group and its opposite are molded by the totality of his life's experience. While he may be able to identify some aspects of these images in terms of his conscious desire to attain particular goals, he may not be able to do so with regard to other aspects whose attractiveness or repulsiveness are rooted in forgotten experiences and not open to rational evaluation. On a conscious level the member simply wants his group to be a certain way by fiat.

When differences in reference groups are causing conflict, especially when members of conflicting groups identify cooperation with each other as antithetical to their ideals, tactics involving attempts at attitudinal change may provide the only long-run hope for resolution. The issue is not likely to resolve itself through the experiences of the opposing groups under conditions of physical separation. But attempting to change someone's reference groups involves the manager in what is clearly a moral issue. Such changes, if indeed they can be created, are likely to affect a man's behavior off the job as well as on it. One who attempts to create such changes must feel secure not only in the belief that he has a right to do so but also in the conviction that if he is successful, the effects he creates will benefit the individual as an independent entity as well as the organizational unit for which he works.

It is also important to consider the possibility that changes in reference groups can have an unintended snowball effect. Groups which start out hating each other, through joint experience under conditions where cooperation is necessary for survival, may not only learn to get along with one another but also come to like each other. As a result, they might become more concerned with each other's welfare than with the joint activity the instigator of the change was most concerned with. For instance, if two ethnic groups at the blue-collar level in a factory go from enemies to allies, their newfound friendships might create more headaches for management in terms of strikes, slowdowns, resistance to incentive systems, and so on than the results of their former hostilities did. Attempting to change reference groups is indeed a complex matter. In many cases a manager might be better off trying to stop conflictful behavior through physical separation in some degree, living with the costs of surveillance and the potential for more conflict involved. His own values and knowledge of what is likely to happen may be put to a major test if he chooses the attitudinal change approach.

Conflict which derives from differences in groups' perceptions of a just distribution of rewards appear to be somewhat less rooted in protagonists' personalities, and its resolution through attitudinal change may have a less pervasive effect on personal and firm life. The mere contention that another group should be attacked because it is getting more than it deserves involves a logical argument with a logical solution—reduce the group's rewards to what it deserves. In this respect, the unconscious desires of the individuals involved are less salient. However, belief in a given equation for reward may be deeply rooted in the superego and is likely to be hard to change without positive experience under a new system.

Change in perceptions of a just equation for reward may affect family life. A man who gradually comes to believe that performance is a more important requisite for reward than seniority may find himself taking fewer days off, evaluating his friends in a different way, raising his children differently. For these reasons, attempting to change conceptions of distributive justice involve many of the same risks and moral dilemmas that attempting to change reference groups does.

Perhaps one way in which attitudinal change of this kind is less problematic is that the acceptance of a common equation for reward in and of itself is not likely to encourage stronger primary ties between two groups. Therefore, the threat of overreaction against the intervening party is less evident.

Conflict resulting from differences in work norms appears to be even less a part of the combatants' personalities, and reducing such antagonism through attitudinal change tactics is likely to have less pervasive effects on participants' personal lives. This is not to say that different work orientations themselves are not ingrained in the protagonists' superegos. They very well may. The point rather is that the conflict which derives from such differences can be resolved in ways that require personalities to be changed relatively little. A man may prefer a given task orientation, but this does not mean that he is incapable of understanding when his own preferences do not meet task demands. The task of the intervening party here is not to change a conflictee's work orientation but to change his reasoning about the apparently illogical behavior of the people he disagrees with. As in the case of changing attitudes about distributive justice, the resolution of differences in work norms through attitudinal change is also less likely to encourage the development of strong primary ties between former enemies. One can easily understand and accept the rationale for doing things in different ways under different conditions without becoming enamored of persons who perform tasks that are different from one's own.

Finally, conflict stemming from competition for scarce resources appears to be the least rooted of all the sources in the personalities involved, and attempts at its resolution through attitudinal change are likely to involve the fewest moral dilemmas. Definitions of what scarce resources are, or how they should be used, do not have to be changed; only the attitude that one group will gain access to resources at the expense of another. This may involve a change in the notion of who should use the resources under different conditions, but such a change should have little effect on the basic desire to benefit from the resources on the job or on how one might use them at home where the situation can be defined as clearly different. Likewise, on the job, a clearer understanding of the logic of resource distribution should benefit the intervening manager, since members of the conflicting groups can use it as a goal for making sure that resources are distributed to other groups according to this logic and thereby used to the maximum benefit for their own.

## INDIVIDUAL DIFFERENCES WITHIN GROUPS

In this paper we have focused on sources of conflict which derive directly from a group's social structure and norms. It seems worthwhile mentioning in closing that differences in individual personalities and roles add another dimension of complexity to the conflict process. For no single group member is likely to perceive his group's ideals, equations for reward, work norms, and resource priorities in exactly the same way that any other member does. While there may be considerable consensus on these issues, individual differences are bound to exist. Likewise, particular members are likely to feel different levels of allegiance to viewpoints held by most of their cohorts, to be attracted in different degrees to alternatives offered by other groups and individuals, and to be willing to stop conflict or to change their minds under different conditions.

This is especially important to note where attempts at conflict resolution involve negotiations between group representatives. The personality of each representative may be just as important as the social structure and norms of his group in determining how successful the negotiations will be. A representative might find one solution agreeable which the majority of his group's membership would reject. He might forego other solutions which his constituents would prefer.

Not only is the personality but also the status of a representative within his group worth noting. As a leader he might be in a position to change group opinion. Were he simply a member in good standing who did not hold a leadership position he would be less likely to do so. While members at the bottom of the status hierarchy would hardly qualify for the job of representative, e.g., members who deviated a lot from group norms or those who had lost battles for controlling positions and were alienated toward the group as a whole as a result, their behavior should also be considered for the negative roles they might play in the creation of conflict itself and in any attempt at resolving it. Such individuals might seek to misrepresent their groups or reveal internal tensions or negative feelings toward other groups as ways of getting back at the other members for their low status. They might do the same things simply out of their own misunderstanding of their groups' positions and policies.

In any case, any assessment of intergroup conflict should involve not only analysis of each group's shared perceptions and feelings but also of the perceptions, feelings, and statuses of the particular persons involved both in the conflict itself and in any attempts at conflict resolution which might be considered. The same tactics for handling intergroup conflict noted above can be applied to particular interpersonal relationships as well. The intervening manager should consider the use of a variety of tactics in conjunction with each other, some focusing on individuals, some on groups as whole units, in his attempts to cope with the intergroup conflicts that fall under his domain.

# Suggested List for Further Reading on Managing Group and Intergroup Relations

## Suggested Readings on Group Issues

KENNETH F. BERRIEN. *General and Social Systems,* Rutgers University Press, 1968.

FRED E. FIEDLER. *A Theory of Leadership Effectiveness,* McGraw-Hill Book Company, 1967.

ROBERT BLAUNER. *Alienation and Freedom,* University of Chicago Press.

ROBERT BLAUNER. *Alienation and Freedom,* University of Chicago Press, 1964. 1955.

GEORGE C. HOMANS. *The Human Group,* Harcourt, Brace and Company, 1950.

WALTER BUCKLEY. *Sociology and Modern Systems Theory,* Prentice-Hall, Inc., 1967.

JOSEPHINE KLEIN. *Working With Groups,* Hutchinson University Library, London, 1963.

THEODORE M. MILLS. *The Sociology of Small Groups,* Prentice-Hall, Inc., 1967.

## Suggested Readings in Intergroup Issues

WILFRED BROWN. *Exploration in Management,* William Heinemann Ltd., 1960.

A. K. RICE. *The Enterprise and its Environment,* Tavistock Publications, 1963.

MELVILLE DALTON. *Men Who Manage,* John Wiley and Sons, 1959.

TOM BURNS AND G. M. STALKER. *The Management of Innovation,* Tavistock Publications, 1961.

ROBERT BLAKE, HERBERT A. SHEPARD, AND JANE S. MOUTON. *Managing Intergroup Conflict in Industry,* Gulf Publishing Co., 1964.

M. SHERIF (ED.). *Intergroup Relations and Leadership,* John Wiley and Sons, 1962.

LEONARD R. SAYLES. *Managerial Behavior,* McGraw-Hill Book Company, 1964.

# Index of Cases